SEARCHING FOR
MY SLAVE ROOTS

SEARCHING FOR MY SLAVE ROOTS

FROM GUYANA'S SUGAR PLANTATIONS TO CAMBRIDGE

MALIK AL NASIR

WITH CARINYA SHARPLES

WILLIAM COLLINS

William Collins
An imprint of HarperCollins*Publishers*
1 London Bridge Street
London SE1 9GF

WilliamCollinsBooks.com

HarperCollins*Publishers*
Macken House,
39/40 Mayor Street Upper,
Dublin 1, D01 C9W8, Ireland

First published in Great Britain in 2025 by William Collins

1

Copyright © Malik Al Nasir 2025

Malik Al Nasir asserts the moral right to be identified as the author of this work in accordance with the Copyright, Designs and Patents Act 1988

This book uses archival source material from the Sandbach Tinne Collection, available on Cambridge Digital Library https://cudl.lib.cam.ac.uk/collections/sandbachtinne/1

A catalogue record for this book is available from the British Library

ISBN 978-0-00-846448-6

All rights reserved. No part of this publication may be reproduced, stored in a retrieval system, or transmitted, in any form or by any means, electronic, mechanical, photocopying, recording or otherwise, without the prior permission of the publishers.

Without limiting the exclusive rights of any author, contributor or the publisher of this publication, any unauthorised use of this publication to train generative artificial intelligence (AI) technologies is expressly prohibited. HarperCollins also exercise their rights under Article 4(3) of the Digital Single Market Directive 2019/790 and expressly reserve this publication from the text and data mining exception.

This book is sold subject to the condition that it shall not, by way of trade or otherwise, be lent, re-sold, hired out or otherwise circulated without the publisher's prior consent in any form of binding or cover other than that in which it is published and without a similar condition including this condition being imposed on the subsequent purchaser.

Typeset in Dante MT Std by Six Red Marbles UK, Thetford, Norfolk

Printed and bound in Great Britain by CPI Group (UK) Ltd, Croydon

This book contains FSC™ certified paper and other controlled sources to ensure responsible forest management.

For more information visit: www.harpercollins.co.uk/green

*This book is dedicated to my ancestors who were
enslaved by the Sandbach Tinne dynasty. May
this go some way to lifting the silence of their
anguish, and ensure that future generations
will never forget their immense sacrifice,
so that we could exist.*

'The great force of history comes from the fact that we carry it within us, are unconsciously controlled by it in many ways, and history is literally present in all that we do.'

– James Baldwin

CONTENTS

Glossary of names	xi
Preface	1
Chapter 1: Andrew Watson	13
Chapter 2: Back to de sugar cane	32
Chapter 3: I heard him cry in a most affecting manner	63
Chapter 4: The air of England was too pure for slavery	85
Chapter 5: Hunted victims	123
Chapter 6: Three or four hatchets	142
Chapter 7: The Demerara Rebellion – a licence to preach to the Negroes	172
Chapter 8: A large and liberal atonement	211
Chapter 9: Extending to slaves practically all civil rights but freedom	231
Chapter 10: Emancipation, finally – but not really	244
Chapter 11: These good-natured savages	259
Chapter 12: Mercantile monsters	280
Chapter 13: We the people	308
Epilogue	313

List of illustrations	327
Acknowledgements	329
Glossary of terms	333
Notes	341
Index	375

GLOSSARY OF NAMES

Adamay Patricia Bevaun (1953–2020), relative of the author; linked to family land

Adela Tinne, formerly enslaved; mother of Sophia

Agnes Maud Watson (b. 1880), daughter of Andrew Watson (footballer) and Jessie Nimmo Armour; Watson's first wife

Andrew Watson (footballer) (1856–1921), son of Peter Miller Watson; marine engineer

Andrew Watson (uncle) (1803–1837), brother of Peter Miller Watson

Ann McKenzie Robertson (1772–1835), second wife of John Gladstone; mother of W. E. Gladstone

Ann Robertson, daughter of Eliza Thomas and Gilbert Robertson

Anne Robertson (née Forbes) (1748–1826), mother of Christian Watson (née Robertson); later Traill

Annetta Watson (c. 1850–1889), daughter of Peter Miller Watson; later Stevenson

Alexine Tinne (1835–1869), daughter of Philip Frederick Tinne; explorer and photographer; inherited wealth from firm's activities

Ann Parker, née Sandbach (1803–1890), daughter of Samuel Sandbach; married Charles Stuart Parker (ii)

Banastre Tarleton (1754–1833), British general and politician; defender of the slave trade in parliament; neighbour of Samuel Sandbach in Everton

Beryl Watson, daughter of Frederick Adolphus Watson, 'diamond seeker'

Camelle, member of staff at Guyana General Register Office

Catherine McInroy, free woman; mother of Grace Ann McInroy, the Black daughter of James McInroy

Charles Sandbach Parker (1864–1920), descendant of Sandbach and Parker families; partner in Sandbach, Tinne & Co.

Charles Parker Sandbach (d. 1869), botanist who the pteridophyte genus Parkeria is named after

Charles Stuart Parker (i) (1771–1828), founding partner in Robertson, Gordon & Parker, Robertson Parker & Co., Grenada; McInroy Parker & Co., Glasgow; McInroy Sandbach & Co., Demerara; and Sandbach, Tinne & Co. Liverpool.; married Margaret Rainy (1774–1844)

Charles Stuart Parker (ii) (1800–1868), son of Charles Stuart Parker (i) and Margaret Rainy

Charles Stuart Parker (iii) MP (1829–1910), son of Charles Stuart Parker (ii) and Ann Sandbach; Partner in McInroy Parker & Co., Glasgow; McInroy Sandbach & Co., Demerara and Sandbach, Tinne & Co. Liverpool; married Ann Sandbach, daughter of Samuel Sandbach and Elizabeth Sandbach, née Robertson

Chloe, enslaved person registered under Sandbach

Christian Douglas (b. c. 1665), wife of George Robertson; royal lineage to Plantagenets

Christian Robertson (1781–1842), daughter of Reverend Harry Robertson; married James Watson; mother of Henry Robertson Watson, Peter Miller Watson. Later married Thomas Stuart Traill

Christian (Chrétien) Théodore Tinne, brother of Philip Frederick Tinne; had a child with enslaved woman

Colin Robertson (1764–1863), brother-in-law of John Gladstone

Divie Robertson (1766–1850), of St Martin-in-the-Fields, Middlesex; married Jane Rowland; brother-in-law of John Gladstone; father of Rev. Divie Robertson

Eliza Thomas (1787–c. 1850), daughter of Dorothy (Doll) Thomas and Captain Joseph Thomas (in Grenada); Eliza was the mother of Ann and Henry by Gilbert Robertson, brother of Christian Robertson

Elizabeth Moore (1782–1870), wife of James McInroy

Elizabeth Robertson Sandbach (1782–1859), wife of Samuel Sandbach; niece of George Robertson; sister of Christian

Elizabeth Sandbach (1806–1881), daughter of Samuel Sandbach and Elizabeth Robertson; cousin of W. E. Gladstone

Eric Phillips, deputy chair of CARICOM reparations commission; representative of Guyana to CARICOM

Evan Baillie, chaired government claims committee for slavery compensation

Evelyn Stuart Parker (1870–1936), descendant of Sandbach and Parker families; partner in Sandbach, Tinne & Co.

Florence Mary Watson, née Caldwell (Flo) (1920–), wife of Reginald Wilcox Watson; stepmother of the author

Frederick Adolphus Watson, a diamond seeker. Related ancestor of the author through Beryl Watson

George Baillie, Bristolian merchant in Grenada

George Garnett, colonial figure; Tinne family connection through Henry Tinne Garnett

George Rainy (1790–1863), nephew of George Robertson; partner in Sandbach Tinne & Co., and main representative in Demerara; involved in the Highland Clearances

George Robertson (1756–1799), slave merchant; partner in Robertson Parker & Co.; uncle to Elizabeth Sandbach, née Robertson and Ann Parker, née Robertson; founder of the Sandbach Tinne dynasty

Gilbert Robertson, brother of Christian; had mixed children

Gilbert Robertson Sandbach (1848–1907), son of Gilbert Sandbach and Margaret Maxwell; continued the family's involvement in colonial enterprises

Gilbert Sandbach (Revd.) (1817–1882), son of Samuel and Elizabeth; father of Gilbert Robertson Sandbach

Grace, enslaved person registered under Sandbach

Grace Ann McInroy, daughter of Catherine McInroy

Henry Robertson, son of Eliza Thomas and Gilbert Robertson

Henry Robertson Sandbach (1807–1895), son of Samuel and Elizabeth; inherited the Hafodunos estate in North Wales; partner in Sandbach Tinne & Co.

Harry Robertson Watson (1801–1836), brother of Peter Miller Watson

Henry Tinne Garnett (c. 1828–1879), descendant of the Tinne family; partner agent of Sandbach Tinne in British Guiana

Helen Jane Gladstone, daughter of John; became a nun; opium addict

Isabella, enslaved person

Jack Gladstone (c. 1800– (after)1823), enslaved leader of 1823 rebellion; enslaved on John Gladstone's plantation; suspected member of Gladstone family despite reputedly being the son of Quamina (which is suspect)

Hugh Munro Robertson (d. 1819), brother of Christian Robertson; twin with George; shipwrecked in *The Demerara* in 1819, all on board were lost

James Capellen Tinne (1847–1914), son of John Abraham Tinne; partner in Sandbach, Tinne & Co.; married Margaret Louisa Huntson

James McInroy (1759–1825), partner in Sandbach, Tinne & Co.; died 1825; his son, James Patrick McInroy, also partner

James Parker (Capt.) (1729–1815), father of Charles Stuart Parker (i)

James Watson (c. 1765–1808), father of Peter Miller Watson and William Robertson Watson; Factor and Chamberlain to Lord Henry Dundas, Earl of Orkney

James Watson Jr (b. 1809), brother of Peter Miller Watson; did not go to Demerara

Jeanne Marguerite Tinne, sister of Philip Frederick Tinne; died in Demerara

John Abraham Tinne MP (1807–1884), son of Philip Frederick Tinne; partner in Sandbach, Tinne & Co.; married Margaret Sandbach, daughter of Samuel Sandbach and Elizabeth Robertson; chair of the Royal Geographical Society

John Ernest Tinne (1845–1925), son of John Abraham Tinne; significant role in the firm in late nineteenth and early twentieth centuries; treasurer of Liverpool School of Tropical Medicine; treasurer of the Blue Coat School, Liverpool

John Gladstone (1764–1851), major slave owner; plantations in Demerara and Jamaica; architect of the slavery compensation scheme and its largest single recipient; chair of the Liverpool West India Association; involved in the founding of the Liverpool and Manchester Railway; father of Prime Minister W. E. Gladstone

John Waddell, involved in Sophia Tinne's case

Judith, enslaved person

Karen Budhram, deputy archivist at the Walter Rodney Archives, Demerara

Lawrence Dundas (Sir) (1712–1781), 1st Baronet; landowner and investor; son of Thomas Dundas and Bethia Baillie

Lord Dundas (1742–1811), Henry Dundas, 1st Viscount Melville; inherited slave plantations

Margaret Roscoe (1812–1852), granddaughter of William Roscoe; married Henry Robertson Sandbach; resided at Hafodounas Hall; patron of the sculptor John Gibson

Margaret Sandbach (1811–1868), married John Abraham Tinne

Maria, enslaved person

Mary Elizabeth Traill (1841–1892), daughter of Thomas Stuart Traill; married Robert Ormond; half-sister of Peter Watson' co-executrix of Peter Miller Watson's estate

Mary Rosina Sandbach (1815–1882), one of the Miss Sandbachs

Matthijs (M. S.) Tinne, brother of Philip Frederick Tinne, merchant in Demerara

Mercurius, family member; husband of Adamay Bevan, author's second cousin

Michael Gibbs, artist

Minkey (Mincky) Rose, manumitted enslaved woman

Miss Traills (group), teenagers in 1832. The Traill sisters who hosted their cousin W. E. Gladstone as a young man

Mr Euston, estate manager murdered on a Sandbach Tinne plantation

Patrick Parker (c. 1802–1874), brother of Charles Stuart Parker (i); son of Captain James Parker; timber merchant in Virginia

Peggy, enslaved person

Peter McLagan Jr MP (1823–1900), Scottish politician; first non-white MP in Scotland; son of Peter McLagan, partner in Sandbach, Tinne & Co.

Peter McLagan Sr (1774–1860), father of Peter McLagan MP; partner in Sandbach, Tinne & Co.

Peter Miller Watson (1805–1869), sugar planter in Demerara; father of footballer Andrew Watson; owned two plantations and hundreds of enslaved people. Managed entire British Guiana operation for Sandbach Tinne. Great-nephew of founder George Robertson

Philip Frederick Tinne (1772–1844), Dutch merchant; co-founder of Sandbach, Tinne & Co.; moved to Demerara in 1796 and became a full partner in 1813. Colonial official in Demerara; head of the Court of Policy

Philip Frederick Tinne (Jr) (1836–1869), son of John Abraham Tinne; continued the family's involvement in the firm

Phyl Hall, modern descendant of William Sandbach

Reverend Harry Robertson (1448–1815), father of Christian Robertson, Elizabeth Robertson and Anne Robertson, a.k.a. the Three Fair Maids of Kiltearn; brother of George Robertson (Grenada) Doctor of Divinity; resided at the Manse of Kiltearn, Scotland

Reginald Daniel William Watson, half-brother of Reginald Wilcox Watson by George Edward Watson and Mable Rawlins; partner was Henrietta Smith; children were Sibyl Melvinna Boilers, née Watson and Whithyelene Amelia, née Watson

Robert Forrester, lawyer in Guyana who assisted the author with land issues

Robertson Gladstone (1805–1875), son of John Gladstone; active in Demerara

Roze Catharine Sandbach (1760–1824), Samuel Sandbach (of Grenada) bequeathed his slaves and £100 per year plus a plot of land in St George, Grenada, to 'Roze Catherine Sandbach, my daughter, a free mulatess'

Rupert Andrew Watson, son of Andrew Watson (footballer); inherited shares in the East Kilbride Rail Road in New South Wales when he emigrated to Australia

Samuel Sandbach (1769–1851), co-founder of Sandbach, Tinne & Co.; mayor of Liverpool; high sheriff of Denbighshire; married Elizabeth Robertson; nephew of Samuel Sandbach (Grenada)

Samuel Sandbach (uncle) (1730–1800), early Grenada slaveholder; left three houses in Brompton Row, London, to his nephew Samuel Sandbach, co-founder of Sandbach Tinne

Sibyl Melvinna Boilers, née Watson, first cousin of the author; daughter of Reginald Daniel William Watson; sister of Whithyelene Amelia Watson

Solomon Marsham, doctor in Sophia Tinne sale

Sophia (possibly Oxley), enslaved daughter of Adela Tinne (property of P. F. Tinne) and Bass Oxley

Sophy McInroy, mother of Adela Tinne

Stephen Small, Professor Emeritus at Department of African American Studies, UC Berkley; from Liverpool

Susey, enslaved person

Thomas Stuart Traill (1781–1862), Scottish physician and professor; father of Mary Elizabeth Traill with Christian Traill, formerly Christian Watson, née Robertson; President of the Liverpool Athenaeum; editor of the Encyclopædia Britannica; President of the Royal Scottish Society of the Arts

Vanessa Joan Johnson (b. 1982), great-niece of the author; granddaughter of Whithyelene Watson

William Ewart Gladstone (1809–1898), prime minister; son of Sir John Gladstone

William Robertson Watson (1807–1876), brother of Peter Miller Watson; guardian of Annetta, ancestor of the author

William Sandbach, slaver owner and plantation owner; owned Banana Estate in Grenada

William Robertson Sandbach (1813–1891), son of Samuel and Elizabeth; partner in Sandbach, Tinne & Co.

William Roscoe (1753–1831), considered an abolitionist, historian and writer from Liverpool; grandfather of Margaret Roscoe, the wife of Henry Robertson Sandbach; co-founder of the Liverpool Athenaeum; banker; ship owner; botanist

William Walker, governor in estate correspondence

William Wilberforce, abolitionist MP

Whithyelene Amelia Watson (1926–2012), first cousin of the author; daughter of Reginald Daniel William Watson, the author's uncle

PREFACE

> *'Nigger! Nigger!*
> *Pull the trigger.*
> *Bang! Bang! Bang!'*

'Daddy, what's a Nigger?' I asked naively, as I walked home from my first day at Cross Farm County Primary School in Netherley, a new council estate on the outskirts of Liverpool. It was 1973 and I was six years old. My father, Reginald Wilcox Watson, was a towering figure of a man (six foot one tall), with a dark complexion derived of his Afro-Guyanese heritage. I heard him suck his teeth as he glanced down at me, with an awkward scowl on his face. 'Skunt!'[1] he muttered under his breath. 'Take no notice of that,' he declared, with an air of utter contempt in his voice.

We walked on in silence for a few minutes, along the pristine, newly laid black tarmac path that extended from the site of the new school across the oller, towards our new home. The 'oller' was the term people in Liverpool used to describe an unkempt area of wasteland. As Netherley was only built in the late 1960s, there were still areas that were undeveloped, and others that were still under development. Indeed, the school itself had only opened in 1973, despite most of the new families moving into the surrounding council housing during 1969 and 1970 – as we ourselves had done.

As the estate had no primary school at first, the local comprehensive secondary school, Netherley Comp, was used to house infants, juniors and seniors for the first few years, and I had attended the infants' there from 1971 to 1972.

When Cross Farm finally opened, I recall my excitement at the thought of going to a brand-new school along with my three siblings, all of whom – like myself – are of mixed racial heritage. On our first day, we were all led into the school assembly hall and the headmaster, Mr Talbot, welcomed us and introduced himself and the other new teachers. He had brought in a reel-to-reel tape machine, rigged up to a PA system, to broadcast a story across the hall to the hundred or so school children, who by now were all sitting in their respective year groups, cross-legged on the wooden floor. As my siblings and I were each a year apart in age, we were all separated from one another but at first it didn't occur to me, as I was so excited to be in my new school. Mr Talbot pressed the button, the music started and then horror struck. 'Black Sambo! Black Sambo! Living in the jungle all alone. Except for big black Mumbo and big black Jumbo.' I was immediately distraught. I turned to look for my siblings and caught sight of my little sister Michelle a few rows back, who looked like she was about to burst into tears. All the white kids were laughing, and I saw several of them pointing at us and saying, 'Black Sambo!' It was a baptism of fire, our innocence was gone, and we were at the start of what was to be a childhood characterised by racist slurs, aggression and trauma.

My eldest sister Jacqueline's dad – Kermit Lewis – was a Jamaican, but at that time, I didn't know that she had a different father. We'd never met him – and neither had she. We only found out in our teens some years later when the subject came up. At that time, we assumed that we were all my dad's kids. The other three of us – my elder brother Reynold, my younger sister Michelle, and myself, Mark – are all Reg's kids and our mother is Sonia Parry, a Welsh woman from a small village in North Wales called Dyserth, in the parish of Saint Asaph. Her father was Elvin Parry from Holywell in North Wales, whom we also never met and her own mother, who'd died when my mother herself was still a child, was Elsie Knight, from Chorlton-cum-Hardy in Manchester, England. My mother came to Liverpool at the age of seventeen and soon fell pregnant with Jacqueline. We later discovered that Kermit had gone to prison and left my mum as a young single white woman, with a black child. My mother took up lodging in my father's house and that's where our family – as I knew it – began. Kermit never reappeared and no one mentioned it, which is why we assumed we all had the same father. It had also never occurred to me that having a white mother and a Black father was something unusual, until we moved from my birthplace in the more cosmopolitan area of Toxteth in south Liverpool, to Netherley on its outskirts.

Toxteth was close to the River Mersey, and as Liverpool was a seaport with a substantial coastline, peppered from one end to the other with docks and shipyards, it had always been a place where seamen from around the world had visited, settled, and formed communities – and intermingled with the local white women. Historically, Toxteth had been a very affluent area, boasting some of Liverpool's most exquisite merchant houses from the Georgian and Victorian periods, when the city had been at the epicentre of the British Empire and the most prolific port in the abhorrent transatlantic trade in enslaved Africans. But as Liverpool's significance as a port began to wane in the post-World War II era, Toxteth had gone into a state of decline, along with the rest of the city, and had now become synonymous with the Black ghetto that had evolved, as the mercantile classes moved down south to London and the Home Counties, and more Black and foreign immigrants moved in.

Many of the Black seamen took advantage of the economic decline and bought up these old merchant houses, as they were relatively cheap. Seamen usually came home with cash they had been unable to spend, due to the long voyages they undertook. This resulted in the emergence of Black communities with a degree of relative economic independence, as they were usually excluded from white society in all but the most menial of employment roles – with few exceptions. Many went away to sea and had Liverpool as a base, buying their houses and having kids with local white women, as there were few Black women in those days in Liverpool. Others worked in or around the docks in shipping-related roles, as rope-makers, carpenters, dockers or security guards. In the post-war era, boarding houses in many UK towns would have signs in the windows stating 'No dogs, no Irish, no Blacks', and Liverpool was no exception.

When the post-World War II economy started to move again, there were massive labour shortages in Britain, due to the sheer levels of casualties during the preceding wars. A call had been sounded in the Caribbean for post-war labourers to come and work in the British factories, on the docks etc., and Black workers came on ships such as the *Empire Windrush*, which docked at Tilbury in 1948 with hundreds of West Indians who'd answered the call, and who are now referred to as 'the Windrush generation'. These Caribbean men would often walk from city to city, stopping off in doss houses along the way for food and overnight shelter, before carrying on the next day. My father, who'd come over long before the Windrush generation, was one such man. He'd reputedly walked the 200 miles from London to Liverpool, and when he arrived in Toxteth and connected with others from the Caribbean, one of them remarked: 'Look 'pon de slow train comin'.' That was how my father got his Liverpool nickname, 'Slow Train'.

There was also a post-war baby boom, as British people were encouraged to have children in order to replenish the population decimated by two world wars in the preceding three decades. And for that, they needed midwives. Enoch Powell, a British Tory politician – and in the opinion of many immigrants an absolutely loathsome man – was health minister from 1960 to 1963. During his tenure, he'd invited nurses from the Caribbean colonies to come to

Britain, pushing the narrative of Britain as the 'mother country', a 'land of plenty', where immigrants could find work in the National Health Service.[2] This time, many West Indian women embarked upon journeys to Britain to take up these vacant posts, and Caribbean nurses populated the nascent NHS as midwives, while many unskilled labourers became hospital orderlies. But just five years later, the same Enoch Powell was calling for them all to be sent back to the Caribbean, decrying the concept of 'multi-culturalism' and making his now infamous and menacing, racially charged tirade, often referred to as the rivers of blood speech,[3] (a reference to a Roman poem about war) about the effects of uncontrolled immigration, and also in response to the passing of the Race Relations Act 1968.

There were many Black people in Britain before the Windrush generation. My father was born in 1918 in what was then the colony of British Guiana, on the Caribbean coast of South America. It was a plantation-based colony with strategic waterways such as the Demerara River, which became famous for 'Demerara sugar' and its rum. What was not generally alluded to, however, when talking about Demerara, was its pre-eminence as one of the most prolific slave-based sugar economies in the Caribbean during the preceding centuries. My father, like many others, grew up in the cane fields, doing the gruelling and dangerous work of cutting sugar cane and wading through the flooded fields, wielding his cutlass to both harvest the cane and fight off the poisonous snakes that resided there.

His father – George Edward Watson – was a school master of African origin, with some Scottish ancestral genes in him. George was from the rural province of Berbice on the eastern side of British Guiana, in what was formerly a Dutch colony, where many of the villages had either Scottish or Dutch names. The regional capital of Berbice, called New Amsterdam, is situated on the eastern side of the Berbice River. Just across the river, on the western bank, is the infamous Blairmont sugar refinery.

My father's mother was called Olivia July, a woman of mixed African and Amerindian heritage from Meadowbank in Demerara.

British Guiana adopted a new name in 1966, the year I was born and the year of its own independence from British colonial rule. It ceased to be British Guiana and became the Republic of Guyana. Having left the capital Georgetown (named after King George III) in 1936 at the age of eighteen, my father had spent the next three years as a colonial merchant seaman, travelling the globe, before World War II broke out.

After serving on the supply ships from the outbreak of the war in 1939 – when he was just twenty-one years old – until 1942, my father decided to voluntarily enlist in the Royal Navy, reputedly joining his first fighting ship that same year in Greece. He continued his national service for the next three years, until the end of the war in 1945.

After the war, like many British colonial seamen, my father decided to reside in the UK and after moving around between Tiger Bay in Cardiff, London and Manchester, he settled and bought a house at 53 Upper Warwick Street in Toxteth, Liverpool. This is where the family lived when I was born in 1966. I was three years of age in 1969, when Liverpool Corporation (forerunner to Liverpool City Council) decided to place a compulsory purchase order on my father's house and forced him to sell it to them, so they could demolish it to build Toxteth sports centre. It was this action that took my father, and many other black seamen, from being independent homeowners in multi-racial communities to being dependent on Corporation housing as tenants in poor white communities, precipitating the situation in which we now found ourselves in Netherley.

As we continued along the black tarmac path, my father, having taken some time to absorb the shock of my disturbing question about what a 'Nigger' was, declared, 'Spartacus, don't you ever be an Uncle Tom!' (When I was a kid, my dad and his Guyanese friends used to call me Spartacus, after the revolutionary Thracian slave who took on the Romans. All Guyanese people had nicknames, and sometimes you'd only learn their real names at their funerals.) 'Daddy, what's an Uncle Tom?' I asked. 'A white man's bootlicker,' he retorted.

The black path – as we called it – was to take on new significance as the months went by and people settled into the new Cross Farm County Primary School. Gangs had already begun to form on the council estate and there was always trouble, which would often make its way into the school. Netherley was fast becoming a violent place, even the smallest of kids on the street were getting involved. When a fight happened in school – usually at break time in the school yard – kids would gather and start making a kind of tribal monkey chant: 'Ooh, ooh, ooh, ooh, ooh, ooh.' Whenever you heard that noise, you'd stop what you were doing and run over to see who was fighting. It was very primal behaviour that had somehow woven itself into schoolyard lore, and as such, everyone adopted it and participated. Sometimes it would continue after school, and the black path was usually where it took place. Regardless of what happened in the week, Fridays were always fight days, and after school, kids would gather on the black path, according to their territorial groupings. These weren't gangs in the formal sense, but you fought according to your territory.

We lived in Peckmill Green, and our two neighbouring streets were Brittage Brow and Glebe Hey. They were at one end of the black path. At the other end was Tothail Turn, Moxen Dale and Langshaw Lea. The school was opposite Tothail Turn on one side, and as the black path went past the school, it extended across the oller, which was strewn with rubble and was about the size of a large football pitch. If you crossed the oller diagonally you'd arrive at Brittage Brow, and that's where my mate Steph Taylor lived. Steph lived with his dad and two older brothers. We had become mates in school. I'd been getting bullied after school by an older kid, who'd wait for me every day at the end of the school yard on the black path. When he saw me, he'd punch me in the stomach, wind me, and as I curled over gasping for breath, he'd run off laughing. One night, the same kid asked me to hide in a small coat locker, about a foot wide and perhaps four foot tall. Naively I got in and he closed and locked the door. I was trapped and the school emptied. My mum came looking for me and the cleaner heard me banging and let me out after about half an hour. I was traumatised by the experience. Steph invited me to join his gang, and I did. After that, I never got touched. We did, however, join forces with our streets for the Friday night after-school fight, on the black path.

For the fight we had to gather our 'ammo', which consisted of stones, sticks, bricks and bottles – anything that could be thrown at the enemy. Steph gave me a nickname, 'Parro', after my mum's surname, Parry. Scousers – as they call people from Liverpool – had a thing about putting an 'o' on the end of everything and shortening it. So, Robert would become Robbo, Thomas would be Tommo and so on. One Friday, Steph and I came out of school and were walking up the black path, 'Come 'ead, Parro,' he said – which in Scouse vernacular means 'come on' – 'let's get our ammo for the fight.' Steph and I cut diagonally across the oller towards Brittage Brow. We came across a rubble heap with some building debris and crates from the shops' rubbish that had been dumped there. I grabbed a crate and started sifting through the rubble for good ammo. I gathered a few 'halfies' (half a brick) and saw some bottles on top of the rubble. I started to climb the heap to get to them and felt something stab me in the foot. I jumped back, dropped my ammo and realised that I'd stood on a broken milk bottle. As my foot pressed down on the curved sliver of the broken bottle, the thick glass under the sole of my shoe, forced by my body weight, pivoted the upper sliver downwards, through the side of my shoe and straight into my foot. 'Oww!' I shouted as I jumped back. Steph was startled. 'Are you okay?' he asked. 'Steph, get it out!' I squealed. Steph knelt down, grabbed the bottleneck and wrenched it out. A few of the other kids came to see what the fuss was. 'Parro's wounded!' declared Steph. 'Are you still gonna fight, Parro?' one of the other kids asked. In that moment, I gathered myself, I felt a sense of courage coming over me, a chance to show my boys that I wasn't scared, I was wounded but I had to represent for my streets. The blood was filling up my socks and I could feel it squelching in my toes. 'Yeah, I'm still gonna fight. Get me my ammo!'

We grabbed the crate and made it back across the oller to the black path, where the streets were already gathering at either end. I saw my brother Reynold there. He was with some older kids from his year group. 'Steph, we need a plan!' I said. 'This is what we should do. I can't run 'cause I'm wounded, but I can still fight. Give me the ammo and a few kids. We'll hide behind the bin shed on that house in Tothail Turn. When the fight starts, you all retreat so they think they've got you on the run. When they chase, we'll come out from the side and ambush them, then you all run back.' And that's exactly what we did. In the commotion a kid called John Murphy threw a halfie and it hit my brother Reynold on the forehead, cutting his head.

My ambush, however, was a success and made me a bit of a hero the next week in school. The wounded warrior who masterminded the ambush, that won the battle on the black path. I was to become somewhat notorious after that, but not necessarily in a good way. I was only eight years old. School had got wind of it, and we were hauled in for questioning by Mr Talbot. Both myself and Reynold being wounded was all he needed to conclude that we were the instigators. That was to be the start of a campaign by Mr Talbot to get us out of the school, which eventually – in my case – succeeded.

At Christmas 1974, my father was working for Netherley Property Guards. No one else had wanted to work, but he'd volunteered. His job was to guard the cargo sheds at the docks. He'd got up and put on his brown uniform with his peaked top hat and left at 5 a.m. to await the bus that was due to take him to work. It was a horrendous winter that year, and the snow was at least a foot deep. As kids we loved it. A white Christmas was always a source of celebration for us, but for my father, standing for hours knee-deep in snow, waiting for that bus was to prove fatal.

My mum had been working at the Meccano factory which made toys, so that year, we had a lot of presents to open. You could build things with a Meccano set. We got Raving Bonkers Fighting Robots and Dinky Toys, like the Pink Panther cars with a ripcord that made them speed across the lino on the floor. On the fighting robots, I was Muhammad Ali. It seemed like a happy day until my father came in looking utterly freezing. I thought he'd been to work and come home early for Christmas, but in fact he never got there, because despite those hours waiting in the freezing snow, the bus never came. I recall he went straight to bed without opening his presents and that day he had a stroke in his sleep. When he awoke, he couldn't move. An ambulance was called but the damage was already done. My father was paralysed from the neck downwards. He was now a quadriplegic, and he would never walk again.

At eight years old, I was too young to understand what all that meant, but the ambulance took him away and we only saw him occasionally after that, mostly at weekends. He would arrive in an ambulance from Broadgreen hospital, and they would push him into the house in a wheelchair. They had put a special hospital bed with a hoist in our living room and that had now become a permanent fixture of our new corporation house in Netherley. My father would sit almost motionless in the chair watching TV, and we would carry on playing, as if nothing had changed, occasionally disturbed only by his need to go to the toilet, or to be hoisted in and out of the bed. Putting him on the toilet took three of us, one under each arm and one to move his legs. Looking back, it was quite traumatic to see him like that but at the time we all adjusted and just got on with it. He would occasionally say to me, 'Spartacus, I still gwan take ya back to de sugar cane, when I get me legs back.' Of course, he never did, but that seed grew inside me over the years to come, and the desire to one day go to Guyana was rooted firmly in my soul.

After my father got sick, things took a downward turn for us. Netherley was by now an extremely hostile place. The council had built these sprawling new estates, with a mixture of houses and enormous flats, similar to what they call the 'projects' in America. The flats extended from the top of the estate to the bottom and housed literally thousands of families, stacked on top of each other. There were very few recreational facilities, and no thought on the part of the urban planners of that era as to what the social impact of creating brand-new communities with tens of thousands of complete strangers might be. They emptied all the post-war tenements and Victorian slums from the city centre into these new estates. Communities that had evolved over generations were ripped apart. No one knew anyone else, and neighbours had no idea who was moving in next door. The one thing that they all had in common – with a handful of exceptions – was that everyone else was white. That year, of the 100,000 people that were moved in, we were one of about six black families, four on our side of the estate and two on the other side.

During that era, people put their kids on the streets to 'play out' and we were no exception. The kids got up to all kinds of skulduggery and that's how the gangs had started to form on the estate. Territories got carved out, and fights had begun to break out everywhere. The place was becoming a hotbed of violence and crime. I don't recall how many times I heard the word 'Nigger' on the streets, as it was a daily occurrence. This was the era of 'Golliwogs' on Robertson's jam jars and their adverts were on the TV. 'We're off to Robertson's land. See you at tea-time' was the strapline, as the ridiculous trope of the happy Negro 'Golliwog', prancing merrily over Robertson land to bring jam to white kids, was displayed to the masses. People would see us in the street and start singing 'See you at tea-time'. I recall coming home from school with another kid and his father was walking with us. His father jokes, 'You've got a disease, haven't you?' I looked at him wondering what he meant. He turned to his son, motioning his head towards me, and said, 'He's suffering from a case of jam-jar-jir-itis,' at which point both he and his son burst out laughing at me. I was in shock, but I just dropped my head and carried on walking, as if nothing had happened. I really didn't know what to say. His father wasn't finished though. 'You need to go back to where you came from,' he said, 'Robertson's Land!' They again burst out laughing at me. At this point, I just wanted to shrink out of sight and be forgotten, it was so demeaning. What's worse, not only did they think they had the right to humiliate me (an eight-year-old child) like that, but they also really didn't see the problem with it.

That was typical of most white working-class people I encountered in those days, and as such, their racism began to shape our lives in ways over which we had absolutely no control. Being told to 'go back to where you came from' had a profound effect upon me as a child. Not only did it make me feel that I didn't belong where I was, that I was not welcome on this estate, in this city, or even in this country, but it also made me ask myself, 'Where did I come from?' A question that would dog me for the rest of my life.

CHAPTER 1

ANDREW WATSON

> *If you are on the road to nowhere, find another road.*
> *– African proverb*

It is hard to imagine how I found myself standing in Richmond cemetery, on a bright spring Saturday in April 2021, looking at the clean white surface of a refurbished marble gravestone. The inscription, inlaid with new lead lettering, bore the name of a man who had unknowingly changed my life. A man I hadn't even known existed until I watched a 2003 BBC Scotland documentary some eighteen years before. That documentary was entitled 'Andrew Watson, Scotland's Lost Captain'.

Previously forgotten to history, Watson has since been recognised as the world's first international Black footballer, a trailblazer in both Scottish and English football in the late nineteenth century. His grave was only discovered in 2021, after the UK government's public release of the 1921 population census, putting an end to speculation as to his final resting place, which had previously been thought to have been in India or Australia. At the time of his death, he'd been living at 88 Forest Road in Kew, on the outskirts of London, not far from the cemetery where he found his final resting place.

I had long been frustrated by the misinformation that had been circulating about Watson, much of which was predicated upon speculation in the documentary about his family origins in Demerara and his mixed heritage. Born at a time just after Britain emancipated the enslaved Africans in its Caribbean colonies, but while slavery was still rife in America, Brazil and many Spanish colonies, Watson's familial origins were enshrouded in mystery.

Having researched Watson's family extensively since seeing that first documentary in 2003, I wrote a few articles in 2019 which expanded on Watson's origins, bringing me to the attention of a Black film producer in Scotland called David Donald. David had also become fascinated with Watson's story and he was keen to revisit the subject, as the hundredth anniversary of Watson's death was nearing in 2021. He reached out to my literary agent, and we started talking about what a follow-up documentary about Watson might look like. David soon discovered how frustrated I was by the misinformation that had been stirred by the first documentary when he informed me that BBC Scotland were planning on re-screening it, complete with details that we now knew conclusively to be inaccurate and misleading. I implored him to go back to BBC Scotland and convince them that a new documentary should be commissioned, and offered to act as a consultant, sharing my contacts and much of my own research with them. David did just that, and BBC Scotland commissioned his Glasgow-based company (14th Floor Productions) to make it.

It was a huge triumph to finally get an outlet to redress the historical inaccuracies around Watson. Not only had he quickly become a major find in the annals of football history, even Scottish history, but he'd become a central figure in my own history.

David enlisted the Black football icon Mark Walters, who had over 600 professional games under his belt, plus eleven England caps, in his twenty-year career. His professional pedigree included a four-year stint in Scotland at Glasgow Rangers under manager Graeme Souness, who was also to feature in the newly commissioned documentary, entitled 'Mark Walters in the Footsteps of Andrew Watson'.

Finding myself behind the lens, when David brought Mark to Liverpool in March of 2021 to shoot one of the film segments, was a watershed moment for me. Filming on the Liverpool docks, built from the proceeds of the enslavement of Africans and at the very epicentre of the transatlantic slave trade, was quite profound. I felt rather emotive talking about this historic figure, who was something of an enigma, but one whom I'd spent years trying to get to know – delving into dusty archives, travelling around the world, and carefully piecing together documents and fragments of oral history.

In April 2021 I travelled from my hometown of Liverpool by train to London Euston, where a driver was waiting to taxi me to Richmond for the unveiling. I was filled with a mixture of excitement and trepidation throughout the whole trip. This had been the culmination of a long search, not only to find the truth about Andrew Watson, but more so, to find the truth about myself.

Upon arrival at the cemetery, I called the producers, and they guided me to the grave. When I arrived at the graveside, I noticed it was covered with a tartan blanket and surrounded by film crew and other participants. I caught sight of Mark Walters, the presenter of the documentary, and made a beeline to greet him, having not spoken since the Liverpool shoot a few weeks before. I saw several Scottish flags and a group of people wearing Scottish national team colours. These turned out to be representatives from the London branch of the infamous Scottish football fans, known as the Tartan Army.

Representatives of King's College School in London – where Watson had once studied – and other organisations with historic links to his academic and sporting career, such as the Corinthians from London, had also arrived with wreaths to lay on his grave. When it was time to lift the tartan tarpaulin, a lone piper in full regalia, kilt, sporran and dagger, stepped forth and delivered a superb rendition of the hymn 'Amazing Grace'. Though it had evolved into one of the most famous Black gospel songs, its lyrics were actually written in 1772 by a repentant former slave owner, Revd. John Newton – an historical fact lost on most Black people, who sing it with such fervour to this day.

With one of the many Black footballers to have followed in Watson's wake standing beside me, I saw for the first time Watson's grave, refurbished thanks to a fan-based crowdfunding campaign. Mark Walters was visibly enthused, having only discovered this remarkable Black Victorian football pioneer in the process of making the film. Walters would later recount his own career playing in Scotland, contrasting his experiences with those of Watson; the latter had also played in Glasgow at Parkgrove between 1874 and 1880, close to where Rangers now play and where Walters himself played from 1987 to 1991.

In an emotive testimony in the film, Walters reminds his former manager, Graeme Souness, of the racial slurs he'd endured both on and off the pitch, along with the regular hail of bananas, darts and coins that would be hurled at him whenever he got the ball. By contrast, there was little evidence that Watson faced anything like the racial abuse that the Black players of the 1980s suffered; that might have had something to do with Watson's social standing, during an era when football was largely 'a gentleman's sport' and Watson, despite being Black, was very much a part of the Victorian upper middle class.

I read the epitaph once more to myself: *In Memory of Andrew Watson. Born May 24th 1856, Died Mar. 8th, 1921. 'Resting.'* It is a simple inscription for a truly remarkable man. Not only was Watson a sporting legend, but he was also the key to an astonishing family history that criss-crosses Scotland, England, Australia, India, the Americas, the Caribbean and beyond, encapsulating the complexity, cunning and callousness of the British Empire and its chief source of income: slavery.

However, what began as a quest to unravel his family history also became a search to find my own.

My journey had begun nearly two decades before, in Aigburth, Liverpool. I was watching TV at home late one night when a documentary came on, 'Black Flash: A Century of Black Footballers in

Britain'. Though I wasn't particularly interested in football at that time, the opening sequence included Liverpool FC's Emile Heskey, one of the club's prominent Black footballers. I was intrigued, so I watched on. As the documentary progressed, historical black figures such as the footballer Arthur Wharton, who played for Preston North End at the end of the nineteenth century, and Walter Tull, who signed for Tottenham Hotspur at the beginning of the twentieth century, fascinated me. I'd had no idea that there were black players during the Victorian era. This was a revelation. Contextualising the Black experience in football revealed just how deep racism runs in the veins of British society. Hearing about the experience of Walter Tull on the field, not being able to play for England because he was Black but being able to do military service in World War I, where he gave his life for Britain – despite being Black – was a bitter pill to swallow.

There are no commercial adverts on the BBC, but they do showcase their own content in between programmes, so as soon as 'Black Flash' ended, the BBC announced that there was a further documentary airing straight afterwards that would show another Victorian Black footballer, one who'd preceded Arthur Wharton (long thought to be the first black footballer) by at least a decade. That man was Andrew Watson. By this time, they had my full attention.

I watched the subsequent documentary, 'Scotland's Lost Captain', with awe, and when the screen filled up with an old sepia-tone photo of Watson standing, surrounded by his white teammates, gazing straight into the camera, I thought, 'he looks like a boss'. And lo and behold, he was a boss – the captain of the team, no less. I immediately noticed the wavy loose Afro-style hair peeking out of the sides of his floppy Victorian football cap, the eye line, nose and chin, the way the shoulders slope down and the chest rises up. This man looked just like me – and not only that, we also shared the same surname. My name is Malik Al Nasir now – I changed it when I became a Muslim in 1992 – but prior to that, it was Mark Trevor Watson.

I'd adopted my father's name at the age of eighteen having been born with my mother's name.

As I was watching the documentary, thinking this guy looked like my double, the phone rang. It was my mum. 'There's a documentary on the BBC!' she declared. 'I know, I'm watching it,' I retorted, somewhat in a state of shock, while glued to the screen and my seat. 'He looks just like you,' she said.

'I know. It is freaking me out, there is so much similarity.'

My mum went on, 'I'm looking at the picture on top of the telly of you as a kid, and the picture of him underneath, and it's like looking at the twin of someone from a hundred years ago.' My mum had a picture of myself and my siblings as infants and there was a picture of Watson, in what the BBC described as an 'orphanage in Halifax'. I was later to discover that it was not in fact an orphanage but an elite boarding school, where rich merchants sent their children to be educated. It was one of many misrepresentations in that first BBC documentary, which purported to support a narrative of Watson being 'hidden away' due to the supposed 'shame' of his white merchant father, having an 'illegitimate black child' at a time when such unions were frowned upon. The fact that his education was paid for by his white father's accountant – on Bentley Road in Liverpool – was also used as supposed evidence of the need for discretion, to hide the shame of his Black child. I was later to discover that this whole narrative was nothing more than an attempt to perpetuate tropes that were diametrically opposed to the truth of the matter.

We were both astonished. At first I was wondering, could there be a connection? I'd never been to Guyana, and my father had long since passed away, but my own mum was telling me we were 'identical', so I couldn't be imagining this. I knew at that moment that I had to find some answers, to dig deeper into the life of this astonishing historic Black footballer. Little did I imagine on that fateful night that the search for Andrew Watson would go on for the next twenty years of my life, and that the discoveries I would make while on his trail would not only inform both his history and my own, but would be a catalyst for a whole new field of study, whose ramifications would go way beyond football to the very heart of the British establishment and its global empire.

Ironically, I had spent the previous two decades trying to escape football and anything to do with it. Watching 'Black Flash', and hearing of the racism experienced by Black footballers John Barnes and John Fashanu, had only reinforced my views as to why, at that time, I hated football. I'd played football as a child. In Liverpool, it's like a religion. Though I'd never wanted to be a footballer – I didn't think I had the skill – you can't live in Liverpool and not at least follow the football. It comes with the territory. As a young kid, I was a football fanatic, I loved to play the game, I used to collect the Panini football stickers, I knew every player and every team. But one day when I was about eleven, everything changed.

It was 27 August 1977, and Liverpool were going head-to-head with West Bromwich Albion at Anfield. Back then I was living at Greystone Heath Community Home in Great Sankey, Warrington, the care home I'd been put into at the age of nine after my father's tragic paralysis. At the weekend, when they let us out for home leave, me, my friend Colin and a couple of other kids from Greystone would go to a match, if Liverpool had a home game. We preferred to go in the Kop end. Only Liverpool supporters were allowed in the Kop, but in the Anfield Road Stand – 'the Annie Road end', as we called it – visiting supporters mixed freely with home fans.

To get into the Kop in the mid-1970s cost 70 pence, but the Boys' Pen was only 35 pence. The Boys' Pen had the worst view in the whole stadium, right up in the far right-hand corner of the Kop (if you were facing the Kop with your back to the pitch), but we figured out that if you threw your coat over the barbed wire that caged you in the Boys' Pen, you could climb over into the Kop and run down the open terraces to the front.

That day when West Brom came to Anfield, the stadium was packed with more than 48,000 supporters. Both the Kop and the

Boys' Pen were crammed full, so my friend Colin and I were forced to head to the Annie Road end, with the West Bromwich Albion supporters. It was to be a decision that I would regret for decades to come.

As we waited in the stands, I was already feeling apprehensive. Bottles were being thrown overhead, and grown men were shouting at each other and swearing. That was quite normal for the Annie Road end at that time, and that's why we never usually went in there as kids. It was wild. The teams started filing out of the dressing rooms, through the tunnel and onto the pitch. The crowd started to roar, and the players began to warm up, jogging on the spot, tapping the practice balls around and stretching their limbs. The Liverpool manager at that time was Bob Paisley, successor to the legendary Bill Shankly, and the team seemed unbeatable. It was like Liverpool were winning everything and hardly ever lost a game at home. These were considered the footballing golden years for the club.

But that day in 1977 marked a turning point for me. In those days most teams in the league didn't have any Black players – Liverpool had never had one – but West Brom had two, Cyrille Regis and Laurie Cunningham. As soon as Cunningham joined his teammates on the field, the monkey chants started, and bananas were being lobbed like yellow missiles through the air onto the field. Then a chant broke out in the crowd, 'The National Front is a white man's front! Join the National Front.' I saw straight, white arms being raised high in Nazi 'Sieg Heil' salutes. My mum had told me about the National Front. 'They don't like Black people,' she said. 'If you ever see them, run! If they catch you, they'll hurt you.'

I completely freaked out. I forced my way through the crowd to get to the back of the terraces. I'd lost Colin in the crush, as the opposing fans had already started fighting with the Liverpool fans. As there was no separation, it was complete chaos. I was an eleven-year-old Black kid, among thousands of angry grown-up white men who were throwing bottles, chanting racist Nazi propaganda and openly attacking one another, with no one on the terraces to control them. I was petrified. I managed to get to the exit gates. By that point I was frantic, hyperventilating, trying to explain to the security guard at the doors that I needed to leave immediately. 'I'm not allowed to open these doors during the game,' he insisted. 'They stay closed until the match is over.' I begged him, 'Listen to them, listen to what they're saying! You've got to let me out.'

He looked at me strangely, as if to imply, 'What's the big deal? They always shout that.' Finally, perhaps seeing the extent of my distress, he opened the gates and let me go. I ran all the way to the number 27 bus stop and cried my eyes out on the journey home. When I got in the house, I headed straight for the bedroom, ripped up every single Panini sticker, every football book, all my treasured collection and threw them all away. I never willingly played football again. After I'd officially left local authority care in 1984, if anyone came to my house and turned on the football, I switched it over. If I went to someone else's house and they put football on, I left. I never went to a football match again – not until many, many years later. It was like a switch in my head had just gone off. Everything to do with football seemed tied to racism. The beautiful game had showed me its ugly face, and I wanted nothing more to do with it.

Watching the documentary about Andrew Watson a quarter of a century later was a shock to the system, not just for the possibility of my personal connection to this iconic figure, but for his remarkable story itself. How did Watson, a Black man born in 1856, not just play football, but captain Scotland's national team – three times? All while – at least according to the records – receiving hardly any racial abuse, and without much attention being given to his race or colour at all. It required more digging, and the more I dug, the more nuanced was the picture that emerged.

But I wasn't the only one now digging into Watson. Ged O'Brien, founding director of the Scottish Football Museum, had first discovered Watson while looking through Scottish Football Association annuals dating back to 1881 and unmatched photos at the archives of the Scottish club Queen's Park. During his research for the documentary 'Black Flash', he'd noticed something different about one member of Queen's Park and Scotland's team – that same team who had thrashed England's national side 6–1 on 12 March 1881 at The Oval, hammered Wales two days later 5–1, and again triumphed over their English rivals on 11 March the following year – this player was Black. The name 'Andrew Watson' in the official line-up may not have said much about the player's origins, but the Black man that O'Brien spotted in the official photographs spoke volumes.

This discovery brought into the spotlight not only a footballer, but an architect of the game itself, and a gentleman. I was determined to find out more and discover if we shared not just the same ancestral family name, place of origin, mixed heritage and looks, but the same bloodline.

As a young man, I'd briefly followed in my father's footsteps and had a five-year stint at sea. I was semi-literate when I left the care system aged eighteen, but used my time at sea to learn to read properly and afterwards started to devour books at an ever-increasing rate. One such book was Alex Haley's *Roots*, which had made a huge impression on me. But unlike Haley's saga, tracing a familial line through slavery's so-called 'middle passage' from West Africa to North America, I was to find that my story – and Andrew Watson's – hinged on the legacy of European slavery and colonialism in the Caribbean and South America, specifically the British colonies of Grenada and Guiana.

From the first Watson documentary on BBC Scotland, I'd gained some initial clues. 'Born in May 1856, Andrew was the son of a wealthy Scottish sugar planter, Peter Miller, and a local girl by the name of Rose Watson,' explained journalist and presenter Stuart Cosgrove in his distinctive Scottish lilt, as the screen hovered over a map of the vast British empire and archive images of men hacking sugar cane, indigenous families outside a straw hut, and lines of Indian labourers. The film portrayed Watson as the product of an illegitimate, shameful liaison – but the story I was to uncover painted a very different, much more complex and nuanced picture.

Andrew Watson was born in British Guiana, which, while it is located on the northern coast of South America, was considered part of the Caribbean, or what was then known as the West Indies. People assumed it was an island like Trinidad, rather than being on the South American mainland. By 1856, the year Watson was born, enslaved Africans in the British Caribbean colonies had been officially 'emancipated' for twenty-two years – a date still celebrated annually in Guyana on 1 August as Emancipation Day.

Census records from British Guiana, dating back to 1851, give some further indication of the world Andrew was born into. In that year, the population numbered 127,695 – in addition to an estimated 7,000 'aborigines' who were not included in the census. Of those who were included, the overwhelming majority (86,451) are described as 'Natives of British Guiana', with the remainder hailing from Barbados and other West Indian islands, from Africa, or from Madeira in Portugal; alongside them were 'Coolies' (a derogatory term for Asian indentured labourers)* mainly from Madras and Calcutta in India, or from Shanghai in China. Guiana also had a coloniser class of its own, consisting of 'English, Scotch, Irish, Dutch, French and Americans'.

Interracial mixing had long been part of life in the colony, so Andrew's mixed parentage would not have been at all unusual there. The 1851 census, in fact, records 'mixed' as the second largest ethnic group, behind the sizeable African population.

My first step, upon discovering Andrew Watson, was to go online and try to find any of his ancestors. As Watson was born in British Guiana, his birth records were not held in the UK, but by the time

---

* The word 'Coolie' is very much pejorative by today's standards – as is the term Negro – but I use them both within the text, as they were the terms of the day, and appear throughout the archive and the literary canons of the period.

of the 1861 census, he was already in Britain – at Colwich Farm, Colwich, Staffordshire, to be exact, with his older sister, Annetta. The siblings are described as 'visitors' hailing from 'Demerara'.

Five years later, in August 1866, Andrew Watson was 'admitted by Mr. Cox'[1] to the Grammar School of Queen Elizabeth at Heath, near Halifax – the type of school where the records list future graduates from 1845 to 1875 under the note 'Cambridge is meant except where otherwise stated'. He is captured again in the 1871 census, aged fourteen.

There is only one photo of Andrew Watson as a child, when he's boarding at Heath Grammar School. It is not the best of photos: a small, blurry image of a boy scowling under a large, peaked cap, his hair poking out of the side. I think about what life would have been like for him, surrounded by a sea of white faces, away from his mother and his home.

Growing up in care from the age of nine myself, albeit only miles from my family home, I knew how rough it could be. In September 2003, just months after the Andrew Watson documentary aired for the first time, I finally got compensation and a public apology from the Lord Mayor of Liverpool for what was for me a traumatic and horrific experience in the local authority care system. Back then, even things that should have been easy proved a challenge – like combing my loose afro hair. I remember my mum got me an afro comb, one of those ones with the long metal prongs, but the staff at the children's home took it off me because they thought it was a weapon, despite calling me 'scruffy' for having unkempt hair.

This was in the 1970s, a century after Andrew Watson was at school, and yet he had a secret weapon that likely would have shielded him from many of the judgements about his hair and skin colour. It was his privilege, money and the patronage of one of Britain's most powerful families.

From Halifax, Watson went on to King's College School in London, where he stayed from 1871 to 1874. He then matriculated at the University of Glasgow in 1875 to study mathematics, civil engineering and natural philosophy under Professor William Thomson, the famous physicist, engineer and inventor who later became the 1st Baron Kelvin, better known simply as Lord Kelvin. But Watson never completed his graduate studies. Instead – in 1875 – he had a footballing stint at Maxwell FC in Glasgow and appointed himself vice-president of Parkgrove, a football club he'd invested in, and where he had been team captain since its founding in 1874.

At first glance, it looks as if Watson has thrown in the academic towel – and with it, his future career prospects. But at the same time as he is climbing the ranks of Scottish football, official documents show him pursuing his own business interests, and steadfastly working his way through the training necessary to become a chief engineer. In 1877, he marries Jesse Nimmo Armour, the daughter of a joiner, and on the marriage certificate he is recorded as an 'apprentice mechanical engineer' living at 97 Shields Road, Pollockshields, Glasgow. This is a man on the move, in more ways than one. In the space of four years, between 1877 and 1881, his address in Glasgow changes four times.

He co-establishes Watson, Miller & Baird – where he's described in the Post Office Glasgow Directory of 1800–1801 (at 35 Mitchell Street and 54 Union Street) as a 'wholesale warehouseman'. His wife Jessie gives birth to two children, Rupert Andrew Watson in 1878 and Agnes Maud Watson in 1880, when his address is 1 Rutland Crescent, Kinning Park, Glasgow. This time, his occupation is described as 'Railway Shareholder'.

Watson was also invited to join Queen's Park FC, who were at this time the biggest football club in the world. A glowing profile from the *Scottish Athletic Journal* of 1885 calls him 'Courtesy and unostentation personified' both on and off the field, praising how he plays the ball, as opposed to 'charging his opponent'.

Unlike the English players, who would take the ball and run up the field, the Scots developed the passing and running game, with the idea that you're only as good as your team. It's in direct contrast to the English system, which was far more utilitarian in nature, and where it was very much a game of 'every man for himself'. In the 1870s, the Scottish footballers who were the founders of this new passing system became known as the 'Scotch Professors'. They were football's elite, and Watson was one of a number of Scottish players paid by English clubs to teach their players how to play with their heads, using strategy, and not just their feet, relying solely on speed and power.

But money wasn't the goal for Watson. In fact this paid work, along with his border-hopping to play in both Scotland and England, laid him open to criticism about where his priorities – and loyalties – lay. The amateur form of football that he played was seen as a gentleman's game, and if you wanted to play, you were expected to have the money to support yourself – something Watson was clearly able to do. Amateur players financed their own kit and considered the idea of being paid to play the game somewhat reprehensible. Amateur clubs were for 'men of substance', and receiving wages for playing was considered beneath them. This is evident in the early days when Watson had put his own money into establishing Parkgrove FC.[2]

In 1882, Watson's wife Jessie died. By this point, Watson was living in Tottenham, London, and was in the thick of the English game. As well as the London Swifts and the Pilgrims, he played for the Corinthians – considered by some at the time to be among the best teams, not just in the country but the entire world, and known for their famous 'Corinthian spirit', an ethos built on sportsmanship, fair play and love of the game. Watson, however, did still make appearances north of the border with Queen's Park, perhaps to keep up his links with the club, or while visiting his children, who were now living with their grandparents, John and Agnes Armour, in Glasgow. In the next three census records, his children Rupert Andrew Watson and Agnes Maud Watson remain at the Armours' residence at 75 Houston Street, Glasgow, on the site of what today is an industrial estate and a railway terminus. As Andrew was training as a steam engineer, and later became a 'railway shareholder', one wonders whether this was a convenient location for his training, or for his business when he was with Jessie before she died. In the later Scottish census records, Andrew Watson does not appear at all.

Looking deeper into the Armour family line, I discovered a document citing the death of John Armour, Andrew's father-in-law. The record is signed by his widow, Agnes Armour, and refers to a 'claim for aliment at the instance of the deceased against Andrew Watson'. It's essentially a child-support demand for 'the maintenance and education of his two children' over a period of no less than fourteen years. What really caught my eye though was the details of the person the claim was addressed to: 'Andrew Watson, Chief Engineer, S.S. Darién c/o West Indian Pacific Steamship Navigation Company, Liverpool'. The document is dated 2 April 1901. This is the same ship, *Darién*,[3] that four months later was forced to bring back forty passengers from Colón, Panama, where a battle was raging over the separation of Panama from Colombia. A *New York Times* article from 16 August 1901 (also in the *St Louis Republic*)[4] reported the British Consul protesting at 'Jamaicans being conscripted by the Colombian Government to fight against the rebels'. Meanwhile, the passengers, docking in Liverpool, reported 'atrocities on both sides', including a government soldier who was 'found, shot in the abdomen, and with both legs amputated . . . a reprisal for the torture by the Government of political prisoners'. The tensions on the isthmus of Panama persisted, and even ten years later we get a sense of the unease in the region. The presence of Jamaicans to build the 'railways and canals' is also noted, another factor that would take on greater significance as my research evolved.

The hostilities in Panama were to endure, and Watson must have witnessed these on his travels. The shifting demographic of the region was being impacted by colonial powers exploiting the prowess of both the indigenous people and the descendants of the enslaved to build canals and railroads. Their agenda to press their colonial power base, and of course to exploit the regional Black and indigenous labour force, is amply described in *Stanford's Compendium* of 1911, just seven years before my father was born:

> At present no group of Carib speech is known to inhabit any part of the isthmus, although there are traditions that some of the warlike tribes in the central districts south of San Bias came originally from the Goajira peninsula, which is still held by a powerful Carib nation. In recent years they have nearly all been absorbed in the general population – a mixture of Indians, whites, and Mulattos, in which the coloured element is most pronounced. It is due to the large number of Jamaicans who were attracted to Panama by the high rate of wages on the railway and canal works, and many of whom afterwards settled in the country. The movement, unless arrested, must eventually assimilate the isthmus to those parts of the Antilles where the African element predominates.[5]

It is not known whether Watson was on that particular *Darién* voyage in 1901, but it gives a sense of the transnational political climate at the time he sailed on the ship, and in the ports to which he would have docked on its regular routes. Up until then, I'd only found references to Watson being an 'apprentice' and 'second engineer', including records of five journeys as second engineer with the *Louisiana*, when he was living at 17 Fairfield Street in Liverpool, and thirteen journeys as second engineer with the West Indian and Pacific Steamship Company (another variation on the company name referenced by Agnes Armour in her claim against Watson). I wanted to know why he was sailing with this line. Clearly the name SS *Darién* was a reference to the failed Scottish colony of Darién on the isthmus of Panama.

But here was proof of the huge professional climb he made, taking him from a trainee to a qualified first-class chief engineer, with the Liverpool Marine Board in May 1893. Clearly, this also would have meant he was away at sea for long periods of time, so would not have been able to look after his children personally, particularly after the untimely death of his wife. But why didn't he appear to provide for the children? This question dogged me for some time. When Andrew died, he left shares in the East Kilbride Railway in New South Wales, Australia, to his son Rupert,[6] who went to Australia to collect his inheritance. The census of 1911 hints at another connection between father and son. Rupert Andrew Watson, by now thirty-one, was still living with his sister, Agnes Maud Watson, his grandmother – John Armour's widow – 'a boarder', and a 'potato buyer' by the name of William Matheson, but Rupert's occupation was no longer 'scholar' – he was now, like his father, a 'marine engineer'.

It's easy to draw the conclusion that Andrew was an absent or neglectful father, but I know well that real life is not as black and white as official documents. To this day, there is still a space on my birth certificate next to 'Father's name' due to him being married to someone other than my mother. My dad had the same gap on his birth certificate, due to his own father being married to someone else. Meanwhile, in the BBC documentary, Andrew Watson is accused of altering his records to add 'Watson' to the surname of his father, Peter Miller – the assumption being that his mother's maiden name was Watson (ignoring the 'M.S. Rose' that follows her name on his marriage certificate, indicating her 'maiden surname'). This was a blatant misrepresentation by the BBC of what was on the marriage certificate. We now know conclusively that Andrew Watson's father was not Peter Miller, as the BBC initially alleged, but Peter Miller Watson, as Andrew correctly stated on his marriage certificate. This suggests that his mother was in fact married to Peter, as her maiden name is Rose. I did more digging and discovered that Hannah (aka Anna) Rose was in fact the mixed-race daughter of Andrew Rose, Peter Miller Watson's business partner.

Their marriage would have been a civil marriage; if Hannah, like most of the Black and mixed-race women of Demerara at that time, was not a Christian, she could not have been married in a church. The marriage may not have been recognised in Britain, despite being valid in Guiana. In Britain, church weddings required banns to be published in advance to announce the proposed betrothal and allow time for any objections to be raised. In Demerara, it was common to hold civil ceremonies when one of the parties was not a Christian. Such marriages were witnessed by a magistrate rather than a clergyman, and no banns were required. The practice led to many white Europeans in Demerara taking a 'free woman of colour' and marrying her in a civil ceremony without banns. Then, despite 'being a wife in all respects', though 'not allowing her to sit at the table', these women were sometimes discarded by their white husbands. As such, often, upon his return to Europe, the white man asserted 'plausible deniability'. In those days, if the man and the woman were seen together socially they could be construed as being husband and wife, so Black women were generally forbidden to attend social events. Similarly, if such a white person died, they would often be regarded as having 'died unmarried and without issue', when in fact they were in civil partnerships with coloured or Black women and had children with them in the colonies. Such common behaviour was generally tolerated in families that enjoyed the spoils of plantation slavery and grew rich from its evil proceeds, turning a blind eye to the grotesque conduct of their affluent relatives and often also to their mixed-race offspring.

When Andrew Watson lost his father, he was twelve years old and the details on his marriage certificate are 100 per cent accurate, despite the BBC's claim in the first Watson documentary. For me, it's too late to change my birth record to include my actual father. My dad died on 9 October 1981 when I was fifteen, and to get his name on my birth certificate now would require taking the case before a judge and a lot of bureaucracy. However, what I can do is fill in some of the blanks and tell the story that the documents alone cannot. I realised that I couldn't do that in England; looking through an

English lens gives a somewhat skewed perspective, especially where slavery and colonialism comes in, due to the deliberate erasure of Black familial data and a purposeful lack of proper records. I needed to go to the birthplace of my dad and Andrew Watson and figure it out for myself, from oral histories and other fragments of evidence. I needed to go to Guyana.

CHAPTER 2

'BACK TO DE SUGAR CANE'

A man who knows nothing is not aware of his ignorance.
– African proverb

Guyana had always been present in the background of my adolescence, though none of our family ever actually went there during our childhoods. In Toxteth, where I was born, my dad had lots of Guyanese and West Indian friends. But when the local government implemented their dispersal policy, designed to break up Black communities and scatter them around Liverpool, and we were dumped on that white, working-class estate in Netherley, we pretty much lost contact with the West Indian community. From time to time, my dad would take me to one of the two barber shops back on Granby Street in Toxteth that could cut Black people's hair. There was Jax, a white guy who spent his whole life cutting Black people's hair, and then there was Peewee & Smalley.

Smallie (Mr Small) was a typical West Indian man, talkative, funny, and seemingly content with his lot in England as a barber. His kids however had greater ambitions. His son Stephen Small, for instance, became a professor in the department of African American Studies at Berkeley in California, where he specialises in slavery studies to this day. But the Smallie I knew was my dad's friend – and occasional drinking companion – in that little barber's shop, which provided a small window into their West Indian world; a world that seemed alien to me in Netherley, but somehow provided the faintest of threads to a history to which I somehow belonged but was otherwise disconnected from. We would spend the whole day there, I'd get a haircut, and my dad would sit drinking Wray & Nephew white 'overproof' rum[1] and chatting with them in their thick patois. If you went there in the morning, you got a good clean cut. If you went in the afternoon, they'd be pissed, and you'd get a slightly wonky cut.

Sometimes my dad would reminisce about his childhood in Guyana. When he said, though, 'One day, I gwan' take you back to de sugar cane,' it seemed like a rather random statement of intent and to be honest, I had at that time no solid reference point to attach such a declaration to.

'What do you mean, Daddy?' I asked inquisitively. He said, 'We used to cut cane, son; you know?' 'What was that like?' I asked. He said, 'Well, you have to be careful of de snake. I take my cutlass and chop de snake.' Sugar cane, cutlasses and snakes – that was all I knew about Guyana and my dad's adolescence. There was a very definite cultural chasm between father and son. A yearning to go to Guyana had been etched into my soul, but it would be decades before I could cross that bridge.

When I finally did get to Guyana, I asked some people about their experience of the cane fields. After slavery had ended, many formerly enslaved Africans refused to cut sugar cane any longer, and so would instead 'dig shovel', meaning to dig the huge canals that were used to transport the cane from the plantation to the refineries on the coast, floating on vessels they called 'punts', ready to be processed into sugar, and to be exported to Europe and the west.

I'd distinctly heard my father say that he'd 'cut cane', so while 'digging shovel' may have been prevalent among Black people in Guiana, it was not necessarily universal. It seemed that as the times shifted, and the demographic and racial polarisation between the formerly enslaved Africans and the indentured Indians became more clearly delineated, attitudes towards societal roles became more entrenched and would later be the source of rancour between the populations that had been brought there by the Europeans from Africa and Asia.

My dad left British Guiana around 1936, just three years before the start of World War II, where Guiana was to play an important part in the war effort. As well as sending a small contingent of troops, mainly volunteers, it was there that the bauxite used to make aluminium for aircraft, ships and other war machinery was produced. During the war, production of bauxite in the country intensified, and British Guiana became the world's second largest producer. Realising its significance, German U-boats attempted to sink ships leaving the country, so additional protection was provided, including by the United States Air Force, operating out of the Atkinson Field base in British Guiana, one of a number of sites leased by Britain to its chief ally.

Like most veterans, my father was traumatised by memories of the war, often getting emotional when he talked about 'the waterfront'. He was an aggressive man, a tough seaman who came from a rough neighbourhood. Even after the war had ended and he remained in England, he was known to keep an axe behind the door – the next best thing to a cutlass. It is said he once chased a man down Berkeley Street in Liverpool with that axe. He could also be hot-tempered at home. My mum once told me that when I was born, with this wavy hair – so unlike my brother's afro – my dad had at first denied me, accusing my mum of 'going with a coolie man' and beating her due to his unfounded suspicions. Watching the Andrew Watson documentary long after my father had died, and seeing his hair, so much like mine, had felt like a vindication for my mum – not that she needed vindicating, it was my father's own insecurities that should have been checked. When my dad was discharged from one of the merchant ships he had sailed on in 1940, his discharge book stated he was a 'Fireman and trimmer' and that he did 'National Service'. Beyond that, I don't know much about his war career and only have his ration book.

Years later, when he had a stroke and had to go into hospital, Guyana became even more remote. We rarely saw his friends other than at Christmas, when my dad would come home for the holidays and throw his usual Christmas party. Christmas was no different at our house than in most English homes; before his stroke, my dad didn't really cook, so it wasn't like we were sitting around eating Guyanese pepper pot. We lived in a white neighbourhood with two white women, my mum and Flo – the woman we called our nan. The only Guyanese or Caribbean thing about our home was my dad, his patois and the 78s on the record player like Lord Kitchener's 'Muriel and the Bug', whose saucy insidious lyrics were lost on us kids, but we loved the melody . . . 'A bed bug, that found himself into Muriel's treasure. That bug was really clever to find that area . . .' and Harry Belafonte, whose lyrics still stick in my head to this day: 'Yellow bird up high in banana tree' or 'Jus' give me a redhead before I'm dead'. We had an old radiogram; it was like a piece of furniture, about five feet long, two feet wide and two feet high, perched on four legs. The veneered wood-like finish made it look like a cabinet, but when you lifted the top, it had a transistor radio and a built-in record player. The records spun at different speeds and the old 78rpm records were 10in in diameter, thick, brittle black vinyl. If you dropped them, they'd shatter. All the old calypso reggae records were on 10in. We used to mess about with the speed dial and deliberately play records at the wrong speed. Our favourite was Aretha Franklin's 'I Say a Little Prayer'. It was a 7-inch record, which played at 45rpm, but there was a button on the radiogram which could switch it to 16 rpm, which slowed it down considerably and made her sound like the drawl of a man's voice. When it opened with 'The moment I wake up, and I put on my make-up' in a deep man's tone, we found it hilarious.

Occasionally we saw my dad's best friend, an old Guyanese man they called 'Lucky' and whom I knew as Uncle Lucky. He'd lost three children in a fire, so I'm not sure how he got the name, but he'd known my father in British Guiana before he left around 1936. They'd both left on the ships and had both settled in Liverpool, and they maintained their friendship right up until my father had a stroke. Even afterwards, Lucky would still come and see us once in a blue moon, but then I went into care, my dad passed away and those connections were cut off. We fell out of touch, until one day some years later, when I saw a man staggering drunk out of the betting shop on Berkeley Street, just off Princes Road in Toxteth. Somebody I was with said to me, 'Oh there goes Lucky, drunk again.' He was too far gone to properly talk to, but I'd seen his face now, I knew who he was. The next time I saw him, I caught him sober and explained who I was. It was actually Lucky who gave me the nickname Spartacus, when I was about three years old and already a bit of a rebel, so he remembered me instantly. We sat down and I said, 'Look, I want to know more about my father. I want to find out some history about him and my Guyanese roots. I want to find people who knew him.'

He said, 'I can arrange that, Spartacus.' He took me over to the Alexandra pub at the back of Princess Road, right opposite his bungalow. He said, 'Wait here,' and left. I got a pint and just sat there, not sure what was going on. After a while all these old Guyanese men started to trail in, saying 'Where Slow Train boy at?' referring to my father's nickname. Soon I'd been introduced to Sour-pot, who used to cook with vegetables that were on their way out, Yank, who always wore American clothes and insignia, Panama, who had spent years in jail after killing his wife with an axe, Choppers Balls, Dukie, Ovid, Scarano, Parris, Skeet . . . on and on they kept coming. No one used the others' real or full names, maybe they didn't even know what their real names were. But I found out many things about my father that day.

Old man Skeet told me that he had been on a merchant ship with my father in World War II and had paid off the ship[2] in South Africa, because the company had sold the ship. The crew had to wait for another ship to come and collect them. My mum had once told me that my dad had been in South Africa and had got a woman pregnant. This was, of course, during the era of apartheid and the white police had apparently raided a shebeen in the Black township where they were staying, beat the woman and kicked the baby out of her.

At the time that she'd told me the story, I didn't know much about apartheid, and it sounded so fantastical I thought it was just a tall tale. I'd asked Skeet if he knew anything about my dad in South Africa and it turns out that Skeet was with him. He told me the whole story: 'We arrived in South Africa and the company sold the ship. They put all the white officers in a hotel and all the Black crew were sent to – what looked like – a barn with straw on the floor.' Skeet said, 'Your father wasn't having it, and he gathered the crew to head for a township.[3] We went to a shebeen.*

We moved in,' he said, 'and one of the women there fell pregnant to your father. The white police raided and beat her, and she lost the child.' I asked him for more details, but he said, 'I'm not sure your father would have wanted me to tell you everything.' So I left it at that. Skeet died soon after and the rest of the story died with him. But without such oral histories, much of what I was later to learn might not have made as much sense as it eventually did.

Even my dad's nicknames help paint a picture of his life. Up until he left Guyana, they called him 'Lard Oil', because he used to eat bread and dripping. That's how Lucky knew him before they came to England. Then, when he went on the ships, he was 'Sea Lawyer', as he was one of the few Black men on board who was literate, because his father was a school master. As he had the ability to read the rules on the ship and assert the rights of the crew, his crewmen turned to him as a sort of shop steward, even though the Black crews he sailed with at that time were generally not unionised.

From then on, I would go to Lucky's bungalow periodically to check in on him. People were always coming and going. Lucky seemed to be a pivotal figure in the Liverpool Guyanese community, and sometimes you'd hear snippets of oral histories that you would never get anywhere else. One day while I was there, Sour-pot popped in and said two really significant things to me. One of them was that my dad was in the Royal Navy and signed on a ship in 1942 in Greece.

---

* An unlicensed club in the township that had rooms at the back.

I knew he'd been in the merchant navy, but sure enough when I acquired my father's discharge book, lo and behold, there was his record of Navy service that same year. The other thing he said to me was that my dad lived in Weldaad, a former Dutch village on the west coast of Guyana's Berbice River. Sour-pot, whose real name was Gerald Alfred, may not have been the best at choosing fresh vegetables, but he was like an elephant when it came to details. He remembered the minutiae, and if he said that was how it was, you could be pretty sure he was right.

Hearing these stories about my dad was illuminating. When he died, Flo hadn't invited us to the funeral, or even told us he'd passed away. She'd cremated him and had his ashes scattered. I only found out that he'd passed away through my brother, who had been told by a neighbour that he'd happened to bump into. It was heartbreaking. There was no grave for us to visit, no ashes, nothing. It was shortly before that that we had realised that Flo was not – as we thought – our nan but was in fact my father's wife. And while she tolerated his relationship with our mum, she harboured a bitter resentment to us children, as she herself was unable to have kids.

When Sour-pot told me in 2007 he was going to Guyana the following year, I knew I had to go with him. Now I could learn more about my dad and, at the same time, fill in more details about Andrew Watson's family. All I had to go on was Sour-pot's word that my father had lived in Weldaad, my father's discharge book, which listed his 'next of kin' as his mother, Olivia July, living in Meadow Bank Village on the East Bank of the Demerara River, and the certificate of my dad's marriage to Flo, which listed my grandfather as George Edward Watson.

I'd been working in the US and Jamaica on some music projects and decided to take a trip to Guyana to research a book on Watson. I'd commissioned an author – Tonya Leslie – from New York to write a children's book on Watson, and we had decided to go there together to do the research. It was also a chance for me to fulfil a childhood dream of going 'back to de sugar cane'. Tonya was originally from Belize, but we had actually met some years before as undergraduates at Liverpool Institute of Higher Education (which later became Liverpool Hope University) and we had kept in touch. Tonya regularly visited Belize, and was more familiar with the South American style of third world protocols that we might encounter than I was.

We set off on a flight from New York to Georgetown in Demerara with a sense of anticipation. As the aeroplane descended into Cheddi Jagan International Airport, the jungle below us suddenly transformed into massive tracts of flat land. The cane fields were evident on an industrial scale. Seeing them from a bird's-eye view, I got a sense of the sheer magnitude of the sugar production operations, and I thought of my dad out there, just cutting, cutting, cutting, all day long in the blistering heat and humidity.

For years I'd been looking at images of this coastal land. Now it was as if I was entering the map, and the view had switched from 2D to 3D. We touched down and taxied up to the airport terminal, a simple, single-storey concrete building in cream and terracotta, planted around with colourful flowers, bright palms and broad banana leaves. It had taken me more than forty years but, finally, I'd reached my fatherland. As clichéd as it sounds, it felt like coming home and I was consumed by a sense of belonging.

We dumped our bags at Le Meridien Pegasus – a cylindrical hotel located close to the stone seawall – in Georgetown, the capital of Guyana. This vast seawall structure snakes along the coast to protect Georgetown from flooding and was constructed back in the days when the Dutch ruled over this land. We only had five days in Guyana and plenty to do, so we got to work straight away. While Tonya headed for the Walter Rodney National Archives, I packed my handheld camcorder, notebook and pen and spent the next few days on the road, talking to anyone and everyone I could.

I first arranged to meet one of my dad's contemporaries, a man known as 'Hundred' (apparently after the number of women he had slept with). Lucky had told me that Hundred was the only person still living in Guyana who had known my dad before he left the country. It was evening when we met at Hundred's home in Campbellville, a tightly populated neighbourhood just outside Georgetown's bustling city centre. As the sun went down, the glaring heat of the day mercifully subsided, and a smattering of fireflies appeared. I'd never seen them before and watched in fascination as they danced about us, dots of bright light against the gradually darkening skies at dusk. I asked Hundred what he remembered of my father as a young man. 'Your father lived in Tiger Bay,' Hundred told me.

'Yes,' I said, 'When he came over to Britain he was living in Cardiff, in Tiger Bay.' 'No,' Hundred shook his head. 'Tiger Bay right here in Guyana.' It turns out my dad went from one Tiger Bay to another – the first in British Guiana, the next in South Wales – both busy, dockside areas with a reputation for being somewhat rough. Cardiff's Tiger Bay had boomed during the industrial revolution, attracting seamen and other workers from more than fifty countries around the world, including countries in the Caribbean. Though its name has since been changed to Cardiff Bay, its history as the oldest multi-ethnic community in Wales lives on. Meanwhile, in Guyana, Tiger Bay remained the kind of area you're warned not to visit alone. I asked Hundred how my father survived in a place like that. 'How you mean survive?' he chuckled, 'Your father used to run Tiger Bay.' I knew my father liked to settle his affairs with his fists (then there was that axe) but I had no idea he'd been a bit of a gangster.

The next day, Hundred and his son Brian, a union man with dreadlocks and a greying beard, who he had co-opted for some assistance, took me to Meadow Bank, the village my father referenced in all his seaman's Department of Trade records as the home of his next of kin, his mother, Olivia July. Today its strategic riverside location, close to the mouth of the Atlantic Ocean, makes it a popular base for the newest colonialists, international oil and gas companies, keen to exploit Guyana's offshore oil reserves. But when I visited Meadow Bank in 2008, its reputation was more street than slick. I was warned not to go at night, so we arrived in the heat of the day. I got chatting to some of the residents, telling them about the family connection and why I was there. One woman told her son, a boy of about ten or eleven, to show me the spot where my grandmother's house used to be. 'What's it like around here?' I asked him, just to make conversation while we walked. 'Deh call it Murder Bank,' he replied somewhat knowingly. The friendly advice I'd received – to come during daylight hours – suddenly made more sense.

The community were welcoming though, and freely shared local gossip, telling me how Olivia, along with other elderly residents, was swindled out of a few properties she'd owned by a sheisty lawyer called Llewellyn John, who later became a government minister. I tried to track him down at his offices but had no luck, his secretary told me he wouldn't be around for a few days and offered no useful information. Now it's too late: Llewellyn John passed away in January 2021. In an obituary, the local paper, the *Stabroek News*, described him as being 'well known for his expertise in civil matters, such as those related to land'. Whether that included land in Meadow Bank, I guess I'll never know.

Other than the few neighbours who remembered her, there were no traces of Olivia remaining in the village – at least that I could ascertain on that short visit – nor members of the July family. I turned to the phone directory and happened upon a July living further up East Bank Demerara, just off the Soesdyke Highway (a long stretch of road leading to the town of Linden in the Upper Demerara-Berbice – Region 10 – the home of bauxite in Guyana, and on the road to the vast, green interior).

Terrence 'Terry' July leaned forward expectantly on the sofa, his white vest against his brown skin, silver-framed spectacles magnifying what seemed like slightly nervous eyes. His leg was bandaged, and his foot swollen in what looked like a form of cellulitis. I held the camcorder up and asked him to introduce himself on tape and tell me about our family.

'My mother's name is Margaret July,' he said.

'And who is her mother?' I prompted.

'Her mother's name was Helora July.'

'And what's her relationship to Olivia July?'

'They were, um . . .' He paused. 'What is it, bai?'

'Niece?' suggested his wife, Alita, an Amerindian Arawak woman with cropped hair, peering over oval glasses.

'Niece,' he repeated, uncertainly.

'Olivia July was your grandmother's niece?' I said, looking for confirmation.

'Niece, right!' he said with a relieved smile.

'So Olivia July was your mother's cousin.'

'Cousin?' He paused. 'Aunt! Because they were so close – something like that. So long ago this thing, I tell you . . .'

Oral history brings stories to life and can add colour, details and interpretations that you won't find in a dusty archive or on an official document. But it can also make your head spin. Though I never quite clarified how Terry and I are related, he did remember Olivia living in Meadow Bank and shared memories that helped bring to life the grandmother I never knew. 'Olivia! She was a wonderful person. She used to make lovely chocolates and gingerbread.' Terry also remembered that, though she was a double amputee (according to her former neighbours she had lost both legs), Olivia still used to come to the door of her home and invite them in to share 'old-time stories'. At that time, he said, most of the properties in the village belonged to the July, Lewis or Cane families. Olivia was a savvy businesswoman and would sell the chocolates and gingerbread right from her porch to make money. I reminisced about my father, who lost a leg after his stroke when a bedsore in his foot became gangrenous. I wondered if either mother or son knew of the other's similar fate, or indeed had ever met again after he'd left.

Hundred told me, 'I'm too old for all this travelling around,' but having linked me up with Brian, he said he was sure we would find what we were looking for. Brian made himself available for the week to show me around and give me an insight into the lie of the land. He lined up a driver, Raj, a young man of Indian origin who became part of the quest, chipping in his own encouragement and tips as we went. I told them about my journey to seek my family's roots back through slavery and colonialism, as they took me up to the seawall. 'There is the jetty where they used to bring in the slaves from Africa in the colonial times,' said Brian, pointing to some stakes of wood just about visible above the water, 'and the East Indian indentured slaves,' he added. Those who came from India are usually referred to as 'indentured labourers', but Brian wasn't far off. The conditions that the new arrivals from India lived in were not dissimilar to those of the enslaved Africans who'd preceded them. It felt fitting to have an Afro-Guyanese and an Indo-Guyanese showing me around the country that their ancestors were brought to, and at one point I couldn't help myself as I shouted out those famous words of Martin Luther King Jr. 'Free at last, free at last. Thank God almighty, we are free at last.'

I decided to follow Sour-pot's lead that my dad had at some point lived in Weldaad, a coastal community in the Mahaica–Berbice area, otherwise known as Region 5. In Guyana, most villages on the eastern side of the Demerara River are off the coast road that stretches from Georgetown, the capital, east towards Mahaicony and then on to Berbice, interrupted only by the mouth of the Berbice River. The road is bumpy and neglected in parts, sometimes little more than a dust track, while in other parts, tarmac glistens in the midday sunshine. Miles and miles of plantations veer off both to the south into what was once dense Amazonian rainforest, and on coastal land to the north, reclaimed from the sea. I was fascinated by the topography of the landscape and wondered how people traversed these vast plantations without motor cars. Brian told me, 'People used to walk miles from village to village. How you think ya' father got the name Slow Train? Guyanese people from dem times walk everywhere.' The gravity of what he was telling me started to sink in as I began to contextualise the myth that surrounded my father. Every so often, we had to stop or slow down, as there were cattle, horses, donkeys and goats arbitrarily walking the same road as us, haphazardly manoeuvring themselves with scant regard for the danger posed by a passing vehicle. I looked up at the dense blue sky and caught sight of a flock of blue-and-yellow macaws flying overhead. The majestic scene was like something from a Disney movie. I had never seen such a beautiful and spectacular sight. At home we have flocks of grey pigeons, white seagulls and black starlings, but nothing like this. I was filled with wonder and anticipation for what lay ahead.

After a few hours, we finally arrived in Weldaad. My excitement at this point was palpable, although I feared that I wouldn't find anything – that my efforts would be futile and that the whole journey, whilst intriguing on many levels, would turn out to be a dead end. Undeterred by the nagging doubt in my mind, I set about the task at hand. I started to run the tape in the handheld camcorder to record the moment, to capture a sense of what this place was like and, if indeed this was the land my father trod, to have a record of it for posterity.

I began by randomly stopping passers-by and asking for any information on Watsons in the village but drew a complete blank. I spotted the post office and motioned to go inside. I figured if anyone knew of any Watsons in the village, they would. But again, they confirmed that there were none. There was a guy coming out of the post office dressed in camouflage military fatigues, riffling through some paperwork, trying to get it into his pocket. I approached him and we struck up a conversation. Unsurprisingly, when I asked his name, he replied in true Guyanese fashion, 'They call me Soldier.' I asked him if there was anyone in the village who knew the history of the place, particularly family history. Soldier told me there was a rice farmer called Mr Hamilton who 'knows a lot of family history'. We headed off to Mr Hamilton's farm, realising that if any Watsons had ever been here, they probably weren't here any longer.

When we arrived, a tall thin man of brown complexion, dressed neatly and with a very polite and calm demeanour, dismounted from his tractor and approached us with a welcoming smile on his face. He didn't much look like a farmer, I'd expected someone shabbily dressed in muddy boots, but he was very well turned out, and his tractor looked new and expensive. Behind him lay acres of neatly tended rice paddies; he was clearly doing rather well for himself. He greeted us and I proceeded to tell him who I was and why I was there, and again asked if there were any Watsons in the village. Mr Hamilton was also doing genealogical research – not into the Watsons, but into the White family. We spent some time exchanging stories, in the hope of finding a correlation between our research, but alas, it soon became clear that none existed. Mr Hamilton suggested that I leave my number and he would let me know if he heard about any Watsons. For now, he suggested that I try seeking out the elders of the area. He told me that the oldest man in the village was Gerald Jocelyn Blockman, born two months before my father and at that time he was just shy of his ninetieth birthday.

I had never had the chance to really talk to my father about what life in Guiana was like back then, and I never knew about Weldaad until Sour-pot told me, so when I finally met this wizened old gentleman, with a peaked cap and dark, leathery skin, it was probably as close as I was going to get. Gerald recalled attending St Jude's Anglican Primary School in Lichfield and then Belladrum Secondary School before leaving school at thirteen – not uncommon for boys at that time. A life of odd jobs followed. A little rice work, a little farming, running a bakery, gold digging – 'anything you think about being in Guyana as a poor man'. He'd worked at the Bath and Blairmont sugar estates, and to get there, he would take the omnibus train from Belladrum (the next village along from Weldaad) eastwards to Rosignol in Berbice on the banks of the Berbice River. Blairmont wasn't just a plantation, it housed the main sugar refinery in Berbice and sat strategically at the mouth of the Berbice River, which let straight out into the Caribbean Sea. It was also nautically closer to Britain, which would reduce the duration of the voyage from Demerara to the UK.

If he was working in Port Mourant or Skeldon, he'd take the ferry over the river to the capital of Berbice, New Amsterdam – moving even closer towards where Guyana borders Suriname, or Dutch Guiana as it was known until its own independence in 1975. Its proximity – directly across the mouth of the river from the infamous Blairmont sugar refinery – gives it further strategic importance. The steam train no longer exists in Guyana, though the ferry still carried passengers and cars over the Berbice River up until recently, when they constructed a bridge.

Gerald told me that he remembered my grandfather, George Edward Watson, the school master. 'To visualise him now take me a little time,' he admitted, but it was enough for me. It was as if the past was coming to life, and I started to feel like I was walking in my ancestors' footsteps. He told me of the team that came from Belladrum School to Weldaad to play cricket, and the man who brought them, known as 'Teacher Watson'. He couldn't recall much more, but this was the validation that I needed to confirm Sour-pot's story that my father most likely did spend time with his father in Weldaad, though it was clear they'd never settled there. We set off back to Georgetown with a renewed sense of purpose.

The following day, a trip to the National Archives would shed more light on this genealogical jigsaw. In the records of the Colonial Registrar's Office, I found a document called 'Persons Entitled to Vote in the Election of Members of the Colleges of Electors and Financial Representatives . . . in and for the Counties of Demerary and Essequibo'. Near the bottom of the list for Electoral Division No. 1 was a name that would help to redress the erroneous story previously told about Andrew Watson's parentage. It stated, 'Watson, Peter Miller', registered by 'his attorney William Jones, Georgetown'. Peter Miller Watson's abode is listed as 'Absent' and his qualification to vote given as 'Part Proprietor' of 'Pln. [Plantation] La Bonne Intention, and of one undivided third of Pn. Zeeburg, by Letters of Decree and Transport, Having More Than Three Acres of Land Under Cultivation'.

The date of registration is 13 December 1855, and the document is dated 14 January 1857, meaning that at the time it was prepared – four months before Andrew Watson was born – Peter Miller Watson was absent from the colony, and so may not have been present to witness – let alone register – his own son's birth. I decided to release what I'd found about Andrew Watson and Peter Miller Watson online. A part of me said, 'Don't! Keep it. This is important. One day it will matter.' But there was another part of me saying, 'There is a public interest.' And there definitely interest. In fact, a flurry of research was triggered by the new details I'd posted, including the birth and baptism records of Peter Miller Watson of Crantit in Orkney, son of James Watson, Chamberlain to Lord Henry Dundas, the Earl of Orkney. All the Andrew Watson researchers, such as Llew Walker – who went on to write *Andrew Watson: A Straggling Life* – and historian David Alston, who manages the website 'Slaves and Highlanders', dug in deeper and took it to a whole other level.

The premise of the BBC documentary that Andrew Watson was hiding illegitimacy – that his parents weren't married because there were no marriage banns published – was gradually being eroded. Peter Miller Watson's will refers to Andrew and Annetta Watson as his 'Natural Children', while in the will of his half-sister, Mary Eliza Traill, there are references to Andrew and Annetta as Peter Miller Watson's 'natural born children'. I would argue that, while their parents' marriage may not have been recognised in England, this form of 'irregular marriage' was legal under English colonial law and Dutch and Scottish law, as well as under the civil laws of Guiana. Andrew Watson had every right to claim legitimacy, as he was born under that legislature – he clearly named his father as Peter Miller Watson and his mother as 'Anna Watson – Ms Rose' on his marriage certificate to Jessie Nimmo Armour. Since his father referred to him in his will (while Andrew was still a minor) with the surname Watson, we can clearly establish that as a child, his father knew him by no other surname, a fact that is borne out in all Andrew's school and census records.

There is also a phrase, often used in Guyana to this day, of 'reputed wife' or 'reputed husband', which essentially recognises common-law partnerships – those not registered as civil or religious marriages. But Peter Miller Watson and Anna Rose did register their marriage, according to the British Guiana Colonists database – an Australian website digitising material from various global sources, including the Centraal Bureau voor Genealogie and Algemeen Rijksarchief at The Hague, the Rhodes Library at Oxford and individuals with ancestors from British Guiana's colonial era. It may have been the case that, as both Peter Miller Watson and the children were now in the UK and the colonial civil marriage was not recognised, Peter used the term 'natural child' in his will to avoid any difficulties with his intended distribution of his estate. The children would have had no way to prove their paternity had he not done so. However, if they had all been in Guyana at the time of his death, this would most likely have not been an issue. Perhaps this is where the discrepancy lay.

When I started looking into Andrew Watson's ancestry, I largely ignored the English side, because apart from the census records, I couldn't find anything on his life in England beyond his schooling in Halifax. My research focused on Scotland, looking through the Scottish parish registers and combing through the banns and marriages on the Scotland's People website. Only when I got to visit Guyana did I realise the true extent of the Scottish influence there and its legacy, from Scottish surnames and place names to pictures of white Scottish ministers in all the churches I entered. There was even one in Georgetown called St Andrew's Kirk. Generation after generation, decade after decade, the Scots were there. In fact, had the Acts of Union not been passed in 1707, Guiana would probably have been a Scottish colony.

Peter Miller Watson, moreover, wasn't the only Watson to come seeking his fortune. He was one of five brothers born to James Watson (1770–1808) and his wife Christian, née Robertson (1780–1842), and registered at birth in the parish of Kirkwall in Orkney. The *Genealogy of the Families of Douglas of Mulderg and Robertson of*

Kindeacre with their Descendants sparingly captures the brothers' lives. The eldest two brothers, Harry Robertson Watson (1801–1836) and Andrew Watson (1803–1837), are both said to have died in Demerara at the age of thirty-four, their deaths less than a year apart. Peter Miller Watson is recorded as having 'died unmarried at Weylea, near Guildford, 22nd April 1869', and 'without issue', which we know to be incorrect. His younger brothers William Robertson Watson and James Watson both died in Scotland. Other than James (who it seems didn't join his brothers overseas), all are said to have died 'unmarried' – no children are mentioned. It was a fact that I saw repeated throughout my research, where the white Scottish clansmen spent most of their adult years in the colonies and were recorded as having 'died unmarried and without issue'.

Since beginning my research into Andrew Watson and our possible family connection, some sceptical historians have asked, 'How could you be related to him?' The presumption might have been that if none of Peter Miller Watson's brothers had children, and nor did any of his grandchildren (Andrew Watson's children), the family line ended with them. However, I was convinced there was more to the story. I couldn't believe that while the Watson brothers spent years in Demerara and Berbice, all four who went there remained unmarried and only one of the four produced any children. Validation came from the words of the brothers themselves – specifically a series of letters they wrote to their mother Christian and their stepfather, Dr Thomas Stuart Traill (1781–1862), Christian's second husband after James Watson's death.

Christian Watson, now Christian Traill, had vast wealth inherited from her rich uncle George Robertson, who'd died in 1799 and left a fortune of £250,000. Christian received substantial annuities from her uncle's will and was in a position to fund Dr Traill's many scientific pursuits, although he too was a significant land owner in Orkney.

The correspondence between the Watson boys in Demerara and Dr Traill gives a fascinating insight into the lives and preoccupations of Scottish colonists in British Guiana. From Demerara and then

Berbice, Harry regularly writes to Dr Traill in Liverpool, informing him of the latest treasures he is sending his way: a 'Warawini Diamond' from the interior, bows and arrows from the indigenous population (one dipped in poison), a rum bottle of three hummingbirds, a snakeskin and a monkey. 'I have several times thought of sending you a Baboon,' he writes in 1821. 'If you would like one, let me know?' To his mother, Christian, he promises 'pots of preserves, a bottle of pickles and a barrel of sugar'. In return, his family sent clothes and other items. On 21 July 1821, Harry enquires after his brother Peter, who his mother has mentioned will soon be coming out to Demerara. 'I trust he will first be fixed in some good situation,' he warns, 'for there are hundreds of young men out here at present who from want of employment are going headlong to ruin.' He reports back on his other brothers too, informing his mother in 1824 that his brother Andrew is again with him. 'He is now permanently settled with me. I have told him very plainly what I expect of him, and he took it all in good part. I have therefore every reason to expect he will turn out a clever fellow and be of use to himself yet.'

What jumped out to me above all, however, were the references to the brothers' relations and children. Peter Miller Watson's brother Andrew writes haphazard, intimate letters, sharing his casual plans for his clerk's salary ('as I get a little capital, I intend to purchase some Cooper Negroes, each of whom will bring in here to the amount of £40 or £50 clear per annum') and nuggets of news, business and gossip, such as 'My marriage is broken off – no more about it'. So much for being unmarried. In another telling letter, a clearly frustrated Peter tells William about money owed by him in Demerara, adding, 'Today the boy Henry came to Town. What am I to do with him? Not having been downstairs for some days, I have not seen the Boy!' It seems that not only has his brother left a mess of his affairs, but potentially a child of colour too. If William had children who remained in Demerara, then Andrew Watson had cousins, and the Watson line in Guyana continued.

I revisited the Scottish census to look for Peter Miller Watson's brothers, and found William Robertson Watson living in Scotland – with Annetta Watson, aged twenty-one, who is described on the document as his niece. So William was back from the West Indies and looking after his brother's daughter. There is no hiding their kinship, no shame. Perhaps just a white man taking care of his brother's mixed-race offspring in Scotland, as his brother Peter did for him with his own mixed-race boy, Henry, in Demerara.

Back in present-day Guyana, in search of contemporary Watsons, Tonya and I scoured the phone book and post offices for clues, whilst Sour-pot pontificated about the old days in the back seat. Further down the coast from Weldaad on the way back to Georgetown, we stopped off in a village called Clonbrook. We parked the car and got out by the post office, a cream-coloured brick building with a red roof, white trim and ragged skirting outside – perhaps the result of one of Guyana's many floods. The windows were shuttered, and vertical blinds hung behind them, but the door was wide open, so we went in and walked up to the meshed counter. We asked if there were any Watsons in the area. A woman behind the desk in a grey pinstripe suit, with a gold necklace and tooth to match, looked up the local pensioners' list – we wanted people with long memories – and there we found a Watson. Beryl Watson to be exact. We asked for Beryl's address, but the post office worker did one better. 'That's my auntie,' she said. It turns out the woman in the suit, Samantha Moira, is Beryl's great-niece. Samantha called Beryl and soon we were on our way to pick her up and go to the home of her cousin, Doreen Butcher, in Victoria.

Out on the veranda, where the air was slightly cooler, I sat next to Beryl Watson. She was wearing a blue striped dress with a blue round-brimmed hat, and her dark eyes had a pale blue ring around the iris that stood out against her black skin. She told me she was born in 1931 and used to be a teacher – though she had long since retired. A plastic table and chairs were pulled up, bottles of vodka and Pepsi appeared on the table, and something called 'Dutch gin' was mentioned, but I politely declined – 'I don't drink,' I said. Time was short so I launched straight into why I was here, filling them in on my family history. In the background, I heard Sour-pot launching into one of his long stories. 'Sour-pot!' I said in exasperation, 'I really need to get this information. I've come a long way for this, you can tell your story anytime!'

What I didn't know at the time was that Sour-pot was sick: he had cancer. He'd actually decided he wanted to die in Guyana, so having settled his affairs in the UK, he'd gone over to resolve his Guyanese affairs. And he did, in fact, die not too long afterwards. I thought we had all the time in the world to talk, but he knew otherwise.

Despite Sour-pot's interventions – though, really, because of his help in putting me on the trail – I discovered that Doreen and Beryl's grandmothers were sisters from the Hall family. Beryl's grandmother, Blanche Hall, had a child with a Watson and that child was Beryl's father, Frederick Adolphus Watson. What the first name of Frederick's father was, the family didn't know.

'He wasn't one who used to talk at all, so you never learn anything from him,' explained Doreen. 'And it wasn't the custom to ask,' chipped in another cousin, Desmond Saul, who was summoned by phone to join us.

'It is a peculiar tradition with the folks of old, children didn't ask questions,' he explained. 'So, a lot of children who may have not been born in wedlock, did not know their lineage.'

They did remember, though, that Frederick had lived in either Weldaad – where my father once lived, and his father too, according to Sour-pot – or the neighbouring 42 Village (also known as Seafield), but had come to live in Victoria as a young man, when his mother died. Victoria is widely accepted as the first village in British Guiana to have been established by a group of newly freed Africans, who in 1839 bought what was then Plantation Northbrook and renamed it, perhaps after the British queen at the time. They weren't the only ones. 'The same thing was happening in all the villages,' Beryl's cousin Doreen told me, 'Cotton wasn't profitable any more . . . so they got rid of it [the land].' Though the trade in enslaved Africans had separated them from their families and homeland, the memories and customs of Africa were not wiped away so easily. Doreen's brother, John, remembered their grandmother saying when they were children, 'Stay away from the Congo people!' – the Watsons, Halls and Sauls being 'Guinea people'. 'In them days,' added John, 'Black people were more conscious of their roots and where they come from.' He mentioned four families in Victoria who retained their African names, or a version of them: Sancho (pronounced Sanko), Kato, Coffy, Kojo. It was interesting to note that the Watsons were regarded as being 'Guinea people', as Peter Miller Watson's family had advertised themselves previously as dealers in 'Prime Gold Coast Negroes'. Guinea was the epicentre of the Gold Coast which sits on the Gulf of Guinea, so the oral history of the Black Watsons being 'Guinea people' accords perfectly with the source of Peter Miller Watson's enslaved Africans.

Though Doreen said, 'All the old people are connected in some way,' and she and Beryl claimed to see a resemblance between Frederick and my father, and between Frederick and Andrew Watson ('the nose, the nose', said Beryl), we still needed to prove the connections. The Weldaad and 42 Village (aka Seafield) links were important to me, but I needed more information. Beryl told me she had a half-sister, Elaine Watson, now living in New Jersey. Elaine's father was also Frederick Watson's, but her mother was one Marion Benn.[4] I called Elaine and went through the family history but after some back and forth, she concluded that there was no connection between my father and her family. Did this mean Beryl and I weren't related? I was deflated but chalked it up as part of the process to sometimes encounter a dead end. Elaine has since passed away, an obituary in her local newspaper naming her (in typically confusing fashion) as Sybil Gwen (Elaine) Watson, yet referring to her throughout the article as 'Gwen'. It wasn't until much later, as I gathered together the material for this book and looked through my records from the trip to Guyana, that I made a connection that gave me hope that Beryl and I might after all be related.

A couple of days after first travelling to Weldaad I got a call. It was Mr Hamilton. He was in a bank in Berbice and happened to overhear two old ladies having a conversation. One of them asked what the other's name was, and she replied, 'Breinburg, but my maiden name was Watson.' When he heard that, he went over and said, 'I met an English guy here who is looking for Watsons. Can I give him your number?' She said he could. I wasted no time in calling up and soon I was in Raj's car again, heading this time to D'Edward Village in Berbice, close to Rosignol, to meet Whithyelene Breinburg (née Watson). Her daughter Adamay was there, as was Adamay's daughter, Vanessa. As soon as I walked in the house, I clocked a photo on the wall.

'That's my dad!' I said.

'No, that's my dad!' replied Whithyelene,[5] who had greying hair and an expressive, youthful face, despite being a healthy eighty-two years old.

'Reg Watson?' I enquired.

'Yes, Reginald Watson,' she agreed.

I did a double take. 'Oh my God! I've got a sister,' I thought, a much, much older sister.

'Reginald Wilcox Watson?' I said, still not quite believing what was going on.

'No! Reginald Daniel William Watson. Reginald Wilcox Watson was my uncle Reg.'

It turned out that we were cousins. Our fathers were half-brothers, both the sons of our grandfather George James Edward Watson, but while my grandmother was Olivia July, Whithyelene's mother was Henrietta 'Tilly' Smith and her grandmother was Mabel Rawlins. Whithyelene showed me a photo of her father (my uncle), a stern looking man in a white suit and glasses.

'He was very strict,' she remembered. 'That man! He was a sweet man too, you know. I believe you take a part of him. Women behind you like rice and peas. I got to watch you!' She wagged her finger at me cheekily.

What my uncle would have made of it, I don't know. They told me Reginald Daniel William Watson's family was very mixed: Indian, White, Black, Portuguese and Indigenous. Whithyelene specifically remembered that he never wanted his daughter to marry a man the same colour as him. 'He'd say, "Alluyuh don't bring none here . . . You must take either Indian mix, mix-Chinese, white and Black mix, but no real Black."' She must have gone against her father's wishes, though, for Adamay was Black, as is Vanessa. Vanessa remembered her grandfather for setting a certain 'standard' everyone had to meet, so much so that, even now, when they go to Georgetown, she says, 'People don't believe we're from Berbice – the way we speak, the way how we upright ourselves.' My ears were still adjusting to the Guyanese accent, but I later discovered that people from Berbice are known for their strong Creole, almost impenetrable to an outside ear like mine. I didn't catch every word the family were saying, but I understood most of the conversation.

Adamay Amelia Patricia Bevan (1953–2020) grew up more with her grandmother Henrietta Smith (1910–1996) – aka 'aunty-Netta' – than her mother Whithyelene, who had moved away to work leaving her daughter behind. Adamay had collected lots of scraps of family history, more so than her mother had. She recalled that my uncle Reginald (her grandfather) had worked on the Blairmont estate as a pump boilerman, and she said the name 'Hannah Rose' rang a bell. It wasn't until I watched the video of our conversation years later, in preparation for writing this book, that I realised the significance of what she'd mentioned in relation to the name Nanny Benn. She said, 'Nanny Benn is grandfather's mother, my great-grandmother . . . she was married to a Watson.' I asked his name. 'William Watson,' she said.

The problem with oral histories is that people do make mistakes, so it's necessary to validate the recollections people offer. Upon researching further, and cross-referencing with the Watsons I met in

Victoria, I find that Marion Benn married Frederick Adolphus Watson, who was a child in 1921 when he came to Victoria. This would put him in my father's age group. So here we have a Benn and a Watson in Berbice, but much later than we need. It somehow posed more questions than answers, but it did validate a connection between the Watsons of Victoria – namely Beryl Watson, Frederick's daughter – and the Watsons of Berbice. But where does William Watson come in?

Reginald Wilcox Watson's parents were George Edward Watson and Olivia July. Initially I suspected Nanny Benn must be Marion Benn, the one who with Frederick Watson had Beryl Watson. To find William Watson – the missing link – and his relation to my grandfather George Edward Watson would require further research, most probably in Guyana. My connection to Andrew Watson's lineage is most likely through his uncle William Robertson Watson, who was a plantation overseer in Berbice.

Name changes and nicknames complicate matters when it comes to researching your family tree, and it seems like everyone – from slavery times to today – has multiple baby daddies and baby mamas. In Guyana, a baby born out of wedlock is called an 'outside child', but I began to wonder, who was actually inside? It seemed that when it came to the white slave owners, the outside child was the norm, the inside child the anomaly. And this brought me back to Peter Miller Watson's letter to Dr Traill, where he refers to 'the boy Henry', no doubt one of William Robertson Watson's outside children. Could he have had a brother named William – also an outside child? Or did 'the boy Henry' grow up and have a child named William, perhaps the father or uncle of Frederick Adolphus Watson? These questions loomed large and could only be resolved with birth records in Guyana, as the oral history, the locational history, and even the land passed down to Whithyelene and Sybil – my cousins – from my grandfather George, all lined up but remained somewhat fragmented.

What really clinched it for me, where the penny dropped and I thought 'This is it', is when I found out about my father's land. I'd heard that my father should have had land in Guyana – in his mother's village of Meadow Bank and in D'Edward Village in Mahaica-Berbice, where his father had lived – but he was disinherited because he never went back, and so wasn't there to press his claim. From Whithyelene and her sister Sybil's family, I learned that my uncle Reginald's mother, Henrietta Smith, also had a child with a man by the name of Richard Kato Simon (1865–1928). Their son, James Simon (1918–?), was the half-brother of Whithyelene's father Reginald. When my grandfather, teacher Watson, passed away, his land around Rosignol and D'Edward Village, where Whithyelene lived, went to Reginald Daniel William Watson and James Simon. My father didn't get a look in, as he'd left the country and to my knowledge had never returned.

Before my father left Guyana around 1936, when Whithyelene was just eight years old, she and her father, my uncle Reg, went to stay with my father in a town called Kitty near Georgetown for a time. Whithyelene remembered it and said he had a woman and a child there with him. She could not recall if the child was a girl or a boy and didn't know the name of the woman, but she recalled my father and referred to him as her 'Uncle Reginald'. This accorded with the accounts of the neighbours in Meadowbank who recalled that a woman and a child had also lived there with Olivia, but in the few short minutes I was in Meadowbank I could not ascertain the names of either. My suspicion was that my father left to go to sea when he was eighteen leaving behind a woman and child whom his mother looked after until she died. Again, I would need to go back to Guyana for further research to establish precisely who they were and if either were still alive.

While I was last in Guyana, to continue connecting the dots, I'd headed for the General Register Office, located inside the same tall, concrete building as the General Post Office. I was met at the door by a young Black man, who was dressed something like a postal worker-cum-security guard, in grey khakis. He stopped me from going up the stairs. 'I want to enter the register office,' I told him. 'You can't!' he retorted. Brian intervened and with a flurry of patois anecdotes, tried to get him to let us in. I couldn't quite understand what was going on, as their accents were so thick and their rhetoric so animated that it became difficult to follow. Then it came to an abrupt stop and Brian turned to me and said with a degree of exasperation and resignation in his tone, 'You have to give he somet'ing. A few dollars.' Imagine the absurdity of it. I had to literally bribe my way into the register at a post office. I have a principle that I don't pay bribes, and I don't take bribes, and I've lived by that mantra for the whole of my adult life. But here I was in a situation where the only thing standing between me and my father's birth record was a few worthless Guyanese dollars, so considering the time imperative and the obvious reality of the situation, I broke my own rule and paid the man to get in.

As if that wasn't bad enough, when we got upstairs, I had to do the same for the female manager, who then appointed the registrar to go and find what I was looking for. I felt physically sick. I was ashamed that Guyana – my ancestral homeland – had been reduced to this level of corruption. It was heart-breaking. But what really broke my heart was the fact that I'd compromised a principle that I'd upheld my whole adult life, even in the most extreme situations.

Everything was manual and complicated and humid and sweaty, but they managed to find my dad's birth certificate, and those of a few other family members that I had identified. That was when I found the blank space on his birth certificate – and learned that he was actually registered not as a Watson, but as a July (the surname of his mother). I also discovered he was born in Grove (East Bank Demerara), about fifteen minutes' drive from Meadow Bank. While I was at the Registrar Office, I took the opportunity to look for Andrew Watson's records too. It had now been five years since the BBC documentary aired and I didn't have the technology to view the VHS recording of the programme that I'd recorded, so I read over articles from 2003 to remind myself of the details. Many cited Andrew's year of birth as 1857, so I hurriedly requested the birth certificate of an Andrew Watson born in Demerara in 1857, only to find . . . nothing. There was no record there. It wasn't until later, after I'd left Guyana, that I realised the newspapers had got the wrong date. Andrew was born in 1856 not 1857. Another dead end.

I decided to pay a visit to James Simon, who lived in Linden, about an hour and a half from Georgetown. Sour-pot had said he'd come with us and show us the way to the address we received from Whythelene. We set out on the long journey, but this time, instead of the coast road, which runs east to west, we took another road, which runs south, directly through the interior.

Starting in Demerara-Mahaica (Region 4), where Georgetown is situated, we headed south in the direction of Brazil. The highway was remarkably well built by Guyanese standards, if somewhat out of place in such a tropical environment. The road to Linden was the most stunning adventure so far on this trip. While on the coast road, I'd seen the vast flat and well-cultivated sugar and rice plantations, the cute wooden houses built on stilts, and the swaying coconut palms and banana trees lining the roads. This was very different. The black tarmac road went through the tropical Amazonian rainforest, cutting a straight line laterally from the coast to the centre of the jungle, and stood out on the landscape like a thick black marker across a green map. On either side, you could see the homes of indigenous tribes, the roundhouses of the Lokono (Arawak) peoples of the region, the tribes from which my grandmother Olivia July emanated. I got a strange sense of another aspect of my origin as I passed by them, having never – until now – acknowledged my ancestral connection to these remarkable and ancient indigenous peoples. Why would I? I had only just found out that I was, in fact, part Amerindian Arawak myself.[6] It hadn't sunk in. My mum had always said that my father had described his mother as fair-skinned, but I had not until now, in all honesty, seriously considered the prospect that she was somehow indigenous, or part indigenous. Once, when I was in New York doing some work at a studio in Brooklyn with a Rasta friend of mine called Sidney Mills from a band called Steel Pulse, Sid had taken me to a local Guyanese eatery, and the woman behind the counter looked at me and declared, 'You're Guyanese!' I recall being somewhat startled as to how she knew that. I then informed her that 'Yes, my father was Guyanese.' She said, 'Yes, I can tell. You're Black and Buck.' That's when I'd first heard the term 'Buck' as related to people of Amerindian origin. My father always described his mother as 'a fair-skinned woman', which I would later discover was because she was of mixed Black and indigenous Amerindian (Arawak) descent, what the Guyanese people used to call 'Buck'. So, someone like me, with brown skin and wavy hair – derived of this genetic racial cocktail – would often be referred to in Guyana as 'Black and Buck'.

The term 'Buck' is derogatory, likened to 'Negro' (which was used to describe enslaved Africans) and terms like 'Coolie'. The pejoration[7] of the word 'Buck' emanated from white settlers in North America, who saw the skin colour of the indigenous Indians as red, like that of a roebuck (a male deer). The white colonists started to refer to the indigenous tribes as 'buckskins' or 'redskins' and when they began to trade with them, the trading currencies used, and the objects bartered, became known as 'bucks', a term that Americans still use to this day as a colloquialism meaning dollars or cash.

We saw some of them cross the road with bows and arrows wearing only loincloths. These remarkable people still lived something of a natural existence in the rainforest, despite all the turbulent history that has surrounded them and encroached upon their natural and pure way of life. We travelled on and soon reached our destination: the mining town of Linden and the home of my newly discovered uncle – James Simon.

I knocked on the door and explained who I was and how we were connected. At all the homes I'd visited in Guyana to this point, I'd received a warm welcome, drinks, food . . . but here, I got no further than the doorstep. I persisted anyway, asking about different family members so I could update my family tree. But he was obviously panicking about the land, thinking I was there to claim it back. And then his wife came out and asked, 'What's going on?' She seemed pissed off. I didn't know if she'd overheard something that she didn't like when he was telling me about the family tree (obviously I was asking about all the children, including the outside children), but I carried on as far as I could. He grudgingly gave me some names, occasionally saying 'you don't need to know that' when I asked about certain relations. He kept repeating the rather pathetic statement, 'Sorry, I can't let you in,' or when he didn't give me a name he'd say, 'Sorry for dat'. It was frustrating, but his evasive attitude told me a lot. The family in Berbice had informed me that it was Uncle James who'd divided my grandfather's land, so I guessed he was hiding details of who got what from my father's share, particularly as he was not my grandfather George's child but rather a stepson he had adopted when he got with my grandfather's wife Mabel Rawlins.

Somewhat exasperated by the experience – and with a mixed sense of stifled accomplishment, having elicited some information, repressing my anger, for having been treated with such disrespect – I just said, 'If you ever come to England, you'd be welcome. I will allow you in my house. But you know, I wish you all the best.' With that, we got back into Raj's car and began the long ride home, leaving Sour-pot in Linden, having realised that he was more interested in hitching a ride than helping out.

What had really excited me about the Linden trip was not my grandfather's land itself, but its scale and position. This was plantation land, bordering the Blairmont estate with its sugar cane refinery, which could have meant that my uncle Reginald and my dad were not working as pump boiler and cane cutter for someone else, but for the family business, as that plantation was previously owned by Peter Miller Watson's family. It is also an area rich with history. Its position, close to the mouth of the Berbice River, made it a very strategic location for bringing in enslaved Africans and shipping out the raw goods that they produced.

I hadn't had much hope of tracing my African ancestry, knowing that the lives and movements of the white plantocracy are more easily traced. But while I may never find out the African names or origins of my Black ancestors who were forced from their homeland, I can place them there, in the home of vast sugar plantations, sugar refineries and slave ships, and of the biggest slave revolt until the Haitian Revolution nearly thirty years later: the Berbice Rebellion of 1763.

CHAPTER 3

'I HEARD HIM CRY IN A MOST AFFECTING MANNER'

*Until the lion tells his side of the story,
the tale of the hunt will always glorify the hunter.*

– *African proverb*

The voices of my white ancestors echo loudly across the years through their private letters, diaries, legal testimonies and other remnants of British colonial bureaucracy. By comparison, my Black or enslaved ancestors appear silent. Even Andrew Watson left no written legacy other than a few official documents – though he was well-educated and born after slavery was abolished in British Guiana – and despite the attention and fame he received at the peak of his footballing career. The voices of his mother, grandmother and other African ancestors are even fainter, since their enslavers would have kept them illiterate – either believing them to be incapable of reading or writing, or in fear of what they would do if they could.

Yet whilst I may not be able to map the Black members of the family tree further back than a few generations, what I can do is get a sense of who they were and the people they lived alongside, via the events they lived through. On the same land where I found my cousin Whithyelene, where my father cut cane, and where my grandfather 'teacher Watson' instructed children living under the shadow of British colonialism, the most famous rebellion in Guyanese history took place. Before I began my research, I hadn't even heard of the Berbice Rebellion of 1763 – or what's known in Guyana today as the 'Great Rebellion'. I knew of the Haitian Revolution that began in 1791 in the French colony of Saint-Domingue, led by the famous Black rebel leader Toussaint L'Ouverture, but had no idea that twenty-eight years before Saint-Domingue erupted, thousands of enslaved Africans in my own fatherland had executed one of the biggest slave revolts in the Caribbean.

Of the three Dutch colonies which formally passed to Britain in 1814 to become British Guiana, Demerara and Essequibo were governed by the Dutch West Indian Company (WIC). Berbice, though, was effectively run by a private society. In 1720, the Berbice Association (also called the Berbice Society, or the Company) was established and by 1762 it had eleven plantations – nine of which exported sugar. It bordered Suriname (Dutch Guiana). There were also some 125 private plantations in the colony. Its defence was funded – at least in theory – by the Company, as historian Barbara Blair notes:

> The Berbice Company was dangerously tight-fisted when it came to paying for the maintenance of its colony's defences. Company soldiers, weapons, and forts were neglected through deliberate cheeseparing . . . There were never enough soldiers, and their rations were poor. They were a private army, of lesser physical quality than Dutch army regulars, and they quickly succumbed to the epidemic when it hit the colony in 1758.[1]

The epidemic or 'the sickness'[2] – thought to be a fever or dysentery – knocked out enslaved Africans and Europeans alike, including the Dutch governor of Berbice, who died in 1760. In 1762, the year before the revolution, the population of the colony, according to official returns, consisted of '346 whites, 244 Indian (indigenous) slaves, and 3,833 Negro slaves'[3] (the free indigenous population was not counted). It was commonplace to do deals with the local indigenous populations to keep the peace around the coastal areas. The enslaved indigenous populace were almost exclusively from the interior, captured by coastal indigenous tribes and sold to the whites in return for goods such as guns and powder. But the enslaved Africans outnumbered the white population by at least eleven to one. Nineteenth-century historian James Rodway stated in the first volume of his *History of British Guiana* that 'in reality, the number of enslaved Africans was likely even higher, given that the figures were taken from the returns for assessing head taxes, which may have been kept deliberately low'. Furthermore, he adds, 'Two slave vessels arrived before the insurrection, while a few deaths among the whites increased the disparity of the numbers.'[4] Given that many enslaved Africans would have fallen foul of the sickness, there would have been extra pressure, and an even greater workload than usual, for those well enough to work. On top of that, food was scarce for all residents of the colony, and as 'planters felt the economic pinch and transmitted their distress to their slaves . . . cruel punishments increased in frequency and intensity'.[5] Or as Alvin Thompson puts it succinctly, 'what hunger did not do – the whip did'.[6]

Many enslaved Africans ran into the forest, or 'the bush' as it was called, and eluded capture. Some were less fortunate. Khan writes:

> Back in the bush, the Negroes were more than a match for the white man. In 1730 the colonists succeeded in capturing eleven bush Negro rebels and killed them by slow torture. One Black was hanged to a tree by an iron hook thrust through his ribs; after being suspended thus for several days he finally died. Two were burned to death over a slow fire. Six

women were broken on the rack and two girls were decapitated. The tortures were endured heroically, and death brought release.[7]

In the most recent account of the Great Rebellion, *Blood on the River: A Chronicle of Mutiny and Freedom on the Wild Coast*, Marjoleine Kars offers a brief sketch of life for the enslaved population of Berbice, who 'toiled in the sun ten hours a day, six days a week' – more at harvest time or when using a tidal mill. The work they carried out was always the most physically demanding and dangerous: 'At any given time, a sixth of adults could not work due to illness, injury, or permanent disabilities.'[8] Cornelis Christiaan Goslinga puts the average period of servitude for slaves in Berbice as just eight years.[9] In addition to working the land, the enslaved Africans were expected to feed themselves by growing vital provisions on small plots dedicated for the purpose, although it meant they were essentially working non-stop. Kars notes that these tracts of land were located far from the main house or deep in the savannah, but 'provided a measure of freedom from scrutiny, yielded a more varied diet and nourished spiritual lives'.[10] However, she fails to add that it gave them the chance to discuss, strategise and plan their liberty, away from the ears of their enslavers.

In a precursor to the explosive events of 1763, a group of thirty-six enslaved Africans bolted for freedom in July 1762, on the plantations of Goed Land and Goed Fortuin, taking with them weapons and ammunition from the house of the absent plantation owner before setting it alight. They headed four hours into the bush, erecting a barricade against any soldiers and militia that might follow. Their strong position initially allowed them to hold off the white forces, two of whom were killed and five injured. But a few days later, recounts Rodway, 'the Negroes were enticed from their defences'. Most were killed, one was executed, two or three were taken prisoner and others were flogged in front of fellow enslaved Africans.[11] One of the rebels was a young man newly arrived in

Berbice from West Africa, who was given the name Coffij – the Dutch spelling for 'Kofi', a name used by the Akan people for a child born on a Friday. He was interrogated by a court made up of members of the governor's council, including one Johan George, and sentenced to be 'broken on the wheel'. This grisly form of execution involved strapping the victim naked to a cartwheel, flat on the floor, and then clubbing them repeatedly – starting with the feet against the iron rim of the wheel and working up to the head – breaking every bone in their body over a prolonged period, before finally crushing their skull, which at the time white Christians considered 'an act of mercy'. Before his death, Coffij, when asked if he 'regretted his actions', is said to have replied that what they had failed to accomplish 'others would soon carry out'.[12] Fittingly, it was another Coffij (or 'Cuffy' as he is referred to in Guyana) who was to realise his namesake's prediction, as the main leader of the 1763 rebellion. Though it had not lasted for more than a few days, the 1762 revolt (and other smaller insurrections that preceded and followed it) must have given the African peoples a sense of renewed hope and determination, as well as exposing gaps in the Dutch defences.

It wasn't hard to see why they would escape at the first opportunity. Those who survived the grotesque tortures of the voyage were subjected to further abuse and inhumane conditions as soon as they landed ashore. A first-hand description from Captain Drake gives us more insight:

> The Blacks were landed at once and two days later were placed on sale in the market. There was a scarcity of hands on the sugar plantations, and good prices were paid for the slaves. The Dutch maids in short green jackets and scarlet petticoats, walked around inspecting the naked Africans as if they were a common thing . . . The darkies were obliged to go through every sort of motion. It seemed at times as if their arms would be pulled out of the joint, or their jaws cracked by some of the Dutchmen. One dame was not

satisfied until she forced a wench to screech by squeezing her breast cruelly.[13]

It was against this backdrop that a deadly game of cat and mouse would be played out for decades. Every uprising among the enslaved resulted in deaths which had to be replenished for the survival of the colony. Whites were always outnumbered, so every loss on their part required some form of emigrant from Europe or the Americas. Labour shortages created both a demand for enslaved Africans and a premium on their purchase price, necessitating more production to see profit. It was a vicious and ruthless cycle. Khan writes, 'Inevitably some Negroes tried to run away. Near was the jungle, a refuge from white terror.'[14]

The enslaved revolutionaries, states Guyanese politician and writer Eusi Kwayana (writing under his birth name Sidney King), understood 'that the moment to raise the banner, was the moment of crisis, when the old rulers were losing confidence in themselves and were beset with more immediate enemies'.[15] Due to underfunding and the dreaded sickness, the military capacity of the white invaders in Berbice was weak, with only thirty-five soldiers fit to fight.[16] The uprising began on or around 23 February 1763 at two privately owned plantations, Magdalenenburg and La Providence, along the Canje River, the main tributary of the Berbice River. After killing two white 'Christians' and three of their own, around 150 enslaved Africans advanced towards the Corentyne River, gathering provisions and weapons on the way and likely inspiring others to join their quest for freedom.

Within a week another rebellion had erupted along the Berbice River at the plantations of Hollandia, Zeelandia, Elizabeth and Alexandria, Altenklingen and Lelienburg – the latter owned by 'one of the most hated planters in the colony', Anthony Barkey (Anthonij Barkeij).[17] It was from here that the rebel African leader Cuffy, and his 'second-in-command', Akkara, came. Under their leadership, several hundred enslaved revolutionaries from both private and

Company-owned plantations along the Canje and Berbice rivers moved towards the colony's administrative centre, Fort Nassau. Within those poorly maintained structures, many of the white enslavers, soldiers and officials were gathered, planning their response to the surprise attacks. Another seventy Europeans had retreated to the house at Peerboom, a Berbice Society plantation named after Abraham Van Peere, one of the directors of the West India Company, who had established the first trading post in Berbice back in 1627. Present among them was Mr J.C. (Johan) George, the man who months earlier had sentenced the young Coffij to a cruel and barbaric execution. He reportedly asked one of the revolutionaries why they behaved 'in such a shocking manner'. The reply came 'that the Christians were cruel to them; they did not wish to have any whites in the colony; they would be gentlemen themselves; all the estates were theirs; and they must be given up'.[18]

Kars informs us that after lengthy negotiations, the following day the revolutionaries agreed to allow the Europeans to board their boats – with their weapons – and retreat to Fort Nassau. Yet as they stepped in their vessels, the revolutionaries opened fire. Through a woman who had been held prisoner at Peerboom and then released, Cuffy sent a message to Governor Wolfert Simon Van Hoogenheim.[19] The letter or note attributed the uprising to 'the stoppages of their allowances by certain masters', which likely related to the food shortages which would have hit the enslaved population hard – though as Alvin Thompson points out, 'Slave resistance had to do with much more than bread and butter issues; it ultimately had to do with the slaves' reasserting their identity as people – individuals with free will – and the capacity to control or influence their own future.'[20] They sent another message too – not a physical one, but conveying a sense of who they were and how they operated. It stated that 'A government had been established among them, and the chiefs kept order by strict discipline.' Accounts in the Dutch literature claim that 'the preacher Jonas Ramring, was dedicated on behalf of the rebel leader Coffy (also Cuffy) to verbally convey the message to the governor that the evil and cruel treatment of the enslaved by the planters was the cause of the rebellion. Eight of those who were considered the worst in this regard were mentioned by name.'[21]

The letters between Governor Van Hoogenheim and 'incoming Governor' Cuffy, which remarkably have survived, give us an insight into the strategies, approaches and characters of the two adversaries. On 3 April, another letter arrived for Governor Van Hoogenheim, now at Dageraad, having abandoned and set fire to the poorly maintained Fort Nassau.

After the fort was set ablaze there were reports in the Dutch newspaper *Nederlandsche Mercurius* of white casualties numbering about sixty, and of white captives including the twenty-two-year-old daughter of 'Raadsheer George',[22] who the 'Opperhooft' (or chief) – no doubt Cuffy – 'took as his wife'.[23] There is a long-established notion that all 'coloured' people were born out of liaisons between white men and Black women, or between their offspring. However, here we have evidence that white women were also having sexual relations with Black men, which would have undoubtedly led to so-called 'coloured' children, in an age where contraception was almost unheard of.

It was common in many African cultures during wars to seize women, marry them and incorporate them into your tribe. This practice differed from that of Europeans, where in war it was common to rape and discard women. There are also rules in Islam about the status and treatment of female captives of war, who would be considered as 'right hand possessions', known as *Ma malakat aymanukum* (ما ملكت أيمنكم) or 'what your right hands possess'). Whoever was the possessor of the captive woman had sexual rights over her but could not allow her to be similarly available to others, so the prostitution of *Ma malakat aymanukum* women was prohibited.

The African Muslims who had freed themselves from enslavement and gone to war with their white enslavers would have seen captive women in these terms, and thus taken them as *Ma malakat aymanukum*, which is what it seems Cuffy did in this case. Male captives of war in Africa and Islamic countries were usually enslaved. The practice was also written into English law at the time. In the English case of Sommersett v. Steuart in 1772, Mr Hargrave for the defence argued:

> It has been said by great authorities, though slavery in its full extent be incompatible with the natural rights of mankind and the principles of good government, yet a moderate servitude may be tolerated; nay sometimes it must be maintained. Captivity in war is the principal ground of slavery: Contract another.[24] Grotius De ([3] J. B, & P. and Pufendorf, b. 6, c. 3, §5,) approves of making slaves of captives in war.[25]

This principle was also commonly held in Europe during the Roman era, while the Normans, who were of Viking descent, preferred the system of serfdom, another form of slavery more closely aligned with indentureship (referred to as 'contract' by Grotius) rather than enslavement. Grotius relied upon Roman law for his principles of 'natural law', whereby law was derived from man rather than God, stating: 'Now the Law of Nature is so unalterable, that it cannot be changed even by God himself.'[26]

Once a female was captured and enslaved by the Romans, there was no limit to the abuse she might endure. European chattel enslavement of Africans was equally barbaric and without regard for the humanity of the captive, male or female, as is clearly seen throughout the western colonialist empires, unfettered by any notion of ecclesiastical constraints such as canon law.

The bearer of Cuffy's letters, John (or Jan) Abraham Charbon[27] – a white Dutchman – had been captured, spared and enslaved by Cuffy as a servant and a letter writer. Charbon survived and in May of 1763 wrote a letter from Curaçao in the Lesser Antilles, which was reproduced in the *Norwich Gazette* of 6 August 1763, and gives a first-hand account of his capture by Cuffy and how he came to be the one to convey Cuffy's demands for 'half the colony. It is a remarkable tale of how Cuffy and his men enslaved white Christian chieftains and made them work for them after administering the lash to them, and treating them with similar contempt to that with which they themselves had been treated by the whites. It also illustrates how quickly the balance of power shifted and forced the white people into the forest, where they struggled to survive. In contrast, the Djuka and other African escapees fled into the forest and built thriving communities that were an ever-present threat to the whites, and from where they were able to raid plantations, freeing enslaved Africans, many of whom remained with the Djuka in their forest communities. Collis writes: 'Previous revolts had taken place there and had never been properly suppressed. Escaping into the forest, the slaves had preserved their freedom and become tribes, living the African life they had been accustomed to before their captivity.'[28]

Charbon wrote:

The Sieur Mittelholzer sent a Negro in the night to me, to desire me to come and join him with all my people, powder and arms, the Negroes having massacred all the Christians below the River.

As soon as I arrived, we charged our fusils, and remained on the watch till next morning, when we took the resolution to go to the plantation of Poitier, where about 30 chieftains were assembled.

In consequence thereof, we repaired there with all our people, who continued faithful to us until they saw the Rebels come to attack us. They then forsook us and joined them. We fired from the windows, and the Negroes from the woods. This work continued from nine in the morning, till seven in the evening. Consala, one of the Negroes of the plantation of Oosterleek, then sent to ask if we would make peace with him: we accepted of the offer. They came out to us, and we concluded an accommodation with them. They promised they would do us no harm and that they would conduct us to the fort; but scarce were we embarked, when they began to fire on us anew, with a great deal of fury. I received three small wounds, one in the breast, and two in the back. In this extremity, we resolved to cross the river in order to save ourselves in the wood, but we had no means of landing. There was a necessity therefore of throwing ourselves into the river, where some of us swam. I had the good fortune, though not without difficulty, to gain the land. My wounds, however, did not permit me to go into the wood farther than gunshot. As I heard a little after a great firing, I thought some vessel was to come to our succour. I ran along the riverside in order to inform myself of this, and I found there the Sieure Mittelholzer lying on the ground and waiting for night in order to save himself. I laid myself down by him, but I had afterwards a good deal of difficulty to get up again.

We wandered eight days in the wood, before we could get to the plantation of Doornboom. Hunger and thrift obliged us to turn to a large fosse[29] on the side of the river: but being in sight of the Negroes, we entered again into the wood, and passed on towards the plantation of Oosterleek, in order to gather some Indian corn. We afterwards entered a few paces into the wood to eat what we had gathered, but scarce were we arrived when we saw a Negro coming towards us with a sabre in his hand: Happily, for us, he did not see us, but ten others who appeared after him perceived us: We endeavoured to hide ourselves; but finding no convenient place, we threw ourselves on the ground at about three toises distant from one another. They discovered Mittelholzer. One of the Negroes would have shot him, but Mittelholzer advancing upon him, cut off his arm with a sabre; seized his arms and afterwards, put off to flight all who were around him.

Mittelholzer, however, afterwards fell into their hands, and I heard him cry in a most affecting manner. It is very surprising that these Negroes did not see me.

I traversed the woods again for five or six days together; but at last, pressed by famine and thirst, I returned to Plantation Oosterleek, the slaves of which as well as those of Doornboom, shewed me all possible favour. But in the evening, there arrived there a vessel full of rebels, who stripped me to my shirt and shoes. They threatened at the same time to give me the next day, 200 lashes with a whip, and then cut off my head. They removed me, however, to the plantation of Holland and Zealand, where I found three Chieftains already in irons, and I made the fourth. On the day after we were all of us beaten, and two of us killed. They kept me in irons for six days, in which time I had at least fifty lashes with a whip. They gave me room, nevertheless, to hope that they would do me no further hurt, as I was young and could write for them. In short, they released me, and I attended them wherever they went.

When they learnt that the Christians were reascending the river with vessels, the chief of the Rebels ordered me to go and find out our governor and ask him if he would make peace with them with this proviso, that he should cede to them the half of the colony. They gave me Johannes and a watch, suffered me to chuse out a pair of shoe-buckles, on condition that I should return; and in default of which I was to expect the cruellest death.

They likewise caused me to be accompanied by two Indians and a Carjaar. I arrived at last at the plantation of Point du Jour, where I found the Governor with the succours from Suriname.[30]

The 'succours from Suriname' he refers to are also alluded to in the accounts of the Dutch soldier Captain John Stedman, who'd been sent to Suriname in 1772 to suppress an earlier revolt, and who complained at having missed the opportunity of being dispatched to Berbice. Stedman had heard the news late and though he applied, he missed the detachment from Suriname that was deployed. At the time of the 1763 uprising, Berbice was far less developed than Demerara and thus more vulnerable to attack. But Suriname's neighbour and fellow Dutch colony was beset with problems of its own. Stedman recalled, 'Suriname was going to send a detachment, but there was a sudden mutiny in the army, which reduced the numbers that could be spared. Perhaps the whole of Guiana could be captured by these terrible ex-slaves.'[31]

Van Hoogenheim's dispatches to the 'incoming Governor' are attributed immediately to 'Coffij', who is described, or describes himself, as 'Governor of the Negroes of Berbice', addressing Governor Van Hoogenheim as 'your late Honourable'. The letter, also attributed to 'Captain Akkara', is a concise, courteous yet warning missive: 'We don't want war; we see clearly you want war,' it states, attributing the rebellion again to a list of specific plantation owners. Van Hoogenheim is challenged to come and speak with the revolutionaries and is told, 'don't be afraid! but if you won't come, we will fight as long as one Christian remains in Berbice.' Perhaps as a bargaining tool, or as a sign of the society they wanted to create, Cuffy promises Van Hoogenheim one half of Berbice and the enslaved Africans on the ships, presumably those who had just arrived. The other enslaved Africans, he says, will go 'high up the river', taking on the upper half of the colony (which in a subsequent letter he names as four valuable sugar plantations: Savonette, Markey, Oost Suoburg and Peerboom[32]), adding, 'but don't think they will remain slaves.' From a revolt against a few individual slave owners, the mutiny grew and spread like wildfire, becoming what was no longer an uprising, states Eusi Kwayana, but a 'revolutionary moment' . . . 'for the slaves had come to realise that there could be no turning back after their challenge, and that they must move on to the stage of national revolution.'[33]

Cuffy's use of letters as a tool of communication, albeit not written in his own hand, give us a sense of who he was. Most likely he and his scribes spoke through interpreters or using Dutch Creole – what Guyanese linguist Ian Robertson terms 'Berbice Dutch', a now extinct language but one that, Robertson found, 'contained more than ten times the number of West African derived forms than could be found in any Caribbean Creole language'.[34] They even developed their own written languages. An Aucaner Bush Negro named Aflakka agreed to collate some of the phonograms from their language and share them with a Dutch government agent called Mr G. deBies, and they were reproduced in 1931 by Ruth K. Khan for her husband's book on the Djuka.

The main Djuka language, 'Talkie Talkie', is a hybrid of Dutch, Spanish, Portuguese, Hebrew and a range of African languages, with the later addition of some English words. Sephardic Jews went to Brazil after the fifteenth-century Reconquista of Spain and Portugal (from where they'd been expelled if they refused to convert to Catholicism – *converso*) and were involved in the slave trade. They brought Spanish, Portuguese and Hebrew languages with them. Khan points out, 'As numbers of the early colonists were Jews, originally from Brazil, Spain and Portugal, as well as from Holland, one still encounters occasional Jewish terms like *tafer* (taboo) among the Bush Negro speech.'[35]

Gold Coast so-called Negroes had been arriving in Guiana since the first settlements of the Spanish and Portuguese in the late sixteenth century. From the time of the first landings, there have been so called 'Bush Negroes' who escaped. This means that their formation as tribal communities in South America preceded the Dutch themselves, who Khan tells us didn't arrive in Berbice until 1613, where 'the Dutch had a small tobacco plantation on the Corantyne river' until it was sacked by local Indians and Spaniards. 'Not long afterwards there came a small number of French colonists and a few Jews who had been driven from their homes in Brazil. They brought their slaves with them' and 'planted sugar'.[36]

I know what it is to discover the power of the written word, and to wield it to fight for your rights and your beliefs. Having been semi-literate when I left care, it was only through the mentorship of the Black American poet and civil rights activist Gil Scott-Heron that I learned how to express myself on the page – from writing poetry and song lyrics, to now undertaking a history PhD at the University of Cambridge (2020–2025). The Guyanese already had a heroic leader much closer to home that they could call on. Why had I never heard of Cuffy till I arrived in Guyana? There, at least, he remains a household name. His achievements are remembered annually on Emancipation Day and daily at Guyana's Museum of African Heritage, while his 1763 monument – as I was to discover on my 2008 visit – still sits in Georgetown's central Square of the Revolution. When I saw it I pulled over and took a picture. The figure had clear African tribal marks and was holding ornate pistols. He looked like a king. I asked Brian, my guide, who he was and he told me the story. That's how I first heard of Cuffy. Ironic that the British and the Dutch knew who he was but never spoke his name. Such was the fear he cast into their hearts with his uprising.

Designed by local sculptor Philip Moore, the initially controversial statue – an abstract rendition – has become an iconic attraction, covered with meaningful insignia and features. The faces on Cuffy's thighs, for example, 'represent the revolutionaries of Guyanese history, like Quamina – a prominent leader of the subsequent 1823 Demerara Rebellion – and Akkara Cuffy's deputy, and the fact that Cuffy considered past leaders to be in solidarity with his revolt'. According to a description by national art gallery Castellani House, the first plaque shows 'Cuffy and his friends communing with the spirits of their forefathers in the dead of the night, to see how best they could overthrow their enemies'.[37]

Despite being a key milestone in Guiana's history, Cuffy's achievements are not taught in the UK, the land of its former colonisers. Perhaps this is what prompted the claim on the front cover of Kars' book to be 'The Untold Story of the Berbice Slave Rebellion'. Guyanese historian Nigel Westmaas cautiously qualifies this 'excessive claim', noting that in fact '1763 is not an untold story for legions of Guyanese, historians and other writers and artists who have probed the rebellion'; he cites A. J. McR. Cameron's *The Berbice Uprising, 1763* as 'the most comprehensive account' and mentions other historians, poets and artists – including Edgar Mittelholzer – to have addressed the rebellion.[38]

But from Kars, we learn that he considered himself to be Amina, which she regards as 'a term the Dutch used for people who had been captured on the Gold Coast of Africa, present-day Ghana'. However, it is also an Arabic word,[39] *Amīna* (Arabic: أمينة, also anglicised as Ameena), the feminine form of *Amin*, meaning 'devoted, honest, straightforward, trusty, worthy of belief (believable), loyal, faithful, obedient of Iman (faith)'. Akkara also identifies as Amina – one of the nations, or communities, of African descendants linked by culture or language (Thompson refers to them both being of 'Akan' origin rather than Amina[40]). In fact, the Amina are held up as well-educated in military affairs and as having been behind earlier rebellions, for example on the Danish island of St John in 1733 and in British Jamaica in 1760.[41] In Berbice, the rebellion spread not just from plantation to plantation, but through allegiances of nations – with the dominant Amina forming the central leadership. When I visited Victoria, that first village in Guyana bought by freed Africans, and Beryl Watson and the Halls spoke to me about the Watson's being 'Guinea people', they were talking about nations. To me it's incredible that these links to our African ancestry have survived some 300 years, and that while I may never be able to trace in detail my African lineage, I know which nation they belong to – and with that something about where in Africa they came from.

A house servant and then a cooper, Cuffy was chosen as the central commander, according to one revolutionary, because he was a 'wise and sensible man'.[42] His strategising is apparent in accounts of the revolutionaries' movements on arriving at a plantation, which involved dealing with any opposition (especially from the estate *bombas* or slave drivers), gathering weapons, slaughtering livestock and raiding gardens for vital food supplies, then burning crops or buildings that were no longer needed – 'making European return difficult'.[43] Supplies were logged and distributed, to arm, feed and maintain not only the rebel fighters but their families too. Everyone was given a job: whether it was engaging in combat, planting vital provisions, acting as lookouts or spies, or gathering and burying the dead according to tradition. So deep, wide and effective were the Black populace's lines of communication that within weeks of the uprising in Berbice, enslaved Africans in Suriname – who outnumbered colonists by an incredible 36,000 to 1,300 – 'could be heard talking and singing about the event'.[44] Suriname was also home to a sizeable number of Maroon communities, established by plantation escapees, who as well as inspiring desertion and rebellion among Africans around the region, were 'directly responsible' for the economic decline of Suriname in the late eighteenth century, and the colonial government's declaration of bankruptcy in 1773.[45]

But it wasn't just men running the show. Kars also shares some fascinating details about the role of women in the rebellion. Amelia from the plantation Hollandia and Zeelandia, described as Coffij's 'sister from the middle passage', was said to have advised the rebel leader. She later testified that she was not his sister by blood but rather in spirit. Other revolutionaries, questioned by the Dutch after being captured, 'claimed at the word of this powerful woman heads rolled . . . One man related that he had even seen her "walking around with a broadsword like a man".'[46] Another woman, Pallas, an advisor to leader Atta, was accused by the Dutch of being 'an instigator of the revolutionaries through pretend magic'[47] – a reference to Obeah, a spiritual belief and practice that survived from West Africa and still exists in Guyana today, despite being made illegal under British colonial rule.

James Rodway's account of the uprising focuses more on the efforts of the governor, the European forces, the remaining 'faithful Negroes' and the indigenous people paid to join the battle against the 'cruel deeds'[48] of the revolutionaries. However, although Rodway leans in sympathy towards the colonists, there are flashes of insight into Cuffy's approach and the revolutionaries' position. For example, when a group of forty-two deserting soldiers escaped along the rebel lines with stolen booty, the few who were not killed were apparently quickly made use of: the surgeon to treat the sick and wounded, and others to clean and repair weapons and train the revolutionaries.[49] Yet we also learn of growing divisions in the rebel group, due to discontentment at the strict hierarchies instilled, the arduous work of planting and farming to sustain the rebels, and political differences between revolutionaries, both African-born and Creole (those born of enslaved Africans in the colonies, and mixed with white European enslavers' bloodlines). Other disagreements are said to have occured over the right approach – diplomacy and negotiation through letters, or full military attack – as well as people's varying visions for what life post-rebellion should entail. 'Some, it appears, sought freedom in an African state that employed coerced labour to participate in the Atlantic economy,' writes Kars, 'while others, wary of a centralising and hierarchical state, desire autonomy to be left in peace to farm their own plots for subsistence and local barter.'[50] By November, a fight between Cuffy and Atta – most likely over strategy, exacerbated by ethnic divisions – resulted in a defeated Cuffy shooting himself, providing a clear path for the new leaders of the revolution.

As time passed and reinforcements for the colonists arrived – from the States General and Berbice Company in the Dutch Republic, Berbice's neighbouring colonies of Demerara and Essequibo, the Caribbean Dutch colony of St Eustatius, Suriname, Britain, and most importantly from indigenous fighters recruited by the Dutch, including several hundred Mazaruni Caribs – the revolutionaries were gradually pushed back. By December, two battalions had arrived under the command of Colonel Jan Marius de Salve and a significant offensive began. 'A major campaign began on December 19th with an offensive against the rebellious Africans. A small fleet sailed up the Berbice and from Demerara, a contingent of company troops advanced overland. In March 1764, more than a year after the inception of the uprising, hostilities ceased.'[51]

Though battles and skirmishes continued right up to the end, most of the rebels eventually either surrendered out of illness and starvation, or were killed or captured. Of the 800 enslaved Africans held at New Amsterdam, 100 faced trial, of whom 47 were pardoned and 53 killed in various gruesome and public ways, such as by being slowly burnt to death, 'broken on the wheel', hanged[52] or tortured by parts of their skin being torn off with red-hot pincers. It was, states Thompson, a grim opportunity for the whites to 'pander to the psychosis of violence which was so much a part of slave society'.[53] The remaining revolutionaries, including the three leaders of the latter part of the rebellion (Accabré, Atta and Fortuin) were hunted down – often by their former comrades and even rebellion leaders such as Gousarie and Akkara, Cuffy's former right-hand man. Another thirty-four were executed on 27 April 1764, and yet another thirty-two after that – although against the wishes of the directors of the Berbice Society, for whom the loss of every enslaved African represented a loss of income. In 1764, the year after the revolution, the population of Berbice was recorded as 3,476[54] – including 1,308 'male Negroes', 1,307 women, 745 children and just 116 'whites'. The white population was now even more outnumbered, nearly thirty to one, but with the backing of foreign soldiers, indigenous expertise and African defectors or those 'loyal' to their oppressors, they had quashed the rebellion and ended the revolution. The Dutch Republic provided a line of credit to the planters and stationed the battalions there for eighteen months. By 1780 the enslaved population had grown to 5,112.

To some, 1763 is seen as a failure. It lasted just over a year before the lashing whip of Dutch rule was once again struck, and the same cruel structure of enslaved Africans lining the pockets of the Dutch was re-established. However, the uprising did bring some changes. In 1772 the Dutch introduced 'The Rule on the Treatment of Servants and Slaves'. Although under Dutch law, enslaved persons could still not go to court, they were now able to report mistreatment – something unknown in other colonial territories. While the Fiscal, who heard their cases, tended to take the side of the white planters, the role was nevertheless 'a check on planters' worst behaviour'.⁵⁵ What was more, despite most revolutionaries being re-enslaved, some stayed free, bolstering the Maroon population of Berbice, Demerara and Essequibo, which in 1782 was reportedly estimated by a French official at 'a little over 2,000'.⁵⁶

Another legacy of the rebellion was the impetus and blueprint (as well as the cautionary tales and lessons) it offered to other would-be revolutionaries. Through the informal Black communication networks that criss-crossed the Caribbean – the enslaved Africans who travelled to other parts of the Caribbean as seamen or to work on other plantations, and through interactions with and between Maroon communities – details of the rebellion would have spread far and wide. The bold actions of the enslaved in Berbice to shake off their oppressors could not have helped but feed the growing sense of discontentment among the enslaved population of South America and the Caribbean, and instil a sense of empowerment. After all, out of the seeds of Berbice – and other rebellions in St John, Jamaica, Suriname and beyond – came the Haitian Revolution of 1791–1804. Eusi Kwayana sees the ripple effects of the rebellion extending even further, citing the anti-colonial American Revolution (1775–1783), the Paris Commune, the October Socialist Revolution and the Cuban perpetual revolution, while noting: 'It contains in embryo, features of all these revolutions and it foreshadowed, as so many other risings have done, some of Lenin's revolutionary principles.'⁵⁷

But the Western lens has a tendency to ignore one defining factor of West African culture – Islam. Most of the countries on the Gold Coast had predominantly Muslim populations who were highly literate in many languages, not least Arabic. The great library of Timbuktu in Mali is a treasure trove of pre-colonial literature, science, philosophy, law and jurisprudence, as well as religion and ethics. The level of literacy in Africa at the start of colonialism was far in excess of that of the general populace of Europe, with the exception of those places ruled by the North African Moors from Mali, Mauritania and Morocco, such as Spain, Portugal, Sicily, Malta and the Balearics. The basic principles of Islam are based upon the memorisation and recitation of the holy book, the Qur'an. Ask any African Muslim today, 'What were the first words revealed of the Qur'an and its first injunction upon the Muslims?' and they will tell you (Read in the name of your Lord who created you from a blood clot) (Surah 96, Verse 1)

'اقرأ باسم ربك الذي خلقك'

This means that it is incumbent upon every single Muslim to read. It is also incumbent upon every Muslim to struggle against oppression. However, when looking at accounts of enslavement, particularly in the Caribbean, from an orthodox Western perspective, Islam is rarely if ever mentioned. Ignoring this element has prompted elaborate explanations for certain supposedly 'inexplicable' phenomena which to a Muslim appear perfectly clear. The body of work on enslaved Muslims is still in its embryonic stages and neither widely referenced nor publicised within the canon of scholarly literature on the subject. I have no doubt that many newly arrived Africans were literate, highly cultured and educated Muslims, who were rendered into the condition in which we found them post-slavery, by the process of enslavement itself, not by any purported predisposition to primitive lifestyles. Such narratives were contrived by white Europeans to justify stripping Black humans of their humanity and attempting to render them into the condition that they accused them of being, i.e. 'illiterate', 'uncivilised' and 'subhuman'.

Apart from its long legacy, the Berbice rebellion had another more immediate impact. The revolution might have ended, but so had the heyday of the Dutch as colonial masters. One third of the plantations in Berbice had been destroyed; the Company's planters and shareholders were hit with a new tax to repay the cost of reasserting dominion over the colony and their enslaved workers.[58]

Towards the end of the eighteenth century, the rising British Empire would seize the colonies – not only of Berbice, but also Essequibo and Demerara – and a new era of enslavement was about to begin, under a new flag, and my white ancestors were at the heart of it.

Many of the strategic tactics employed by Africans in 1763 and their approaches to rebellion were indeed employed by Toussaint L'Ouverture and his followers in Haiti. Only this time, the revolution achieved its aim. Of course, freedom came at a price – not only in blood, but in money too: 150,000,000 francs to be precise, the amount demanded by France for permitting Haiti to dare to become the first Black-led independent republic. Though reduced to 90 million francs in 1837 – about €17bn today[59] – the impossibly huge amount and the punishing interest (Haiti was forced to take out loans with its former colonisers) financially crippled the new republic for the next 122 years, with the final repayment being made as recently as 1947. Rather than making reparations to the enslaved Africans for their kidnapping, torture and exploitation, French slave owners claimed compensation from the government for the loss of their 'property'. Each owner tallied up how many Africans or enslaved persons they had 'owned' and claimed a price per head, some amassing huge wealth in the process. In Britain, the payments to former enslavers totalled £20,000,000 – some £17 bn in today's money. To cover the immense payout, a huge loan was taken out by the government, 75 per cent of which – according to a Freedom of Information disclosure – was underwritten by the immensely wealthy Rothschilds. This was a loan which British taxpayers only finished paying off in 2015, as evidenced by an infamous, ill-advised tweet from the UK's HM Treasury.[60] You may remember sharing a fun #FridayFact that 'Millions of you helped end the slave trade through your taxes'[61] – massively distorting the truth and ignoring the injustice that had been perpetrated against the enslaved populations and their descendants.

CHAPTER 4

'THE AIR OF ENGLAND WAS TOO PURE FOR SLAVERY'

> *This day is published an argument in the case of James Sommersett a Negro, lately determined in the Court of Kings-Bench: Wherein it is attempted to demonstrate the present unlawfulness of domestic slavery in England. To which is prefixed, a state of the case, by Mr. Hargrave, one of the counsel for the Negro.*
>
> – Advertisement, London, 1772

Without the constant threat of rising up against white minority rule on the part of enslaved Africans and those regarded as 'Creoles', it is hard to see how any form of emancipation would have ever occurred in the British Empire. The notion that abolition was somehow a by-product of white Christian benevolence is a fallacy. And as the flames of revolution blazed through the Dutch colony of Berbice in 1763–1764, the Seven Years War of 1756–1763 was drawing to a close. The Dutch had remained neutral throughout that war, which was considered by many to be the first world war. This global battle had emerged out of the French and Indian War in North America, pitting European powers and their colonial vassals against each other over sought-after territories in the Americas, Africa and Asia. The

British – who had allied with the Prussians – emerged from the conflict claiming victory against the French and their Spanish allies, and under the Treaty of Paris, signed on 10 February 1763, Britain gained lands in North America including Canada, the islands of Grenada, Dominica, Saint Vincent and Tobago in the Caribbean, as well as formerly French territories in India and the East Indies. The Prussians were not a party to the treaty, but signed a separate agreement with Austria a few days later, known as the Treaty of Hubertusburg.

The British saw a chance to expand the reach of the 'first British empire' – a fact evident to the Dutch, whose East India territories were monopolised by the Dutch East India Company (Verenigde Oost-Indische Compagnie), arguably the richest company of all time. Its wealth eclipsed that of the British South Sea Company twice over, and it dominated the coveted Far East spice trade. Having stayed neutral in the Seven Years War, the Dutch had incurred none of the costs associated with other European nations during this period, and despite previous invasions of Holland, which had weakened its domestic power base in Europe in the preceding decades, its East India territories remained lucrative and powerful. But, fearing post-war British expansion, the Dutch began to shore up their East Indies defences in late 1763. It was reported in London on 5 August 1763 that 'The Dutch armaments for the East Indies has alarmed our India Company, and therefore they have ordered all the ships they have taken up the last court day, to be fitted out as soon as possible and given orders to their agents to get all the land forces they can, to whom they are given an extraordinary premium.'

Many lowland Scots, sympathetic to England's cause for religious reasons, would have been particularly willing to join them and escape the backlash that had followed the failed 1745–1746 Jacobite uprising, when the English army of Lord Cumberland routed the Young Pretender, aka Bonnie Prince Charlie, at Culloden near Inverness in Scotland, and proceeded to dismantle the Scottish clan system and brutally repress the Jacobites. The period that followed also marked the beginnings of the infamous Highland Clearances, which between 1750 and 1860 saw the eviction of many croft farmers in the Highlands and Western Isles from their ancestral homes by wealthy landowners who wanted to repurpose the land use, with little or no regard for the poor tenants. Other Scots had gone to the West Indies and the Americas to seek their fortunes in the transatlantic trade in enslaved Africans, in which Britain was now emerging as a pre-eminent party, competing with Spain, Portugal, France and a waning Dutch Republic. The latter country had descended into political chaos upon the sudden death of the Stadtholder William of Orange in 1751, which left a three-year-old heir and a legacy of political instability in its wake.

There had been a long tradition of Highlanders serving in three regiments of up to 6,000 men in the Dutch army between 1689 and 1782, known as the 'Scottish Brigade'. Men had been recruited regularly in Scotland during that period to replenish their ranks in Holland, and various agreements between British monarchs and Dutch leaders had allowed both for their maintenance in Holland – mostly at Dutch expense – and their deployment in Britain or elsewhere at the behest of the Crown, should the British monarch summon them. This relationship was complicated by intervening Anglo-Dutch wars, as well as by competing claims to the crowns of England and Scotland in the lead-up to the first Acts of Union of 1706 and 1707, when Scotland lost its independence and became part of the United Kingdom. In 1763, the year of the Berbice uprising, the Scottish Brigade were stood down by the British monarch, who refused to allow the Dutch to recruit further men in Scotland (now part of the UK); here we get a sense of the Scots' trepidation at their plight, caught between warring European powers with their competing agendas and no longer an independent nation with any agency in these matters:

> In July 1763, the Scottish officers drew up a long memorial and presented it to the secretary of war in Westminster. They

were worried in case the ban on recruiting in Scotland, which had been imposed by the War Office, presaged the dissolution of the Brigade and they were at pains to highlight its value and usefulness. The loyalty of the Scottish soldiers to the crown of Great Britain was, they asserted, proven. Not one man or officer had been tempted into the service of the Pretender in 1745, a marked improvement over the Jacobite rebellion of 1715 when a number of officers had deserted to the cause of James III.[1]

Prior to the Acts of Union, when Scotland was a sovereign power with its own parliament, it had, like many other European nations, founded a company with a charter to trade in Africa, Asia and the Americas. The Scottish parliament in 1695 passed an Act for a Company Trading to Africa and the Indies. This was the Company of Scotland. The ill-fated company which took loans from England for the venture was also known as the Scottish Darién Company. Its attempt to establish a Scottish colony in Darién on the isthmus of Panama, ended in tragedy and bankrupted Scotland, precipitating the first Act of Union just eleven years later. The Royal Bank of Scotland was established by the British Crown to collect the debt from Scotland and taxes were imposed upon Scotland's people to service the interest.

During the Seven Years War, Scottish Highlanders had been exposed to the vastness of the British Empire and its potential for economic exploitation. According to the historian Matthew Dziennik, 'one in eight members of the eligible male population of the Highlands served in the army' between the years 1756 and 1783. In return for a period of service to the King – generally three years – Scottish soldiers could take advantage of land grants in colonial North America. Highland loyalty remained strong during the early period of the American Revolution; Highlanders assumed their service in the army would be paid in the form of land grants, as was the case after the Seven Years War, where able-bodied soldiers could convert their pensions into 100 acres of land – plus 50 acres each for their children – in Florida, which had been seized from Spain during the conflict. The Crown had operated this policy of land grants in North America (it notably did not exist elsewhere) due to the vulnerability of its frontiers, the sparse population of European migrants and the lack of value in uncultivated land. It also aimed to foster good relations with trade outposts loyal to Britain in a climate where the existing American colonists were increasingly resistant to British taxation to fund European wars that the Americans felt were not their business. Since many ordinary Scots had struggled in the Highlands under authoritarian landlordism, particularly the Highland Clearances, and with the uncertainty of the future of the Scottish Brigades in Holland, they saw the possibility of having their own property in the Americas as a form of liberty. This created a class of nouveau riche Scots, whose newly acquired colonial wealth started to filter back to Scotland, contributing to the development of its port cities and mercantile centres such as Glasgow, Edinburgh and Inverness. Meanwhile, landed Scottish clans in Scotland itself saw the potential for lucrative overseas holdings, and the chance to participate in the now burgeoning transatlantic trade in enslaved Africans.

Scottish loyalism was somewhat awkwardly rooted in support of opportunities afforded by the British Empire, of which Scotland was now a part, and a belief that the Crown would safeguard their socio-economic interests through the established order of governance in the colonies. To promote their vested interests in the empire, twenty-five Scottish gentlemen set up the Highland Society of London and were soon recognised as an influential body of lobbyists. Post-1763, the Highland residents of the British colonies on the east coast of America were mainly concentrated in the Cape Fear Valley in North Carolina, Georgia, and in the Mohawk Valley, New York, and Darién, Connecticut. They numbered around 20,000 and made up approximately 0.8 per cent of the colonial population.

The attraction of North America was captured in Duncan Lothian's 'A Song for America', which translates from the Gaelic as:

Everyone who has gone there,
Gives a good account of it,
Because they can find good land there,
Only fools remain here.

Ahead of this trend was a young Scottish man called James Parker. I first discovered James during my research into the footballer Andrew Watson's immediate family. I'd acquired a few letters online that were written by Andrew Watson's father Peter Miller Watson while he was based in 'Demerary' (another name for Demerara) during the early nineteenth century. They were addressed to Messrs Sandbach Tinne & Co. in Liverpool and Messrs McInroy Parker & Co. in Glasgow. I had not immediately understood their significance, but in an attempt to widen the net, I sought out anything I could find about these firms. At that time there was very little online, but I did find a deposit at the Liverpool Records Office known as The Parker Papers which appeared to have many letters to and from these companies, so it looked like a good place to start. I was not at all prepared for what I would find.

I cannot overstate the layers of meaning and historical revelations that emerged as a direct consequence of these initial discoveries. Even the street name upon which this archive was deposited was to take on a profound significance. The Parker Papers archive, officially held by the Liverpool Record Office on William Brown Street, consists of a series of papers and letters donated by or relating to the family of James Parker and his son, Charles Stuart Parker; it is to their company that Peter Miller Watson was writing, and chiefly to Charles Stuart Parker (the elder). As I leafed through the papers, I spotted a letter from Peter Miller Watson in 'Demerary' to Charles Stuart Parker. I also uncovered a blue schoolbook-like diary from Harry Robertson Watson, Peter's brother, written in very faint, cursive handwriting and dated 1833, entitled 'Journal of a tour from Demerary'. The first entry stated

'Tuesday 18th June 1833, set out for Bermuda in the Brigantine Belle. Got under weigh [way] at the clock VIIII [9 o'clock]', just two months before Parliament passed the Act for the Abolition of Slavery throughout the British Colonies on 28 August 1833. Harry's brother Peter Miller Watson was in Demerara as early as 1822 and in 1823 had written home to his mother Christian about the enslaved Africans' uprising in Demerara that same year. I found two handwritten notes in the Parker Papers that gave precise timings for one of Peter's subsequent voyages to Demerara, on Friday 4 March 1831 from Liverpool at 2 p.m.

Then I discovered another, about one of his brother Harry Robertson Watson's voyages in that same year of 1831 – just two years before he left Demerara to go on a 'tour', according to his journal of 1833.

I'd discovered Peter's brothers on his birth and baptismal records on the Scotland's People wesbite (the official home of Scottish records and archives), so I knew that there were five brothers born of the marriage of Christian Robertson and James Watson. They were Peter Miller Watson (1805–1869), Harry Robertson Watson (1801–1836), William Robertson Watson (1807–1876), Andrew Watson (1803–1837, uncle to the footballer), and James Watson Jr. (b. 1809). There were also a further five half-siblings from Christian's second marriage to Dr Thomas Stewart Traill.

At that point I hadn't realised that it wasn't only Peter who'd gone to Demerara. Scanning through his brother Harry's diary, it soon became apparent that he too had gone to Demerara, so the later discovery of a handwritten note confirming precise timings of one of those voyages gave me a sense of the timeline and their ages when they started in the family business. Although I was unable to decipher Harry's journal at the time, it intrigued me enough to look into the Watson brothers further. If more than one of them was in Demerara, then the possibility existed that I might be descended from one of his brothers – rather than from him.

Scouring census records from the period, I discovered that another brother, William Robertson Watson, had a ward living with him in the Scottish town of Innerleithen – and that ward was none other than Annetta Watson, Andrew Watson's older sister. The place of birth was shown as 'Demerara – West Indies'. At this time, none of the other researchers had uncovered a sister, so this was a massive find. She showed up in two census records living with William, before she married a white man called John Hunter Stevenson and became Annetta Stevenson. I knew then that I was on the right track.

Finding Peter Miller Watson in the National Archives in Guyana had also given me the confirmation I needed that he was the Demerara sugar planter named on Andrew's marriage certificate, and that he was also the son of James Watson of Crantit, Orkney, factor or estate manager, sometimes referred to as 'chamberlain'[2] to Lord Dundas, the Earl of Orkney. I hadn't got much further than Peter Miller Watson's immediate family on the Scotland's People website, but my visit to the archive at Liverpool Records Office provided me with the spark I needed to blow the story wide open.

I didn't go through all the Parker Papers during my first visit, as at that point I was only looking for Watsons, but I couldn't help but notice the same names appearing again and again: Parker, Sandbach, Tinne, McInroy, Watson, Traill, Robertson, McBean, and McLagan. Sitting in the quiet of this vast library, surrounded by papers, I tried to make sense of it all. The staff told me that photocopies or scans were not allowed, as the heat of copying might damage the documents. This was disappointing, but I'd brought in a small camera, so I took a few snaps. Back home, armed with the new names and a nascent sense of a bigger picture that was yet to unfurl, I expanded my research to include Sandbachs, Tinnes, McInroys, Robertsons, McLagans, McBeans and Parkers, thinking they might offer some clues relating to Peter Miller Watson or Andrew Watson. Searching online, I came across a letter sold through Swann Auction Galleries, part of a collection of 'Printed & Manuscript African Americana'. Lot 12 (which sold for a sizable $800) included a letter 'from Peter M. Watson of McInroy Sandbach & Co., of Demerara, to Messrs. Sandbach Tinne & Co., in Liverpool', dated 3 June 1847.

I kept looking on auction sites to see if I could find any other letters that, I hoped, might be considerably cheaper: £10, £20, £50 . . . I found a few that were being put up for sale by philatelists, who were not interested in the contents of the letters, but rather in the postmarks used in the pre-stamp era. So, wherever I could, I bought them. I managed to get about twelve nineteenth-century letters in total. The deeper I went into these letters, their authors and intended recipients, it dawned on me that the individuals I'd kept coming across in the Parker Papers and in the letters I'd acquired were not just business associates, they were family.

Business partnerships were often bound with marital unions which resulted in extended kinship networks managing multinational corporations with global reach. Peter Miller Watson was not just working with Sandbach Tinne, he was running a significant portion of the family business, as part of a mercantile kinship network whose origin had been established by his great-uncle George Robertson in Grenada (brother of the Revd. Harry Robertson of Kincardine) in the late eighteenth century. In a letter within the Parker Papers, Charles Stuart Parker Jr. describes this partnership with George Robertson as the *'fons et origo'* (the 'source or origin') of the whole mercantile enterprise. This kinship network of mainly Scottish, English and now also a Dutch merchant, stretched across the Atlantic from Grenada and Guiana, through Trinidad, to Liverpool, Glasgow and tentatively Den Haag (The Hague), and later Montreal, Calcutta, as well as Australia, New Zealand and Tasmania.

By 1847, the date of the auctioned letter from Peter Miller Watson, the Dutch colonies of Demerara, Berbice and Essequibo had all been formally ceded to the British.

As I dug deeper into the archives, I continued to expand the family tree. Each familial line presented new narrative trajectories that were harrowing in their subject matter. The flippancy with which they discussed African people's miserable plight, and how they accounted for such people in financial statements as amongst their 'livestock', haunted me, but I was fascinated by the epic tales that were unfolding, challenging much of what I thought I knew of the transition from the early modern into the late modern period at the end of the eighteenth century. I was astounded by the extent of these men's entanglement and the realisation that they were not just figures loosely connected to my ancestry – they were inextricably linked to it. They intermarried on an almost incestuous basis, gave their children each other's first and last names (often as middle names, such as William Robertson Watson, Alfred Traill Parker and Charles Parker Sandbach), and left often huge legacies to one another in their wills, including their mercantile shareholdings, land, stocks, indentures and businesses. But what really caught my attention was how many Black children they had, and how long after emancipation the sexual abuse of Black women continued in the colonies; and how they as a family enjoyed indulging in the sexual exploitation of those they'd enslaved or indentured, as well as their mixed-race offspring.

The letter of 1847 shows Peter Miller Watson and his partners blatantly defying the ban on the sale and transport of enslaved Africans (illegal since 1807 under British law) and continuing to exploit Black and Brown bodies for as long as they could. The auction site transcribed part of the letter, in which Watson reports the arrival of a ship called 'the Parker' (from Sandbach Tinne's own fleet, and named after co-founder Charles Stuart Parker) with 'a cargo of Negroes . . . 115 adult males, 86 adult females, 82 under 14 years, and 41 under 4 years' (clearly referring to them as 'cargo' not 'passengers'), noting that 'there have only been three casualties during the passage – 1 man and 2 children' – which Captain R. says 'may be attributed to the wretched state in which they had lived ashore'. He is clearly accepting zero responsibility for the loss of African lives on board his despicable slave ship.

The coldness of the way these human Black lives are described is chilling. The latter comment confirms that they were in fact trafficked; attributing their deaths to 'the wretched state in which they had lived ashore' demonstrates that they were shipped from a land where they were responsible for their own condition. It is clear, therefore, that they were not previously enslaved, otherwise blame would have been attributed to their former masters for their alleged 'wretched condition'. So, by a process of deduction, we can safely conclude that as late as 1847, Sandbach Tinne were illegally trafficking enslaved Africans into Demerara, post the 1807 ban on the slave trade, post the Emancipation Act of 1833, and post the Slavery Compensation Act of 1837, which they as a family were both among the architects of and its largest beneficiaries.[3]

Peter Miller Watson was born in 1805, two years before the abolition of the African slave trade, to his mother Christian Watson (née Robertson) and his father James Watson, in Crantit in Orkney. He journeyed to Demerara in his late teens to join the family business (established initially in Grenada before decanting to Demerara, by George Robertson, Christian's uncle). A young Charles Stuart Parker (the elder) had arrived in Grenada looking to 'join a House' (the name generally given to a family's mercantile enterprise) but couldn't find one, as all the houses tended to employ and apprentice their own kith and kin. Robertson had initially been in a partnership in the firm Robertson, Gordon & Parker in Grenada, formed in 1790 along with McInroy Sandbach & Co. in Demerara, dealing in 'Prime Gold Coast Negroes', whose produce included items such as cotton, coffee, and sugar from plantations in Grenada and Demerara. The partnership appears to have failed due to some alleged financial impropriety on Gordon's part.

Robertson had previously advertised for an investor partner, the initial stake was £1,000, a huge sum in the 1790s. But when Charles Parker saw the advert, he wrote to his father Captain James Parker (formerly of Virginia, now in London) and asked him for a loan. James Parker agreed and Robertson consented to formalise the partnership, but only after Charles Parker had been apprenticed under him and learned the slave trade. Charles Parker agreed in turn, and the partnership of Robertson Parker & Co. was formed in 1792.

Around the same time, another young man named Samuel Sandbach, son of a yeoman farmer from Tarporley in Cheshire called Adam Sandbach – and whose uncle, also named Samuel, had a plantation in

Grenada with an enslaved workforce – arrived on the island and also began to apprentice as a clerk under George Robertson, which spawned the company McInroy Sandbach & Co. in Demerara in 1790. Robertson Parker & Co. trafficked Africans by the boatloads into Grenada and later to Demerara. They quickly began to make a fortune. To give an example of their business practice during this period, I found a letter from George Robertson in Grenada to James Parker in London dated 25 December 1794, in which he informed Parker: 'Sir, the sloop Speedwell on which we ordered Insurance to Demerary returned yesterday after having landed her cargo of Negroes, safe on the coast.'

It is of note that contemporary records of *Speedwell* at the Royal Museum Greenwich regard this as a '12-gun sloop of the Admiralty', basically a vessel of the British Crown. I can find nowhere any details of HMS *Speedwell* as a slaving vessel, but this letter is clear that the *Speedwell* was shipping slaves to the Caribbean and George Robertson and Charles Stuart Parker (i) the elder were the consignees in Grenada in 1794. References to the *Speedwell* state: 'The Admiralty style full hull model represents the classic style of framing, depicting this well-designed British sloop/ketch. Built at Chatham Dockyard and launched on October 21st 1752, as a support or small transport vessel most likely used to carry important dispatches or high-ranking people given its fine decorations.'

This sanitisation of the historical record is repeatedly evident throughout the course of my research during this period and is indicative of the need for a fundamental reappraisal of historical archives, in order to ascertain the extent of the connection to, or complicity in, transatlantic enslavement. Model makers enthusiastically laud the virtues of this vessel while encouraging manufacturers of such miniature replica kits to be more precise, without the slightest reference to the barbarity of its owners or the depravity of its despicable purpose in the trade of human flesh.

In regard to the recipients of this human cargo, Robertson Parker & Co., such was the success of the partnership, and the business acumen of both his young clerks Sandbach and Parker, that

Robertson married Parker to one of his nieces, thus founding what later became the Sandbach Tinne dynasty. Shortly after his death in 1799, Sandbach married another of his nieces, Christian Robertson's sister, Elizabeth. While Parker was the principal partner with Robertson in Robertson Parker & Co., Sandbach took a minor shareholding in the sister company in Demerara which brought into the partnership another Scot, James McInroy (ii),[4] who already had plantations in Demerara along with George Robertson and Charles Stuart Parker (i). They named the company McInroy Sandbach & Co. Robertson took full advantage of the fact that Captain James Parker (father of Charles Stuart Parker) was based in London and had a full understanding of the business. Captain Parker started to ship supplies to them in Grenada from Bristol and Liverpool and orchestrate their slaving voyages to the Gold Coast on the Gulf of Guinea in West Africa. It was assumed until now that Robertson Parker & Co. did not own any estates, but merely leased them, thus giving themselves the capacity to decant in the event of a calamity such as war or uprising. This assumption, however, is incorrect, as demonstrated in a letter between George Robertson and James Parker on 25 May 1796 from Demerara. Here we gain an insight into Robertson's business mind:

> Our C.S. Parker stated to you in said letter his arrangements with Mr. Sandbach for his payments on the Woodlands, which we think a very advantageous one for us, by getting so large a discount of interest; for reasons explained by him to you, we did not think it proper to announce our being concerned in our landed property, therefore these bills are drawn by him, although you please debit us for the amount, we have therefore to advise of C.S. Parker's . . .
> – draft on you this date, for 2 years sight favouring S. Sandbach £382,, 14,, 1.
> – His [ditto] on you this date, for 3 years sight favouring S. [ditto] £382,, 14,, 1.

This demonstrates clearly that Robertson Parker & Co. did in fact own estates; however, for reasons unclear from this letter, they chose not to declare their ownership.

Born in 1729, James Parker was the son of Patrick Parker, a man of some prominence in the port city of Glasgow, which in 1760 was Britain's foremost tobacco port. He could have chosen to live a comfortable life as a member of the Scottish bourgeoisie but opted instead for a mercantile life in the colonies. During the early to mid-1770s, tobacco firms in Glasgow began recruiting the sons of local merchants as shopkeepers for their flourishing businesses in Chesapeake, Virginia, one of Britain's thirteen American colonies; their presence there dated back to 1707, following the incorporation of Scotland into Britain after the first Acts of Union. Highland elites and merchants tended to establish large, interrelated interests in land, slaves, plantations and timber, with some extending their business networks beyond North America. James was aware of this and became conscious of the possibility of adventure and of forging his own financial independence. In 1747, aged eighteen, he put down roots in Virginia.

James's first job was with renowned Scottish 'tobacco lord' Alexander Speirs. He soon found, however, that it was not possible to conflate the commercial demands of Speirs with his own personal ambitions. From there he moved into factoring, having wrongly assumed like many Scots that there was a lot of money to be made from property management. When he gave up factoring it was with much less capital than he'd hoped. So his entrance into trading was made, in all likelihood, with the financial assistance of his father. In 1758, eager to set up an import-export business of his own, James partnered with a fellow Scot, William Aitchison (also spelled Aitcheson).

Aside from their general trade, Aitchison and Parker became involved in various ventures in North Carolina and the recovery of 'land and slaves for speculators living in Britain and the West Indies'. They also became the owners of cargo ships, and agents for receiving large sums of money. Their client base included the affluent planter class of the Northern Neck, where the Potomac and Rappahannock rivers meet Chesapeake Bay, as well as small-scale farmers on the Virginia–North Carolina border. Their tobacco was exported primarily to Glasgow and Liverpool, from where they imported general merchandise. They also owned a variety of stores and a ropeworks. Both men were married to daughters of Colonel James Ellegood: James Parker to Margaret and William Aitchison to Rebecca.

Most Scots who travelled to Virginia remained clannish and planned to return to Scotland after making their fortune. Parker and Aitchison's marriages into a Virginian family that had been living in Princess Anne County since the 1620s suggests they had, conversely, planned to make America their permanent home. It is certainly the case that Margaret, James's wife, had no intention of leaving Virginia, except when and where it turned out to be absolutely necessary. James's plans to become a permanent resident are also suggested by the impressive two-storey house that he owned near the centre of Norfolk with 'the best garden in that part of the country'. By 1775,

> [He] owned fifty acres of land in the surrounding county, a plot on the eastern shore in Northampton county with a large warehouse, storehouse, lodging rooms, kitchen, and stables; and more than a thousand acres of land in Currituck county – the north easternmost county in the U.S. state of North Carolina. This property allowed Parker to enjoy the ostentatious lifestyle so beloved by the Virginia gentry and to exercise, in the colonies, the status he had left Scotland to acquire. His house was filled with fine glass and china, and he possessed several slaves, a riding chair, and some racehorses.[5]

With a network of businesses rooted in Atlantic commerce and reaching out across colonial boundaries, James Parker had, by the

1770s, become a prosperous and independent merchant of significant means. While he was a supporter of the British Empire, he also believed Americans had a right to manage their own affairs and felt that the British Parliament often exceeded its legitimate authority. He served in local politics, and as a 'Norfolk borough common councilman' from 1763 to 1773. Like the House of Burgesses (the representative assembly in Virginia), he opposed the enforcement of the 1764 Sugar Act, which imposed taxes and commercial regulations on goods imported into the colonies.

Although the Chesapeake Scots only tended to interact with local Virginians at the level of commerce, it seems likely, given their marriage to local women, that James Parker and William Aitchison were more integrated than the average Scot. This did not, however, protect them from becoming largely despised members of the minority Scots population. The colonial community viewed the majority of Scots as loyal supporters of the British Crown, clannish outsiders and parasitic exploiters of financially hard-pressed planters. Parker's pursuit of Virginians through the courts for default business payments created tensions between him and the local community, and inevitably led to his being viewed in a similar vein. He was, furthermore, considered by most to be a 'prickly' character.

After nearly twenty years of residence in Virginia, Parker's pro-colonial sympathies were to be seriously challenged. In 1768, members of the Scottish community decided to immunise their families against smallpox. The residents of Norfolk, given their anti-vaccination sentiments, reacted fiercely to this so-called act of provocation. Parker and his family became victims of mob violence and were clearly affected by their experiences. In 1769, Parker wrote to the Governor of Virginia, Norborne Berkeley, 4th Baron Botetourt, commonly referred to as Lord Botetourt – a British peer and Tory politician – and appealed to him for protection against 'the spirit of rioting and licentiousness' in Norfolk; 'the most innocent and inoffensive persons are not secure from outrage', he wrote. With deep-seated fears about threats to his property and possible anarchy, he shared his view that there would be no possibility of continuing to make a living in America without protection.

Parker believed he had been singled out by particular members of the Virginian community on account of the lawsuits he had initiated against them for outstanding debts. His suspicions appeared to be well founded. Henry Singleton had been hauled before the courts by Parker some months earlier for default of a debt and was later found to be the leader of the mob. The issue of Parker's debt collection practices were raised in court, accompanied by the suggestion that he drop pending lawsuits. Criminal proceedings were launched in the Virginia General Court and dragged on for a year. Some members of the mob were found guilty; most were released without charge. The neutral stance of the Virginia gentry, the court and members of government suggested to Parker they were more than happy to tolerate the behaviour of the mob. Moreover, even though it was not illegal to have engaged in the inoculation programme, Parker was fined for having done so.

The shifting attitude of the Burgesses to increasing metropolitan interference in local affairs had been palpable prior to the 'Smallpox riots'; so too had Parker's ability to sense brewing trouble. By 1769, his fears had extended into the field of commerce. For instance, in October, he shared with his close friend Charles Steuart his worry that the local mob were setting up a 'rope work' in Norfolk that would be in competition with his business. Parker's earlier disdain for imperial injustices faded as he became more worried about the impact of the Virginia 'mob' on the future stability of America. When, in 1769, the local majority adopted a boycott of selected British products in response to the ill-thought-out and unfair Townshend Duties, which taxed goods imported to the American colonies, Parker conversely stood against American resistance, hoping that it would eventually dissipate.

In the midst of the 1772 financial crisis, anti-Scottish sentiment worsened. With the tobacco market entering a depression and planters less able to fulfil their financial obligations, Aitchison and Parker experienced further difficulties collecting debts, even via legal avenues. Problems with the colonists were further exacerbated when the British government passed the unpopular 'Tea Act' of 1773 which allowed the East India Co. to import cheap tea into the American colonies and drive down prices locally, resulting in the infamous Boston Tea Party. It seems that every repressive colonial act was followed by another that compounded the tensions.

When 'colonial patriots' closed the law courts in response to the 1774 Coercive Acts (also known as 'The Intolerable Acts'), the pursuit of outstanding debts became impossible. As the crisis developed, Parker was asked in December 1774 to sign up to the demands of the Continental Association (known as the Articles of Association), an agreement ratified by the first Continental Congress. While it acknowledged the Crown, it effectively imposed trade sanctions on a range of British goods. Parker refused on the grounds that 'he had taken the oath of Allegiance to his Majesty therefore could not consent to do anything that had the least appearance of perjury or ingratitude'.[6] Parker's belief in the superior strength of the imperial Crown was severely tested in 1775 when British authority collapsed in Virginia, but he was, by then, a diehard loyalist.

On 16 November 1775, James Parker accepted a British commission from the Governor of Virginia, Lord Dunmore. His role was Master of Works and Engineers Extraordinary with the rank of captain. On Monday 18 November 1776, in the midst of the American Revolutionary War, he was captured in Williamsburg, branded a loyalist traitor and imprisoned in New London, Connecticut.

Some five months later, around 23 April 1777, he and several others managed to escape. The Parker Papers include letters to James Parker's wife, including one from Andrew Ronald in Williamsburg, Virginia, dated 1 May 1777 informing her that her husband had been reported in the papers as 'a runaway' and describing in detail his escape.

They were being transported to Philadelphia by Captain Lambert, who decided to stop off and get 'inoculated' – presumably for smallpox – on the way. While leaving the prisoners in the charge of another soldier, they were locked up in the 'Doser Gaol', from where they escaped out of a window, travelling nearly 500 miles under the cover of night to reach HMS *Roebuck* off the Capes of Delaware. From there, Parker went on to join the Royal Army in New York, under the command of Sir William Howe, and later fought at Brandywine, Germantown and Monmouth. In further military expeditions he served under General Mathew, General Clinton and General Leslie.

Another letter of 21 October 1780, signed 'Alexander Leslie, Commander in Chief of a detachment of His Majesty's troops on expedition to the Colony of Virginia', describes the 'appointment of J.P. (James Parker) as "Commissioner of captures", with full powers and authority to seize and secure all public stores and property belonging to rebels, also property that is deserted and also all cattle and provisions of all kinds from plantations from which the owners are absent for the use of the army'.

On his way to Virginia from Charleston, South Carolina, on 19 February 1781, Parker was captured again, taken to France (which had entered the war on the side of the American colonial patriots) and imprisoned in a variety of locations. At the end of the war and following his release from a French prison in Caen, James put down tentative roots in London. He had no desire to return to Virginia. His property in Virginia and North Carolina had been confiscated and his family home torched. His wife and children had been forced to flee during the war to a cottage on a small plantation owned by William Aitchison, on the eastern shore of Virginia, and remained there until 1784. He didn't return to Scotland, opting to remain in London where he was instrumental in building his son Charles's new enterprise in Grenada and for whom his contacts and skills proved invaluable.

The tobacco market was in decline and as historian T.M. Devine highlighted in the book 'Glasgow Merchants and the Collapse of the Tobacco Trade 1775–1783', the city's tobacco market during this period never operated at more than 25 per cent of its pre-1776 level. Prior to that tobacco had been more valuable than silver. The collapse was no doubt due to the loss of British territory in the Americas and the reversal of the onerous trade regulations that the Crown had imposed upon the colonists prior to the War of Independence.

Meanwhile, Parker's co-partnership with William Aitchison had been settled and closed in 1777 following the latter's death in 1776. Parker's financial standing and well-heeled background had no doubt shaped his lack of empathy for the indebted colonists of Virginia. He was very much of the 'divinely sanctioned and natural inequality of mankind' mindset. In a letter to Charles Steuart, he notes: 'The author of our being has in His wisdom endowed men . . . with very little different mental and corporeal powers. That difference forever has, and forever will, maintain its power.' [The overplayed 'rights of man' were simply] 'that quantum of freedom and protection which his rank in life intitles him to in the society where he is born and no more at his birth.'

In line with this thinking, James, like many of his fellow Scots, viewed slavery as 'the natural lot of part of mankind',[7] although Mason's characterisation is arguably flawed in that it classifies the enslaved among 'mankind', which the enslavers and the legislation pertaining to the enslaved most certainly did not. The laws of 'property' rather than those of 'people' were applied to the enslaved, and their categorisation as 'livestock' contradicts entirely the notion that anyone outside the abolitionists considered them to be within the ranks of 'mankind'. Nevertheless, Benjamin Franklin shared Parker's view and fought for the maintenance of slavery in the American colonies during the War of Independence, provoked in part by American colonists' concerns over Lord Mansfield's ruling in England on the 'odious' institution of slavery in *Sommersett v. Steuart* – the 1772 case that was to become one of the primary, yet understated, catalysts for the American Revolution.

This is somewhat ironic, given that the 'Steuart' in this famous case was Parker's closest friend and distant cousin Charles Steuart, and 'Sommersett' was an enslaved African he'd owned. The personal letters of Steuart contain descriptive accounts of the American Revolution both from himself and James Parker. They also offer a glimpse into the life and position of the enslaved man called 'Sommersett' (or James Somerset) in eighteenth-century society.

James Parker's wealth and privilege, coupled with his ideas on his supposed 'divine right' to have such wealth and power, was consistent with his reputation for frugality, which did not stop at the colonists of Virginia but extended to his immediate family. He had lofty expectations of his children, of whom like most offspring some excelled more than others. The investment he'd made in the slavery business Robertson Parker & Co. had been built in conjunction with his son Charles as well as George Robertson, and had paid big dividends. His eldest son, Patrick Parker, was conversely characterised by his business failures.

When Patrick became indebted to his father and defaulted, just like the colonists James had pursued with devastating consequences, the results were predictable. Patrick, like his younger brother Charles, had been born in Virginia. Educated in Edinburgh during the war, he returned there around 1783–1784 in order to bring his mother Margaret and sister Susan back to Britain. In 1785 he travelled back to Norfolk, Virginia, with instructions to sell his father's remaining property and its enslaved workforce. James Parker had evidently hoped to cut all ties with the newly independent America he'd fought and lost against and was disappointed when, in 1786, Patrick established a dry goods business in Virginia. James went on to virtually disown Patrick when he married his American cousin, Molly Aitcheson, in 1787 and moved to Charleston, South Carolina, where he scouted for business opportunities. In 1788, Patrick returned to England with his bride and, for a period, father and son were somewhat reconciled. With a degree of trust restored and reassured by Patrick's enthusiastic stories of the amount of money that could be made in America from a lumber business, James Parker had advanced his eldest son £1,000, as he'd later done for his younger sibling Charles.

This loan was to become the unwitting source of long-term tension between the two and resulted in incessant quarrels. As far as James was concerned, Virginians were the 'most unprincipled villains on earth'. To add to his irritation, Patrick ignored his father's advice to move to Grenada where he could have joined Charles in business.

In 1791, despite being financially strapped and unable to pay his father back the money borrowed, Patrick built a house in Virginia. The following year he entered the lumber trade and excitedly informed his father that he had 'shipped a load of staves' and was 'confident of another lucrative contract'. This, he claimed, would enable him to start clearing his debts. In 1793 his dry goods business folded. With operating expenses exceeding his expectations, Patrick again wrote to his father. This time he asked if James would be willing to charter a ship for lumber at an affordable rate; the current freight rates were 'swallowing up all profits'. Ensuing letters record Patrick's viewpoint; he regularly refers to his father's prejudice against the States, his failure to advance the goods that Patrick needed and had requested, and his severe criticism of his son as 'plain not fit for a merchant'. Despite the output of his twenty enslaved workers – said to be producing between 10,000 and 12,000 staves per week – and his estimates of an annual return of £1,200, Patrick's business continued to falter. In that same year, he made the preposterous claim that he'd been unaware his father had given him the £1,000 as a loan, and yet, in petulant tones, promised to repay it. Making further excuses for his lack of business acumen, he blamed his losses on the American Revolution for having made 'shipping scarce' and 'driven freight rates to an unreasonably high level'.

By 1794 James was convinced his son had betrayed him. He wrote accusing him of 'dishonesty and fraud' and expressing his belief that none of the proceeds from his Norfolk lands had been remitted to England because Patrick had instead used them for his own purposes. Patrick continued, nevertheless, to insist his timber was of immense value. He claimed his 1,002 acres of timberland were worth £4,008, his home and enslaved Africans £2,000, his lumber stock £4,000, and accounts receivable approximately £2,600. All told he calculated these and other assets to be worth in excess of £14,000.

Patrick lived an extravagant lifestyle and, despite the size of his assets, remained unable to repay his creditors. In 1795, suffering from a severe illness believed to have been brought on by stress, he travelled to New York to seek medical attention. The last letter he wrote to his father expressed regret for his 'disobedience' and shared details of his plan to return to England. In August, he boarded a ship bound for England but died before setting foot on its green and pleasant lands.

Despite James's disappointment with his elder son, Patrick's younger brother Charles Stuart Parker was very much his father's son. Charles was named after his father's dearest friend and distant cousin Charles Steuart, born in 1725 in Orkney, Scotland, to Charles Steuart (1687–1731) and Marjorie Traill (b. 1691). While I have not established if James Parker and Charles Steuart were blood relations at the time, James's decision to name his son Charles Stuart Parker suggests this is likely, and they were certainly connected later on when Charles Stuart Parker married Margaret Rainy (1774–1808), the niece of George Robertson, his business partner. Rainy's cousin was Christian Robertson (also George's niece), and her second husband Thomas Stuart Traill was a later connection between the Traills of Orkney and Charles Steuart, which would bring Charles Steuart into Parker's family tree.

When Steuart died in 1797, James Parker expressed words of deep sorrow, saying: 'After an acquaintance of fifty years standing & uninterrupted friendship, I can freely say that I never knew . . . a better man.' But even if they were not then related, it should be noted that Charles Stuart Parker's son, George Parker (1806–1860), also married into the Traill family when he wed Anne Traill, the daughter of Dr Thomas Stuart Traill and Christian Robertson. Furthermore, his other son, Charles Stuart Parker junior married Anne Sandbach, Peter Miller Watson's cousin, the daughter of Elizabeth Robertson, Christian Robertson's sister. Seeing the almost incestuous nature of the intertwined business enterprises and kinship networks, it is safe to say that Charles Steuart, though perhaps not a near blood relative, was certainly connected via marriage to what became the Sandbach Tinne dynasty.

Charles Steuart moved to Virginia in 1741, where he initially worked for Robert Boyd, a prominent Glaswegian tobacco merchant. Three years later he moved to Boston to work in the counting house of his uncle, John Traill. But within twelve months he would return to Virginia, where he was employed by Robert McKenzie, the owner of a trading firm. He was also, importantly, a partner in Aitchison & Parker before setting up his own shipbuilding and commercial establishment in Norfolk. We know from his letters that he was an astute businessman trading 'wine, rum, tobacco, molasses, corn and shingles' as well as other products. He was also a trader in human souls. Writing to a client in 1751, Steuart acknowledges receipt of forty-eight slaves. 'One of the women came ashore very sick & is since dead; four of the rest complained a little & two of them had the same symptoms with which the woman was taken.' The same client is asked to be aware that 'Negroes from 14 to 10 years are most saleable'.

Steuart appears to have been impervious to the inhumanity of the trade in enslaved Africans. In a letter to Anthony Fahie, he complained that the two old, enslaved Africans he had sold him were not worth a half of what he had been charged. Steuart, having sold them on, received notice that they were worthless and quoted: 'Their gutts hang out of their fundaments longer than the quill we now write with, & one of them has hardly the use of one arm.'

In addition to his work as a trader, Steuart later became an important official as Surveyor General and Receiver General of Customs for the entire northern region between Quebec and Virginia. He rewarded himself, as a high-ranking customs official, with a painting that depicted him 'wearing a powdered white wig, a beautiful mauve coat with gold buttons, and a shirt ruffle'. It was in his capacity as a customs official that he enforced the tariff duties (Townshend Acts included) that were partially responsible for triggering the War of Independence. It was also in this role that he is known to have travelled widely with his slave, James Somerset.

Somerset, 'a Negro', born in Africa, was one of several enslaved Africans owned by Charles Steuart. While it is not clear whether he had travelled directly to Virginia from Africa or had done so via Jamaica, we do know from the testimony of Captain Knowles that he had been bought by Steuart in Virginia on 1 August 1749. His traders are presumed to have given him his variously spelled name. The tithable records of Norfolk County reveal that as of 1759 he was still known mononymously as 'Summerset'. He stands out as having built a trustworthy, close relationship with his master, one that enabled him to command a degree of independence. As Weiner notes: 'Somerset received a variety of material purchases from Steuart': 'one half-yard of alamode silk at six shillings . . . a pair of stockings for 14 shillings . . . one half-yard of ribbon at one pound and 16 shillings'.[8] This was unusual attire for an enslaved person. Most wore rags or coarse woven sackcloth; to be dressed in ribbons and silks was indicative of a status unusual for one enslaved in America, and more consistent with the English aristocracy who often kept Africans as trophies to symbolise wealth, adorning their exotic pets with finery as a display of ostentatiousness.

On 2 April 1768 Somerset was also gifted £1 in cash, and he was the recipient of praise from Steuart's white colleagues and friends. Nathaniel Coffin, Steuart's customs deputy in Boston, writes in October 1770, 'Mrs Coffin & all my brood are well & join in our most sincere wishes for your health and happiness, don't forget to mention us to our friend Somersett.' In a letter written by Coffin a year earlier, it is possible to discern Somerset's ability to connect with a wider Black community indicated by other correspondence: 'The Children with Sapho and Tombo desire to be mentioned in terms of the highest friendship to able Somerset Steuart.' Here he is given his master's surname; however, he later adopts James as a forename and Sommersett as a surname. Most striking of all are the references to Somerset travelling independently of Steuart while in

America and also in England. A letter to James Parker which Steuart had written from New York revealingly notes, 'About half an hour ago I sent a letter to the post office for your house, and Somerset brought me in return your [William Aitchison and James Parker's] favour.' Richard Murray, Steuart's colleague, also talks of a letter that Somerset had delivered to him and how it was too late at night for him to make a return journey. He states, 'I shall send him into the city tomorrow morning to take a place for the next boat, and he shall take with him what you desire.' It was arguably this freedom of movement that enabled Somerset to make friendships with both Black and white allies, including abolitionists, following his arrival in England aboard the *Earl of Halifax* ship. In his book *Somersett*, Phillip Goodrich imagines a free Black Londoner's response to Somerset on his arrival in the city: 'You tink you so well-off, because you wear silk and velvet? You not well-off. You not free. We free.' Whatever the truth of the matter and the likely provocations he may have endured from other, less fortunate enslaved people in Britain, freedom was for anyone enslaved an ultimate desire. No one wants to be enslaved.

In Virginia, Somerset had seen at least one fellow enslaved African, Joe (aka Josiah Sally), run away from Steuart. Support for abolition was gaining momentum in England and a vocal movement of campaigners were delivering lectures and publishing pamphlets with the aim of promoting the abolitionist cause. Sommersett had been sent to England on an errand for Steuart and upon meeting with abolitionists, became convinced that he should be baptised and abscond from his master. This must have been a very frightening prospect, especially in a foreign land. Many Quaker abolitionists had argued that Africans were 'people' not 'property' and you can't baptise a thing – only a person. Sommersett was well-educated, literate and numerate, and conducted all manner of business on Steuart's behalf. For the abolitionist movement, he must have been the perfect example to contradict the notion of Africans as 'flora and fauna', 'livestock' and 'property', the terms that underpinned the legal

Andrew Watson.

Scotland 6-1 victory against England,
the Oval, London, 1881. Watson captain (centre).

Queen's Park in 1880–81. Andrew Watson is back row, second from the left.

BBC Scotland film shoot at Andrew Watson's graveside, 2021.

Malik arriving at Cheddi Jagan International Airport
in Georgetown, Guyana, 2008.

Rosignol Ferry Stelling – Berbice, Guyana.

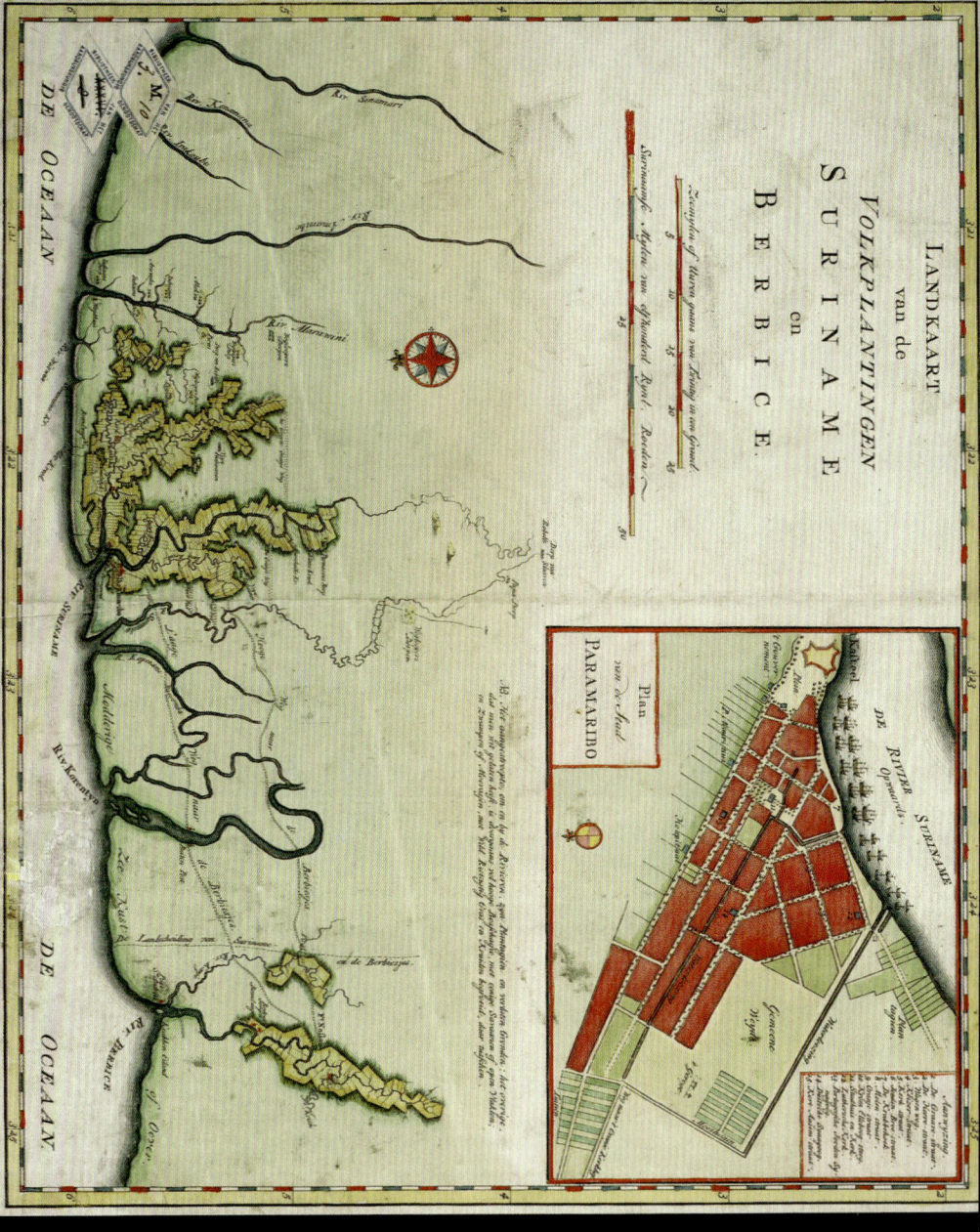

Map of Berbice and Suriname, 1767.

Statue of Cuffy in Georgetown, Guyana.

A return attesting that George Rainy owned 408 enslaved people on Plantation Leonora in 1826. His relative James Robertson was the registrar.

Sugar machinery from the eighteenth and nineteenth centuries at Blairmont in Berbice, a former Sandbach Tinne Plantation, where Malik's father Reginald Wilcox Watson cut cane in the 1930s.

'Mr James Parker who is deemed a prisoner of war.' Williamsburg, Virginia, 1776.

Grenada 25th December 1794

James Parker Esqr

Sir

The Sloop Speedwell on which we ordered Insurance to Demeray ⅋ the 11th Inst Returned yesterday after having landed her Cargo of Negroes safe on the Coast — We have some hopes of this getting to hand in time to stop the Ins.ce, if not already done. —

Mr McInroy is not yet returned from Demy. but we hourly look for him —

The 1st Nov.r mail is just come in which bro.t us your favor covering acc.t of goods ⅌ Harvey they shall be answered when Mr McInroy returns, in the mean time we remain

Sir Your most Obt Servt
George Robertson Parker & Co
⅌ Wa Robertson

A letter from George Robertson in Grenada to James Parker in London, 1794.

Arms of the Company of Scotland trading to Africa and the Indies

> Peter Miller Watson set sail from Liverpool for Demerara on Friday afternoon the fourth day of March 1831 at 2 o'clock

Peter Miller Watson's voyage. Liverpool to Demerara, 1831.

The epitaph of Hugh Munro Robertson.

> Here Is interred the body of Hugh Munro Robertson. A.M. a native of Scotland who in returning from the West Indies in the Ship Demerary of Liverpool, perished with all the crew, on this coast on the night of 16th December 1819.

status of the enslaved rather than 'people' with human rights and 'souls'. But, undeterred, Sommersett was baptised.

When Sommersett escaped his master's service in England in 1771 it was likely something he had been contemplating for years, waiting simply for an opportune moment. He slid unseen into the chaos of London's streets, where 2 to 3 per cent of people were Black, most of them enslaved but also 'runaways, musicians, seamen, actors, boxers, and prostitutes'. Having absconded, Sommersett was baptised in the Church of St Andrew in Holborn, London, where, the scholar Ruth Paley believes, he received the addition of a first name, James. The baptismal record of August 1771 indicates that he was approximately thirty years old and must have therefore been a young teenager on arrival in Virginia. Despite the high reward of two guineas put on his head by Steuart, he eluded capture until the following year when he was imprisoned – fifty-six days after he first made his escape – and transferred to a ship bound for the Caribbean. Steuart handed him over to Captain Knowles, who was shortly destined for Jamaica, on the understanding that Somersett be sold on arrival there. Thus Somersett was 'confined in irons onboard' the *Ann and Mary* prior to the ship's departure.

On hearing of his detention, the abolitionists Thomas Walklin, Elizabeth Cade and John Marlow quickly applied for a writ of habeas corpus. The writ was passed to Captain Knowles, along with instructions to bring Sommersett before Lord Mansfield. Charles Steuart claimed to be 'a kind master', asserting that Sommersett had 'become so vicious, insolent, and insulting, that he had determined to send him to the West Indies'. He believed that the crime lay with Sommersett, not himself or Captain Knowles, and that 'by running away, James Sommersett had robbed them'. James Parker's response to news of Sommerset's so-called betrayal of trust was to refer to him as that 'ungrateful villain Sommerset, [who] if he is decreed yours . . . Should be sent where he be at hard labour during life.'

The case was championed most publicly and fervently by musician and activist Granville Sharp. He enlisted junior counsel in

William Davy, John Glynne, Francis Hargrave, James Mansfield and John Alleyne, who had interceded in earlier cases involving the welfare of enslaved Africans. Sharp had been transformed, writes Simon Schama in his 2006 book *Rough Crossings*, 'from an obscure clerk in the Ordnance Office, to an eccentric but famously resolute warrior on behalf of enslaved Africans in England', and as such paid for the whole of Sommerset's defence team. Sommerset himself had sought out Sharp on 13 January 1772 to ask for his assistance, so he must have known the best person to contact. While not physically present in court, Sharp was there vicariously through his assembled team of abolitionist advocates. He not only shared his research on common law case history with Sommerset's counsel, but also provided evidence of the kind of treatment Sommerset might be subjected to if he was re-enslaved in the Caribbean. This included 'an example of the iron bit used to prevent enslaved Africans from eating cane when labouring in the fields' and another instrument designed to force open the jaws of enslaved Africans on food strike – brutal devices that could also be heated before use, to scald the mouth as a further form of punishment.

The case brought these stark realities sharply to public attention. In the media, a flurry of pro- and anti-slavery letters and articles were exchanged, while in court, the defence employed their best oratorical skills to push the case of their client, giving the impression of Britain as a moral bastion at risk of seeing the 'horrible cruelties' inflicted on enslaved Africans in America brought to its own shores. One of Sommerset's defence team, John Alleyne, addressed Lord Mansfield, pleading: 'could your Lordship . . . endure in the fields bordering on this city, to see a wretch bound for some trivial offence to a tree, torn and agonising beneath the scourge . . .?' As Steven M. Wise puts it in his book *Though the Heavens May Fall*, 'Everyone began talking about Black slavery and the African slave trade, and they didn't stop until both had been abolished.'

Keen to avoid ruling on the case, Lord Mansfield did everything he could to ditch it. In vain, he suggested to one of the witnesses, and others, that they simply procure Sommerset's freedom. He also delayed the case by three terms, well recognising, wrote Eric Williams, the author of the seminal *Capitalism and Slavery*, that 'about 14,000 enslaved Africans and property to the value of £700,000 were involved' (in England alone) and that setting them free 'by a solemn opinion, is much disagreeable in the effects it threatens'. The fact that 'West Indies slave owners' had come forward to cover Steuart's costs shows the worries that proliferated from the case. Finally, on 22 June 1772, Lord Mansfield delivered his judgement to a packed Westminster Hall, to a sea of white faces, but some Black faces too. In a carefully worded summary, he reminded those gathered that 'no master ever was allowed here to take a slave by force to be sold abroad'. After careful consideration, Mansfield discovered that there were no laws on the English statute books that allowed for a person to be enslaved in England. All of the charters enacted in England that had perpetuated the Africa trade related to Africa and the colonies. Unlike the Americas and other colonial territories, England did not enslave Africans for mass agricultural production in England, so despite the colonies being common law territories, their laws were not applied in England. This test of the law resulted in a narrow verdict, that did not explicitly abolish enslavement, however it did de facto force Sommersett's release – to the bewilderment of the enslavers, who feared that abolition would be achieved by stealth as a result of this judgment.

When the words that everyone on Sommerset's side were waiting to hear were read out, a storm was unleashed that would ricochet across the Atlantic and in many ways contribute to altering the course of American history. Mansfield declared, 'I cannot say this case is allowed or approved by the law of England; and therefore, the Black must be discharged.' Immediately after the ruling was pronounced, Somerset and other Black people in the crowds of Westminster Hall are said to have bowed to the Lord Chief Justice and to the bar 'with symptoms of the most extravagant joy'. A few days later, nearly two hundred Black Londoners held a ball at a nearby public house ('five shillings a head and no whites allowed') at which they toasted Lord Mansfield's health.

Not everyone was quite so happy. Racist slave owner Edward Long, in his 'Candid Reflections Upon the Judgement Lately Awarded by the Court of King's Bench in Westminster Hall on What Is Commonly Called the Negroe Cause' predicted swathes of black men coming to England and mixing with low-class white women, so that 'only a few generations on, everyone in England would come to resemble the Portuguese in complexion of skin and baseness of mind'.

It was a monumental decision – as Mansfield knew well, predicating his judgment with the words, 'Whatever inconveniences, therefore, many follow from a decision . . .' Much is made of his statement on slavery that, 'It's so odious, that nothing can be suffered to support it, but positive law.' But while Mansfield's ruling appeared to oppose slavery and was interpreted as an end to the right of masters to own enslaved Africans in England (though not its colonies), that wasn't strictly what he had said. Most scholars believe it would be more accurate to interpret the ruling (of which there are several slightly differing recorded versions) as having withdrawn any perceived authority on the part of masters to coercively transport their enslaved Africans to the colonies where they might be sold. By sending Somerset off to be sold in the West Indies, rather than reclaiming him as his own slave, Steuart was effectively enslaving Somerset on English soil.

In a letter to Fothergill dated 10 October 1772, Sharp reported that West Indian merchants, traders and others – no doubt fearful of losing their golden goose – had formed an association to promote a Parliamentary Bill 'for the toleration of slavery in this Kingdom'. Mansfield's proclamation in the Court of the King's Bench aroused the growing distrust of the British Crown in the colonies of North America. This would be exacerbated after Mansfield's 1783 ruling on the case of the *Zong* massacre, in which 132 enslaved Africans were thrown overboard from the slave ship *Zong* by its captain. He intended to claim their deaths as a loss of property and indeed billed their insurers for £3,960, £30 for every man, woman and child drowned. The owners initially won but a retrial brought the case before Mansfield, who overturned the original decision. The incident has been made famous more recently through popular culture, including the novel *Feeding the Ghosts* by Guyanese writer Fred D'Aguiar and the film *Belle*, about the mixed-race heiress Dido Elizabeth Belle – who was no less than the great-niece and charge of Lord Mansfield. It was he who commissioned the famous 1779 portrait of Belle pictured with Lady Elizabeth Murray, her cousin. Indeed, Mansfield's fondness for Belle was seen by some to have influenced his decision on Sommerset, which 'ensured that laws such as Bermuda's murder statute, would not directly affect blacks living in Britain' – including Belle. The *Zong* case was also publicised widely at the time by Sharp, who had been alerted to the case by a former enslaved African, author and abolitionist Olaudah Equiano, best known for his 1789 memoir *The Interesting Narrative of the Life of Olaudah Equiano, or Gustavus Vassa, the African*. It became a key narrative in the abolitionist cause, which in 1807 succeeded in seeing the Act for the Abolition of the Slave Trade passed in Parliament, thus prohibiting enslavers from going to Africa and enslaving others. It did not, however, emancipate those already enslaved in Britain or its colonies.

While enslaved persons interpreted Mansfield's ruling as having proffered freedom, it would be wrong to assume that it protected them from a continuation of forced deportations. As historian Eliga Gould highlights, Black people had limited access to British courts, and it was inevitable that private kidnappings continued to take place. Not everyone had Sommerset's skill set, education and demeanour. It is recorded, for instance, that in 1790 a young, enslaved girl, Hannah More, was dragged onto a ship in Bristol for onward passage to the islands. Other masters forced their enslaved workers to sign contracts stating they were indentured servants – although their new status would, in theory at least, have given them such rights as a limited period of service and the right to own property. Life in Britain for enslaved Black people was to remain bleak for decades to come, since the ruling did nothing to redress the support denied to them in other areas of public life, including poor relief or the right to a pauper's burial. Williams dampens the impact of the ruling further, stating that it affected 'only an infinitesimal number of enslaved Africans in England' (although Schama puts the Black population of London around 1765 at 'at least five thousand and perhaps as many as seven thousand'). Williams adds that the ruling did not affect those living thousands of miles away on the plantations, where there was no 'underground railway to spirit the Negroes away from slavery'. But he underestimates the power of the decision in and of itself.

Eighteen days after the Sommersett ruling, Steuart received a letter from his friend John Riddell. It demonstrated just one of the ways news of the case was being widely disseminated within the Black community. 'I am disappointed by Mr Dublin, who has run away. He told the servants that he had rec'd a letter from his uncle Sommersett acquainting him that Lord Mansfield had given them their freedoms, & he was determined to leave me so soon as I returned from London which he did without even speaking to me . . . I believe I shall not give myself any trouble to look after the ungrateful villain.'

While there may not have been a sub-Atlantic railway, underground Black communication channels spread the news around North America and the Caribbean at high speed. Schama highlights a slave-owner's advertisement in the *Virginia Gazette* for one Gabriel Jones and his wife, said to be on their way to the coast to board a ship for England, where, it reads, 'they imagine they will be free (a notion now prevalent among the Negroes greatly to the vexation and prejudice of their masters)'. Another owner puts the escape of one of his enslaved workers down to 'the knowledge he has of the late determination of the Sommersett case'. A 1774 pamphlet from Philadelphia promises the enslaved freedom by setting foot 'on that happy territory where slavery is forbidden to perch' – meaning England.

Mansfield's judgement would have automatically entered the common law of colonial America, both North and South, yet it would have been trumped by colonial laws – many of which permitted slavery under law, as in the case of Virginia, where Sommersett had been sold to Steuart. Gould reminds us of the 'zone of conflicting law' which saw England remain silent on brutal, unequal colonial laws and codes relating to slavery: 'even the case of Steuart vs Sommersett sanctioned the colonies' right to modify English common law to accommodate the horror of full-blown slavery, regardless of the institution's legality in England'. Enslaved Africans in North America would need to seek liberation another way. So, when the Governor of Virginia made his famous promise of November 1775 – which became known as Lord Dunmore's proclamation – that any enslaved or indentured person who joined the British Loyalist army against the American Patriots would be 'freed', it must have seemed a hope worth clinging to.

The foundation of Anglo-American race relations and its legal history can be glimpsed, as we shall see, through Steuart's biography. It should be understood that James Somerset was the first enslaved African from America declared free by court order, and that the possible implications of that ruling spread way beyond the borders of England. Any white person could unilaterally manumit an enslaved person that they owned, but they rarely did, and even then it was usually due to their own offspring having raped and impregnated their female slaves. Benjamin Franklin would have been keenly aware of the Mansfield ruling – in fact, Schama places him right in Westminster Hall during the trial, sketching him as 'first bemused, then unamused, then scandalised'.

Franklin was a slave-owner who had long dehumanised Africans by subscribing to the popular idea at the time that they were a lesser, uncivilised people. His newspaper the *Pennsylvania Gazette* was still printing for-sale ads for 'A Negro man' up until at least 1743. He refers to 'almost every slave being by nature a thief', and writes to his mother in 1750 of his two 'Negro servants', saying 'we conclude to sell them both at the first good opportunity' – although his will of 1757 suggests that didn't immediately happen. It stated, 'And I will that my Negro man Peter, and his wife Jemima, be free after my decease.'

Yet in an article about the Somerset case printed in the *London Chronicle* of 18–20 June 1772 (just days before the Mansfield ruling), Franklin sounds like a true abolitionist as he expresses a desire for, at the very least, a law abolishing the African commerce in slaves and the freeing of children of present enslaved Africans 'after they come of age'. He rails against the hypocrisy of 'Pharisaical Britain!,' condemning the British determination 'to pride thyself in setting free a single Slave that happens to land on thy coasts, while thy Merchants in all thy ports are encouraged by thy laws to continue a commerce whereby so many hundreds of thousands are dragged into a slavery that can scarce be said to end with their lives, since it is entailed on their posterity!' Goodrich even writes of Alleyne, one of Somerset's legal team, asking his 'American friend and patron, Benjamin Franklin' before the trial begins for a loan to purchase the necessary wig, robe and other requirements for a barrister, with Franklin now 'insisting upon his addition to the plaintiff's counsel'. Perhaps Franklin thought to subvert proceedings by acting as a saboteur on the defence team.

Whatever his true views at this point, Franklin would have been keenly aware that the ruling would be seen in America as a potential threat to the very institution of slavery – especially given the Declaratory Act of 1766, which asserted the right of the King and Parliament 'to have, full power and authority to make laws and statutes of sufficient force and validity to bind the colonies . . . in all cases whatsoever'. Previously, Parliament's power in relation to the colonies had been limited to introducing new taxes, with colonial laws being approved by the monarch's Privy Council. Steven M. Wise quotes a *New York Journal* article from August 1772, which declared, 'The late decision with regard to Somerset the Negro a correspondent assures us, will occasion a greater ferment (particularly in the islands) than the Stamp Act itself.' Mansfield's decision on the Somerset case wasn't the only perceived threat to the institution of slavery. On 14 November 1775, MP David Hartley (writing as 'G.B.' and referring to himself in the third person) wrote to Franklin with a proposal, that to address the 'vice' of slavery and preserve peace between Britain and North America (or, as he later puts it in the letter, to 'give some chance of preventing blood'), each province in the British colony should accept and implement legislation that 'every slave in America should in all cases be entitled to his trial by jury'. The United States' National Archives notes that much of the letter made its way into a parliamentary speech given by Hartley less than a month later, on 7 December. His proposals were roundly defeated, and likely served only to antagonise American colonists who might well have viewed it as 'one more example of British tyranny'.

For years, Franklin had been battling to create a strong alliance of the colonies of North America. Back in 1751 he had written to his friend James Parker (a different James Parker, born in New Jersey) outlining a suggested structure for the colonies to engage with each other: 'a general Council' led by a Crown-appointed governor in which 'Each colony should be represented by as many members as it pays sums of a hundred pounds into the common treasury'. His vision and argument pre-empted the slogan 'no taxation without representation' that became a rallying cry of the protests against the 1764 Sugar Act and other legislation enacted by the British government to extract money from its colonies in the Americas, prioritise merchandise coming from the British West Indies – as opposed to French and Dutch colonies – and curb the colonies' independence by 'integrating them into a militarily and fiscally unified greater British nation'. This ruling created a compelling pretext to push for American unification and, ultimately, revolution. Although he was later to put his anti-slavery stance into practice and even became president of the Philadelphia Society for the Relief of Free Negroes

Unlawfully Held in Bondage, Franklin's interest in the Sommersett v. Steuart case and pro-abolitionist statements may have been necessary if he was to retain the support of influential Quakers John Fothergill and David Barclay and achieve his personal and public goals, such as wresting authority over Pennsylvania from the grip of its chief executive Thomas Penn (son of the Quaker William Penn, founder of Pennsylvania). Ironically Steuart, the high-ranking Receiver General of Customs for North America, had come to England from Boston, seeking respite from the colonial rebels who opposed the taxes he was tasked with collecting. Perhaps seeing this unpopular figure crushed under the gavel of Lord Mansfield was another handy recruitment tool for Franklin to get colonists on board, as it was soon after his return from England in the wake of the Somerset case that he began to raise the colonist militias for what would become the American War of Independence.

In his book *Somersett*, Philip Goodrich goes further, making the case that Franklin's revolution was in fact 'predicated on one essential element, the legal manumission of at least one individual slave in either the colonies or Great Britain'. He writes that once Mansfield's ruling came in, letters were sent to Virginia plantation owners such as 'Washington, Mason, Jefferson, Madison, Henry, Lee, Monroe, Wythe, Harrison, Carter, Randolph, and . . . Henry Laurens', telling them about the case and essentially leaving it to their imagination as to what it meant for their plantations and businesses, built as they were on the free labour of enslaved workers. To Laurens, says Goodrich, Franklin wrote 'an especially impassioned letter' on the potentially devastating impact that the abolition of slavery would have on his family (as per Franklin's habit, each letter concluded with 'Please burn this after reading'). A profile of Laurens, a powerful slave-owner at the time, records his verdict on Mansfield's decision as 'suitable to the times', though the profile's author notes that this may have been a reference to 'growing anti-slavery sentiment in England', or 'a sneer' at the ruling being delayed long enough to allow the removal of any enslaved Africans in

England – thus avoiding a 'flood of litigation and financial loss'. At the same time as stoking the fears of plantation owners, says Goodrich, Franklin would have had to convince anti-abolitionists that the revolution was not about preserving slavery. The inflammatory letters were sent to North America before the judgement even took place, bundled inconspicuously with some Quaker pamphlets by Franklin's friend Fothergill, to fellow Quaker Anthony Benezet, who was told they were to 'advise slave owners that they could pursue voluntary manumission of their own slaves now' and instructed him to post them after Mansfield's ruling. Just one year after the ruling, a group of about sixty American colonists threw 342 chests of tea belonging to the British East India Company into Boston Harbour in protest at new taxation introduced by the British Parliament in the 1773 Tea Act.

The Boston Tea Party, as it became known, perhaps wasn't what Franklin had in mind. In a letter to the House Committee of Correspondence in Massachusetts, dated 2 February 1774, he cautions, 'if war is finally to be made upon us, which some threaten, an act of violent injustice on our part, unrectified, may not give a colourable pretence for it.' War was indeed upon them and the Revolutionary War, which would rage on from 1775 to 1783, swept up everybody in its path, including the Parker family.

Among most Scots, loyalism had disintegrated by the late 1790s. The Revolution had not threatened the material interests of the Highland Scots in North America in the way their imperial view of the world had originally led them to suppose. Furthermore, the state was unable to garner their support, since it was no longer in a position to offer them the advantage of land grants. The Revolutionary War thus had the effect of diverting a greater number of new Scottish adventurers towards British colonies in the Caribbean. Charles Stuart Parker (1771–1828) figured among their number and would become a key player in the fortunes of my ancestors.

When Charles was born in Virginia just a few months before the *Sommersett v. Steuart* case came to trial, his father James did all he could to ensure that his son received a good education, sending him to Scotland for tutoring and having his friend Charles Steuart look out for him. Charles Parker became highly educated, well versed in the classics, and learned to speak French with fluency. After his mother's death (c.1785–1786), Charles was sent to the Customs House at Port Glasgow. He remained there for eleven or twelve months until November 1787. Soon afterwards, under the guidance of a Spanish priest in Cadiz, he also learned to speak Spanish. He returned to London in early 1789. From London he travelled to Grenada and arrived there in July 1789, as an apprentice to the Scottish merchant George Robertson. And it was here the story of what became the Sandbach Tinne dynasty begins.

CHAPTER 5

'HUNTED VICTIMS'

I suspect that in ten years' time, we'll look back at the study of slavery and try to remember what it was like before we'd heard of the Sandbach Tinne dynasty.

Professor David Olusoga OBE

The Caribbean island of Grenada changed hands between the Spanish, the British and the French and was finally 'awarded' to Britain under the Treaty of Paris in 1783, after four years of French rule (from 1779). An account of this period published in 1964, prior to Grenada's independence, charts the anglicisation that ensued after the British takeover. It included the acquisition of French Roman Catholic churches, appropriating the revenues of Catholic priests and accepting as legal only marriages performed by the Protestant 'established church'. They imposed 'the test', under which only those who had taken the oath against transubstantiation (the belief that bread and wine are transformed into the actual flesh and blood of Jesus) were allowed to sit in the council chamber, or House of Assembly. By the time Charles Stuart Parker arrived on the island to make his fortune at the age of eighteen in 1789, Grenada was just six years into that bout of British rule.

There were many Scots already in the Caribbean when Parker had arrived there, and like his predecessor George Robertson (1756–1799) from Kincardine, Ross and Cromarty, in the Scottish Highlands, he established himself as a merchant in Grenada. Having been apprenticed under Robertson and learnt the business, upon completion of his apprenticeship he took up a partnership. With his classical education and fluency in Spanish, a language still widely spoken in the Caribbean trade with Caracas (Venezuela) and the Viceroyalty of New Granada (present-day Colombia), the young clerk must have quickly proven himself. The following year, 1790, the firm was renamed Robertson, Gordon & Parker.

As Sandbach's uncle – Samuel Sandbach of Grenada (1730–1800) – was also present on the island, having already made his fortune in Grenada, it was a destination of choice for the young clerk. His uncle's slave-trading fortune had already financed the purchase of three townhouses next to each other in the prestigious Brompton Row in London, as well as land in Tobago and a plantation called 'Respect' in Grenada, with dozens of enslaved Africans on it. Contemporary official records relating to Grenada, held in the National Archives, name Samuel Sandbach as a member of the 'council' in February 1789 and again in July 1792, demonstrating that his uncle had a governance role on the island.[1] Although he was not technically in Grenada on these dates (he is marked as absent), the fact that he was on the council alongside fellow Scot Ninian Home (1732–1795), who was to become Lieutenant Governor of Grenada in November 1792, shows the level of influence and power Sandbach's uncle held. When he died, it was stated that he 'left no issue', common for planters who lived for long periods in the Caribbean colonies, but usually an indication that they had mixed-race children with their enslaved women. The three adjoining houses on Brompton Row were left to his namesake and nephew Samuel Sandbach (1769–1851).[2] There were also other family members in Grenada. The slave registers record 'A list of slaves in the lawful possession of Robert Nicholson as attorney of William Sandbach Esq. Proprietor of Banana Estate', and the Legacy of British Slave Owners database has William Sandbach also as the owner of two estates, Resource and Respect, in the parish of St Mark on the northeast tip of the island.

The short-lived partnership of Robertson, Gordon & Parker dissolved due to a falling-out with Daniel Gordon; and, after his removal, the company became known as Robertson Parker & Co. In a letter to his father, dated May 1792, Charles Stuart Parker writes of 'Mr. Samuel Sandbach, a young man about 24', whom he hopes will become part of the business: 'He is . . . a man that we are convinced would render himself useful and agreeable to us. He has an uncle in London who made a fortune here, and I believe is desirous to forward him.' Clearly, his Uncle Samuel was at that point an absentee owner, very rich from his ill-gotten gains, and who had used his influence to obtain a place for his nephew in the new firm, which prided itself on a trade in 'Prime Gold Coast Negroes'. This pattern of 'making a fortune' in the Caribbean and the Americas is illustrated generation after generation and shows just how lucrative it was to steal indigenous people's land and farm it with enslaved labour. There was at that time nowhere in Europe where you could acquire vast tracts of fertile land for free and populate it with an enslaved labour force. To a farming family like the Sandbachs, this was an opportunity not to be missed.

When Gordon left the firm under a dark cloud, Samuel Sandbach took a small share and the company name changed once more, to Robertson, Parker & Sandbach.[3] Parker further cemented their business alliance in 1797 when he married Robertson's niece. That same year on 2 April the partnership was renewed but this time the 'Articles of Partnership'[4] were between George Robertson and Charles Stuart Parker, for six years. It would not last the full term, however, and by this time the partners had all decanted from Grenada to their new principal base of operations – Demerara.

It was on 6 June 1800 that Margaret Rainy's cousin Christian Robertson married James Watson, the union that was to produce Peter Miller Watson and four siblings. James Watson was 'factor of the Earl of Orkney's estate; Thomas, 1st Baron Dundas' (1741–1820),[5] the 'Vice-Admiral Depute of Orkney and Shetland. In February 1807, a Dutch frigate, the *Utrecht*, was wrecked on the island of Sanday during a storm, Watson was required to secure the salvage accruing from it'.[6] Numerous letters in the National Library of Scotland detail cases brought by Watson on behalf of Dundas for wreckages off the coast of Orkney where washed-up cargo was appropriated by locals. It was Watson's job to prosecute anyone doing so, as the salvage rights were Lord Dundas's exclusive preserve. This same Lord Dundas also inherited slave plantations in Grenada[7] (as well as Dominica) from his domineering father, Sir Lawrence Dundas of Kerse (1712–1781) – an ambitious and successful entrepreneur, who from his beginnings as a wine merchant and army contractor rose to become 'one of the most powerful and richest of landowners in Britain',[8] a banker and a major shareholder in the construction of the Forth and Clyde Canal, which opened in 1790, linking Edinburgh in the east of Scotland with Glasgow in the west, with a terminus at Port Dundas, at One Hundred Acre Hill in central Glasgow.

This series of events and liaisons conspired to put the Sandbachs, Parkers and Robertsons in Grenada at the end of the eighteenth century, with the Watsons entering on the periphery in Scotland at the turn of the nineteenth century, each family now intertwined in a violent and abhorrent business portfolio as well as a kinship network, one that was destined to perpetuate itself almost incestuously for generations to come.

Since I started this research, I have adopted two key principles;

1: Follow the genealogy and
2: Follow the money.

This has allowed the story to unravel itself organically, with each new character in the family tree offering an entirely new set of factors to consider. Whilst the corresponding documentation or historical and archival accounts show the changing nature of the businesses, professions, behaviours and outcomes, each variable throws up new questions, as well as some answers. Tracing where their money was made and to whom it was passed on, helped to build up a picture of their lives, firstly in Grenada at the source and also in the UK, both before and after they embarked upon their colonial endeavours.

What perhaps yielded the most unexpected sources of new information was the response to my decision to share some extracts from my research in the media. One such response was from a descendant of William Sandbach (b. 1807). The lady's name is Phyl Hall and, like me, she'd been looking into the family tree, though she was following an entirely different Sandbach line. Phyl told me about her lineage within the family: poor farmers who apparently never inherited anything from their rich relatives. She shared a list of records from the Slave Registers of former British colonial dependencies, 1813–1834. The document reveals the names of a group of enslaved Africans owned by the Sandbach family in the parish of St Andrew, Grenada:

Owned by Rose Sandbach:

Peggy, 42
Grace, 40
Maria, 36
Judith, 34
Catharine, 33
Edward, 32
Chloe, 24
Susey, 14
Eliza, 14
John, 7
Isabella, 6

It is of note that they are mostly women and girls, with just one man and one boy. The names and ages of these eleven people – recorded as being either from 'Grenada' or 'Africa' – bring a humanity to what is otherwise an amorphous group of individuals, quantified and valued like livestock. Upon further investigation of the British Colonial Dependencies Slave Registers 1813–1834, I discovered that William Sandbach was classed as the enslaver in 1817 of 502 individuals, ranging from babies to some over eighty years old, on the island of Grenada.

What also stands out is the name of the owner of those initial eleven enslaved people that I discovered: Rose Sandbach. In the will of Samuel Sandbach (the uncle), the second person he mentions in his list of bequeathments is one 'Roze Catharine Sandbach, a free mulatess, my daughter'.

I was disturbed to see that the mixed-race child of a white enslaver and an African or Creole woman whom he'd enslaved and raped (she had no choice or agency in whether or not to have sex with her master) was herself bequeathed slaves. Roze (or Rose), a product of that rape by William Sandbach, became a mixed-race slave-owner herself. Clearly, she was now financially independent – a point confirmed by the fact that the same will stipulated she should retain ownership of a plot of land in St Mark's, Grenada, 'now in her possession'. She was also Samuel Sandbach's (his nephew's) first cousin. Sandbach also left his Black daughter an annuity of £100, to be paid every year for the remainder of her life. I was slowly coming to terms with the nuances of enslavement. In those layers of complexity, the very institution itself had become normalised to such an extent that even the children of the sexual exploitation of enslaved Black women by their white masters were, on occasion at least, content to continue the status quo after they had inherited from their own enslaved mothers' rapists.

Roze Sandbach was far from the only freed so-called 'mulatress' or 'mulatto' (a derogatory term used to describe a female or male of mixed white and Black origin) in Grenada at the time. Historian

David Alston suggests that Charles Stuart Parker himself fathered two 'mulatto boys', Charles and James (or Jim), who were 'sent to Scotland for education in 1791'. Given that this was only two years after his arrival in Grenada, when Charles would have been just twenty, is illustrative of the convention that when a white man arrived in the colonies, he should first take an enslaved woman or a Creole as his mistress. The women generally had no right to refuse. Rape of enslaved men and women was de facto legal, as enslaved Africans were considered as 'property' not 'people' and had little or no recourse to justice at that time.

In 1783, Grenada's population was recorded as including 1,125 free coloureds (185 'English' and 940 'French'), living alongside 24,620 'slaves' (16,240 'English speaking' and 8,280 'French').[9] What is important to note from these figures is that there were considerably more French 'free coloureds' than English. By 1795 their number had doubled – much to the alarm of the British authorities.[10] The measures designed to reduce the powers of the French populace of Grenada, such as the prohibitions on non-Protestants in civic office, were even more pronounced for French free coloureds. Restrictions included tight controls on public gatherings, and laws requiring free coloureds to carry a lantern at night. 'Eventually,' recounts the historian Kit Candlin, 'mixed race subjects would have to undergo the humiliation of having to prove their free status by presenting evidence to a series of convened courts.'[11] One of those subjects was the wife of Julien Fédon, a coloured free man. She was directly impacted by the strict regulations, resulting in her detention in prison for several weeks. Fédon was himself the owner of enslaved Africans (another instance of the normalisation of enslavement, even among the children of the enslaved and their enslavers), but despite the apparent acceptance of the status quo, events like this led even free coloureds like Fédon to rise up. He was soon to become the leader of a massive rebellion of enslaved Africans and free Creoles.

Ninian Home had become Lieutenant Governor of Grenada in

November 1792, and he was well aware of the potential spark of insurrection. In July 1793, he wrote to his brother in Scotland, reportedly declaring that 'he feared the minds of the slaves in Grenada would be poisoned by the immigrants from the French islands, slaves and coloured people[12] propagating the doctrine of liberty, equality and fraternity'.[13] In another letter, Home writes that there exists 'too great a mixture' in the island's population.[14] He was right to suspect trouble was brewing. *Le Déclaration des droits de l'homme et du citoyen* (Declaration of the Rights of Man and the Citizen) of 1789, extended in 1791 and 1794, granted full citizenship to free coloureds and emancipation to enslaved Africans in France's Caribbean territories. The French Revolution was not only taking place on European soil, its doctrine was permeating through its colonial territories as well. In fact, a revolutionary army 'and some Jacobin administrators' had been sent from France under the command of the so-called leader of the French Revolution in the West Indies, Jean-Baptiste Victor Hugues, 'to establish "Liberty, Fraternity and Equality"' among French Caribbeans'.[15]

In February 1795, Hugues (sometimes spelled Hughes) signed a declaration in French and English which directly addressed itself to 'the Commanders in Chief of the British forces in the Windward Islands', pledging that the 'assassination of each and every individual Republican (of whatever colour he is, and in whatever Island it may happen) shall be expiated by the death of two English officers – our prisoners. The Guillotine shall at the first notice thereof, perform this act of justice.'[16]

Any Frenchman or 'traitor' who did not comply with the Republic's forces, it added, would be 'outlawed' and their property seized. The *History of Grenada* records how that same February, just one month before they staged their own uprising, Fédon's fellow 'mulatto' co-conspirators, Charles Nogues and Jean Pierre La Valette, travelled to Guadeloupe to see Hugues. When they returned, they appointed Fédon as Commandant-General of the insurgents in Grenada. They also brought with them 'arms and ammunition, caps of liberty, national cockades and a flag on which was inscribed in large letters Liberté, Egalité, ou la Mort'.[17] What is important to remember here is that those leading the battle were not all impoverished enslaved Africans; these were free, educated and well-connected 'coloureds' or 'mulattos'. The British feared them, but they were likely also jealous or resentful of the fact that people of colour should have such power, wealth and relative autonomy. Having once had the freedom to create wealth, the French coloured population were now, under the British, being treated as second-class citizens. Whether or not their primary motivation was to protect their own rights and property, they wholeheartedly adopted the language and principles of the French republic and 'revolution' was inevitable.

Fédon and his followers would have been keenly aware of the American War of Independence, that battle against British rule, and of the Haitian Revolution that began just four years earlier in 1791. Somewhat bizarrely, Fédon had been a signatory to a public letter in 1790 from a group of French inhabitants of Grenada asking the government for protection against 'idle and disorderly vagabonds' who had come from Martinique 'to disturb the peace' and wanted to 'kill all the Coloured people of Grenada, for the reason, no doubt, of their subservience to Great Britain'.[18] Devas suggests that this appeal 'may have not been sincere', or the local government 'showed no interest' in it.[19] Perhaps it was a veiled threat from the group, warning the newly returned British, who had also come to 'disturb the peace', that their lives were also in danger. What is clear, however, is that Fédon's fortunes, property and freedom were bound up in the political turmoil. By 1794, he owned a house in Gouyave, plus a '360-acre Belvidere [sometimes spelled 'Belvedere'] estate with 96 slaves engaged in the cultivation of coffee, cocoa, and sugar'.[20] His brother Jean, meanwhile, is recorded as purchasing a coffee plantation of 139 acres in St John that same year. Another twist in the tale to compass how an anti-slavery revolt could have been orchestrated by a Black man who himself had owned enslaved Africans.

The rebellion was to be led by a group of wealthy so-called 'mulattos' and co-signed by disgruntled French Catholic whites, whose rights had also been curtailed by the British. However, it is important to note that the enslaved Africans rose up against their oppressors and swelled the ranks of the rebels in considerable numbers; without them, the rebellion would not have been possible. Many who took part may have been new arrivals to the island, as from 1791 to 1793, 25,000 Africans were brought from their home continent to Grenada alone.[21] Others may have been increasingly aware of their legal rights under the French which were now being usurped by the British. Prior to Ninian Home's tenure, a dispatch from Grenada's former governor, Edward Matthew (appointed Governor-in-Chief in 1784, and namesake of Fort Matthew), dated 13 April 1788, shared an extract from the minutes of a rare court case 'relative to the Tryal, Sentence, & Execution of a White Man (Richard Brigstock, also called Richard Preston) for the Murder of a Negroe (an enslaved woman called Anna Ritta)'.[22] It's not often you come across the conviction of a white man for the death of a Black person, even today. The historians Morgan and Rushton point out that 'The argument hinged on the humanity of slaves rather than their legal status, and, by extension of mediaeval law in the Magna Carta, the prohibition against lords killing their unfree subordinates, the villeins of the manorial system.'[23] This argument in law defeated the de facto assumption proposed by the defence that 'no freeman ought to suffer death for the murder of a slave' and unusually, Preston was hanged on 14 April 1788.

The combination of a growing demand for justice and a groundswell of Black resistance – from the Haitian Revolution of 1791 to the Second Carib War on St Vincent in 1795 – proved incendiary. In Grenada, the fuse was lit close to midnight on 2 March 1795. Fédon, his second-in-command Stanislaus Besson and approximately a hundred coloured men and slaves 'took by surprise' the town of Grenville Baye, or La Baye.[24] In the early 1800s an account of the events published in *Encyclopaedia Britannica* (later edited by Peter Miller Watson's stepfather Dr Thomas Stuart Traill in 1852), recounts the story in scandalised terms, painting the picture of an unholy alliance between 'the disaffected Negroes' and 'numbers of white people who were charmed with the extravagant doctrine of liberty and equality'.[25] Together, we are told, they 'plundered the dwellings and store houses; dragging the innocent, the astonished inhabitants into the streets, setting them up as marks to be shot at'. Eleven English inhabitants were killed before the rebels proceeded to Belvedere, the estate owned by Fédon where he had established his headquarters. The notion that the English captives were 'innocent' is of course absurd, given the fact that slavery was a crime against humanity, albeit legalised by unscrupulous parliaments across Europe, yet reports of the time are keen to portray the English as such. In one report they are described as 'hunted victims' and 'defenceless', in contrast to the so-called 'rebels' who are categorised as 'inhuman wretches', 'ruffians' and 'a Race of Monsters' that carry out their actions 'with all the wanton cruelty, which savage ferocity could devise'.[26]

Simultaneous rebel attacks were launched in Gouyave (also known as Charlottetown) with prisoners taken on estates across the island. It was not until the morning of 4 March that the rebels entered the island's major port. Candlin states that 'at around half past ten, a washerwoman came running into St George's convinced that "the enemy" was marching on the town'.[27] Others followed her from the river, claiming that they too 'had heard distant drums and had even seen troops moving into position up the road'. The British troops braced themselves for an attack.

Colonial reports of the uprising are, as one would expect, presented from the perspective of the authorities or British observers. However, as with Cuffy's rebellion in Berbice in 1763, we can find small snippets about the rebels when reading between the lines of the official accounts. A colonial account of events 'by a sincere well-wisher to the colony', planter Thomas Turner Wise, recounts how in Gouyave, 'all the white English inhabitants were seized in their beds, and tied and sent to a camp, which, it then appeared, the insurgents must have been long preparing at Belvidere, an estate very high up in the mountains . . . belonging to one Julien Fédon, a mulatto'. This gives us a sense of the careful planning that the rebels had undertaken before launching their revolt. Other letters quoted by Wise, capturing the British military movements, give small but humanising glimpses of the rebels. There is the ceremony they hold 'under the cover of the darkness of the night' to pay 'homage' to visiting chiefs (and, the writer of the letter suspects, to keep awake the British soldiers); the resourceful blacksmiths turning 'bills' (used for cutting tree branches) into more deadly 'pikes'; and the 'rebel who was captured' boldly wearing a national 'cockade' or rosette in his hat.

Another revealing report records the movements of Governor Ninian Home, who at the time the uprising began was in St Andrew's. Keen to return to St George's, but wanting to avoid running into any rebels on the road, he decided to take the sea route. As he and his men debated their best course of action, they didn't notice that someone was paying close attention, an enslaved African whose wife had reportedly been taken and possibly sent to England by Governor Home.[28] At the first opportunity, this man called 'Orinoco slipped away from the house and made all haste to the rebel camp in the mountains'.[29] Word soon reached the rebel leaders, and an ambush was quickly organised.

As Ninian Home passed Gouyave, now bobbing in a dinghy in an attempt to escape detection, he was fired on and surrounded by canoes before being brought ashore and imprisoned at Fédon's HQ. A missive from the rebel chief, written in French and dated 4 March 1795, gives us further insight into Fédon's style of leadership. In the letter, he proudly announces his coup – the capturing of 'le Tyran [tyrant] Ninian Home' and other Englishmen – and calls on others to submit within two hours or face 'tous les Fleaux d'une Guerre desastreuse' (all the scourges – or plagues – of a disastrous war): namely punishment by death and the burning of all their possessions.[30] He also clearly shows where his allegiances lie, directly quoting from Hugues' February declaration, as well as introducing himself as *'Commandant General des Forces de la Republique Francaise, et Officiers en Service actual'* and signing off the letter as *'de la Republique Francaise une et indivisible'* (from the French Republic, one and indivisible; or as Alexandre Dumas – himself the son of a mixed-race military general from Saint-Domingue, Thomas-Alexandre Dumas Davy de la Pailleterie, and the grandson of a white Frenchman and an enslaved African woman – was to memorably put it in his classic 1844 novel *The Three Musketeers*, 'All for one, and one for all'). Now that the French Republic had clearly stated that it would defend all French, whatever their skin colour, the Republican mantra *'une et indivisible'* would have been an especially significant and empowering motto for Fédon.

The British were overwhelmed and overpowered. Around this time, yellow fever was spreading so quickly through the Windward Islands that by 1794, in Grenada, 'Every house was the abode of death'.[31] Furthermore, according to the 1801 'Report on the Petition of the Proprietors of Estates in the Island of Grenada', on the day the rebellion began there were only 293 men in the British garrison who were fit for duty.[32] With the governor imprisoned at Fédon's HQ, Kenneth Francis McKenzie, the Attorney-General and President of the Grenada Council, stepped in to take over the top job. One of his first actions was to write to the commanding officer of the St Andrew's regiment and ask him to 'immediately assemble all the white men, who can possibly be spared from the necessary defence of your quarter'.[33] His specification of 'white men' may seem telling, given the colour of the rebels; however, in a letter sent to Colonel Horsford the same day, he suggests the Colonel 'arm a number of able trusty Negroes'. Perhaps mindful of Hugues' racially inclusive declaration, McKenzie also issued a proclamation promising a pardon to all rebels (except those involved in the murders in La Bay), as well as 'a reward of 20 Johannes's [£40], to any person bringing in any of the said insurgents dead or alive'.[34] He then sent a distress call to Grenada's neighbours for help. In response,

Trinidad's Spanish governor reportedly sent forty soldiers, while Martinique deployed British troops. St Vincent was too busy dealing with its own uprising – the Second Carib War – to boost the colonialists' defences. Dispatches to the British government provide further insight as to the progress of the uprising. McKenzie's first missive as governor, dated 28 March 1795, described the unfolding events as 'a general insurrection of the French free coloured people'.[35] He reported:

> The Negroes are daily joining the insurgents and desolating the estates; all of which have been plundered, and a number in the neighbourhoods of the town have been burnt. From our latest accounts they have 350 men armed with musquets and 250 armed with pikes, bayonets, &c., and are joined by about 4000 Negroes. Their chief is a Mulatto of this Island, two or three leaders have joined them from Guadeloupe, and many of the French inhabitants of this Colony, some of them people of property.[36]

By the end of March, Fédon's camp reportedly numbered 7,200, including 4,000–6,000 enslaved Africans and 600 whites and free coloureds – the second group armed with muskets and bayonets, with the larger group of enslaved fighters having cutlasses and pikes. By contrast, the British defences at this point numbered some 500 regulars and 380 militiamen.[37] The rebel operation must have been highly organised, as not only did Fédon quickly set up his base camp, but his troops were recruiting and training new members. On 24 April McKenzie sent an update to his superiors in the UK, noting with some panic that 'from the long continuance of this insurrection the defection among the plantation Negroes has become general, and the enemy are daily training them to arms'.[38] Some, however, did abandon the uprising – and it is they who reportedly informed McKenzie that Home and other prisoners had been 'massacred'. It was not until May that McKenzie's first letter arrived on the desk of the Home Secretary, the Duke of Portland, in London – although, the British National Archives note, 'the British government had heard rumours of the uprising before then'.[39]

The slow initial response of the British and their concentrated position in the port capital of St George's had given Fédon time and space to gather provisions, supplies and fresh support. However, as in Berbice in 1763, these resources gradually ran dry and put the rebels in a weaker position to overthrow the British reinforcements when they finally arrived. By May 1795 a 'Black Corps' of 300 'trusted slaves' had been dispatched to the woods, terrain they would have been more familiar with than the British.[40] Further support arrived over the following months, while a 'concerted attack' was launched in June 1796 by Lieutenant General Sir Ralph Abercromby who brought a fleet, having been dispatched by Scotsman Lord Henry Dundas, Secretary of State for War since 1794 under the premiership of William Pitt.[41]

In the middle of the chaos was another Scot – James McInroy Sr (1759–1825) – who had first come to Demerara in 1782 and owned ships which traded between Demerara, Carriacou and Grenada, as well as West Africa and the UK. McInroy soon had his own sugar plantation in Demerara,[42] and by 1790 had established a store there too.

In 1790 when he was joined by George Robertson, Charles Stuart Parker the younger and Samuel Sandbach, and they had established the company McInroy Sandbach & Co., they would not have known that their business was to come to an abrupt end there. By the time of Fédon's rebellion in 1795, George Robertson and Charles Stuart Parker were both in the UK, 'with the aim of establishing new business contacts'.[43] On hearing the news, the two held back their travel plans until notice that it was safe came from Demerara. McInroy, however, was in Grenada at the time and very much in the thick of it.

In April 1795, when Ninian Home was captured by the rebels, he was reportedly executed by being put through a sugar grinder; such was the hatred resultant from the extreme cruelty meted out by the whites to the enslaved Africans. Records of enslaved people in the Caribbean being boiled alive in molten sugar were commonplace.

Somehow McInroy managed to dodge the rebels and head for the harbour where the company's sloop, the *Rambler*, was anchored, and he and a few close friends made a lucky escape with the help of their 'Negroe crew'. In a letter to his father dated 27 November 1795, sent from Tobago, Charles Stuart Parker recounts the dramatic journey that McInroy faced after leaving Grenada. On its way from Trinidad to Demerara, he reports, the *Rambler* and its crew of about fourteen was 'seized by a French privateer with some fifty to sixty men onboard'. The armed ship 'grabbled the Rambler twice but without success. In her last attempt the captain and three or four men were killed.' Parker credits the 'miraculous escape' to the 'brave behaviour of our Negroes on board the Rambler which are perhaps unparalleled'.[44] This would suggest that the enslaved Africans who crewed McInroy's ship were more cognisant of the conflict with France than the rebellion. It also illustrates how these white enslavers relied on their enslaved Africans for their own protection, even from their fellow white Europeans competing for their share of the Caribbean pie. Parker is unsurprisingly quick to move on to money matters, noting the '£9,000 sterling property on board' that McInroy managed to smuggle away, adding that 'the said sloop, Mr McInroy, and our property are all safe' and, that after reaching safety, 'All the goods were sold from the Rambler which closes our Union sales.' While there are post-rebellion records of William Sandbach's presence in Grenada in the nineteenth century, I have so far found no records of Samuel Sandbach, Charles Stuart Parker, George Roberson or James McInroy after McInroy fled the island in 1795. It appears from the records that they decanted their business to Demerara and didn't go back.

By July 1796, McKenzie reported the death, escape or imprisonment of many rebels, leaving only 'a desperate band of Free coloured men and Negroes in the woods'.[45] The human and financial toll of the uprising was immense. Some 7,000 enslaved Africans died; and sugar works, rum works and other buildings on sixty-five sugar estates and thirty-five coffee estates were destroyed.[46] According to Edward Cox's detailed overview, government forces captured and punished most of the principal actors; 'Fédon, however, evaded the victors and reportedly perished at sea whilst attempting to escape by canoe to Trinidad.' Other accounts claim he was caught and executed in 1796.

After the rebellion was thwarted, McKenzie's preoccupation became what to do with those detained, and, inevitably, to the public cost, which he estimated (from the start of the rebellion) to total more than £230,000, not to mention the fact that the island was making no income during this period.[47] One prominent Scottish plantation owner in Grenada, George Baillie, cousin of Bristolian slave trader and politician Evan Baillie (sometimes written as Bailie), led the battle for financial support from the government. George worked for his cousin's company, Garraway & Baillie. According to historian Nicholas Draper, Baillie himself said that 'after great perseverance, and being three times refused, I succeeded in my application to Government for a loan, to the extent of one million and a half, for all the sufferers'.[48]

Baillie portrays Prime Minister William Pitt as initially being averse to any financial aid – 'lest it might become a very dangerous precedent'. What Baillie doesn't mention in his narrative, Draper points out, is that the parliamentary process for compensation began within months of the rebellion's beginning – in fact, before it had even ended. In June 1795 'a petition of merchants trading to St Vincent and Grenada was referred to a committee, and Royal Assent was given to the Bill on the 27/06/1795, for a total loan of up to £1.5M'.[49] Unsurprisingly, Baillie was the main beneficiary of the loan, receiving some £260,000. A substantial share also went to the firm Alexander Huston & Co. There is no mention of Sandbach, Robertson, Parker or McInroy in Draper's overview of the Grenada loans or in the subsequent Act of Regis of 1806 where the loan was extended, before some of the recipients eventually defaulted. The money didn't save Baillie. He and his partners did eventually pay back the loan, plus interest – no doubt helped by repeated delays to the repayment dates and the fact that Evan Baillie was chairing the committee appointed to investigate the financial claims of Grenada and St Vincent merchants and planters.[50] Despite this, by 1807 George Baillie was bankrupt.[51]

The decision of the government to award a loan is interesting in itself. As Draper suggests, there are three main reasons they may have done so: guilt at not sufficiently protecting the island, pressure from influential individuals, and 'systemic intervention'. When the second-largest recipient of the exchequer loan, Alexander Houston & Co., failed to repay in full, the government did not ask their guarantors to settle, they simply liquidated the company. Most accounts suggest that this was in 1800, but this is questionable, as an act of Regis of 1806 extends the loan period to them. Draper concludes that 'the state and slavery in the 1790s were still in the perceived symbiotic relationship that had characterised them before the rise of abolitionism.'[52] The government was not really protecting the company but rather the continued use of enslaved labour.

In contrast to Baillie, Samuel Sandbach, James McInroy, Charles Stuart Parker and George Robertson flourished. We know from Robertson's will of 1799, for example, that he left c. £250,000. However, even before the rebellion, the family had also been investing in businesses and plantations outside Grenada, and the colonies of Demerara, Essequibo and Berbice were now the focus of their attention.

James McInroy and George Robertson's nephew Harry Robertson (1774–1795) were already established in Demerara. On 4 April 1796, a hand-written note from the Parker Papers reveals the Robertson family 'received the melancholy news of our dear hopeful son Harry's death at Demerary on the 28 December 1795'. The unknown writer may have been thinking of Fédon's rebellion and the deaths that ensued when they referred to it as a 'Fatal year!'

Perhaps the plan had always been to shift focus to the colonies of Demerara, Essequibo and Berbice, but the tumultuous events in Grenada must have sped up the process.

That year was no less fatal for Fédon and many of his followers, bringing not only death, but an end to their battle for freedom from British rule. Yet although the uprising did not ultimately succeed, Fédon's name lives on in Grenadian popular culture and folklore. When the United States invaded the island in 1983, prompting a new Grenada revolution, Fédon became a popular name for children. A commissioned portrait of Fédon by Michele Gibbs 'was less a likeness than an ideological reinterpretation'. This 'heavily Africanized image of the mulatto leader' became the official portrait of Fédon and he was again co-opted into the new uprising. Although Fédon's goal had been to establish a French republic on the island – or according to some modern-day reports 'a Black republic'[53] – others caution that 'he did not specifically request an extension of the rights of Afro-Grenadians'.[54] However, as Professor Shalini Puri points out, in 1983 this almost didn't matter. 'The revolution's version of Fédon's rebellion told it as a story of Black rebellion and claimed it as the prehistory of the revolution.'

Not long after escaping Fédon, James McInroy had fathered a mixed-race daughter, Grace Ann (born c.1796), with Catherine McInroy (who in 1817 is recorded as a free woman in Demerara, suggesting some form of marriage, either regular or irregular). He later left £400 to his daughter.[55] The following year, in Glasgow,[56] he married Elizabeth Moore, a girl of about fifteen or sixteen, born in the Dutch West Indian colony of St Eustatius, to parents who were both born in the West Indies (St Eustatius and Montserrat).

CHAPTER 6

'THREE OR FOUR HATCHETS'

> *The ruin of a nation begins in the homes of its people.*
> *– African proverb*

Demerara is famed for its sugar, but also for its rum. Many brands that emerged during the period of enslavement endure to this day and have continued to be exported worldwide. Evidence of the involvement of Sandbach Tinne, its subsidiaries and its precursor organisations in this liquor trade includes a label for 'Genuine Black Diamond Demerara Rum' which named the 'sole exporters' to Canada as Sandbach Parker & Co., Ltd of 'Demerara, British Guiana, Est'd 1790'.

Two hundred years prior to the arrival of George Robertson, Charles Stuart Parker, Samuel Sandbach and James McInroy,[1,2] a tale of the riches of Demerara had lured successive generations of colonists. Sir Walter Raleigh's claim to have discovered 'El Dorado', the fabled lost city of gold, proved popular with the general public, and no doubt contributed to the continued fascination with the legend which has inspired books, films, and even an award-winning Guyanese 'El Dorado' rum – which is still produced by a former Sandbach Tinne subsidiary, Demerara Distillers, to this day. In 1595, Raleigh had travelled to Guiana to seek 'El Dorado'; keen to win favour with

Queen Elizabeth I, he returned from his tropical expedition and promptly published *The Discovery of the Large, Rich, and Beautiful Empire of Guiana – with a Relation of the Great and Golden City of Manoa*.[3] Raleigh boasted, 'The country hath more quantity of gold, by manifold, than the best parts of the Indies, or Peru.'[4]

While Raleigh had been searching for El Dorado, the Dutch were busy creating trading posts, and in 1613 established settlements at Demerary and Essequibo.[5] By 1621, the Dutch West India Company had formally established the colonies of Berbice, Demerary and Essequibo, so at the time of the arrival of the Robertson, McInroy, Sandbach and Parker families, some 170 years later, the Spanish conquistadors had long gone, and the Dutch planters, colonists and administrators had firmly taken root.

In his elaborate report of his first visit to Guiana, Raleigh had painted the indigenous peoples as 'brutal', 'barbarous' and 'ruthless'. Yet his report also provides some interesting insights into the early enslavement of indigenous Arawaks, and particularly the sexual exploitation by the Spaniards of indigenous women and girls. It was considered bad luck to have women on board warships, so the early Conquistadors would have likely gone months without seeing a woman, only to be met by topless natives when they arrived in the West Indies and South America. It is noteworthy that the 'barbarous' behaviour the Europeans attributed to the native people was more aptly a description of themselves. An account from that period records the transactional nature of such encounters, in explicit terms:

> Among many other trades, those Spaniards used canoas to pass to the rivers of Barema, Pawroma, and Dissequebe (Essequibo) . . . and there buy women and children from the cannibals, which are of that barbarous nature, as they will for three or four hatchets sell the sons and daughters of their own brethren and sisters, and for somewhat more even their own daughters. Hereof the Spaniards make great profit; for buying a maid of twelve or thirteen years for three or four

hatchets, they sell them again at Margarita in the West Indies for fifty and a hundred pesos, which is so many crowns.[6]

The region had become the focus of a land grab for competing European powers, lured by the natural wealth, the native women and the relative ease with which they could both be seized and exploited. By 1663, King Charles II had 'issued letters patent to Lord Willoughby' granting 120 miles of territory 'between the Copenam and Maroni rivers[7] . . . Later this colony would be ceded to the Netherlands by the Peace of Breda.'[8] Under article 3 of the Treaty of Breda (1667) the Dutch ceded New Netherlands (now the states of New York, Connecticut, New Jersey, Pennsylvania, Delaware and Massachusetts) to the British, and the British ceded the territory of Suriname (previously granted to Willoughby) to the Netherlands. This established the Netherlands as a significant regional power in the Caribbean, with a stronghold in Suriname to the east of Demerara, Essequibo and Berbice.

Like the Spanish, the Dutch exploited enslaved labour to build settlements, plantations and wealth. Indigenous Arawaks never adapted to enslavement. Their unique understanding of the jungle terrain gave them a distinct advantage when escaping captivity, in that they could easily disappear into the jungle and survive without much difficulty. This was after all their own habitat. Efforts were made to encourage coastal tribes to bring their war captives from the interior for sale as slaves to the Europeans, on the promise that if they delivered their enemies to the Europeans, the whites would not enslave them. A similar tactic was used in West Africa with the coastal tribes such as the Kru people of Liberia, Ivory Coast and Sierra Leone. Kru tribesmen would help facilitate the capture and transport of enemies from the interior and would be paid for every captive by the whites on the coast. Many of the Kru tribe would also sign on as seafarers on the slave voyages, being excellent seamen. It is thought that the English word 'crew' is derived from the Kru tribe, in that ships would sail light from Europe and pick up 'Krumen' on the Gold Coast before embarking on their transatlantic voyages. Like the coastal Arawaks of the Guianas, the Kru of Liberia and Ivory Coast never succumbed to enslavement, but like the Arawak, they became complicit in it, in order both to save themselves and, in most cases, to profiteer.

Once the European whites had established that they could effectively collude with coastal tribes, both in West Africa and along the Caribbean coast of South America, the traffic in enslaved Africans to the Caribbean went into overdrive, thus affording the whites extensive free labour for the macro-infrastructure that would provide the basis for industrial cash crop production in the Americas and the Caribbean.

At the forefront of those infrastructure projects in the Guianas were the Dutch. They are often credited with establishing the system of canals, trenches and sluices that drained much of Guiana's coast, turning it from a fertile but muddy wetland into land fit for planting and living upon. Guiana's topography is similar in some ways to that of Holland, in that the western coastal areas are largely either on or below sea level. This experience of developing sea defences and land reclamation from the sea that had evolved in earnest in Holland in the sixteenth century, but whose origins go back to the thirteenth century, was put to good use in the seventeenth century in engineering the sea defences and irrigation systems of Guiana's fertile and flat costal landmass. However, while the work in Holland was done primarily by serfs, at the behest of the *Heren Regeerders* (ruling lords), the extensive digging of canals and the construction of dykes, pumping stations and sluices in Guiana was done by enslaved Africans.

Guyanese social historian Walter Rodney points out that in order to create the estimated 49 miles of drainage canals and ditches, and 16 miles of waterways for transportation and irrigation, 'slaves moved 100 million tons of heavy, water-logged clay with shovel in hand, while enduring conditions of perpetual mud and water'.[9] Each plantation located along the coast or the banks of the Berbice, Essequibo or Demerara rivers, was made with front, side and back dams, to keep out seawater and bring in river or rainforest water for irrigation, drainage and transportation. A Dutch map from 1798 (see the second picture section) gives a vivid sense of Guiana at this time.

It illustrates the colonies of Essequibo and Demerara and all their plantations, colour coding those that produce coffee, sugar, cotton and cocoa, and plotting rice and tobacco cultivation too, as well as churches and 'Indian' villages or huts.[10] An earlier map, made in 1765, depicted the results of a vast measuring exercise carried out by A.L. de Saffon, who concluded: 'I have measured the land granted between the rivers of Essequibo and Demerary along the coast, containing altogether ten thousand, one hundred and twenty-five acres, having left a path of sixty feet between each plantation.'[11]

This was the landscape Robertson, McInroy, Parker and Sandbach found when they arrived in Demerara one or two decades later. In October 1797 George Robertson wrote from the colony to James Parker in London, regarding a shipment of 104 bales of cotton, with instructions on how much they should be insured for. A detailed map from 1798, which names the owners of land along the coast of the three colonies, also lists 'Robertson & Parker' on one lot between Mahaica and 'Maicouny' (now Mahaicony) at Mahaica Creek, and 'Robinson & Parker' (perhaps misspelt) on Leguaan Island.[12] A Robertson is also listed for 'Saardam', between Mahaica and Demerara, though it is not clear which one this refers to. What we do know is that in 1799, a year after this map was produced, George Robertson died in Demerara. In a rather desperate letter dated 24 March 1799, his nephew Gilbert Robertson (1774–1839) broke the news of his death to Charles Stuart Parker the elder and shared plans for a funeral the next day, to honour 'my dearest uncle and ever to be respected friend'. The letter describes how on the way home from visiting a Mr Hopkinson on Leguaan Island, George Robertson was caught in 'heavy showers' and developed a feverish illness, which resulted in his death some days later. Stubbornly, he had refused to take his prescribed medication, which, Gilbert sorrowfully writes, 'might have been his salvation'. The letter then switches to more practical matters. Gilbert was keen to reassure Parker that he had everything under control, noting, 'I have been in the country long enough to acquire a thorough knowledge of all the affairs of the concern . . . I can by a prudent & faithful discharge of the important duties left to my charge, prevent you from experiencing that uneasiness of mind.'[13]

Another letter, dated 26 February 1802, gives a hint at why Gilbert may have been so keen to reassure Parker. In the letter, the Revd. Harry Robertson (brother of George Robertson) asks James Parker what he thinks of Charles Stuart Parker the elder going to Demerara for his health instead of stopping at Madeira. Referring to an evil spirit or deity that pushes people to seek riches, the good reverend bitterly notes, 'Mammon must have a sad hold of his [Parker's] heart, and he was kind enough to remember to forget, leaving orders to pay my annuity till he returns. This only betwixt ourselves, but it was not very handsome.'[14] This is clear evidence that the supposedly righteous Revd. Robertson was also a direct beneficiary of enslavement, receiving an annuity from Parker. In a letter the following year, Robertson calls Parker a 'truly a strange fish' and complains, 'He has never wrote here since returning from Demerary. I really don't envy him, poor man. However we shall make all our claims in due time, the parting with money is like losing his vital blood.'[15] Parker had married into the Rainy family on 4 December 1797.[16] Perhaps this is why George Robertson leaves money in his will to 'Mrs Parker' (aka Margaret Rainy) rather than her husband C.S. Parker the elder himself; Parker's reputed stinginess perhaps extended even to his own wife.

George Robertson also gives us a clear sense of the immense wealth that could be procured through slave trading and plantation cultivation at that time. In a document entitled 'Calculation of the respective proportions accruing to the heirs of George Robertson made 1st Oct. 1799',[17] we can see a total payment of £234,395 (and change) made over a five-year period to some familiar names including Gilbert Robertson, Gilbert Rainy, George Rainy 'and wife' – namely Ann Robertson, sister of both George and the Revd. Harry.

It was the following year, 1800, that Christian Robertson married James Watson, the grandfather of Black footballer Andrew Watson. At that point she was extremely eligible. Not only was she a preacher's daughter, having grown up at the Manse of Kiltearn in Ross-shire with her father, the Revd. Harry, but she was also now extremely wealthy in her own right. The will of her slave trader uncle George left her various annuities including £8,005 19s 3d (£560,160 in today's money[18]) annually on 1 May (1800, 1801, 1802, 1803 and 1804) a total of over £40,000 (approx £3,000,000 in today's money) over five years, as well as a further lump sum of £6,000 on 9 March 1799, plus £1,064 10s on 9 March 1800, as '1st instalment on the estates'[19] (income from the plantations), £2,200 2s on 1 May 1801, 2nd instalment on the estates, £2,165 8s on 1 May 1802, 3rd instalment, £948 2s 8d, 1 May 1803, 4th instalment, £996 6s 11d on 1 May 1804. In total, Christian inherited over £54,000 between 1799 and 1804 (approx. £5,000,000 in today's money), all the proceeds of enslavement and the brutal maltreatment of Africans and Afro-Caribbeans.

A total gross valuation of the two slave owners' – George Robertson and Charles Stuart Parker the elder – estates in 1799, just before his death, was £541,325 (£51,654,484 in today's money) with a net value after the payment of all debts and liabilities of £235,238 19s 12d (£22.5 million in today's money). Robertson and Parker were 50-50 shareholders, so half of that estate value was Robertson's, on top of the income over those subsequent five years (1799–1804), plus all the cash-in-hand when he died.

We have an account of the betrothal of Christian Robertson to James Watson from the 'Memoir of Mrs Traill' written about Christian by her second husband, Dr Thomas Stuart Traill:

> In October 1798 [just prior to the demise of her uncle George] Miss Christy Robertson, then in the full bloom of youthful beauty was first seen by her future husband,

Mr James Watson,[20] a Lieutenant in the Regiment of the Isles, then quartered at Inverness. They first met at a ball, during the festivities of the Northern Meeting, in Inverness; at which Miss Robertson made her first public appearance. Her elegant dancing and engaging manners attracted general notice, and she was led out by Lord Macdonald the Colonel of the regiment. Mr Watson was introduced to the young lady by an intimate friend of the family and early sought an opportunity of seeing her at Kiltearn. Mr Watson was about ten years her senior – a man not of shewy manners – but of gentle address, of considerable reading, of natural good taste, an excellent musician, of strong good sense, and of sterling worth. His discrimination speedily discovered the excellent qualities of Miss Christy, and she was assiduous in his attentions. He soon left the militia, on receiving, through the recommendation of his friend Mr Miller of Dalwinston,[21] the management of the Orkney estates of Lord Dundas.[22]

Samuel Sandbach and C.S. Parker the elder had formed the Demerara business of Sandbach Parker & Co. in 1790. This was in addition to their other concerns. A few months after Miss Christy's 1798 'first public appearance', the loss of her uncle George Robertson in 1799, and the winding up of Robertson Parker & Co., events precipitated the formation in 1801 of a new company – McInroy, Parker & Co. – with its headquarters in Glasgow. The following year, a Liverpool branch was added, when Samuel Sandbach moved to the city along with James McInroy. A letter sent from Demerara to C.S. Parker the elder in Glasgow, dated 28 August 1802, shows how much of a family business it had become.[23] The writer, presumed to be Gilbert Robertson,[24] asks whether Parker might be in need of a 'young lad', namely his brother Hugh Munro Robertson (1787–1819),[25] 'to work in the firm's counting house, as his parents feel him not yet ready to fulfil his desire to come to this colony'. Perhaps mindful of Parker's appetite for money, he added, 'whatever expense may be incurred . . . I will cheerful repay'. It seemed that during this period, Parker the elder was central to the day-to-day running of the operation. Also in 1802, Christian's sister Elizabeth Robertson – another of the late George Robertson's nieces – married Samuel Sandbach. In fact, these two women, together with their cousin Margaret Rainy, were the triangular hub uniting the spokes of the Robertson, Rainy, Parker, Watson and Sandbach families into one powerful wheel. That same year, a notice in the *Lancaster Gazette* of Saturday 27 November identified another business entity, that of S. Sandbach & Co. It reported the arrival from the 'West Indies' of the ship 'Margaret & Eliza (Capt. Stephenson)', a brig of 163 tons owned by McInroy & Co., 'from Demerara, with 1 puncheon' Rum, 1 half butt wine, 8 bales cotton, 50 bags coffee for S. Sandbach & Co.'[26] It appears at this point that both James McInroy and Samuel Sandbach had briefly formed their own companies, and while doing business together, did so for a short time as separate companies.

In December 1804, the Revd. Harry Robertson wrote to James Watson complaining about C.S. Parker the elder, hinting at the administrative power that Parker wielded:

> I feel myself incompetent to decide upon the state of accounts betwixt you, but I lean to Gilbert's state. I fear nothing decisive can be done till Mr Parker returns, which I suppose will be about May or early in June . . . Mrs Parker wrote me that he had made arrangements for my drawing a certain sum if necessary, in his absence. Wonderful consideration! We must however carry fair with him on various accounts & particularly for fear he brings the legacy tax &c upon us. I don't even advise you to write Gilbert on the subject till Parker returns & then we shall have time to correct errors.[27]

From this narrative, again we learn that the affairs of the holy man – the good Revd. Harry Robertson, Doctor of Divinity – are inextricably wound up in the income from plantation enslavement. He was clearly not at all passive in this regard when it came to the distribution of wealth, particularly the immense fortune his slave trading brother had amassed, which was now being administered by Parker as his brother's business partner. This calls into question his assumed religious morality and reinforces the notion of how intertwined enslavement was with the Church, particularly in Scotland. The same can be said of another Sandbach Tinne partner, George Rainy (1790–1864), whose father was the Revd. George Rainy. As I researched the genealogy of this family, the clergy were present in almost every line, with slave traders as sons, brothers and fathers; even daughters and nieces were sometimes involved in ownership of the enslaved or married to enslavers.

In advertisements from the period, we also see another new entity emerge – McInroy, Sandbach, McBean & Co. William McBean's brother was married to the sister of James McInroy, yet another partner.[28] Two public notices, both published on New Year's Eve 1803 in the *Essequibo and Demerary Gazette*, show the company offering for sale a 'fast sailing sloop' and imported items, 'beef and pork in barrels, soap and candles, tallow in kegs, and butter in firkins'. As well as selling such products, shipped from Boston, Cork and beyond, by 1807 the company had diversified from shipping enslaved Africans to offering freight or passage on 'the ship Juno' heading to Liverpool and the 'Brig Margaret' going to Glasgow.

The Liverpool maritime and social historian David Hollett, in his book *Passage from India to El Dorado: Guyana and the Great Migration*, includes an appendix of the 'combined fleet list of McInroy, Parker, Sandbach, Tinne & Company of Liverpool, 1795–1901'.[29] The list is extensive, with descriptions of some forty-nine vessels owned directly by the partners. Other ships were leased periodically, and contra-agreements existed with more distant family members who also had shipping lines. The accounts demonstrate that they used each other's ships for convenience on favourable terms not generally afforded to non-family merchants. Prior to 1807, the company also sold 'to the highest bidders' a different and more profitable product – humans. An advertisement from 1805 promotes the public auctioning of 'A boat captain, three boat Negroes and a washerwoman', while a runaway notice from the *Essequibo and Demerary Gazette* shows that the family were on the front line of the trade in enslaved Africans, with Charles Stuart Parker the Elder senior dealing directly with escapees:

> Strayed on Sunday last, out of a parcel of new Negroes sold by Mr. King, a new Negro man from the Gold Coast; he had on a check lap and is supposed to have separated about Paradise estate. Any person taking up a Negro of such description is requested to inform B. Lustall Esqr. at Froes Amis, or Chs. Parker Esqr. at Woodlands, Mahaica, – A Joe reward will be given. Demerary, 29th June 1805.[30]

The reward of a 'Joe' refers to the Portuguese Johannes coin that was also used as currency in the three colonies during this period, along with the Dutch guilder. In another advertisement, also from 1805, the family firm entices potential buyers with '233 prime Gold Coast [west coast of Africa] slaves' for sale 'at their store on front of Plantation Werk & Rust'. Research conducted by Dr Alice Kinghorn into Bristol's connections to Sandbach Tinne & Co., traces the comings and goings of a ship called the *Minerva* between Bristol, the Caribbean and Cape Coast Castle – the notorious slave holding pen in modern-day Ghana. For example, after depositing a shipment of enslaved Africans in Barbados, the ship immediately returned to the Cape Coast, and having loaded up, headed back to the Caribbean on 5 November 1803. At Demerara it disembarked 'two hundred and eighteen prime Gold Coast slaves, – Chantees', Fantee's and Coromantee's'. Once again, the stores of McInroy, Sandbach, McBean & Co. provide the location for this grotesque sale of human beings.

Dr Kinghorn cites a letter sourced by Scottish researcher Alison Clark of the University of Edinburgh, a descendant of James

McInroy, showing that business links between the slave traders, the Parkers and the Bristol-based Andersons existed as early as 1796. In a letter to his son, Charles Stuart Parker the elder, James Parker in London wrote, 'John and Alex Anderson have been telling to me their intention of sending a large cargo of Negroes to your market. If so, you may believe if it is my power, I will get them to you. I would not however have this keep you a day longer than you intend staying.'[31]

The Andersons (led by John Anderson) were leading Bristolian agents from 1770 until the early 1800s.[32] Between 1796 and 1807, twelve ships from Bristol arrived in Demerara, eleven of which were owned by the Andersons.[33] James Parker's role here is interesting. After escaping the American War of Independence, he set up in London and became key to the family's trade. Prior to his demise, George Robertson and his apprentice C.S. Parker the elder ordered goods for their stores from James Parker, and James extended lines of credit in London to supply his son and his son's partner George Robertson with products from Glasgow, Bristol and Liverpool, including musket shot, gunpowder, and whatever they needed shipped out to the colonies. While Parker the elder was a partner in the firm Robertson Parker & Co., and a 50 per cent shareholder, his father James appears to have been acting as an agent. After the dissolution of Robertson Parker & Co. in 1799, new companies – and later new partnerships – were formed to carry on the family business. We can see how the partnerships were reconfigured after George Robertson's death in a document entitled 'Glasgow profit & loss acc', dated 31 December 1810, for the Glasgow arm of the family business, McInroy Parker & Co. This shows how the money was divided up at this time: James McInroy and Samuel Sandbach each have three-eighths and Charles S. Parker the elder has the remainder, rendering dividends that year of a healthy £4,232 13s 11d (£196,927 in today's money[34]) for the former two, and £2,821 16s (£131,284) for the latter.[35] It is interesting to note that while the company does not bear Sandbach's name, he is a joint major shareholder with a bigger share than Parker, whose name does appear. This is indicative of the tripartite arrangements between Liverpool, Glasgow and Demerara. Each of the partners held shares in each other's 'House' in varying percentage splits, while each House bore a different name with prominence being distributed according to major shareholdings. The absence of Sandbach's name from a House where he had a bigger share than Parker suggests that at some point after its formation he grew his shareholding, but for continuity of trade left the familiar trading name as it was. There were also side businesses with numerous ownership configurations which often involved one or more plantations, or ships, or other concerns, and while they would use the House for things like shipping goods or selling commodities, paying the House a commission, the side business shareholdings would be between one or two partners only.

The cotton estates of Woodlands and L'Amitié in Demerara, for example, were purchased by Charles Stuart Parker the elder and Gilbert Robertson, nephew of the late George Robertson, in 1800 and employed fifty enslaved Africans at that time.[36] Gilbert Robertson was never a partner in the House, but used it for his own business concerns, as did Peter Miller Watson and others.

Woodlands was managed by Gilbert Robertson, who had been working for his uncles since 1794, when he was about sixteen years old.[37] Professor Cassandra Pybus notes The Demerara Gazette 'has numerous references to Gilbert between 1800 and 1836 as a prominent planter and agent for the company Robertson, Parker Sandbach'. There is also a letter in the Traill Papers at the National Library of Scotland which recounts Gilbert Robertson's business, running a coffee plantation called 'Brothers' for McInroy Sandbach & Co., in Berbice, and the enslaved under his hand in 1832:

> The slaves are at present quiet & orderly in this Colony but I much fear a rigid adherence to all the exactments contained in the last orders in Council would create much mischief. I am making a good coffee crop on the place (the Brothers) for

Mr McInroy. The father of the present proprietor purchased it in 1817 with 130 slaves & added 27 more making in all 157 & there is now 221 making a clean increase of 64 in fifteen years after deducting the deaths. I mention the circumstance to you as one that I reflect upon with pleasure.[38]

I expect his reference to 'last orders in Council' related to the implementation of some amelioration measures for the enslaved, prior to the 1833 Emancipation Act. The amelioration measures had been passed in London in the House of Commons on 16 March 1824 following the Demerara uprising of 1823; however, the enslavers often challenged these measures, arguing that the particular account of the nuance of their respective colonies required delay in implementation. Many petitions were submitted to Parliament, debated and often referred to the Privy Council, which further delayed implementation. Having conducted a debate on the 'conditions of the slaves' with regard to the powers for the enslaved to purchase their own freedom without the approval of their masters,[39] a petition by the enslavers in Demerara and Berbice not only delayed implementation, but caused all the orders of Council that had already been implemented allowing enslaved people to purchase their freedom without their masters' consent to be rescinded, pending a consolidation of the provisions across the Caribbean colonies.

Historian David Alston points out that Gilbert's older brother, William Robertson (1773–1837), was also in Demerara, and two more brothers would later follow. While Gilbert's accounts of himself appear productive, Charles Stuart Parker was not entirely pleased with Gilbert's record. Alston quotes a letter sent by Parker to his wife in which he shares his concerns: 'I am sorry to say that accounts of Gilbert Robertson (from him we have heard nothing) are far from flattering, he is over his head in debt, I see nothing for it but compulsive measures to get what can be got out of his hands.'[40]

However, in an 1803 letter the Revd. Harry Robertson gives a sense of the challenges of living under changing colonial powers, as control of the colonies switched between European hands: 'By a letter from Mr Sandbach (who is a plain sensible unassuming young man), I learned that he heard from Gilbert of date the 4 Dec'r and that he was fortunate enough to have shipped this year's crop before the colony was given up to the Dutch or rather the French.[41] A reference to France's occupation of the Netherlands (which was renamed the Batavian Republic, 1795–1806). Napoleon subsequently made his brother Louis king of the Netherlands in 1806, de facto rendering Dutch territories into French jurisdiction.'

Despite the large sums of money involved in these slavery concerns, as well as the ever-evolving geopolitical factors that could adversely affect their blood-soaked businesses, the partners and their employees were keen to avoid spending money wherever they could. Charles Stuart Parker the elder was now an absentee planter, yet he was clearly still involved in the management of his assets in Guiana. In a letter to Peter McLagan dated 18 December 1819, sent from Glasgow, he writes of moving enslaved Africans from L'Amitié plantation to Woodlands, 'placing the whole Gang under the eye of the Manager' and potentially selling off the smaller gang, both to consolidate the plantations and to increase the land under cultivation by 'removing the Negro housing'. By this time there were hundreds of enslaved Africans in both so-called 'Gangs', and the idea of rationalisation to save costs and drive up profits had no regard for the fact that the workload of the gang that remained would increase once the other gang were 'sold off', and the remaining gang would be forced to work both plantations. From this letter, we also adduce that Samuel Sandbach is Peter McLagan's uncle:

> The plan you suggest is certainly judicious that the houses of the L'Amitie Negros should be removed to, or renewed at Woodlands thereby placing the whole Gang under the eye of the Manager – at same time I am not ill pleased with the reminder so you make of the distance the two Gangs keep from one another, as it may induce us at some future day to

offer the smallest Gang the L'Amitie one for sale. Concerning the Woodlands we may be sufficient in number and value to keep up a cultivation of cotton on the best land on both places – As you have so good an opinion of the L'Amitie Gang, I wish you would recommend to the proprietors of Caledonia to take them for pushing the cultivation there. Your uncle I am sure would join me in accepting a lower price from this concern than from any other purchaser for these very obvious reasons – there should be actually no change of masters, no risk of payment, and if a good bargain, we should reap our share of advantage, if you have the smallest wish that he may say what you would think them worth to you and Mr Sandbach, approbation can be asked.[42]

UCL's Legacies of British Slavery database shows Woodlands and L'Amitié as separate plantations in 1798 and again in 1817, by which time they belonged to C.S. Parker the elder and McInroy & Parker respectively, with 303 collectively enslaved. By 1826 the numbers on the combined plantation had dropped to 266. The letter above demonstrates that they were combined in 1820 for several reasons. They feared the two slave gangs coming together and staging a revolt, so they kept them apart, but inevitably they enacted the plan drawn up in 1819, and having sold the smaller enslaved gang after leasing them out to Plantation Caledonia, they made the remaining gang do more of the work. This would increase cultivation and profits without business risk, as they would also then be able to knock down the slave housing on L'Amitie to increase the cultivatable land and thus increase profits further, but it would also demonstrate the exploitation and inhumane treatment that would eventually contribute to the enslaved Africans' uprising of 1823.

By the time of emancipation in 1833, we can see from the compensation claims by the owners of both plantations that they were now treated as a single plantation. The UCL Legacies database records them as 'Woodlands and L'Amitie – British Guiana, Demerara':

Estate Information (5)
   1798
   [Name] L'Amitie [Crop] Cotton
   L'Amitie, shown as plantation No. 35 under the subheading 'De Mahaica a Demerarie,' proprietaire 'Postleth Waithe,' 500 carreaux, Coton.
   Carte Generale . . . Demerarie 'Liste des habitations . . .' (1798) University of Amsterdam Library 'Suriname 1599–1975.'[43]
   1817
   [Number of enslaved people] 106(Tot) 51(F) 55(M) [Name] L'Amitie
   Geo. Rainy att'y of Ch. S. Parker prop'.
   T71/397 L3 1646
   1817
   [Number of enslaved people] 197(Tot) 89(F) 108(M) [Name] Woodlands
   Geo. Rainy att'y of McInroy & Parker prop'.
   T71/397 W3 1636
   1826
   [Number of enslaved people] 266(Tot) 118(F) 148(M) [Name] Woodlands and L'Amitie
   In lawful possession of the executors of James McInroy deceased by their attorney George Rainy
   T71/417 1475–1481
   1832 [Number of enslaved people] 286(Tot) 127(F) 159(M) [Name] Woodlands and L'Amitie Belonging to Pl'n Woodlands and L'Amitie in lawful possession of Will'm McInroy by his att'y George Rainy.
   T71/429 35–42[44]

To manage their network of businesses, letters were exchanged relentlessly. The partners also appear to have rotated their tenure in the West Indies, particularly in the early days before settling into a relatively sedentary set of triangular trading roles between Liverpool, Glasgow and Demerara. The partners in the UK were constantly exerting influence, either through lobby groups such as the West India Association or by pulling the strings – in many cases – in both civic offices, such as Liverpool Town Hall and the Houses of Parliament.

Their business letters were usually signed on behalf of the companies in Glasgow, Liverpool and Demerara, so sometimes it's a process of deduction to ascertain who is the author, but some letters bear personal names and are addressed to individuals, which helps to gain a more personalised account of proceedings. A system of codes or 'marks' was also used, some of which related to people, some to business entities, some to ships, and some even to the names of the plantations they managed, owned or part owned. Marks are made up of letters of the alphabet or symbols, and as well as shortening the names for convenience, they also provided some discretion, as only those who had the cipher could understand to whom, or to what, the mark related.

The colonies of Demerara, Berbice and Essequibo were captured by Britain from the Dutch in 1796 and only briefly restored to Dutch rule between 1802 to 1803, following the Treaty of Amiens which ended the Anglo-Dutch war.[45] In his clearly racist but revealing narrative of 1855, *The History of British Guiana*, Henry G. Dalton reproduces the capitulation of 18 September 1803, signed by the former governor of Essequibo and Demerara, Anthony Meertens, and 'P.F. Tinne, Secretary'. This was Philip Frederick Tinne (1772–1844) who, like his grandfather and father before him, served as *greffier* or translator of foreign languages to the States General of the Netherlands.

The Tinne name had already made its mark in the colony of Demerara. The previous capitulation by the Dutch to the British, signed at Fort William Frederick on 22 April 1796, bears the signature 'M. S. Tinne, Secretary ad interim'.[46] In fact, in his *History of the English Church at the Hague 1586–1929*, Fred. Oudschans Dentz cites at least four Tinnes who died in Demerara, including Philip Frederick's cousin, Matthijs (or Matthieu) Tinne (b. 1761) – presumably the 'M.S. Tinne' mentioned above – who was Receiver General and later Secretary of the colony. He died on Turkeyen Estate, aged fifty-one, followed not long after by his wife, Jeanne Marguerite (Philip Frederick's sister). There was also Philip Frederick's brother Chrétien (or Christian) Theodore, Secretary to Governor Meertens, turned Receiver then Deputy Secretary to the Court of Policy. He was buried in 1812 on Turkeyen Estate, leaving behind the mixed-race son he had fathered by an enslaved woman, Mary.[47]

While Dentz's history is revealing, I came across a document written by the Tinnes themselves – 'A Short history of the Tinne Family for three centuries' by Dr John Ernest Tinne, which includes translated extracts from 'Reminiscences d'une Vie Unimportant' by 'Philippe Frederick Tinne, 1772–1844'. Early on, we find eighteen-year-old Philip Frederick in London for the first time, sharing his first impressions on meeting King George III. 'I was struck by the haggard look of the King, who had only recently recovered from the fit of mental derangement, which had almost necessitated a regency, but which returned some years afterwards.'

The brief account hints at how well connected Philip Frederick must have been to attend court and meet the King and Queen within days of arriving in England. A few years later, in 1793, he replaces his cousin Matthijs as Secretary to the Grand Pensioner V.D. Spiegel, but leaves after less than a year, due to 'the general confusion which followed the invasion of Holland by the French'. In 1796 he takes up his cousin's offer to join him in Demerara, only for the colonies to undergo their own revolution en route.

On approaching the river into Demerara, Philip Frederick records, Captain Milne 'informed us that the Colony had surrendered by capitulation a few weeks previously to an English force commanded by General Whyte'. Yet the capitulation is more strategic than anything, a move designed to keep out the French, and Philip Frederick soon lands on his feet and is presented to Governor Beaujon. In this account of his arrival, Philip Frederick refers to Victor Huguet, Governor of the French Antilles, who 'was committing all sorts of horrors there'. He also gives an interesting insight into previous French incursions into Demerara itself. He states, 'Already some months before . . . the repose of the Colony had been endangered by the plots of some factious men, among whom were numbered several Frenchmen, who had formed a club on the model of the Jacobins of Paris. The club was closed, and the evil stopped.'

Tinne also refers to an 'insurrection of the slaves' on the western coast of Demerara in 1794, which 'was followed by the execution of a number of Negroes'. He is referring to a response to the uprising in 1795 against what were called the 'Bush Negroes' (escapees who had created successful Maroon colonies within the interior and raided the plantations for supplies). He goes on to note that 'Several of these wretches were broken alive on the wheel, and a woman who passed for a sorceress and whom the blacks believed to be invulnerable was burned to death.'[48]

White men ruled these colonies with what the evidence shows was savage barbarity. Far from regretting the arrival of the British, Philip Frederick Tinne seemed glad (or at least happy to follow the official line), noting that their arrival led to an improvement in the 'treatment of the Blacks'. He claimed that after that initial British takeover, 'torture was abolished, and the [Dutch] punishment of the Negro criminals on the wheel or by the mutilation of their ears soon ceased . . . people were far from imagining at that time, that the abolition of slavery and a complete emancipation of the Blacks could ever take place! Nobody would have believed in the possibility of such a thing, and if anyone had had the boldness to predict that one day it would be an accomplished fact, he would have run a great risk of being charged with high treason.'[49] However, subsequent accounts from the 1823 uprising illustrate that that was simply untrue.

It turned out to be an auspicious time for a Dutch–English translator to arrive in the colony. There was a great need there for people with dual language skills. Tinne states, 'I was not long in finding lucrative occupation there. I was appointed sworn interpreter, and the Police Court assigned to me a salary of 1200 fl. for translating into bad enough English, the reports of its sessions and the rules or ordinances having the force of law which it published.' Dutch was also the official language in Berbice, so Philip Frederick was able to almost double his workload by doing the same work for that colony's government, as well as lawyers and solicitors, adding another 1,100fl. to his income.

In 1797, he was appointed as Secretary to Governor Beaujon. In his reflections, he paints a picture of a highly creolised and mixed society. Referring to the governor, he observes:

> My poor governor had for his wife a woman, a Creole like himself, from Curacao, with whom he lived on fairly bad terms. She was very jealous, and not without cause, for her husband was passionately in love with a mulatto woman, and this attachment being known to Madame Beaujon was frequently the subject of lively quarrels between them, for which they made use of a Spanish patois in use at Curacao. An old Negro woman, once the nurse of the Governor's wife, intervened in them, and the quarrel sometimes became so animated that it could be heard from the street, although nobody understood anything of it.[50]

He then adds a personal connection, sharing that the 'mulatto' woman in question, Marie Viendri, had been the mistress of his cousin and brother-in-law Matthieu, before his second marriage to Sophie de Laval.

In 1802, when the colony briefly returned to Dutch hands

following the Treaty of Amiens, a new governor was appointed. This was Anthony Meertens, of the Bristolian family with whom Tinne was acquainted before setting out for Demerara. However, the British were soon to return. In September 1803, Philip Frederick records in his memoir, 'An English squadron appeared in our waters . . . [and] summoned Governor Meertens to surrender the Colony. A grand council of war was convoked. The Batavian garrison, reduced to a small scale by a frightful epidemic, was entirely insufficient to resist a vigorous attack with which we were threatened, so an agreement to capitulate was soon reached'.

In the company of two members of the Police Court and two officers of the garrison, Philip Frederick took a launch to the flagship of the British fleet. He recounted that:

> On the morning of the next day (if I am not mistaken the 13th or 14th September) we went on board the frigate 'Happy', which was anchored to a considerable distance from the coast, and on which were to be found the British General and Admiral. The articles of the capitulation were soon arranged in conformity with the conditions drawn up in advance at the Council of War, and which were accepted by the British commandants without any changes.

Despite the handover, there was little change for most Dutch colonists. Philip Frederick became Colonial Secretary and continued to build up his investments (and coffers). By 1805, he had acquired two coffee plantations, Vauxhall and Westminster, with 'Messrs F. Martin, Overmaker and Pasquier', later becoming sole owner of both.[51] The following year he married Anne Rose, the sister of Peter and Andrew Rose (and the aunt of Anna or Hannah Rose, the mixed-race daughter of her brother Peter Rose and the mother of the Black footballer Andrew Watson). Philip Frederick met Anne through her relative Mrs Cummins, and together the couple travelled to London in 1810. But the following year, he received news that his brother Chrétien was in poor health, and he returned to Demerara on a McInroy, Parker & Co. ship. As he noted himself, 'I was far from foreseeing then that less than two years later I was to become partner in this commercial house.' In fact, it was while stopping in Glasgow that he met his future partners, 'Messrs. McInroy and Parker', before travelling to Edinburgh to pay a visit to his mother-in-law in the company of his brother-in-law Andrew Rose, who also had to return to Demerara.

Philip Frederick next travelled back to Liverpool during the war of 1812, which pitted England against North America. He recalled, 'we had several alarms owing to the uncertainty that each vessel that signalled us might be an American corsair'. Yet after such adventures and his 'active life' in Demerara, he found himself feeling 'rather dull' in the coastal town of Greenock, Scotland, so he proposed to James McInroy that he join the family firm. His suggestion was approved, and he was dispatched to Demerara 'to extend their connections in that Colony with the aid of a credit of £30,000 which would be placed at my disposal'. Given the Dutch colonisation of Essequibo and Demerara, Philip Frederick's fluency with Dutch in addition to his Scottish connections would have served him well. No doubt McInroy and Sandbach saw him as a handy intermediary who could help them smoothly navigate the colonies' shifts in power from Dutch to British, to Dutch and back again (and occasionally French, a language he was also fluent in). Throughout this period, trading and legal matters in the courts of policy continued in Dutch – with the guilder as the currency right until the formal 'ceding' of the territory from Holland to Britain which took place in 1814.

It is no surprise then that Philip Frederick joined the family firm in December 1813, just weeks before the British formally took over the colony, and Sandbach Tinne & Co. officially went into business, first with McInroy Parker & Co. in Glasgow, then with Sandbach Tinne & Co. in Liverpool and McInroy Sandbach & Co. in Demerara.[52] The partnership was formalised in 1815 and renewed in 1822 with a deed of co-partnership for all three business entities. The network was now triangular, between Glasgow, Demerara and Liverpool. 'It would,' notes David Alston, 'remain one of the most successful trading companies in the Caribbean.'[53]

The journal of J.C. Cheveley, a clerk with commission merchants John and William Pattinson Bros,[54] gives a sense of the family's reach and involvement in every aspect of the colonial plantation economy. In 1821, he writes of visiting 'the tall gaunt-looking store of Messrs McInroy Sandbach & Co., looked up to as the Rothschilds of Demerara, rich and influential'.[55] Cheveley is quoted as writing,

> Many estates were heavily mortgaged to them, their whole business connected to the arrangements to which the mortgagers were strictly tied down. All the sugar must be shipped home in their ships, under their agency both here and at home, and so much every year, all plantation stores to be brought of them; and other pickings, highly profitable to the mortgagee, who got full rates and commissions, considerably more so than planting was to unfortunate mortgagers, who got about as much as would just keep them on their legs. Other produce such as coffee and cotton was subject to like conditions.[56]

He goes on to describe George Rainy the younger as 'slow-spoken' with 'a sharp visage, high thin nose, and a cold, quiet, calculating grey eye', noting that 'He and his coadjutor Mr George Buchanan brought enormous gains to the Liverpool House and to McInroy Parker & Co., in Glasgow, though they dealt fairly, their business was moneylending.' Not surprising then, that they would soon after be involved in the creation of the UK's first joint stock bank, the Bank of Liverpool.

In Scotland, 'Demerary' was becoming a household name. A letter from Anne Robertson to her daughter, Christian Watson, from 1806 showed the women of the family to be highly informed and interested in colonial affairs, negating the common notion of the 'Victorian housewife', ignorant and under the thumb of her husband. Anne writes to Christian:

> It is not fixed yet when my dear Hugh goes for Demerary. Indeed, it touches me to the heart that no other plan has cast up for him. George Robertson, Hugh Munro the smith's son & Sir Hector's late valet Donald Aird all go at their own expense this summer to Demerary. They are three genteel lads & if spared have a good chance to do well. The boy Hugh you saw with us had indented to go there and another lad from this Parish & a son of McLenan the Plaisterers.[57] The last three are indented each for 3 years.[58]

Robertson also refers to a 'long letter from Mrs Parker', presumably the wife of Charles Stuart Parker, in which she reports buying 'a good many bales of cotton that grew on Kiltearn Estate belonging to Gilbert Robertson & Gilbert Rainie'. These women are not just aware of shipments and cargo, they are actively buying imports – although the fact that these goods are produced by enslaved labour, on the plantations named after their Scottish homes, is not mentioned.[59]

The letter also reveals that independently funded opportunists were not the only ones making their way to the West Indies. The lower classes were also seeking opportunities, but as indentured workers. In his *History of British Guiana*, Dalton described the large number of Scottish immigrants as 'for the most part of humble extraction, uneducated, and glad to accept of any opening that presented itself', adding, 'they exemplified the well-known caution and parsimony of their race, and, from the humblest, gradually rose to fill some of the highest situations'. In fact so numerous were the Scots, and so familiar was their habit of building tight networks, that even the enslaved Africans noticed their clannish nature; according to Dalton, 'the shrewd Negroes applied the term of "Scotchmen" to the large shrimps which they were in the habit of hawking about for sale, because of the habits of these creatures in clinging one to the other.'[60]

The letters I found in the Sandbach Tinne archive add colour to this image, giving a sense of the dramas and diversions that pervaded colonists' lives. In a letter from Demerara dated 13 January 1822, Peter McLagan wrote supportively to James McInroy about the manager of one of their estates, a Mr Euston: 'He makes the people do their duty, but not with severity, which is not used or allowed on that Estate or any other that I have under my charge, the people know my sentiments on that & would soon inform me if done & they are quite contented & have not for some years given me the smallest trouble. What the truth of the matter is, it is easy to guess.'[61] McLagan even admits, 'it is true the Estate has been very unfortunate in loss of Negroes & short crops', although he says he does not 'at all attribute that to his conduct'. This conduct is hinted at by McLagan's worrying assurance that 'I believe that he has entirely given up sporting since that accident happened' and 'I do not think the gun was for himself'. Another letter, from McInroy Sandbach & Co., in Demerary, to Messrs McInroy Parker & Co., dated 14 January 1822, mentions the deaths of James McKenzie, who 'had become very much addicted to drink', and his 'only Negro', who had died a few days before.

Looking at the trading records of the firm, you would be forgiven for forgetting that in 1807 the British Parliament had passed the Slave Trade Act (officially An Act for the Abolition of the Slave Trade), which prohibited travel to Africa and the procuring of slaves and trafficking them to the colonies. It did not emancipate those already enslaved or prohibit the enslavement of the children of those already enslaved. Despite the best efforts of the West India Society, founded in 1782 to maintain the trade, it was now illegal to transport slaves from Africa or between colonies. However, there continued an illegal trade, sometimes carried out with the complicity of the authorities, especially given the tight relationship between government, royal family and planters, all of whom still owned enslaved people. The main slave traders' lobby group in Britain, the West India Committee, held a banquet in or around 1814 which welcomed no less than HRH the Duke of York, HRH the Duke of Clarence, the Earl of Liverpool, the Rt. Hon. George Canning MP and the Rt. Hon. Robert Peel, Prime Minister.[62] According to Dalton, 'Slaves continued under certain restrictions and regulations to be imported into the colony, in limited numbers, from other sources for many years afterwards, or until 1823.'[63] And of course you could still 'breed' those already enslaved on the plantations.

Once again, contemporaneous advertisements give us some insight into what plantation life was like at this time. A 'for sale' classified ad from the *Essequebo & Demerary Royal Gazette* of 5 September 1807 gives explicit details of the contents of 'The Estate commonly called Friends Retreat & Expectation, situated on the West Sea Coast Berbice', including 370 acres of cotton, 86 of plantains and 25 'in excellent pasture, well fenced'. The buildings include two 'Logies' or dwellings for multiple slaves, measuring 50ft by 24ft – although it lists 'Negro houses' too, suggesting a difference in quality or use. There is also a 'good new gin house', hospital, fowl house, pigeon house and kitchen. Along with the cattle are listed 'one hundred and twenty-five Negroes of all descriptions, very healthy, mostly young, with a fine shew of Creoles' (Creole women were the preferred sexual victims of the white enslavers who would rape them at will). A letter from McInroy Parker & Co. in Glasgow to Messrs Sandbach Tinne & Co., dated 23 June 1817, gives a sense of the scale of money being exchanged. The writer of the letter, seemingly discussing the potential purchase of Plantation Leonora, writes, 'Mr Parker however seems inclined towards your plan, & will have no objection to join Messrs Sandbach & Tinne in the purchase on joint account each one third at the price stated in the letter of ƒ600,000 [c.£3,000,000 in today's money].'[64] Leonora then became their biggest and most profitable plantation, earning in excess of £100,000 per year thereafter according to the financial accounts for the period. More money came out of Leonora than any other plantation, constituting almost 20 per cent of their entire revenue in some years.

A letter to Messrs McInroy Parker & Co. from a trio of investors, signed 'N. French, Eliza French, Donna French', shows how many other women were also banking on slave-worked plantations to enrich their coffers. The note, dated 13 May 1823, refers to a dispute over Plantation Phoenix Park, and the writers express their concern that the enslaved Africans attached to the plantation will be 'sold off too cheaply'. They even refer to 'the bill talked of in Parliament to be brought out & passed against the slave trade', nothing 'that ought to enhance the value in the different colonies'.[65] Also revealing is a document titled 'British Slave Indenture' and dated 15 June 1820. This agreement between Peter Rose (brother-in-law of P.F. Tinne), William Gordon (the elder), William Gordon (the younger), Alexander Crombie, Philip Frederick Tinne, Patrick Rose and Andrew Rose (also brothers-in-law of P.F. Tinne) records the number of enslaved persons held at Plantation Hope (a plantation in Essequibo) in 1817 and 1818. On 1 July 1817, 162 male and 93 female enslaved Africans are recorded. The following year, between 21 May 1817 and 30 May 1818, sees the arrival of 28 males and 36 females – taking the totals to 190 and 129 respectively. The 'Cowan auction notes' for the document describe other sparse details collected: 'The name, color, age, occupation, condition (healthy, weak, invalid, cripple, good, sickly, superannuated, sores, able, old, swelled legs, etc.,) and country of origin is listed for each (many just list 'Africa' as country of origin).'[66]

Even more shocking is the story from Hugh Munro Robertson, the aforementioned brother of Gilbert Robertson who moved to Liverpool in 1804 to work under the direction of his brother-in-law, Samuel Sandbach, before in 1806 following in the family footsteps and sailing out to Demerara. Alston remarks on his 'intense friendship' with Thomas Stuart Traill (future husband of Christian Watson), and what can only be called love letters that he writes from

Demerara, signing off 'Yours to the end of time' and declaring 'Write me soon . . . when you want to write anything on snug subjects regarding either of ourselves, you might (to avoid any being the wiser) call yourself Marcus & me Julius.'[67] In addition to managing Plantation Kiltearn in Berbice, owned by his brother Gilbert, Hugh acted as an on-the-ground assistant to the naturalist Traill, collecting samples of flora, fauna and cultural artefacts, sending reports and descriptions of his new home. His botanical and zoological research was accompanied by some dark observations, including 'how common the venereal disease is among the Negroes . . . in fact a person runs a greater risque in this Country than among the fair nymphs (i.e. prostitutes) at home, unless they are very wary.' In other records, his own abuse of the enslaved Africans is brutally apparent.

Robertson[68] had written to his close friend Dr Traill in Liverpool that 'The slave girl Susannah' (born 1796 or 1797 to c.1851) 'was no more than twelve years old' when, in 1808, she 'gave birth to her first child, fathered by George Munro' (1766 or 1767–1824, aged forty-two at the time) from Easter Ross, the owner of Alness in Berbice, a plantation notorious for its harsh discipline. One account has him telling the enslaved woman that he wants her little daughter. The mother 'says she's not old enough' and to 'wait until she's older'. But Munro brutally rapes her anyway and by the time she is twelve, the enslaved helpless little Black girl has borne the child of her white Scottish paedophile rapist. She bore him two more children before she was sixteen.[69] In a letter from 1806, we see the common assumption that 'having been purchased, enslaved females were considered sexually available'.[70] Munro on another occasion called an enslaved woman to his bed but she refused. In retaliation he gave her thirty-nine lashes, it being legal under British colonial law to whip an enslaved woman with up to thirty-nine lashes for such a crime.[71] The depravity and barbarity of the Sandbach Tinne family in Demerara towards those they enslaved was endemic and largely normalised. What was worse, much of what they did to those they enslaved was actually legal; even that which they did illegally rarely caused them a problem, as their family sat in high civic office in the colonies, Britain and Holland, and in many cases were the lawmakers themselves.

Another account has Gilbert gifting his brother 'a little boy newly imported from the Gold Coast . . . about 11 years old, a very good natured smart little fellow'. In his letter to Traill, Hugh Munro Robertson outlines his plans to groom the child to cater to his needs: 'I will have the complete training of him myself, I can make him do anything I please, he is really a fine creature – he has always a complacent smile on his countenance & seems (& I think really is) quite happy. I have got him smartly rigged out – he is very desirous to please & I really think the poor little thing has conceived an attachment to me already.'[72] Perhaps it is fitting that Hugh Munro Robertson was on board Samuel Sandbach's ship the *Demerara* when it went down off the coast of Ireland on the night of 16 December 1819 on its return to Liverpool.[73] He drowned at sea and I'm sure there were many on his plantation that let out a sigh of relief at the demise of their serial abuser. Including that little boy.

CHAPTER 7

THE DEMERARA REBELLION – A LICENCE TO PREACH TO THE NEGROES

*A single blow of a blacksmith is equal to a
hundred blows of a goldsmith.*
– Indian proverb

On 18 August 1823, somewhere between 9,000 and 12,000 enslaved Africans gathered on the public road that snakes along Guiana's coast, in what was to become the largest slave uprising in the colony's history. The first plantation to rise up was Success, the property of John Gladstone, Member of Parliament for Woodstock, Lancaster (1820–1826) at the time of the uprising, and later Berwick-upon-Tweed, (1826–1827). John Gladstone, a corn merchant, had become rich and influential, largely through the produce of slavery, with his shipping and underwriting business, and later his plantations in Jamaica and Demerara, but also through his second wife's family, which included Francis Humberston Mackenzie, 1st Baron Seaforth (1754–1815), a British politician, soldier, and later a botanist, who was Chief of the Mackenzie clan, and Governor of Barbados from 1800 to 1806.

John Gladstone is perhaps best known today as the father of

William Ewart Gladstone, the MP who would later become Britain's four-times and longest serving prime minister. William was just fourteen years old at the time of the uprising, and as a young man, was being nurtured amid the merchant class of Liverpool and its surrounding suburbs. Those who would influence the young Gladstone included his aunts, uncles and cousins on his Scottish mother Ann McKenzie Robertson's side of the family; among them were Christian Robertson, who was Ann's third cousin, and Christian's sister Elizabeth. Charles Stuart Parker the elder,[1] who was married to another of W.E. Gladstone's mother's Scottish cousins – Margaret Rainy – would also have an input into the development of the young Gladstone.

We get a sense of this predominantly Scottish influence on the future prime minister from W.E. Gladstone's own diaries. On Monday 17 September 1827, at the age of seventeen, Gladstone wrote, 'Called on Mrs Moss, & the Sandbach's where we saw Mrs Parker.'[2] The footnote reads: 'Wife of Charles Parker, Gentleman of Aigburth near Otterspool'.[3]

On Friday 6 January 1832, the twenty-two-year-old Gladstone wrote, 'Miss Traill's came.[4] Concocted a letter to the Albion, with Robert on Paganini,[5] hinting that he ought to give of his money to the charities.' The footnote reads, 'Niccolò Paganini (1782–1840) violinist and composer.'

It seems that the young Gladstone enjoyed the company of his female cousins very much. He wrote the following day: 'The Miss Sandbach's came, plenty of music – in which – I did little there below. And I did that little ill. Sat up late writing a letter to father on my future profession.'

How interesting that such a pivotal moment should occur in what was to become the momentous career of William Ewart Gladstone, straight after meeting two sets of girls from the Sandbach Tinne dynasty; first the Miss Traills, ages 15 to 20, then the Miss Sandbachs, ages 16 to 25 – probably Elizabeth Sandbach (Mar. 1806–1881) age 25, Margaret Sandbach (8 Jan. 1811–1868), on the eve of her twenty-first birthday (and who three months later married John Abraham

Tinne), and Mary Rosina Sandbach (May 1815–May 1882), aged sixteen at the time of the meeting.

It is impossible to know what was discussed with all of these young Sandbach and Traill women, but what is not in dispute is that they all met him in succession, they enjoyed entertainment together and at the end of the second night, he immediately sat down and wrote a letter to his father concerning his future career. Something in these encounters must have caused him to ruminate on the direction of his life, and clearly the Sandbach and Traill families had a profoundly important role in his early years and in influencing his future career direction. In Sydney Checkland's biography of the Gladstones, he notes that young 'Willy', as he was referred to, often travelled with his parents in an attempt to broaden his horizons beyond their homes in Rodney Street, Liverpool, and Seaforth House, their suburban mansion on the outskirts of the city. He recounts that 'in London, before renting the Grafton Street house, the Gladstones usually stayed with Colin Robertson in Russell Square or Divie Robertson in Bedford Square'.[6] Both Colin and Divie were enslavers with plantations in the Caribbean and they were the brothers of Gladstone's wife Ann McKenzie Gladstone (née Robertson). Colin and Divie owned outright – or held mortgages over – at least four plantations in Jamaica, with hundreds of enslaved people.[7]

In September of 1826 at age sixteen Gladstone had also written, 'Made 14 calls . . . Mrs Traill';[8] the footnote reads, 'Wife of Thomas Stewart Traill, physician associated with John Gladstone in various good works'. There is irony in the perception in Britain of John Gladstone as a man of 'good works'. These diaries were published in 1968, the editor being an Oxford professor, Michael Richard Daniell Foot CBE. Eminent historian though he was, he fails entirely to make the familial connections between the Gladstones, the Traills, the Parkers and the Sandbachs, as is clear from his footnotes. This take on British history, which has become the common thread in many works of the colonial era, is lacking in coherence due to the omission of the familial connections which were at the heart of how business was transacted in the eighteenth and nineteenth centuries. Liaisons such as those mentioned in the young Gladstone's diaries were often the precursor to a marriage, where young women 'came out' and young men proposed. The eligibility of both the men and women of the day was vested in the 'standing' of their families, often determined by wealth, status and connections to the landed gentry or aristocracy.

The Gladstones, Sandbachs, Tinnes, Robertsons, McKenzies, Watsons and Traills had all of those things, and the incestuous degrees of familial intermarriage were aimed at maintaining those assets within the family. But what they also had were copious amounts of Black children from the Africans that those family members who went to the colonies often enslaved and raped. The brutality with which they operated, beneath the veneer of the 'pious', 'charitable' and 'philanthropic' Christian gentleman who built churches and schools in Liverpool, Glasgow and The Hague, was evident to anyone who set foot on one of their colonial slave plantations.

It is significant that the 1823 uprising began on Gladstone's plantation, given how prominent John Gladstone's family were. Gladstone chaired the enslavers' lobby group the West India Committee of Liverpool, and also held a mortgage over another sugar plantation in the Essequibo Islands–West Demerara region of Guiana, called plantation Vreed-en-Hoop; upon the death of its owner Jonas Fileen in 1822, Gladstone bought the estate outright. It was later the subject of debate in Parliament, when the question of emancipation was raised, and the then Under-Secretary of State for the colonies cited it 'for the purpose of showing what a destruction of human life had taken place in the West Indies, from the manner in which the slaves were worked'.[9] He was referring to the high mortality rate on Gladstone's plantation, where seventy of the hundreds of enslaved Africans on that plantation had been worked to death in the scorching heat of the tropical climate.

John Gladstone's assets in Demerara were entangled in many ways with those of the Sandbach Tinne dynasty. Both had substantial operations in Demerara; both were of primarily Scottish origin (although Sandbach himself was English and P.F. Tinne was Dutch, their wives and business partners were all Scottish); both were headquartered in Liverpool; and both had their own shipping lines. Gladstone owned Seaforth near Liverpool, named after the Scottish Loch Seaforth in the Outer Hebrides (there are numerous Earls and Marquises of Seaforth in his second wife's family tree) and Sandbach owned most of Aigburth (both Seaforth and Aigburth were considered outside of Liverpool, though Aigburth was later incorporated). Sandbach also had properties in the merchant community of Everton on St Ann Street, at that time also outside Liverpool. Sandbach had married Elizabeth Robertson (George Robertson of Grenada's niece), and John Gladstone's second wife (Ann McKenzie Robertson) was Elizabeth's third cousin, thus connecting the Gladstones and the Sandbachs by marriage. Ann McKenzie Robertson was the mother of Prime Minister W.E. Gladstone but was also third cousin to Christian Watson, the mother of Peter Miller Watson. Thus, the Watsons and the Gladstones were also cousins.

The Black footballer Andrew Watson – Christian's grandson – died on 8 March 1921, and was buried in Richmond cemetery in Kew on the outskirts of London. At the time of his death he was residing at 88 Forest Road, Kew. His death certificate records the cause of death as '(1) pneumonia. (2) cardiac failure.' His profession is described as 'Marine Engineer'. His death notice, published in a Richmond newspaper[10] described him not only as the 'son of the late Peter Miller Watson' but also 'cousin of the late Right Honourable W.E. Gladstone and C.S. Parker'.

The family connection is further illustrated in a book on the Douglas and Robertson genealogies, which has John Gladstone (b. 1764) marrying Anne, daughter of Andrew Robertson and Ann McKenzie, on 29 April 1800.[11] This means that John Gladstone's father-in-law was a first cousin of George Robertson (Christian Robertson's great-grandfather, not to be confused with her Uncle George who left her an inheritance) who married Christian Douglas, and went on to produce the Robertson line at the heart of this story. Christian Douglas could trace her bloodline back to royalty; Egidia, the daughter of King Robert II, and her husband Sir William Douglas are linked to the Plantagenets, the Bruces (Robert the Bruce) and the Stewarts (Mary Queen of Scots), as well as King James I of England. Joan Plantagenet (1327–1385), great-granddaughter of King Philip III of France (1245–1285) and granddaughter of King Edward I of England (1239–1307) is described as 'The fair maid of Kent'.

The three Robertson sisters (Christian, Elizabeth and Margaret), all descended of Egidia's line, and are collectively referred to as 'the three fair maids of Kiltearn'. The second picture section shows the bloodline.

This is in addition to Gladstone's mother-in-law, Ann McKenzie, being third cousin of Samuel Sandbach's wife Elizabeth Robertson. This incestuous entanglement would be repeated throughout the Sandbach Tinne dynasty for generations to come. The connections of the Watsons and the Robertsons through George Robertson and Christian Douglas to the royal line, are also illustrated in the second picture section.

An 1805 letter from Anne Robertson (née Forbes, 1748–1826) in Kiltearn, Scotland, to her daughter Christian Watson in Crantit, Orkney, suggests a closeness and admiration for the Gladstone family. 'Annie would tell you what a splendid entertainment she was at on New Year's Day at your acquaintance Mrs Gladstones.[12] It was on that day her son was baptised, but I will forbear any more of her news, as I am confident you had all this from herself. Mrs G was always my favourite of that family, and I would just expect her great fortune would not spoil her agreeable temper and disposition. I am much pleased that herself and our friends are in such friendly habits.'[13]

This was four years before William Ewart Gladstone was born and demonstrates that the Robertsons were inextricably linked to the Gladstones throughout William's life. The Gladstones were not always quite so admiring in return. In a letter to John Gladstone dated 18 December 1828, his son Robertson Gladstone wrote from plantation Vreed-en-Hoop about his visit to Demerara and told him that his agents, McDonald, Watson & Co.: 'having a store of their own is right in the teeth of your interests . . . Harry Watson,[14] although clever enough in business, does not appear to apply himself. Andrew Watson, his brother is one of the best of them.' Here he is referring to the older brothers of Peter Miller Watson. Robertson Gladstone advises his father John to find alternative agents, noting, 'I have seen one or two instances since I came to the colony which convince me that they [McDonald, Watson & Co.] have enjoyed our business as a good thing much too long.'[15] As well as the business Sandbach did with Gladstone, clearly, the Watsons also had his business for a time.

John Gladstone was central to the events of 1823. Such was his connection to the rebellion that in August 2023, which marked its 200th anniversary, his direct descendant Charles Gladstone and other family members travelled to Guyana to issue a formal apology for the family's role in slavery and mark the launch of the University of Guyana's International Institute for Migration and Diaspora Studies, to which they had donated £100,000. In a report by the *Guardian*, Charles is quoted as saying, 'John Gladstone committed crimes against humanity . . . He was a vile man. He was greedy and domineering. We have no excuses for him. But it is fairly clear to me that however you address it, a lot of my family's privilege has stemmed from John Gladstone.' However, another Gladstone was also at the heart of the rebellion, not in the corridors of power at Westminster, or in a Scottish counting house, but in the cane fields of East Demerara.

Jack Gladstone was an enslaved man working on Plantation Success, and is remembered as one of the leaders, if not *the* leader, of the 1823 rebellion. The events of 1823 still permeate; particularly the significance of the rebellion in the wider battle for abolition, and the question of who Jack Gladstone was. Can we really believe what has been said about him, and his role in this seismic event in British colonial history?

The uprising received huge attention in Britain and beyond, not just for its size and the violence that ensued, but for the involvement of a lay clergyman, Revd. John Smith. He was a member of the London Missionary Society who was preaching at Bethel Chapel on Plantation Le Resouvenir, located right next to Gladstone's Plantation Success in Demerara. The involvement of Revd. Smith led to a lengthy parliamentary debate, the transcript of which is useful for gathering a sense of how the rebellion unfolded, who was involved and what the attitudes back in Britain were towards the main protagonists. Also informative are the many court reports, personal letters and other documents used in the trial of Revd. Smith, including his own diary. Collectively, these accounts all prompted intense political, religious and media dissection in the aftermath of the 1823 Demerara uprising.

Smith had arrived in Demerara on 6 March 1817 to expand upon the groundwork done by his predecessor, the Revd. John Wray. Wray had sought 'license to preach to the Negroes' and it had occasionally been permitted in Demerara and Berbice, chiefly because the planters came to understand that once the enslaved workers had embraced Christianity, they worked harder, stopped drinking and were less likely to fight. The Dutch had strictly forbidden 'preaching to the Negroes' as they feared that any enslaved person who was baptised would then claim equal rights with their 'white Christian brethren'. But profit won the argument with a few planters, and Wray made a convincing case. The news of it soon spread.

As the colonies of Demerara, Essequibo and Berbice were formally ceded by the Dutch to the British under the terms of the Anglo-Dutch Treaty of 1814, the Dutch retained trading rights and received £2,000,000 in compensation, and 'John Gladstone and his friends could settle down to the long-term development of their estates in Latin America'.[16] In a statement of assets compiled by

Gladstone himself, we can see how his fortunes evolved. For his West India assets alone (which would include plantations and the supposed cash value of those enslaved by him upon them) he records a value for 'Demerara' in 1820, prior to the uprising, of £100,000[17] (£5,743,040 as at 2017).[18] This could also be calculated using the Bank of England's inflation calculator – to date – at [19]£8,121,683. By 1828 that had doubled to £200,000 and by the passage of the Emancipation Act of 1833,[20] he valued his Demerara assets at £296,000, plus £40,000 for his Jamaica assets, bringing his entire West India assets at the onset of abolition to £336,000 (£33,608,380 according to the Bank of England inflation calculator and £22,781,236 according to the National Archives calculation. In either event, it constituted over 50 per cent of his total net worth at the time).

After the territory was ceded formally to the British, Dutch law was no longer applicable and preaching was tolerated only under strict licence, and was still limited to those few plantations where the owners agreed. From Wray's diaries we get a sense of the political mood, both within the colonies and in Britain, and amongst the abolitionists in Parliament. Their accounts are telling, in that they illustrate the timeline of the proselytisation of the enslaved Africans in Demerara and Berbice, in parallel with the proceeds of enslavement being used for the development of the poor of Britain, along with the establishment of the educational institutions in Liverpool and beyond, that were being founded by the rich enslavers and their philanthropical frontmen like William Roscoe and Thomas Stuart Traill. Wray writes:

> The men of 1819, however, so unprivileged as they seem to have been, could lay claim to benefits enjoyed which were unknown to their fathers of 1789. The British slave trade had ceased to exist, nor could any slave ship be seen riding at anchor in our rivers or docked at our ports for renewal or for being refurnished with its horrid gear; whilst every great modern Missionary and Bible and Tract Society had begun its

career and got well on its course; as also had the great Educational Societies.²¹

Wray was no doubt referring here to academic startups like the Liverpool Institution (est. 1814) which spawned many others, and laid the foundations for much of the modern educational system that we have in the UK today. He would also have been aware of the works of the Society for Promoting Christian Knowledge (SPCK) and the Society for the Propagation of the Gospel (SPG), who had long argued a business case for propagating the gospel among the Africans as a means to replace hostile enslavement with willing subjugation to Christ, to facilitate exploitation of minerals in Africa, and produce in the Caribbean and the Americas. This would later manifest in the 'colonialist business model'. Evidence of this can be found in a *Missionary Intelligencer* of 1851, where Henry Townsend (1815–1885), a British missionary in West Africa, argues for abolition and to replace slavery with colonialism, facilitated by proselytising among the Africans, so as to exploit them for minerals and labour once they were subjugated to European Christianity: 'It is as Christianity takes root in the land, that the productive energies of Africa and her vast commercial capabilities will open and afford the materials of a trade more lucrative than that which even India has yielded.'²² We also discover from this letter that many of those he was seeking to convert were Muslims. More converts meant more revenues, and enslavers, flush with cash, began donating.

By 1827, there were fifty-two clergymen plus three 'Native clergy', and fifty-four societies promoting Christianity in British Guiana, bringing an income to the Church Missionary Society that year of £46,473 from individuals and £36,972 from the societies – a total revenue of £83,445 (£7,410,516 according to the Bank of England inflation calculator and £5,657,679 according to the National Archives calculation).

Townsend revealed his loathing of Islam, which predominated in West Africa during his tenure: 'Christianity is divinely beneficial in its influence; individually it converts, nationally, it ameliorates. It raises man from the degradation of heathenism; it frees him from the harsh repulsiveness of Mahomedan fanaticism; the intellectual powers are developed; and the torpid or perverted energies are quickened into action or directed into a healthful channel.'[23]

This propaganda was instrumental in perpetuating the false narratives of the illiterate barbaric Africans, and ignored the fact that Muslims in West Africa were among the most literate populations in the world. Most in what is now called Nigeria, where Townsend was situated, spoke, wrote and read Arabic and at least two other languages. Hausa and Fulani were both written in Arabic script prior to Europeans' arrival in West Africa. The Library at Timbuktu in Mali housed over 300,000 written volumes in numerous languages dating back to the eleventh century. However, as soon as an African was dragged aboard a slave ship, all of that was stripped away from them: reading and writing were forbidden, often on pain of death, or at least a flogging. Religion was also suppressed, although many practised in secret. Names were changed, tribal origins were obscured, as successive generations of enslaved Africans and their offspring were acculturated into the illiterate and subhuman status that the white Europeans had attributed to them. They were now ripe for conversion and a new form of subjugation, which would not be regulated by the white man's whip on their Black bodies, but rather by the white man's God on their eternal Black souls. This new business model gained traction after the 1823 uprising and Gladstone's explanation for the uprising inadvertently led to mass conversion in the aftermath.

Gladstone was initially blamed for the uprising. It was, after all, on his plantation where it all began, putting him in the sights of the white enslavers who'd lost money or crops and had family members killed and injured. The whites also killed and executed enslaved Africans, quantifying this as a 'loss of property' for which they collectively but unsuccessfully sought compensation from the government. Gladstone deferred blame wherever he could, as was his way, and this never changed. We see subsequent examples of this in how his son tried to explain away the seventy deaths on Vreed-en-Hoop as everybody's fault but Gladstone's, some ten years after the uprising, but the reports of gruelling all-year-round sugar production, a ruthless overseer, and the cruel treatment of those enslaved, came to light in the testimonies that followed the uprising. Wilberforce and his abolitionist friend Fowell Buxton MP had drafted a motion in February 1823 and produced an abolition manifesto. News of their intention to present the motion to Parliament reached Gladstone, and when it was presented, the Liverpool MP William Huskisson wrote to Gladstone saying 'the Government did everything in its power to prevent Buxton's motion altogether'; in May 1823, meanwhile, a motion was passed that 'the House take into consideration the state of slavery in the British colonies'.[24]

Gladstone ironically considered himself somewhat religious and often financed the construction of churches, some with schools attached, such as St Andrew's Episcopal Church on Renshaw Street in Liverpool and St Thomas's Church in Seaforth, as well as St Thomas's in Toxteth, Liverpool, and St Thomas's in Leith, Scotland (which was built in 1835 in honour of his second wife Ann McKenzie Robertson, who died after a long bout of an incurable illness).

After Buxton's motion of 1823, Gladstone and others were forced to take stock of the conditions on their plantations and his appointed representative, attorney Frederick Cort, gave him a utopian report of happy, well-behaved slaves, content and obedient. When pressed for a more accurate account, Cort reported that 'should the planters be deprived of the whip over women, he felt they had no alternative to solitary confinement'.[25] Until this time, if a white man wanted to rape a Black woman or girl, it was *de facto* legal to do so; if she refused to be raped it was considered insubordination and she could legally receive thirty-nine lashes with the cat o' nine tails (a leather whip with nine knotted strands that would rip flesh from bone). If Buxton's motion led to a successful bill, the whipping of women and girls would become illegal, and then (Cort contended), the only way for a white man to punish a Black woman or girl for refusing to be raped was to lock her in solitary confinement until she was compliant. It was clearly felt that the whip was essential to maintaining the white man's legal right to rape Black women. Fearing 'bloody revolt, Cort was much concerned with the security of the colony; holding as we do our dominion over the Negros's by a mere spell'. This was a recognition that pitting the overwhelming numbers of the enslaved against the few whites with guns was untenable, and a new way of exploiting and controlling them was needed.

When the inevitable uprising occurred later that year, Gladstone blamed everyone, from the enslaved themselves to the priest who taught them to read so he could minister to them. As calls for compensation started to emerge, Gladstone quickly changed gear and blamed George Canning, the Liverpool MP who was appointed Foreign Secretary in 1822 and had proposed a bill passed on 16 May 1823 that would offer amelioration measures to the enslaved in the British Caribbean colonies. Gladstone claimed that the enslaved Africans had become confused and thought they had been freed and that their owners refused to acknowledge their rights; and therefore, they rose up due to 'a tragic miscommunication regarding measures to alleviate the harsh conditions experienced by the slaves'. Canning's resolution read:

> That it is expedient to adopt effectual and decisive measures for ameliorating the condition of the slave population in His Majesty's colonies: That, through a determined and persevering, but at the same time judicious and temperate enforcement of such measures, this House looks forward to a progressive improvement in the character of the slave population, such as may prepare them for a participation in those civil rights and privileges which are enjoyed by other classes of His Majesty's subjects. That this House is anxious for the accomplishment of this purpose at the earliest period that shall be compatible with the well-being of the slaves themselves, with the safety of the colonies, and with a fair

and equitable consideration of the interests of private property.[26]

By 'private property' he meant enslaved Africans.

The sheer number and determination of the enslaved who took part in the uprising illustrates that their desire for freedom and justice was unquestionable, contrary to the initial claims of Cort that they were 'happy' and 'obedient'. Any notion that the enslaved people were 'quite content' with their masters was a fallacy that Gladstone and others promoted in Liverpool and Parliament to deflect the blame onto Canning, using it as leverage to gain government compensation. Writing about Canning's use of diplomacy in the Caribbean to bring about 'gradual abolition', the historian S.A. Simeonov comments that in 'Administrating abolitionist pressure, Canning's Foreign Office promoted amelioration as a gradual reform approach which defused both the most violent excesses of slavery and the uncertainties of immediate abolition.'[27] This was a compromise designed to reassure people like Gladstone who had fortunes at stake in the event of immediate abolition. But now, that same initiative which he'd encouraged his own son, William Ewart Gladstone, to promote later on in Parliament, was being weaponised by Gladstone to avert blame from himself and to secure compensation for his losses and those of his fellow enslavers, whose favour he sought to regain.

Demerara was a land where order was kept by the white merchants with the most brutal violence and depraved barbarity. Smith's diaries record an occasion when he and his wife, Jane, sat in their house on Plantation Le Resouvenir and each silently counted the number of lashes being inflicted on an enslaved person outside. He counts 141, she 140.[28] The manager of Le Resouvenir at the time of the rebellion was a man named John Hamilton, who it is said was having an affair with one of the enslaved women working in the house – who also happened to be Jack Gladstone's wife. Hamilton had been installed in the position after the previous manager Adrianus Van der Haas was, according to the diary of Revd. Smith, 'discharged for his cruelty to the Negroes'.[29] In 1812, forty or fifty enslaved Africans had complained to the Fiscal about him, saying that 'the manager flogged them severely for every trifling fault and . . . had flogged in a "most shameful manner" an enslaved man named Hector, and that Quamina, the leading carpenter, had received ninety stripes from the manager, plus more from the drivers, just because he had not been able to complete his day's work.'[30] Even by the barbaric standards of nineteenth-century British law, which prescribed 'no more than 39 lashes', these excesses were extreme and ruthless.

Van der Haas's sister-in-law was the owner of the estate following the death of her husband. White women were no less ruthless than white men when they came into plantation ownership, and they were not passive bystanders, but were often engaged in the operational aspects of enslaving and running plantations bequeathed to them. Mrs Van der Haas's plantation Le Resouvenir was later mortgaged to McInroy Sandbach & Co., with George Rainy given power of attorney.[31] A letter from Philip Frederick Tinne refers to 'debts for the erection of the sugar works . . . hanging over the estate' and mentions an unnamed 'young man of colour of the name of Van der Haas, now a student at Leyden (the most prestigious university in the Netherlands), to whom she has made advance of money'.[32] This suggests her husband, her brother-in-law, or herself may have had a Black child in Demerara. Tinne promises that 'Mr Rainy will enquire into the matter and see what can be done about it, as well as respecting the chocolate affair.' In a pitiful letter, widow Van der Haas writes to the company:

> Having now completed all that was desired from us and placed our property in Demerary under the entire and exclusive management of your House, we cannot but trust in return that you will not leave us destitute . . . We begin to be short in table and bed linen and have been compelled in these awful sickly times to deny ourselves even a necessary glass of wine – also to dismiss our manservant and one of our female domestics, so that now we have only one woman to serve us.[33]

This testimony supports other accounts of the way Sandbach Tinne did business. They were money lenders and when you were indebted to them, all your business had to go through them on terms favourable to them, to such an extent that their mortgagees were trapped in deals which were financially to their detriment. It is telling that their business practices in the early nineteenth century would be the very foundations of the exploitative modern banking system we inherit to this day.

On Gladstone's Plantation Success, the Revd. Smith noted in his journal, 'the Negroes work excessively hard, and have but little to eat'.[34] Since his arrival in Demerara, twenty-seven enslaved people had died on the plantation. 'The people have scarcely any time to eat their food,' he added in November 1821, 'they have none to cook it, eating for the most part, raw yellow plantains. This would be bearable for a time, but to work at that rate, and to be perpetually flogged, astonishes me that they submit to it.'[35]

A slave register of Plantation Success dated 1817 gives us a sense of the lives of the male and female population enslaved there. Roles listed under 'Employment' for men include carpenter, boatman and cooper; and for both sexes 'Field' and 'Jobber'. One elder, sixty-six-year-old Lucinda, is listed as a 'Yaws nurse' – yaws being a chronic skin infection. Other descriptions found under 'Condition' include 'Weakly', 'Able', 'Leprosy', 'Diseased', 'Sores', 'Healthy', 'Sickly', and 'Epilepsy'.[36] The document is signed by John Gladstone's attorney, Frederick Cort, and 'Registrar' James Robertson. The enslaved also faced being uprooted at any moment. A letter dated 13 July 1818, from McInroy Sandbach & Co. in Demerara to Messrs Sandbach Tinne & Co., Liverpool, refers to the sale of '126 Negroes, at £160 per head, payable . . . at 2, 6 and 12 months without interest. One third of the gang is for the plantation Uitvlught, to increase the gang and replace those sold.'[37]

Despite the control they wielded, the same letter suggests the plantation owners who lived in the colony (which at the time of the rebellion was only about 75 of the 200 proprietors, according to Dalton)[38] were in constant fear of an uprising. A postscript refers to a Bill that 'had passed the House of Commons authorising the Privy Council to grant licences for the importation of slaves into these colonies from Dominica and the Bahamas'.[39] The writer expressed concern, adding, 'from the description we have heard of them, they are a very dangerous set.' No doubt he feared a repeat of the successful Haitian rebellion of 1804.

Months before the Demerara uprising, a letter from McInroy Sandbach & Co., Demerara, dated 24 June 1823, reported that 'the measles have been severely felt & occasioned much loss'. Amid 'heavy and almost constant rains', the epidemic has hit all but has been chiefly fatal amongst the Negroes . . . they have lost 4 or 5 at Plantation Coffee, 2 or 3 at Plantation Leonora since the 1st of this month'. They go on to complain how 'work had to be suspended for weeks'.[40]

In April 1823, a motion calling for the gradual abolition of slavery in all British colonies was presented to Parliament by Thomas Fowell Buxton – whose legacy is still remembered in Guyana today through the village of Buxton, which was bought and named by freed Africans after emancipation. Buxton's motion was defeated on this occasion; however, the Anti-Slavery Society (formed in 1823) of which he was a member had clout, with other members including abolitionist MPs Thomas Clarkson and an ailing William Wilberforce. It was through this endeavour that Canning's 'amelioration measures' were finally introduced to reduce some of the vilest conditions endured by the enslaved Africans. These included a prohibition on the whipping of female slaves, and on slave drivers carrying whips in the field. The new laws were sent out to the colonies by Lord Bathurst, the Secretary of State for the Colonies. In Essequibo-Demerara, the authorities were slow to adopt the measures; in fact, Governor John Murray sat on them for over a month before members of the Court of Policy finally passed the necessary resolution in August 1823. It is of note that all but one member of the Court of Policy was themselves a planter, including Philip Frederick Tinne.

In a letter from McInroy Sandbach & Co. dated 29 June 1823, the writer alludes to 'discussions that have agitated the colonial interest and of the manners contemplated', presumably the rules in question.[41] 'The communications from Government have only lately arrived,' continues the letter writer, 'and we are not yet prepared to give that deliberate opinion on the subject, which we would wish to form.' They decry the hasty response of 'Proprietors on your side, some of whom have never crossed the Atlantic', and in words that would come to haunt them just weeks later, they insisted that 'nothing but the greatest tranquillity and subordination prevails universally here, and no apprehension is entertained of any contrary feeling in disposition'. Their pathological brutality was clearly ingrained, and the notion of easing the burden of those they had enslaved by giving up the brutal and depraved behaviours afforded by their white privilege was lost on them. But they were also in a state of absolute denial as to what was the inevitable outcome of their barbarity.

Enslaved Africans were not members of the Council or Court of Policy, but little that happened in the colony was not in earshot of an enslaved person of one description or another; a driver, a house boy, a nanny, all would overhear conversations and come to know what the discussions of the white people were, and this would spread quickly amongst the enslaved population. Some speculated that 'the King of England has ordered full emancipation' but the Governor and the planters were ignoring his wishes and denying the enslaved Africans their freedom. Others believed their working days had been reduced, giving them more time to tend their provision gardens and go to church.[42] Jack Gladstone heard the rumours and used his connections to spread the word. Jack's job was head cooper, a skilled job which included crafting the wooden barrels such as hogsheads which carried sugar or puncheons that housed rum, ready to store and ship the plantations' produce abroad. As the author Thomas Harding points out in his book *White Debt*, Jack's managerial role would have meant that he 'travelled without escort or supervision to Georgetown when he delivered the hogsheads of sugar to the shipping houses'.[43] This would have afforded him more freedom than most and provided the opportunity to gather and spread news at a fast pace, and to effectively plan how they would overthrow their masters and claim their freedom.

Jack sent a letter to members of their Bethel Chapel congregation to tell them of the injustice, which demonstrates that, unlike most of the enslaved, Jack was literate and somewhat educated. This would have been a contravention of the wishes of Governor John Murray, who Revd. Smith records in his diary as threatening, 'If you ever teach a Negro to read and I hear of it, I will banish you from the colony immediately.'[44] Jack would have had further status through his role as one of Bethel Chapel's 'teachers'. The position of the man recorded as his father, Quamina, was a deacon of the chapel since March 1817 – a month after Smith arrived in the colony.[45] The archive of the Council for World Mission contains, among other documents, correspondence from Quamina, who was a regular visitor to the home of Revd. Smith and a trusted friend and advisor of the missionary and his wife.[46]

Records were kept of Jack's trial, but they are not wholly reliable. His words may have been misheard or anglicised by the court interpreter or scribe. Though the fact that Jack's testimony and the evidence of other enslaved Africans was heard at all is quite remarkable. In Demerara and Berbice, unlike other British colonies at the time, slave testimonies could be heard in court. When they were mistreated, slaves could also appeal to the Fiscal for redress under the Rule on the Treatment of Servants and Slaves, though justice was rarely delivered in their favour.[47] Harding shares three such horrific stories: the enslaved man nailed by his manager in a coffin though he was still alive, the overseer starving his workers, and the owner repeatedly raping teenage girls on his plantation.[48] Little wonder that Harding notes Demerara was known as one of the most violent colonies in the British Caribbean.

In terms of Jack Gladstone's trial, there are suspicious comments made which denote a more nefarious agenda afoot, as when he reportedly says, 'From the hour I was made prisoner by Captain

McTurk up to this time, I have received the most humane treatment from all the whites; nor have I had a single insulting expression from a white man, either in prison or anywhere else.'[49] In lines added to his statement by Robert Edmonstone (one of the court interpreters and also co-proprietor of Messrs McDonald, Edmonstone & Co., for whom Cheveley worked), Jack was made to blame the Methodists, reportedly stating that 'Parson Smith knew the whole plan.'[50] Who was pulling his chain, putting words in his mouth and instructing others to record his testimony in such terms? This is all highly suspect for someone who had supposedly just led a slave uprising against his white masters, especially when other insurrectionists were being 'broken at the wheel', decapitated and having their heads displayed on the roadside on spikes, or at the very least having the flesh ripped from their bones. Why was he being so well treated?

Whether or not Jack and his fellow enslaved Africans considered themselves Christian or religious, the Church undoubtedly provided them with a degree of authority within the enslaved community, reading material to practise or learn literacy, and the means to gather in large numbers. MP John Williams spoke disparagingly in Parliament of Revd. Smith's 'sale by him of Bibles, testaments, and primers to the Negroes' and 'the miserable details of presents made of ducks, chickens, and yams to Mr. and Mrs. Smith'.[51]

Yet these details in fact suggest a flourishing system of bartering among the African community, and a keenness for reading. In Revd. Smith's letters we find that the chapel was frequently filled, with both Africans and Creoles (meaning those born in the colonies of mixed race) attending in their hundreds. An 1824 edition of *The Mirror of Literature, Amusement, and Instruction* illustrated the scene: 'Some of the free black girls come to the Chapel in fine white lace veils and silk stockings, with a reticule to hold her pocket handkerchiefs, and their fingers sparkling with gold and diamond rings. Many of the slaves, on the contrary, come almost naked.'

Going to church at all showed fortitude, with some managers forbidding the enslaved from attending and even sending spies to report on those who did.⁵² In mapping the leaders of the rebellion to their church roles, John Coffey at the University of Leicester has found some overlap, with five so-called 'ringleaders' previously serving as 'teachers', supplementing and advancing the work of Revd. Smith by spreading the Christian message to other plantations.

The church also afforded a connection to England. Harding mentions Quamina in 1817 sending a letter to the head of the London Missionary Society, which explains the difficulties his fellow Africans face in attending church: 'Our masters and managers . . . try every means to stop it in working us so late at night . . . they are watching us like a cat would for a mouse.'⁵³ From this we know Quamina was illiterate at the time, as the letter is written by a Moses Chisholm, and signed with an 'x' by Quamina, Satin, Bristol and Asaar. It gives a sense of the growing assimilation of Black people in the Caribbean and Africa through the missionaries, who had long made the case that it was better to abolish the abomination of enslavement and focus upon the Christianisation of the Africans so they could be controlled via the church. They argued that if they could be converted in Africa, they would give up their resources freely to the whites and subjugate themselves willingly to the Church of England. This not only removed the need to enslave them for profit, but also provided a more lucrative business model, one that today we call 'colonialism'. The extent of this assimilation into white western belief systems is demonstrated in this early connection between not only the enslaved in Demerara and the white abolitionists in England, but also their fellow Christians in Africa, and is illustrated in a letter which states how 'joyful are we to hear how gladly the people in Africa are receiving the gospel'. Concerted efforts were being made to build another 'house of worship', and the form of church services that could be found at Bethel Chapel, is suggested by the news that 'one of our brothers has died . . . which is a very great loss to the church for he was the singer'.

Before their arrival in the colonies, to spread their truncated version of the Christian word in the form of 'the Slave Bible', John

Smith and his predecessor John Wray – writes Da Costa – were advised to expect 'ignorant babes'.[54] Instead they found a people whose system of meanings they ignored and often took at face value, men and women of flesh and blood, seasoned in their struggles against managers and masters.'[55] In turn, she continues, the enslaved Africans 'appropriated the missionaries' language and symbols, and turned their lessons of love and redemption into promises of freedom'.

It is important to look at what else was happening in the colony in the months preceding the rebellion. When historian David Olusoga visited John Gladstone's other former property in Demerara, Plantation Wales, for his documentary *Britain's Forgotten Slave Owners*, he noted financial losses in accounts for that same year of 1823. In the years before 1823, the price of sugar, cotton and coffee had all declined, explains Da Costa, 'when the European market began to be flooded with sugar from Brazil, the East Indies, and other colonies in the Caribbean'.[56] Prices reached their lowest point in 1822 and 1823, just £61 and £59 respectively, compared to highs of £99 in 1814 and 1815;[57] however, produce continued to flow from the colonies of British Guiana. In 1823, 36,962,174 lb of sugar, 1,265,035 gallons of rum, 1,123,667 gallons of molasses, 5,986,435 lb of coffee and 2,065,957 lb of cotton were produced in Demerara alone, with quantities of sugar and molasses increasing – not decreasing – in this tumultuous year.[58]

In addition to the market downturn, there had been the epidemic in Georgetown in 1823, which brought production on the plantations almost to a standstill as referred to previously in the letter from McInroy Sandbach in Demerary to Sandbach Tinne in Liverpool in July 1823, a few weeks before the uprising. From that account we understand that:

> There has been a serious mortality in almost all the districts of the colony. It began with a sort of influenza or cold, accompanied with severe fever and is succeeded by the

dangerous disease of pleurisy in some cases, and dysentery in others and has, in one shape or another, been so general that we may say for the last four or five weeks, little or no work has been done on most estates.[59]

The writer promises, 'when this sickness abates, there are large quantities of canes to be taken off'. Yet in a postscript of 25 July, they add, 'We have accounts from Woodlands of yesterday, where they continue very sickly and have lost 5 creoles within the last 24 days'. The alarming death toll didn't stop them pressing ahead with an order for 'two steam engine boilers for Leonora and Jalousie (plantations) and some other articles', as they [like other planters] switched their attention from cotton to sugar.

In this environment, the lives of the enslaved Africans became even more desperate:

> For the slaves, all these changes meant longer hours of work, a faster pace of labor, less time to cultivate their own gardens and provision grounds, or to go to the church and the market, diminishing supplies of food and clothing, more rigorous supervision and punishment, and more frequent separations from family and kin. Slaves responded to these pressures with increasing rebelliousness.[60]

In 1823 the African and Creole slave population of Demerara and Essequibo numbered 74,997, a decrease from 1820 when the total stood at 77,376, but still a significant number.[61] In comparison, in 1817, only Jamaica had a larger enslaved population (346,150). Among those who rose up, Da Costa adds, 'There were head people and field workers, men and women, Christians and non-Christians, free Blacks and slaves, Africans and Creoles, Blacks and Mulattos, young and old, Coromantees, Kongos, Popos, Mandingos, and probably others whose identities are lost to us. If a common experience united them, it was slavery.'[62]

The rebellion began around six, on the evening of Monday 18 August 1823. Conch shells were blown and drums beaten to signify to those on Plantation Success and neighbouring plantations that the time had arrived to down tools, seize control and make the white man finally give them the freedom they deserved. As they went from house to house, the enslaved Africans gathered what weapons and stocks they could find, but under the orders of Quamina and Jack Gladstone there was to be no violence. In the end, two white men did die defending their property at Plantation Nabaclis, but most overseers and plantation owners who were found, were simply given a taste of their own medicine and put in the stocks.

A number of women, it was said, took the opportunity to liberally slap their masters in the face and hurl well-deserved abuse at them, such as Rosey from Grove (the plantation where my own father was born), who was struck and sent home with her hands tied behind her back, before being put in the stocks for three days – away from her still-breastfeeding child – simply for stopping work due to a pain in her bowels.[63] She later left the estate without a pass and went to the protector of slaves. In the uprising, the women did not only wield slaps and harsh words; some also bore arms. Amba is said to have carried a musket on her shoulder and told her fellow rebels, 'you allow one Buckra man to knock down so many of you? Take for me gun and shoot him.'[64] The uprising surged through the cool evening air, catching plantation after plantation in its fiery trail:

> Slaves spoke of laws coming out from England. They spoke of 'rights.' They spoke of the King, of Wilberforce, and of 'the powerful men in England.' They used their masters' whips and put their masters in the stocks. They broke doors and windows, destroyed furniture, set buildings afire. They whipped managers and masters, stole their clothes and money, drank their wine. And when whites fired at them, they shot back. By the middle of the night, the old African

shells and drums were silent. Only the sound of European guns was heard.⁶⁵

That night the Smiths were visited by four servants representing four key local figures: Lieutenant-Colonel Goodman, Charles Wray, president of the Court of Justice, merchant Richard Chapman, and 'a Mr. Robertson', possibly slave-owner Gilbert Robertson (1774–1839) or his mixed-race son, Gilbert Robertson (1794–1851).⁶⁶

A detailed account of the Demerara uprising from the military perspective is provided in the writings of Cheveley, who would have been forced to join the ranks of the British military force to swell their numbers and, when the rebellion was sparked, to quell its flames. Cheveley was even there when Governor Murray and his troops met a group of the rebels on the road between Plantations Le Resouvenir and La Bonne Intention (a plantation that was later co-owned by Peter Miller Watson). The story is picked up by Odeen Ishmael in the introduction to his edited copy of the Parliamentary debate:

> Governor Murray asked them what they wanted, and they replied, 'Our right.' He then ordered them to surrender their weapons, but after they refused, he warned that their disobedience would cause them to lose whatever new benefits the new regulations aimed to provide. Further, Murray asked them to go home and to meet with him at plantation Felicity the next morning, but the slaves bluntly refused this invitation . . . That night the slaves seized and locked up the white managers and overseers on thirty-seven plantations between Georgetown and Mahaica in East Demerara.⁶⁷

In the days immediately following the rebellion, between ten and fifteen enslaved rebels were killed at Dochfour estate, six at Good Hope, six at Bee Hive plantation and forty at Elizabeth Hall.

Governor Murray declared martial law and sent Lieutenant-Colonel John Thomas Leahy into the fray with the 21st Fusiliers and the 1st West Indian Regiment. In a reversal of the enslaved Africans' march from Success to Stabroek, the soldiers made their way eastwards from the capital, at each stop regaining control of the plantations that had fallen: Vryheids Lust, Brothers, Montrose, Felicity, Chateau Margot, Mon Repos, Good Hope, Annandale, New Orange Nassau, Friendship, Vigilance, Elizabeth Hall, Hatcheries and Bachelor's Adventure.[68] At Nabaclis alone, twelve supposed ringleaders were shot, fifteen were executed at La Bonne Intention, and at Beterwerwagting the heads of murdered Africans were hacked off by the whites and stuck on poles at the entrance of the plantation.[69] Yet it was at Bachelor's Adventure that the biggest massacre of enslaved lives happened on 20 August. Cheveley was again present and recounted the events. Jack is said to have shown Lieutenant-Colonel Leahy a copy of a letter signed by plantation owners confirming they had not met violence from the rebels. This carefully prepared document, however, did not inspire the colonial forces to show the same restraint. When the enslaved assembly refused to surrender their arms, the troops opened fire. In less than fifteen minutes it was over.[70] Leahy estimated the number of dead at 100 to 150 Africans and Creoles, although in his introduction to the parliamentary discussion, Ishmael puts the number closer to 250. By any stretch of the imagination, it was a massacre. On the other side, just one soldier was killed – accidentally shot by one of his own. An amnesty, as usual, was then issued by the governor in the hope that the rebels would return to the plantations where they had been enslaved and resume their work filling the coffers of white men and women in Britain and Holland.

Gladstone had recently formed an elite cabal with fellow enslaver and Bristolian politician James Evan Baillie (MP for Bristol 1813–1834). They called it the British Guiana Association. After news of the uprising in Demerara, they convened a meeting on 23 October 1823 at the Thatched House in Bristol, and passed resolutions asking the King to express his displeasure by means of 'a Royal proclamation declaratory of His Majesty's high and marked displeasure at the late revolt'.[71] James Baillie MP, who chaired the meeting, commended Demerara's Lieutenant Governor and fellow Bristolian enslaver, John Murray,[72] for his apparent 'gallantry, zeal and good conduct' despite his brutal massacre and barbaric behaviour in the suppression of the uprising. They also sought to defend themselves in advance of any reports to the contrary, declaring that 'in no one instance did the Negroes engaged in the insurrection make any complaint against their masters of their treatment', blaming instead 'evil designing persons' for misleading 'the Negroes'. It is clear who these 'evil designing' people were in their minds, the missionaries and most notably the Revd. John Smith. They called for 'proper restrictions on the transit of missionaries from these Kingdoms to British Guyana' – and, sensing the opportunity, as was Gladstone's way, stated that they were entitled to 'full compensation from Parliament' for their 'serious loss of property'. In Parliament they had their sympathisers, their opponents, and those who sat somewhere in between. Henry Broughton MP, who instigated the parliamentary debate of 1 June 1824, declared 'they [the masters] have not only covered themselves with disgrace, but they may, if cooler heads and steadier hands control them not, place in jeopardy the life of every white man in the Antilles'.[73] He called for 'a just and humane administration of law in that colony, as may protect the voluntary instructors of the Negroes, as well as the Negroes themselves, and the rest of His Majesty's subjects, from oppression'.[74] Yet Broughton was in no rush to see the enslaved Africans freed, apparently 'for their own good'. The King did not in fact issue 'a Royal proclamation declaratory of His Majesty's high and marked displeasure'; he did the opposite and proclaimed his displeasure with the brutal manner in which the rebellion was put down. However, I'm certain that this was not out of concern for the enslaved, but rather as a rebuttal to Baillie and Gladstone's demand for compensation, which was denied.

The responses of enslavers such as John Gladstone are captured in those same minutes of the British Guiana Association of 23 October 1823, where James Baillie MP (listed as the Chair), drawing – no doubt – on his experience in Grenada during Fédon's rebellion of 1795, and seeking to get the most out of the situation as possible, passed resolutions where the committee praised the 'wisdom and firmness displayed by His Excellency General Murray', and called for 'not less than twelve hundred Troops' and 'two Vessels of War' to be garrisoned in Demerara to protect against further insurrection.[75] Baillie went on to give a sense of the situation in Demerara, two months after the rebellion: 'By the latest accounts from Demerary there was still a considerable number of insurgents about, and amongst them, two notorious leaders . . . the insurrection cannot be considered as having been entirely quelled, and that is impossible, but very great alarm must remain in the minds of all persons here interested in the Colonies, until further accounts shall be received.'[76]

On the plantations, of course, business resumed swiftly. A 'wanted to hire' notice dated 23 October 1823 calls for 'fifteen to twenty effective Negroes, to pick coffee' on Plantation Alliance, Canal No. 2. The advertiser is McInroy Sandbach & Co.[77] However the family do make some references to recent events in their correspondence. A letter from McInroy Sandbach & Co. in Demerara on 14 April 1824 refers to 'the late disturbance' and notes that 'the measures adopted against them ['the Negroes'] were disapproved of by the King'.[78] There is also a letter from eighteen-year-old Peter Miller Watson to his mother, dated September 1823, which gives his own somewhat naïve teenage take on the 'insurrection' and ongoing trials:

> It appears all to have arisen from the base representations of the two Methodist missionaries here, who with the view of extorting money from the deluded Negroes, informed them of papers having come from the King directing that they should be immediately freed, and that if that was not the case, the only way was to take it by rising in a body and

slaughtering all the white men . . . The two Methodist parsons are in Gaol and will no doubt meet with a reward suitable to their crime by being hung opposite to the chapel in which they formerly preached that Gospel which has brought so many hundreds to an untimely and disgraceful end. The number of prisoners now remaining to be tried is about 150, none of whom can hope to escape the rigour of the law. I heard from Berbice about two days ago. They are all well and the Negroes are quite quiet.[79]

Watson accuses the missionaries of trying to extort money from 'the deluded Negroes' and encouraging them to seek redress, if needs be by 'rising in a body and slaughtering all the white men'. It is perhaps Watson to whom Smith's predecessor at Bethel Chapel, John Wray, refers when he complains of the accusations issued against him:

Had this false report originated with people in the colony in an inferior situation of life, without influence either here or in England, I should have passed it by in silent contempt, but unfortunately, Messrs. Atkinson and Watson are among the people of influence and respectability, the former being a planter and lately one of the first merchants in Berbice, at present holding important and serious office of a vestry man of the Church of England, and also some years since a Lieutenant in the Berbice Militia; the latter at the head of a large mercantile house in the colony.[80]

A letter from Andrew Watson to his mother from Demerara in November 1823 indicates that they, like Cheveley, were conscripted into military service. He writes: 'At present I have scarcely time to scribble off a few lines before going on guard. We are so much taken up with military affairs that we have scarcely time for anything . . .

I see Peter every day on parade. He makes a very good soldier and looks very well in his uniform.'[81]

Despite apparently making a 'very good soldier', Peter Miller Watson is keen to get back to the business of making money. He writes again to his mother on Christmas Eve 1823:

> Our time here is so much occupied with a military duty, that we have enough to do to get through with the business of the store & counting house . . . I have been enrolled in the Rifle Corps since September. We are out drilling every afternoon from 4 to 6, which makes the thing very tedious – and we have to keep guard on every seventh night, but I understand that martial law is soon to be over on the 2nd of January 1824, which I hope may be the case, for I shall then be enabled to do my business with ease and will have no difficulty in keeping the books up, which at present is rather hard.[82]

Finding the leaders of the rebellion was seen as a priority, and a reward of ƒ1,00 (Dutch guilders) was offered for the capture of Quamina, Jack Gladstone and several others. The McInroy Sandbach letter of 14 April 1824 denotes not only the state of vigilance that followed the uprising, but a fear that the measures taken to suppress it would only make it worse. In summary, it states, 'There are rumours of movements among the slaves, chiefly on the East Coast, but no plot has been discovered . . . The militia in the country districts has been reassembled and that of the towns has resumed part of their former duties.'[83] The enslaved people suspected that 'the King disapproved of measures taken against them after the late disturbances, given the speedy dismissal of the 21st Regiment and its Commander, and the Governor and Fiscal. However, the present Governor has a copy of a despatch to the new Governor approving the steps taken during the insurrection and desiring him to use equally rigorous measures.' So, it appears that the King's 'displeasure' was a ruse to defuse the volatile situation, and the replacement of the offending officers was meant to reassure the enslaved. However, on the back channel, the new Governor was authorised to be just as brutal as the last, if there was a resurgence of rebellion.

On 16 September 1823 the authorities had finally caught up with Quamina, who had escaped into the back dam and had no doubt been looked after by other rebels, those who remained on plantations, and the self-liberated Maroons living deep in the forest. As David Alston notes, 'from the last decade of the eighteenth century until emancipation in 1834, Maroon communities were larger, more resilient and more enduring than has been recognised.'[84] Both Quamina and Jack Gladstone are said to have referred to Maroons' willingness to join the insurgents, 'with reports, attributed to Jack Gladstone, of "a thousand Bush Negroes" who might come from Wakenaam Island in the mouth of the Essequibo River'.[85] Indeed one of the enslaved people who escaped from Plantation Success earlier in 1823, a driver named Richard, returned the very same day the rebellion broke out, and was the one responsible for putting the manager of the plantation, John Stewart, in the stocks.[86]

Da Costa's account of Quamina's death is moving and gives a sense of this African-born elder, who had died still technically enslaved but free.[87] He took his last breath in the back dam of Chateau Margot, where he was found with the help of hired Amerindian 'slave catchers'. He was ordered to stop, but instead calmly carried on walking into the bush. He was shot in the arm and temple. Later, in his pockets were found a knife and a Bible.[88] The authorities did their best to remove his dignity, hanging his body in chains by the side of the road at plantation Success, but Quamina's constant battle for freedom and justice is still remembered in Guyana today. In 1985, Murray Street in Georgetown was renamed Quamina Street – a posthumous victory of sorts for Quamina over the old ruthless Governor John Murray. Revd. Smith is also remembered in Guyana. This

English Methodist, who had been tried for four offences, was imprisoned for seven weeks before his trial came to court. He was sentenced to be hanged and sent to the prison, where he eventually succumbed to the tuberculosis that he had been battling after the epidemic of 1823. He died on 6 February 1824, days before notification arrived from England commuting his sentence and freeing him from prison. Ishmael records that soon after, the enslaved Africans 'began referring to him as the Demerara martyr'.[89]

Justice for Revd. John Smith and Jack Gladstone is sought even today. In 2022, MP David Lammy, who is of Guyanese heritage, asked Parliament to pardon seventy of those convicted for their role in the rebellion. In a letter to the then-justice secretary, Dominic Raab, the *Guardian* reports that Lammy wrote: 'The full pardoning of both John Smith and Jack Gladstone would be a significant step in Britain's acknowledgment of its role in the history of slavery. Both John Smith and Jack Gladstone were pioneers of the abolition movement, and they must be remembered and celebrated as such. It is for this reason that I am requesting a pardon through the exercise of the royal prerogative of mercy.'[90] Attempting to evade British culpability, Raab responded somewhat absurdly that it was up to the president of the now independent Cooperative Republic of Guyana (himself a descendant of indentured Indians) to do so. Reminiscent of the Ku Klux Klan lynch mobs of the Southern states of the USA, many enslaved people like Quamina had been tried on the spot – or not at all – and death was administered instantly by hanging or firing squad, or by being 'broken at the wheel', their bodies subsequently often mutilated and given no semblance of dignity, even in death. After the immediate suppression of the uprising, a show was made of the administering of so-called 'justice', with a court martial established on 25 August by Governor Murray. This oversaw the lengthy trial for Revd. Smith, who as a white person was at least entitled to a modicum of due process. According to Ishmael, 'Over 200 Africans were beheaded by Governor Murray and their heads placed on stakes at the Parade Ground in Georgetown and from Plaisance to

Mahaica in East Demerara . . . In addition, there were other sentences, including solitary confinement and flogging of up to 1,000 lashes each. Some were also condemned to be chained for the rest of their servitude.'[91]

The most unusual and intriguing of the cases, to me, is that of Jack Gladstone himself. After he was captured and arrested, Jack was charged with 'causing, exciting and promoting revolt and rebellion against the peace of our Sovereign Lord the King, and also for having . . . been actively engaged in such revolt and rebellion; and further, for acting as a chief or leader or headman in such revolt and rebellion; and also aiding and assisting others therein'.[92] On 22 September 1823, just over a month after the revolt, he was found guilty. Yet he had support from an unusual corner – Sir John Gladstone himself.[93] In a letter to the governor, the MP highlighted the 'good behaviour, intelligence and usefulness' of the man who had instigated the uprising on his estate. Cort, Gladstone's attorney, added his support, noting the potential negative impact that news of Jack's execution would have on his fellow enslaved Africans and, ultimately, on the plantation's profits. The letters worked. Jack's sentence was commuted and later he was sold and deported to St Lucia. Harding, too, cites a letter from Governor Murray arguing that Jack Gladstone's anti-violence strategy was something to be commended, despite his leading role in the events of 18 August.[94]

I believe that there is more to the story. The Gladstone family have always been seen as absentee plantation owners, but it is not impossible that another white Gladstone found his way to Demerara in the late 1700s and produced mixed-race offspring. After all, Robertson Gladstone was out there in 1824. Jack is regularly described in letters from the period and the trial notes as the 'son of Quamina'. The surname 'Gladstone' could have been used to distinguish him from the other 'Jack' on Success, recorded in a slave directory of August 1817 as a twenty-five-year-old field slave born in Africa (Jack Gladstone was twenty-two at the time and is listed as born in 'Demerary').[95] But could it be that Jack had a white Gladstone father, who gave him the

'European nose' he is described as possessing in the wanted notice calling for his arrest?[96] One of Gladstone's brothers, perhaps, or another relative of John Gladstone, who didn't want to see his son hanged on the gallows and asked John Gladstone to step in. I have seen no plantation records that mention other slaves called Gladstone, which raises the spectre of doubt about Jack's parentage. Quamina, after all, was the one appealing to Jack not to kill the whites, yet Quamina was summarily executed and hung in chains, while Jack was mysteriously spared. Did Quamina know who Jack's white father really was? Had he been instructed to claim Jack as his own, to cover the scandal of his birth in the family? With John Gladstone blaming everyone from missionaries to MPs for the uprising while he had headed the West India Association since 1807, why would he personally intervene to spare the life of the main protagonist in the uprising and call upon his allies to do likewise? As Peter Miller Watson's mother Christian was Gladstone's wife's cousin, it appears he was calling upon all his allies to ensure the blame locally fell on Quamina and not Jack, and on Smith and Canning rather than John Gladstone himself.

There are questions here still to be answered. John Smith, a white Christian priest, was sentenced to death for inciting the rebellion. Jack Gladstone was a black slave who led the rebellion, yet they commuted his death sentence and sent him into exile with a good reference. A letter from Robert John Wilmot-Horton, the Under-Secretary of State for War and the Colonies, dated 16 March 1825, notes: 'with respect to the fate of the slave Jack, I think it is right to inform you that he has been removed from Demerara and enrolled as a military labourer in St. Lucia.'[97]

'It is for the sake of the Blacks themselves, as subsidiary to their own improvement, that the present state of things must for a time be maintained. It is because to them, the bulk of our fellow subjects in the colonies, liberty, if suddenly given, and still-more, if violently obtained by men yet unprepared to receive it, would be a curse, and not a blessing; that emancipation must be the work of time, and, above all, must not be wrested forcibly from their masters'[98]

Of course, the Africans were well prepared for freedom. According to the parliamentary report, those taking part in the proceedings 'proclaimed that their action was a strike and not a rebellion'. This is a significant framing of the events that took place. Just as Harding decides in *White Debt* to refer to the rebels as 'enslaved abolitionists', others equate the action with a modern-day union strike.[99] In his article 'The Demerara Rebellion of 1823, collective bargaining by slave revolt', Christian Høgsbjerg calls the action 'surprisingly modern in its strike-like character'. However, Da Costa suggests such actions were common, albeit on a considerably smaller scale:

> When norms for labour performance, food and cloth allowances, and medical assistance were violated, slaves protested. From law and custom they derived notions of 'rights.' And it was in the name of these 'rights' that, individually or in groups, slaves went to the fiscal to complain, rejected their allowances (when these were insufficient or spoiled), did not perform their tasks when they thought the assignment was 'unreasonable,' and from time to time even resorted to strikes, collectively refusing to do any work until their demands were met.[100]

In a letter from McInroy Parker & Co., dated 10 March 1818, the writer notes, 'Captain Ring brought in a report of the whole gang of Turkeyen & Henrietta, having in consequence of a quarrel with their master, gone off in a body, but from Mr Rainy saying nothing about it, was concluded that they had returned to their duty.'[101] Just over a week later, another letter adds 'a fine piece of news . . . Mr Bessey & his Negroes at Turkeyen are always at war. The whole gang has left him several times & yesterday the whole were in town at the Fiscal with a complaint, & it is thought that the Fiscal will look into this time.'

Others were less favourable to the rebels, including MP Wilmot

Horton, Under-Secretary of State for the Colonies, who declared in Parliament that 'the principal leaders in this insurrection were high in the confidence of their masters; they were trusted, they were well fed, they were well paid and, if I may be allowed the expression, they were in comparative circumstances of affluence and prosperity.'[102] It was a myth perpetuated by many, including Baillie and Gladstone, in the Demerara Association communiqué with Parliament and the King. Keen to show the apparently benign nature of slavery on his estates, as Checkland pointed out, John Gladstone obtained a report from his estate manager and attorney Frederick Cort, who had initially dutifully reported back 'that it was rarely necessary to punish the slaves and that they were generally happy and contented'.[103]

Disguising himself under the pen name Mercator, John Gladstone embroiled himself in a lengthy exchange of views in the *Liverpool Mercury* with abolitionist James Cropper.[104] If slavery was to be abolished, he demanded there must be full compensation for slaveholders. Again, he claimed his slaves to be well-treated and comfortable:

> The Slave, when guilty of crime, is tried in the same manner as his master. No driver or overseer can punish beyond six lashes for any offense. Connexion by marriage is encouraged, and its lawful fruits of increase rewarded. Families cannot be separated, but, when disposed of, must be sold together. In cases of sickness, able medical aid is provided; and in old age, when invalided, every comfort is afforded and continued. Their dwellings are roomy and commodious, their labour regulated and moderate.[105]

Of course, this was a complete fabrication; Gladstone's own reputation had come under intense scrutiny and was the subject of both public and parliamentary debate, particularly in the wake of the uprising. John Gladstone and other planters signed a petition on 11 February 1824 reminding government that 'we hold our plantations in your Majesty's colonies by grants or purchase from the Crown . . . Negro slaves were brought by your Majesty's British subjects from Africa to your Majesty's West India Colonies and sold by them to planters under the sanctions of Acts of the British Parliament.'[106] Gladstone, it was obvious to all, had plenty of reasons to see slavery continue and to paint life on his plantations as a kind of favour to the enslaved Africans. However, increased interest in and publication of accounts of plantation life revealed its true horrors to the British public and beyond, as Da Costa summarises: 'The slave uprising showed clearly where the lines of loyalty were drawn. It forced people to take sides and to make their commitments clear . . . It made public, for a moment at least, the slaves' secret life. It removed the mask of benevolence and exposed in its nakedness all the brutality of the masters' power and brought into the open their growing opposition to the British government.'[107]

What really clinched the public's interest were the documents sent by Revd. Smith's wife, Jane, to the London Missionary Society, including a transcript of the trial, a copy of the Reverend's journal and other documents. These were forwarded to the media and shared widely, triggering huge public coverage and interest, particularly when it was revealed that Revd. Smith had died before his pardon from the King arrived.[108] On 12 June 1824, *The Mirror of Literature, Amusement, and Instruction* shared Smith's story, noting, 'this event has excited great interest in the religious world, and numerous petitions have been presented to Parliament; praying that the sentence on Mr. Smith may be reversed.'

This was a turning point. The details of the violence and inhumanity of the British in suppressing the Demerara Rebellion garnered more support for abolition. Smith's testimony, in which he gives a solid account of the rationale for preaching to the enslaved, also instigated a wave of evangelical fever.

Prior to 1823, when people spoke of a 'Christian', in Demerara, they meant a white person. Missionaries of course existed already, and before the 1823 uprising – as William Wilberforce reminded his fellow MPs – the House had 'declared its determination to ameliorate the condition of the slaves in the West Indies; and, more especially, by a course of religious instruction gradually to prepare them for the safe participation in those civil privileges which are enjoyed by their fellow-subjects in this country'.[109] In fact, in 1811 Lord Liverpool, Secretary for War and the Colonies, issued a circular making it clear that the government supported the religious 'instruction' of slaves.[110] Yet it was after the events of 1823 that Black people were allowed to become literate again, and to read and write in earnest, but this time in English rather than in their native tongues. Christianity hastens its spread among Black people in the Caribbean and in Africa as a direct consequence of the rebellion. Where once Peter Miller Watson decried the missionaries in Demerara and the *Royal Gazette* of February 1822 declared, 'If we expect to create a community of reading, moral, church-going slaves, we are woefully mistaken',[111] the promotion of the doctrine among the enslaved was promulgated. Ironically, Christianity had provided the moral justification for the enslavement of Black people, and when that argument was turned on its head by John Smith's testimony, the Sandbach, Tinne, Traill, Robertson, Watson and Gladstone families all began endowing missionaries. Charles Stuart Parker left money in his will to the Moravian missionaries. There were many clergymen in the families, including the Revd. Harry Robertson, Peter Miller Watson's grandfather; the Revd. George Rainy, father of Sandbach Tinne partner George Rainy; the Revd. Gilbert Robertson, minister of Kincardine; Christian Bain's father, the Revd. John Bain, minister of Dingwall; and many more. The families had for a long time also been involved in the building of churches.

When the Slave Bible was created and propagated by the SPCK, records were published in newspapers listing who had contributed to its production and propagation among the enslaved in the Caribbean. It illustrated clearly that the largest contributions came from the same slave traders that previously had said 'no' to Christianity for those they enslaved. Among them are Samuel Sandbach, Philip

Frederick Tinne, John Abraham Tinne and George Rainy. The idea of gradual emancipation with Christian assimilation had firmly taken hold since the testimony of John Smith, and the very religion that had enslaved the African was rebranded as their means of redemption, albeit a heavily censored version.

In 1831 William Ewart Gladstone gave a speech at the Oxford Union, where he challenged the immediate emancipation of the enslaved and favoured what he termed 'gradual manumission',[112] a doctrine that his father no doubt preferred, with 'religious instruction'. The young Gladstone entered Parliament the following year in 1832, having been gifted the safe Nottinghamshire Conservative seat of Newark by the Duke of Newcastle. His father bought his own seat with bribes, so for a seat to be handed to his son was no surprise. When the subject of emancipation came up for debate in Parliament, W.E. Gladstone was quick to defend his father, claiming that the seventy deaths on his plantation referred to in Parliament were 'due to old age' and that the plantation manager was a 'kind man'. He also gave a slew of other excuses to defend his father's infamously ruthless and barbaric regime. His intervention was a timely one, as he was now in a strategic position to help shape how the abolition of slavery was to be administered, as well as seeing his father's reputation – which had been severely tarnished by the uprising – restored.

CHAPTER 8

A 'LARGE AND LIBERAL ATONEMENT'

> *A tree is bent while it is still wet.*
> *– African proverb*

The Demerara Rebellion may have been quashed but the colony's planters and managers could not rest easy. Protests, uprisings and daily acts of resistance continued right up until slavery would finally be officially abolished in most British colonies. However, subsequent to abolition, it still continued due to the system of apprenticeship and other forms of servitude which followed, as is evident from letters and other documents from the period. After the 1823 uprising, the Demerara-based partners and employees of McInroy Sandbach & Co. kept their counterparts in Glasgow and Liverpool informed, not only of crop production levels and profits, but the mood of those enslaved on their plantations. In a letter from McInroy Sandbach & Co, from Demerara dated 14 April 1824, the writer recounts that 'we were yesterday alarmed with a report that the Coffee Grove buildings burnt down, which fortunately turned out to be . . . one range of Negro houses'.[1] While no explanation is given for the fire, which may have been a domestic accident, the tone of the remainder of the letter is apprehensive:

Surmises of fresh movements among the Negroes, chiefly on the East Coast, have been afloat for the last few days, on the approach of the Easter holidays, but the most rigid investigation has not been able to detect any plot, so far as we can learn . . . There is reason to believe that some excitement exists in the minds of the Negroes from the idea that the new Governor momentarily expected, may bring them something favourable.[2]

The new governor, Sir Benjamin d'Urban, had no such intent, having received a dispatch 'approving of all the steps taken during the insurrection & desiring the latter to use equally vigorous measures if the occasion should call for them' (a sentiment which had also been recounted in Peter Miller Watson's letter home to Scotland). The events of 1823 and particularly the trial of Revd. John Smith had only heightened planters' hatred of missionaries. The plantation owners saw it as a vindication of their long-expressed alarm concerning missionaries' involvement with enslaved workers, which had deepened following Britain's abolition of the slave trade in 1807. The Society for the Conversion of Negro Slaves had been founded in 1794 with a bequest. In 1808, the so-called Slave Bible was published, a copy of which was displayed in the 2023 exhibition 'Enslavement: Voices from the Archives' at Lambeth Palace Library.

A description of the Slave Bible and its contents is an utter indictment of the complicity of the Church with the enslavers to edit the 'word of God', in order to ensure the continued servitude of the enslaved Africans. This was the beginning of a two-tier system of apartheid within the Church itself that remains to this day. The narrative at Lambeth Palace, home of the Church of England and the seat of its power, having assessed the text, recounted the following:

Whereas a standard Protestant Bible contains 1,189 chapters, this version contains only 232. It excludes 90% of the Old Testament, and 50% of the New Testament. Many references to freedom and escape from slavery were removed and some passages encouraging loyalty and submission to masters were emphasised. For instance, the text skips directly from Genesis 45:28 to Exodus 19. It includes the Ten Commandments (Exodus 20), but the first 18 books of Exodus, in which the Israelites escape slavery in Egypt, have been removed.[3]

The volume, which consists of 'select sections of the Holy Bible for the use of the Negro Slaves', was published on behalf of the Society for the Conversion of Negro Slaves.[4] Yet even though they extrapolated the sections relating to service and obedience, and agreed with the plantation managers and slave owners what would be taught to those whom they'd enslaved, discontent still ensued. In his description of the 1808 arrival of missionaries from the London Missionary Society in Demerara, Dalton declares: 'Had the missionaries' exertions been strictly directed to the regeneration of the depraved heart of the slave, and their religious zeal been tempered with moderation and discretion, much misunderstanding would have been averted . . . they had, notwithstanding, imbibed in all its bitterness, the strong prejudice which at that time existed in England against the planter.'[5]

What is evident from parliamentary debates at the time was the emergence of a rationale for British enslavers to rebrand themselves in an effort to cast off the now toxic moniker of slavery.

In Georgetown on 24 February 1824, a public meeting was held, at which it was resolved 'That the Court of Policy be forthwith petitioned to expel all missionaries from the colony, and that a law be passed prohibiting the admission of any missionary preachers into this colony for the future.'[6] However, the case of John Smith and the Demerara Rebellion had created a demand for more narratives of plantation life, and of the cruelties experienced by the enslaved Africans. In June 2024, Britain's *Daily Mirror* newspaper reprinted an extract from Dr Pinckard's 'Notes on the West Indies' that records the writer's impressions on visiting a slave market in Demerara:

> The poor Africans who were to be sold, were exposed naked, in a large empty building, like an open barn. Those who came with an intention to purchase, minutely inspected them, handled them, made them jump, and stamp with their feet, and throw out their arms and legs; turned them about; looked into their mouths; and, according to the usual rules of traffic with respect to cattle, examined them, and made them shew themselves in a variety of ways, to try if they were sound and healthy.[7]

Pinckard captures vignettes of couples and families separated, including two friends (or possibly brothers) who celebrate when they are sold together, describing them as 'exhibiting all the purest signs of mirth and gratification . . . Satisfied to toil out their days, for an unknown master, so that they might but travel their journey of slavery together.' In the wake of such emotive (albeit romanticised) portrayals of slavery in the public press, the cause of John Smith was taken up, and a new urgency to Christianise the enslaved was felt.

Evangelical proselytisation in foreign lands, of course, was nothing new. In a document named 'Chronological Chart of the Progress of the Church Missionary Society', we find missions dating back as far as 1646 when 'Eliot preaches to the N. A. Indians',[8] as well as a mention of a 'Moravian Mission among the Hottentots'[9] (a derogatory name for the ancient Khoesān people, now thought to be the ancestral forefathers of the modern humans) in a region of South Africa in 1736. In 1827, a mission founded in 'Br. Guiana occupied' is recorded. The Quaker movement had been calling for abolition for many years, yet they represented only a small sect of the Church. They did not have the capacity of the Catholic Church, for instance, or even the Church of England, but their message was now starting to resonate. In time, even the planters began to see religion as a solution, although their goal was to manage their enslaved Africans and hold off the abolitionists. Their rationale was the false notion that 'we are the representatives of God and Jesus, because everyone knows this is our religion; we are white, God is white, and Jesus is white'. The iconography created in churches reinforced this fallacy. They assumed that the supremacy of the white man, once reinscribed in religion, would force the enslaved Africans to submit to being controlled by them, even if they were emancipated.

As we have seen, the Church itself had long invested in and supported slavery. The moral argument disseminated to justify this involvement was that Black people were 'not on the boat with Ham and Shem and were therefore not the progeny of Noah or Adam'. Black people, it was said, 'developed as a separate subspecies' that 'evolved from apes, separately from Homo Sapiens', and therefore could be classed as 'flora and fauna' – as was done with Aboriginals in Australia – or, in the case of African enslavement, as 'property'. John Smith's testimony, however, asserted the humanity of the enslaved Africans in ways that could not be undone. Christian abolitionists knew that a moral argument alone would make little impact, so some made a business case for colonialism, telling the slave owners that the mineral resources in Africa are far richer than anything you could cultivate from the enslaved Africans in the Americas, and if you Christianise them, you won't have to fight them for it. They will willingly give it to you.

Colonialism began in earnest after the abolition of the slave trade but went into overdrive after the death and the testimony of John Smith. The Christianisation process started with the building of churches and schools for the enslaved and was entwined with a massive resource grab in Africa which saw cocoa, palm oil, gold, ivory and other produce and commodities flow back to Europe, alongside minerals and materials needed to power the industrial revolution, such as iron, bronze and copper. The Society for Promoting Christian Knowledge, which still has its headquarters on Euston Road in London, and the Society for the Propagation of the Gospel, both expanded their reach and started sending more missionaries to proselytise to the enslaved population and the indigenous peoples of both the Caribbean and Africa.

A *Church Missionary Intelligencer* of the mid-nineteenth century recounted the colonising methods used by the missionaries to make inroads into so-called 'heathen' lands. Britain, its royal family and wider aristocracy had long bought into – and expanded – the trade in humans from Africa, yet in the *Intelligencer*, the missionaries focus on the Africans as the ones who were perpetuating the system of transatlantic slavery, which up until then, white Europeans had conceived, developed and dominated. After the abolition of the African slave trade in 1807, the British missionaries took the moral high ground and delighted in blaming the Africans for being the architects of their own misery, taking little or no responsibility for what they themselves had created – an international demand for human beings in bondage. They stated, 'we must feel how necessary it is, not merely to coerce the native into an abandonment of the traffic, but to disincline him to do it, so that even if the opportunity of resuming it were presented to him, he would refuse to do so.'[10] The writer continues, 'This can be affected only by the dissemination of Christian truth and light amongst the native tribes.' Ironic since the same Christians had at that point spent three hundred years justifying the enslavement of Africans and profiteering from its barbaric fruits. These missionaries were not only evangelists, but were also the foundation of what we today call the diplomatic corps. If you look at these missionary intelligencers, they are like diplomatic briefings. They have detailed maps and illustrations; breakdowns of the tribes, the demographics of the region, the customs and food of the people; intelligence on who-hates-who and how to exploit the tribal divisions. And every time they went to a location, the local intelligence was updated for the next missionaries. These were not only religious figures but scientists, botanists, cartographers, doctors, teachers and more. The irony was that they could only reach the remote locations targeted by their missions on board the ships and boats of the slave traders. The quid pro quo was 'we get the souls – you get the minerals'.

After 1823, the Christianisation of the enslaved was accelerated. In accounts of the Berbice Rebellion of 1763, the term 'Christian' had been used as a synonym for a 'white man' – anyone else was a 'barbarian', a Muslim (or so-called 'Mohammedan') a heathen, etc. As the public mood in Europe gradually shifted towards proselytisation of the enslaved, the notion of the enslaved as Christians took root, although worship was still segregated, as can be seen from the picture of Christ Church (second picture section), founded in the exclusive Georgetown neighbourhood of Cummingsburg in 1834 'as a proprietary chapel'.

It was formed by sixteen former members of St George's Cathedral. A mezzanine was installed where the formerly enslaved and now indentured Africans were permitted to worship, separated from the whites who sat below. Two back stairways allowed segregated access for the formerly enslaved congregation, to minimise contact between them and the whites during church services. Christ Church was not formally consecrated until 1841 due to a dispute with St George's Cathedral, an Anglican church administered by the Church of England. Clergy were appointed and sent from England; the building was also owned by them. This led to tensions with some of the enslavers, who felt that they had no control of what was said or who was saying it. This resulted in a breakaway in 1834 where the founders formed Christ Church, owned the land and the building, and appointed their own clergymen. The anger of the Church of England from this loss of control led to a rift which delayed the consecration of Christ Church until 1841.

Samuel Sandbach's mansion (which is now the president's residence) is almost opposite the church, separated only by the Promenade Gardens founded in 1853 on the old parade ground, and filled with botanical specimens from all over Guyana (further evidence of the enslavers' and colonialists' obsession with botany). Evidence of a Sandbach Tinne connection to Christ Church can be found on a monument with a eulogy that still hangs on the wall there, dedicated by the Tinne family.

It is evident from the records that Philip Frederick Tinne and Anna Tinne (née Rose, 1785–1827) witnessed Henry Tinne Garnett's parents' wedding.¹¹ It is also of note that Henry Tinne Garnett's mother was a child bride.

In 1827, the 'Report of the Incorporated Society for the Conversion and Religious Instruction and Education of the Negro Slaves in the British West India Islands for the Year MDCCCXXVI [1826]' was published.¹² The document included examples of the new drive to spread Christianity among the African population of the Caribbean, which bears 'ample testimony to the beneficial tendency of the plans which have been adopted, at the suggestion of the West India Bishops, for the religious instruction and education of the Negroes, and to the steady progress which sound religion is making in their Lordships dioceses'. Behind this drive were not only church leaders, but politicians and plantation owners themselves. Future prime minister and founder of the police force Robert Peel was listed as a 'Vice President' of the society, while the governors include Lord Kenyon and a Joshua Watson. The report praises 'the zeal and liberality with which the work of religious instruction and education is upheld in the West Indies' and 'those proprietors of estates, and other persons connected with West India interests resident in this country, who have given active and liberal support to the branch associations of the Islands, with which they are respectively connected'. Donating to such organisations became a way for slave-owners to absolve their consciences, believing them to be (in the words of the report) 'a charitable and pious work which cannot fail, under divine providence, of being productive of the most substantial blessings'.

The list of subscribers to the society is also revealing. As well as Lord Kenyon, Robert Peel and Joshua Watson, one can find royal subscribers including the Duke of Clarence (with an annual subscription of £10); the Duchess of Clarence (donation as before); and the Duke of Gloucester, with a one-off donation of £31 10s. From the planters, £1,000 is donated by the West India Planters and Merchants of London, and £100 each by the West India Planters and Merchants of Liverpool and the West India Planters and Merchants of Glasgow, organisations whose members included Samuel Sandbach and Charles

Stuart Parker. Other individual or corporate donors include Bristolian slave traders James Baillie (£220 annually), Evan Baillie & Sons (£500), abolitionist MP William Wilberforce (£5 annually), even the British *Guardian* (£1 1s annually). The Sandbach Tinne family, inevitably, make an appearance, with Samuel Sandbach and Philip Frederick Tinne donating £2 2s apiece on an annual basis. Other names jump out too, which could be connected to the family: George Watson of Jamaica, the Revd. J.J.D.D. Watson of St Albans, and a few 'persons of colour': Miss J. Rainy, Miss S. Watson and Miss E. Watson.

The involvement of Wilberforce is unsurprising, though his contribution is eclipsed by those of James and Evan Baillie, two of Bristol's most notorious enslavers. In May 1823, just months before the Demerara uprising, Wilberforce had submitted a petition calling for the end of slavery. In an address supporting his colleague's motion, Thomas Fowell Buxton referred to Wilberforce as 'the father of the cause' and added his own call for justice:

> For the tens and tens of thousands suffocated in the holds of our slave ships – for the tens and tens of thousands of emaciated beings, cast ashore in the West Indies, emaciated beings, 'refuse men'[13] (for such was the mercantile phrase) lingering to a speedy death – for the tens and tens of thousands still more unhappy who, surviving, lived on to perpetual slavery, to the whip of the taskmaster, to ignorance, to crime, to heathen darkness – for all these, *we owe a large and liberal atonement*. And I do thank God, we still have it in our power to make some compensation.[14]

The form of the proposed 'compensation' or 'atonement' was to include various elements, but above all, declares Buxton, 'we may give him the truths of the Christian religion, which, as yet, we have withheld.' He imagined a time when maintenance, education and religious instruction was provided to the children of the enslaved, that 'we may raise them into a happy, contented, enlightened, free peasantry'. Religion was seen as the guiding tool, and Buxton was keen to assert that slavery was not only 'repugnant' to the principles of the British constitution but to those of 'the Christian religion'.

In the report of the Incorporated Society for the Conversion and Religious Instruction and Education of the Negro Slaves in the British West India Islands, Demerara and Essequibo, there is mention in a news update, of the division of the two colonies into 'parochial districts'. This meant that 'the society has been released from the very heavy expense which it had incurred in providing for the religious instruction required'.[15] These savings were passed on to the West India bishops 'for the maintenance of catechists and schoolmasters', while a further sum was 'voted in aid of the school recently established in Georgetown under the superintendence of Lady d'Urban (wife of the Governor)'. The school was described as being for 'the religious and suitable education of free coloured girls; a numerous class, and in many instances, from their orphan condition and other circumstances, peculiarly the objects of pity'. Other expenses recorded include books such as the new lectures on the Gospel of St Matthew by William Marshall Harte, published only in 1824. A 'statement of receipts and expenditure' for the year 1826 recorded where the remainder of the donated money was spent, such as £625 towards 'moiety of salaries to the four Demerara chaplains'. Dalton cites another example of 'improving efforts of civilisation' that followed, including the formation of vestries and later, an act for 'regulating and preserving registers of baptism, marriages, and burials, in the United Colony of Demerara and Essequibo'.[16]

In the baptismal records from St George's Cathedral in Georgetown for the year 1828, we get a snapshot of the blatant apartheid operating within the Church, in the manner in which the records for whites, enslaved Africans and free people of colour were delineated. Whites had their full details recorded; name of child (a person), Christian and surnames of both father and mother, date of birth (as distinct from date of baptism), profession of father, abode, etc. For the enslaved it records 'slave woman' or 'infant slave' (not a 'child') and instead of the parents' Christian names, surnames and profession of father, it simply states, 'belonging to' and the name of the owner; either a person, a company, a plantation or 'the government'. In the case of a 'free' person of colour – usually manumitted by their white father, or born of another free-born person of colour – it says, 'free child' (i.e. a 'person' because they have part white blood) followed by the name of both parents, validated by three 'sponsors'. At the bottom of this entry are a 'free woman' and 'her children' with Christian names and no surnames and no details of father, just a reference to their abode as 'Demerara river'.

So, at the behest of their owners, enslaved adults and their existing children were being baptised, and in some cases multiple baptisms of enslaved people were taking place each Wednesday. This suggests enslavers were demanding that their enslaved captives be mass baptised, so they could – in their twisted logic – attain the 'blessings' that their clergy informed them of, through the SPCK and the SPG. This can be seen in page after page of the baptismal records from this one cathedral alone. Similar things were happening at churches all over the colony after the uprising of 1823.

The systemic racism that permeated the laws during the period of enslavement was construed into Christianity, in order to indoctrinate the enslaved Africans with a diluted version of the religion which redacted any notion of freedom from bondage. Meanwhile congregations were segregated and a system of cataloguing births and baptisms developed within a racial hierarchy that placed all whites as humans on top, all enslaved Africans as property on the bottom and those of mixed blood as an anomaly in the middle, with partial human status – but without full rights – due to their mixed white heritage.

Elsewhere in the West Indies, the impact of this large-scale Christianising mission was already being felt. A submission from Jamaica to the report notes that on Seven Rivers Estate, 'every adult can repeat the Lord's Prayer, the belief, and some of the commandments. The children are able to repeat as much as the adults, and many of the older children much more.' The number of baptisms and marriages of enslaved people is recorded, where once marriage was discouraged or not permitted. And there is clearly an emphasis on behaviour, with references to congregations that are 'very large, and behave with decorum', where 'an astonishing degree of regularity and subordination has hitherto prevailed', or how 'religion is manifestly advancing among the Black population and producing daily better habits'. In one parish, the children are given 'a uniform Sunday suit . . . which was desirable, not only in point of neatness, but as giving additional importance to the attendance at Church, in the estimation of the slaves themselves'. These 'achievements' are celebrated by the report's writers, who insist:

> It is a fact, now well established in every reflecting and unprejudiced mind, that religious instruction has hitherto imparted generally to the slaves a character for virtue and integrity, to which they were before comparatively strangers; and, in making this observation, they are borne out not only by their cheerful submission to the authority of 'the powers that be,' but also by the social order and harmony, the decent exterior and demeanour, which so strongly attest the improved habits of industry, now so prevalent amongst them.[17]

Slave-owners had previously shown little concern for the wellbeing of the people they had enslaved, yet the promise of a submissive workforce appealed to them, particularly following the events of 1823. The report continued that 'a further extension of religious knowledge . . . would furnish the best possible antidote to any attempts that might be made to unsettle their minds or render them less satisfied with their present condition'. With children receiving religious instruction (on some plantations) every day, the chance to mould the next generation of enslaved workers would have seemed like a winning strategy to the plantation owners. Thus the business case that John Smith and other missionaries had made, had now came to pass.

The racial hierarchies being developed through this system of religious conversion are also evident. One report from Morant Bay, Jamaica, refers to a proposal 'to select from amongst the free coloured inhabitants, a person of unblameable reputation, qualified for catechizing and teaching the children on such estates as might be accessible to him, as well as for superintending the Sabbath School'. A free coloured person is recommended 'for two very obvious reasons': getting a white instructor at the same rate would be very difficult, and as 'an individual of this description would have no ulterior object in view to divert his mind from the important work before him; and . . . being already inured to the climate, he would be less liable to suffer from its effects'.[18] In another document, charting the Missions of the Church in British Guiana, indigenous Amerindians are encouraged to take over African jobs on the plantation:

> For every Indian who attends a place of worship once, immediately feels that he must attire himself decently as the rest of the congregation, or go no more. Hence, he finds himself compelled to work for the estates, either in thatching, wood-cutting, or in cleaning trenches; nay, in the beginning of the present year, during the strike of the Negroes, Indians were employed, in one instance, in cutting sugar canes. Thus, he benefits not only his own family, but the planter, who is in want of labour, as well as the merchant and manufacturer of the goods of which he becomes a consumer.[19]

In more recent years, the Church has been reckoning with this past. In 2022, priest Guy Hewitt, former Barbados High Commissioner to the UK, was appointed head of the Church of England's Racial Justice Unit to implement the recommendations of the Archbishops' Anti-Racism Taskforce report 'From Lament to Action', published in 2021. Hewitt, who has Indian and Bajan heritage, is well placed to do so, as not only a priest but an Honorary Senior Research Fellow with the Institute of Commonwealth Studies at the

University of London and an Advisory Board member of the Windrush Scandal Research Project.[20] In January 2023, the Church of England announced it was committing £100,000,000 of funding over the next nine years to 'a programme of impact investment, research and engagement' to try and 'address some of the past wrongs'.[21] These wrongs include investing in the South Sea Company, with the proceeds of the Queen Ann Bounty, a fund developed for poor clergy but which made a fortune from the proceeds of enslavement, a mainstay of the South Sea Company with whom it was invested. The company traded in enslaved people, and the Church fund also received donations from individuals 'linked to, or who profited from, transatlantic chattel slavery and the plantation economy'.[22]

While John Gladstone may have blamed the Revd. John Smith and his fellow missionaries for stirring up slave rebelliousness on his plantation, his family were in fact inculcated in religion, with numerous ministers within their own ranks, including high-ranking Church figures. St Nicholas Church in Liverpool has its priest appointed by the Gladstone family to this day.

Wider family members were writing books on ecclesiastical jurisprudence, for example the Revd. Gilbert Robertson (1702–1774) who studied divinity under the Revd. Dr Philip Doddridge of Northampton and was ordained on 7 June 1739. He married Christian Bain, eldest daughter of the Revd. John Bain, Minister of Dingwall.[23] Their children included the Revd. Harry Robertson DD (1748–1815), who was appointed a Doctor of Divinity by the University of Marischal College, Aberdeen, and married the sister of William Forbes, Attorney General of Barbados. His sister Ann Robertson (1750–1833) married the Revd. George Rainy of Creich (c.1733–1810), who was described as 'a very model of a sincere practical Christian and preached the Gospel by his life'.[24] His wife meanwhile is described as 'pious, the impersonation of motherly kindness, and the beau ideal of a minister's wife'. Charles Stuart Parker's wife Margaret is similarly remembered as pious in the family annals: 'From her youth she was distinguished for her piety, her excellent father was wont to say of her that "really Margaret ought to be in the pulpit".' Later down the line, Charles Stuart Parker's son James (1803–1852) married Mary Babington, daughter of Thomas Babington of Rothley Temple, an active anti-slavery campaigner; while Gilbert Robertson Sandbach became Rector of Upper Sapey, Herefordshire. His obituary read that he was

> the second son of the late Rev. Gilbert Sandbach, of Woodlands, Aigburth, Liverpool, and married Miss Rushworth, daughter of a former Governor of Trinidad. He was the senior partner in the well-known firm of Sandbach, Tinne and Co., merchants, Liverpool, being chairman of the Liverpool Exchange Newsroom, in which capacity he was accustomed to receive distinguished personages visiting the Exchange. He was a justice of the peace for the county of Denbigh, a director of the North and South Wales Bank, Ltd., and a trustee of the Gresford Parochial Charities.
> Mr. Sandbach took great interest in Church matters, having acted as vicar's warden at Rossett until Easter, when he was obliged to relinquish the duties owing to failing health. His demise will prove a great loss to the district of Rossett, where he was held in the highest esteem.[25]

The family's actions in Demerara and beyond were far from saintly, yet it seemed that any sins committed while overseas could be atoned for on one's return, which is perhaps why there is a church on the corner of every street in Liverpool, with the most elaborate furnishings, funded by slave traders. Thus, St Ann's in Aigburth, Liverpool, was established by 'Messrs Moss, Booker, Tinne and Parker [all slave merchants] to provide a stipend and free sittings for the poor and humble classes'.[26] Its foundation stone was laid on 27 March 1836, just two years after Britain finally abolished Caribbean slavery. Philip Frederick Tinne's son John Abraham Tinne also financed an English church at The Hague, in the name of his father and grandfather – the church was called St John and St Philip – and in quiet honour of his adventurous sister Alexine. In the *History of the English Church at the Hague 1586–1929*, Fred. Oudschans Dentz commends the Tinne family for their involvement in the development of the church: 'To the memory of John, Philip and Alexine, three people with hearts full of the finest and tenderest feelings, of pious thought and overwhelming love for their fellow men, in whose blood was mingled that of Dutch and English families.'[27] It is of note that the slave traders' names were deliberately juxtaposed with those of saints. As there is no formal canonisation in this church, the inference was meant as a next best option.

However pious their families might have appeared at home in Scotland, England and Holland, life was far from heavenly on their plantations, and the white population continued to be anything but models of Christian piety. Considering that John Abraham Tinne was the second largest individual recipient of slavery compensation after his relative John Gladstone, the notion that he could be faux canonised as 'St John' along with his father who made a fortune from plantation enslavement being compared to 'St Philip' is indicative of the level of narcissism and desensitisation to the rape, murder, mutilation and extreme barbarity that brought them the wealth with which they built such houses of worship, drenched in the blood and misery of the tens of thousands of Black victims who passed through their murderous and depraved multinational business.

Post the 1823 rebellion, relative lawlessness prevailed in the colonies, as the notion of what constituted a 'crime' was purely dependent upon who it was committed against. What would be a crime against a white person was rarely considered a crime against a Black person. In a note dated 11 February 1825, for example, Peter Miller Watson shared the news that 'poor Euston is no more', referring to an estate manager known by that name; he reported, 'He was shot by his father-in-law (McAlpin). McAlpin and his wife were in the habit of quarrelling once a month or oftener and the lady used to fly to Euston for protection – she had done so on this occasion and Euston had carried her home again & was ascending the stair of McAlpin's house, when the father took up a musket & shot him. The shot entered the left arm & lodged in the heart so that he died immediately – the murderer is now in jail, and I hope will be hanged.'[28] Had Euston been Black, no such punishment would have been administered as he would be regarded as disposable property rather than a person. No more attention would have been paid to a horse being shot, had Euston been an enslaved African.

For the enslaved Africans, freedom continued to be constrained in every manner. A document titled 'Latest Returns' lists the slave populations of different Caribbean colonies in 1828–1829.[29] For Berbice, 21,319 males and females are recorded in 1828; in Demerara in 1829 the number is even higher at 69,467 – behind only Jamaica and Barbados. Each of these statistics hides countless individual lives, but to the Sandbach Tinne families, they were still mere commodities or assets in their accounts and vast business portfolios. In a letter, dated 6 February 1826, from McInroy Parker & Co. in Glasgow to Messrs Sandbach Tinne & Co. in Liverpool, a mortgage agreement is outlined for a group of enslaved men: 'Sale of Kensington[30] Negroes £12,323. Interest from 1st Nov. 1821 . . . Jan. 1823 & the capital payable in 6 annual instalments of £2053.12s.3d. each with interest . . . total will be £15,771.4s.4d (four payments as yet unpaid).'[31]

On Plantation Le Resouvenir, where Revd. John Smith had preached, it was back to business as usual. The manager Van Cooten wrote on 3 December 1825 to McInroy Parker & Co. of the 'sales of my 15 bales Cotton . . . Proceeds £191,6,18 and of 60 bales cotton from Le Resouvenir'.[32] Another letter from Demerara, dated 27 November 1825, gives a sense of the scale of the shipping side of the business, which at this time involved six ships being sent to and from Demerary. 'It may be assumed that we can on an average despatch a ship every 2nd openings, or once every 4 weeks, unless our circumstances alter for the worse.' As well as transporting cotton, sugar and other goods over Demerara's 'sand bar' and into the

Caribbean Sea, they often sent more unusual items. In 1826, for example, we find Watson writing to Charles Stuart Parker to inform him of a gift en route, a 'Tiger cat which I have particularly instructed Captain R. to take care of – it is quite tame, and think will be a curiosity in your quarter'.[33] The family would later go on to found a zoo in Liverpool, as evidenced in letters from 1830–1831 between Henry Robertson Sandbach and Lord Derby.[34]

In 1825, one of the founding members of the family businesses, James McInroy, passed away. He left £172,913, about £7,000,000 million in today's money.[35] The partners of the firm were already rich but, ironically, thanks to emancipation in 1833, they were about to get considerably richer. Apart from Peter Miller Watson, most of the family were now based in Scotland or Liverpool. Liverpool is where I live, where I was born. Nearly twenty-two years ago, when I first discovered Andrew Watson, I was working in Everton, supporting asylum seekers unceremoniously deposited into the district in the aftermath of Tony Blair's dispersal policy. Liverpool City Council had refused to accept them because of a financial dispute, but the government had gone ahead anyway, buying two dilapidated tower blocks, scheduled for demolition, for the princely sum of £1 each and sending Liverpool's quota there: Afghans, Congolese, Rwandans, Kosovans, Kurds and others. It was murder – literally. One West African student was kicked to death, kids were beaten on the streets, fireworks were shot through the windows. One reputedly landed on a child's bed and set the bed on fire whilst a baby was in it. I was working as a business counsellor at the time. I speak a bit of Arabic, so I was able to communicate with some of the refugees and helped a number of them to start their own businesses.

The same run-down community I was working in was once a wealthy merchant neighbourhood, physically and socially elevated above the crowded mayhem of the River Mersey. This was where slave traders and merchants came to build their mansions. The area also offers a clear vantage point to the opening of the river, and you can see across 'the bar' as they call the point at which the River

Mersey meets the Irish Sea. As Everton is so high up the hill, you can see the ships on the horizon before they arrive in the Mersey. The local church of St George's is a Grade I listed building famous for its intricate ironwork.

St George's and Everton was the go-to place for the great and the good of Liverpool whose merchants desperately wanted to leave behind narrow streets and pungent town smells inspired by a myriad of businesses associated with the fast-growing port. Everton, with its panoramic views, was an oasis of calm and fresh air for those lucky enough to occupy the mansions and villas that now dominated the ridge in the early to middle 19th century. The church also has records of some of the enslaved people who lived there during the nineteenth century:

1817 – Charles Wallace: An African Negro boy servant to George Seeley, late of Brazil, now of Everton.
    1818 – Nicademus John Nickolas: Born in Santa Cruz, said to be 23 years old and a servant.
    1818 – Antonio Samuel Wylie: Born in Mozambique and carried to Brazil as a slave, a servant of John Wylie.
    1818 – Samuel Barnes: Born a slave in the island of Antigua, a gent's servant.
    1824 – Charles: An African Negro bought at Buenos Aires, about 21 years old servant to Fred Dickson.[36]

Their names are unknown to me, but their stories are familiar. On a recent visit, I explored the graveyard and came across the final resting places of some more recognisable names: Samuel Sandbach, Eliza Sandbach (née Robertson), Gilbert Sandbach, Margaret Tinne (née Sandbach) and John Abraham Tinne.[37]

There was an influx of poor Irish migrants, fleeing the potato famine of 1845–1852, who flooded into Everton, then on the outskirts of Liverpool. This influx caused an exodus of merchants from

Everton to the more lavish suburbs of Aigburth. As many plantation owners scuttled out of the area, those who had died before or during the immigration of poor starving Irish into the community, and were laid to rest at St George's Everton, namesake of the cathedral in Demerara, were the only remnants of that once rich community. It is of note that the cemetery never filled up at St George's in Everton, and it is thought that is because they agreed not to bury the poor amongst St George's rich patrons. When I worked in Everton, I passed by St George's almost daily, not knowing what – or rather who – lay beneath my feet. Today I live in Aigburth, the neighbourhood they moved to after leaving Everton. Somehow my movements seem unconsciously mapped to theirs, not just between my former workplace in Everton or my home in Aigburth but across the seas, to Guyana.

CHAPTER 9

'EXTENDING TO SLAVES PRACTICALLY ALL CIVIL RIGHTS BUT FREEDOM'

He who digs a pit for his brother falls into it.
– Arab proverb

The move towards Christianising enslaved Africans was accompanied by new rules, purportedly designed to improve their quality of life. As mentioned previously, under 'The Rules on the Treatment of Servants and Slaves', enslaved workers could only complain to the Fiscal,[1] who often sided with the plantation owners and managers. After trials between 1823–1824 in Trinidad, which transitioned from Spanish to English law, the British Parliament passed a new slave amelioration Bill in September 1826 which introduced the role of 'Protector of Slaves' to its colonies, something the Spanish had done in the eighteenth century. The responsibility was now increasingly on the managers and owners to keep records of those whom they had enslaved and the punishments inflicted upon them. One such report, dated 28 March 1828, was written by Charles Bird, the Deputy Protector of Slaves in Berbice.[2] As well as noting those who had recorded punishments incorrectly, or had given the 'wrong' punishment (a total of twenty-five), and the number of people sent to trial for 'ill-usage towards slaves' (six), the report also listed details such as how many marriages took place between slaves, how many manumissions were made and how much money had been saved by the enslaved Africans. Despite this, Trevor Burnard notes: 'No field or plantation slave, the Deputy Protector sadly lamented, had deposited a single Guilder in the bank.' This is not surprising, as there was no trust whatsoever in the plantation master, the colonial administrators, or white people in general. Why should there have been?

The Protector was supposed to safeguard the enslaved Africans, yet the information he and his deputy gathered was often misused for ulterior motives. Records of punishments could be used to convince abolitionists in Britain that the 'chastisements' of the enslaved were mere anomalies, and when administered, were somehow 'fair'. This could not be further from the truth.

A curious case brought before the Protector of Slaves that involved Robertson, Tinne, McInroy and Rainy gives an insight into the otherwise obscure history and the sexual exploitation of the enslaved by members of this family, as well as their absolute disregard for the humanity of Black people. Case No. 11 for the year 1830 in the return of the Protector of Slaves in Demerara stated:

No. 11.

1. – The name, age, sex, residence, and mode of employment of the Slave by whom, or on whose behalf the complaint was preferred? – *Sophia*, aged 22 years, female; residing on Plantation Bath and Kenderen Mahaicony and employed thereon.

2. – The Names of the owner or owners, and manager or managers of the Slave, their places of abode, their callings or professions? – The property of the estate of Robert Robertson, deceased, in the year 1819, and who was formerly a butcher of this town.

3. – The time when, and the person through whom, the complaint was first preferred to, or first reached the

Protector? – Complaint preferred on the 1st November, 1829, by Adela Tinne, Black woman, and reputed free, the mother of Sophia, and formerly belonging to P.F. Tinne,[3] late Colonial Secretary, now residing in England.

4. – The substance of the Complaint? – That previous to P.F. Tinne leaving this colony, He gave said Adela a free pass, stating that she was at liberty to go and get herself cured, she being diseased with sores; and further, that she should be free, and her issue after her, if she should ever have any; that subsequently, a Dr. Solomon Marsham offered to cure her for 10 Joe's; that he failed to do so, and therefore she did not pay him. He lived up the Demerara river at the time; that afterwards she got herself cured by another person, and had a child, said Sophia, for Bass Oxley. She then went to another part of the country, leaving said child with her mother Sophy McInroy,[4] who died during her absence, and the said child, Sophia, was left with Doctor S. Marsham, who took upon himself to pawn or sell her to a Mr. Robertson, now deceased, without any authority or claim whatsoever; that said Dr. Marsham kept the free pass above mentioned, and that said Sophia is entitled to her freedom.

5 –The Proceedings taken upon the Complaint, with the date of each successive Proceeding? – The Protector, on inquiry, finds that said Dr. Solomon Marsham was a man of colour, residing up the Demerara River, and that he has been dead for many years; that Bass Oxley and Sophy McInroy are also dead; that the estate of Robertson is now represented by Dr. John Waddell of this town, and that P. F. Tinne, stated to be the former owner of said Adela, and to have given her the free pass, now lives in Liverpool in England, and that he is represented in this Colony by George Rainy merchant. – 2nd November 1829. The Protector summoned Dr. John Waddell. – 16th February 1830. The Protector having requested the Crown Advocate's opinion in this case, receive

the following: – 'The statement of Adela should, in my opinion, be referred to Mr. Tinne, now in Liverpool, to ascertain its correctness. Adela will also prove that Sophia is her child, either by the evidence of the midwife, or some other person. If Adela is an African, she can obtain her manumission for want of registry; if not an African she is still the property of Mr. Tinne, as also her children, during his lifetime; and as Sophia has been registered, she will go to his heirs, but not the others, who will become entitled to freedom.

(signed) S. W. Gordon, Cn Adv.

17th February 1830. The Protector summoned Adela. 3rd April, G. Rainy, attorney of P.F. Tinne, having been referred to, can give no information on this subject, but will write to Mr Tinne about it.'[5]

What is significant is that if Philip F. Tinne had a Black child (Adela Tinne) with Sophia McInroy, a Black child of James McInroy – a partner in Sandbach Tinne & Co. – then a bloodline is established between the partners McInroy and Tinne, something which Dr Alison Clarke, a direct descendant of James McInroy, has always denied. McInroy also had another Black daughter, Grace Ann McInroy (b.1796) in Berbice, to a 'Catharine' (probably an enslaved woman, as she has no surname), a year before he was married in Scotland to his wife Elizabeth Moore on 25 December 1797, at Broomloan, Govan, in Glasgow. According to her grave index, Elizabeth was born on 2 May 1782 in Oranjestad, St Eustatius, Leeward Islands, Dutch West Indies.

Another Scottish Sandbach Tinne partner was Peter McLagan (1774–1860), who had at least two Black children: one, Janet McLagan (b. c.1816), and the other, Peter McLagan Jr (1823–1900). McLagan Sr's mixed-race son went to Scotland, and is found in multiple census records, including the 1841 census at the age of eighteen with his father, aged sixty-five, living at 77 Great King Street, New Town, Edinburgh. In the 1851 census, 'McLagan is enumerated as Peter McLagan Jr., head of the household of Pumpherston Farm. He is unmarried, aged 28, and a farmer of 400 (acres) employing 30 labourers & 6 masons.'[6] His birthplace is given as Demerara. Also in his household are three servants; Jessie Thomson, aged 22, a house maid; Elizabeth Patterson, aged 39, a cook; and David Wardlaw, aged 14, a groom.' He was clearly now a member of the landed gentry in his own right at a mere twenty-eight years of age. He was also destined to sit in Parliament as Scotland's first ever Black MP.

Before his demise in 1860, McLagan senior was also recorded as co-owner of Plantations Coffee Grove and Caledonia with Samuel Sandbach (who had died in 1851). Both plantations feature in the Sandbach Tinne financial accounts, referring to the production of coffee, cotton, cane and plantains. A letter of 3 January 1822, from Peter McLagan senior in Demerara to Sandbach Tinne & Co., in Liverpool, stated:

> The gross cotton in at Caledonia was 60,000, still picking some & had good deal of pods on the trees. No coffee picked I believe since the end of November, the manager says he expects the coffee to turn out 100,000 [lbs] when cleaned off. They are a little scarce of plantains from the very squally weather they had there after the rain commenced . . . They will continue grinding a field or two of canes at Coffee Grove . . . At Brothers, they calculated a few days back at 68,000 gross cotton, still picking a little and the manager says he expected to turn out 50,000 lbs coffee. On the Woodlands a few days back, the manager wrote that he expected what cotton in there would turn out 200 bales.[7]

This demonstrates a huge mercantile interest between McLagan and both Sandbach Tinne and McInroy Parker, as well as an established familial tie through their Black children between all the key partners – Sandbach, Tinne, McInroy, McLagan and Parker.

When combining the information held in the company correspondences with accounts such as the one mentioned in the returns of the Protector of Slaves, we may not see everything that was going on, but it provides a snapshot of the sort of things that might have previously found their way to the desk of the Fiscal, and a residue of evidence to a side of the family that was often deliberately obscured. If not for the numerous twists of fate and deaths of individuals, we may never have known about the Black woman Adela Tinne and her child Sophia. But accounts within the statistics presented in the returns also offered an opportunity to planters to mislead Parliament and the abolitionist movement back in England, to believe that things were better for the enslaved than was actually the case. For example, the number of marriages (something previously strictly forbidden to enslaved Africans) could be used to indicate a happy, loving workforce, as was also reported for the religious instruction they now received and its efficacy in promoting 'good behaviour' as part of the so-called 'civilising' process. The number of manumissions in Bird's report was sixty-four. These factors distinguished the free Africans living in the colony from those enslaved, and was reflected in the census counts. There were a growing number of 'free persons of colour', which intimates that the majority of 'free people' were manumitted because they had white blood in them; the limited numbers of free Blacks would – in most cases – be the mothers of mixed-race children, such as Minkey, Andrew Rose's enslaved African woman whom he manumitted when she gave birth to his daughter Anna (or Hannah) Rose, the mother of Andrew Watson. Such children were usually born of rape and sexual exploitation by white men. Only the owners of the enslaved had the power to manumit an enslaved person, thus affording them their freedom at their absolute discretion, but as we see from Sophia's case, even those manumitted could be arbitrarily re-enslaved, and their children also.

In 1831, the rights of the enslaved were extended further by the Consolidation Slave Ordinance, 'extending to slaves practically all civil rights but freedom'.[8] Yet at the same time as these supposed 'improvements' were being introduced, the low price of sugar was increasing the pressure on the plantation owners, who in turn intensified their demands on the workload of the enslaved. Henry Dalton refers to a diminution in the price of sugar from around 1828 to 1832, which 'added to the general panic' as the possibility of emancipation became more real. He painted a picture of the plantations of British Guiana operating at full capacity. At the same time, both Sandbach Tinne and Gladstone had been undertaking a gradual rationalisation of their enslaved labour force, selling off whole gangs at a premium, knowing that they would be rendered worthless upon emancipation, and ramping up production by squeezing the life out of those who were left to work the vast plantations at an accelerated pace. All of this to indiscriminately maximise profits at a terrible human cost. Dalton states: 'The provision grounds and plantain-walks on estates were left unattended to, in order that all the strength of physical power should be concentrated in the manufacture of sugar and rum. It seemed as if the proprietors had determined that the powers of the slave should be taxed to the utmost extremity, and, like the flagging spirits of a jaded beast, roused to a last superhuman performance.'

This is the same writer who, in earlier pages, had declared that slavery 'possessed some advantages' and that from 'the cradle to the grave every want was supplied and the animal lived, worked, and died without tasting that bitter experience which wrings the stout heart of many a more civilised peasant in the struggle for subsistence'.[9] Again we see how the enslaved Africans were dehumanised and referred to as livestock rather than people, something evident both in the McInroy Sandbach slave auctions, which often occurred in a barn with the animals, and also in McInroy Sandbach and Co.'s accounts where Africans were commodified as assets, mortgaged or rented out to other planters as you would a horse and sold on the auction block like cattle.

The House of Lords, in the 1831–1832 session,[10] discussed the demographic anomaly within the sugar plantation economies of the Caribbean, querying why the population of enslaved Africans was diminishing, despite population growth among the enslaved in other colonies. In answer, the speaker (Thomas Fowell Buxton) retorted that 'the terrible human cost of producing sugar is laid bare'. He declared that 'no slave population in sugar colonies . . . where a large proportion of sugar is grown, has hitherto increased'. The exchange concludes that 'the sugar cultivation is of that hard description of toil, that where it is pushed to a great extent it tends to diminish human life'. It was then asked; 'Do you believe that the labour necessary for the cultivation of sugar is so excessive?' The response was 'I believe that it is.'

In a bid to protect their fortunes, the slave-owners came together once again to petition Parliament. On 7 October 1831, a Mr Goulburn presented a petition from the West India Planters and Merchants of Liverpool in a debate on the Sugar Refining Bill, which proposed importing unrefined sugar from 'foreign' producers, i.e. not from British colonies. The petitioners stated that, according to law, an equal amount of foreign sugar imported into Britain should be exported, once refined – yet they claimed, 'it was well known that this was not the case. This caused some competition against our own colonial sugar in the market,' they complained, 'with the monopoly of which our own planters had been flattered.'[11] They went on to accuse certain sugar refiners of bringing in molasses, which was not subject to the sugar duty; to produce 'refined sugar of an inferior quality' that would be sent abroad, while foreign sugar was used for home consumption without any legal difficulties. There was now, they added, strong reason for believing the monopoly was 'a delusion'. A copy of this petition was also sent, by request, to the Bristol West India Association. It was signed by various Liverpool merchants, including – of course – Samuel Sandbach, Charles Stuart Parker, John Abraham Tinne, Henry Robertson Sandbach, Robertson Gladstone and the influential John Gladstone.[12]

Mercantile lobby groups were commonplace, such as the 'Meeting of the gentlemen appointed by the several committees of the trade in London to confer on the subject of the export of cotton wool from the United States', which took place on 19 March 1813 at the City of London Tavern, with James Baillie MP and John

Gladstone MP on the list of those attending. It was through such powerful lobby groups that slave-owners ensured that emancipation – if it was to be delivered – would be done strictly on terms favourable to themselves. In a parliamentary debate on an anti-slavery petition in 1826, for example, MP James Blair accused 'Methodists and dissenters' of inflaming the public mind by misrepresentation and dismissed the signatories of the petition as unimportant. Interestingly, notes David Alston, 'Mr. Blair was perfectly certain he spoke from good authority; indeed, he had been fully authorised to use the name of his informant, Charles S. Parker, a man of great respectability.'[13]

In May 1823 Thomas Fowell Buxton stated in Parliament:

> We owe large and liberal atonement. And I do thank
> God, we still have it in our power to make some
> compensation. We have it in our power to sweeten a little
> the bitterness of captivity, to give the slaves of the West
> Indies something to render life more endurable, to give them
> something like justice and protection, to interpose a jury
> between the Negro and the brutality of his master's servant,
> to declare that the slave shall not be torn from the cottage he
> has built, from the children he has reared, from the female
> whom he loves, above all, for that is effectual compensation,
> we may give him the truths of the Christian religion, which,
> as yet, we have withheld. For his children, there is a wider
> range of recompense. We may strip them of every vestige of
> servitude; and, by taking upon ourselves, for a season, the
> whole burthen of their maintenance, education, and
> religious instruction, we may raise them into a happy,
> contented, enlightened, free peasantry.[14]

In a remarkable piece of political manoeuvring, John Gladstone MP managed to turn this around so that the ones who received the compensation were the enslavers, not the enslaved. When the idea was first pitched, the West India Committee did not think it was viable, so John Gladstone MP turned to James Baillie MP in Bristol, and together they formed the aforementioned British Guiana Association. On 29 October 1823, Baillie wrote to the Earl of Liverpool stating:

> My Lord
>
> As Chairman of a meeting of the British Guiana Association held on the 23rd last, I take the liberty of enclosing a copy of the resolutions passed at that meeting relative to the alarming insurrection in Demerara to which I entrust your Lordships particular attention,
>
> I have the honor to be
>
> My Lord
>
> Your Lordship's most obedient servant
>
> J. Baillie MP.[15]

The purpose of the British Guiana Association was to get the most powerful of the slave traders to convene a caucus and work out how to get that 'large and liberal atonement' for themselves. Sensing an opportunity to turn misfortune into fortune, Baillie and Gladstone conspired to add legitimacy to their claims for compensation. Among the many resolutions passed relating to the Demerara uprising of 1823, condemning the Revd. John Smith and Canning's amelioration measures, they resolved that 'whereas by measures thus emanating from this country, a serious loss of property has been occasioned, it is the opinion of this meeting that the sufferers are entitled to a full compensation from Parliament, and this Association will unite with them in taking the most efficient measures for attaining this object.'[16]

Once they had agreed on a proposed compensation package that they felt they could sell, they approached the Liverpool West India Association again, and this time were successful. With no more need for the British Guiana Association, it was disbanded; and with the might of the Liverpool West India Association[17] behind it, the proposed compensation was transformed from a loan to a grant. It was then redirected from Buxton's proposition to compensate the enslaved, to Gladstone's proposal to compensate the enslavers, leaving the enslaved with absolutely nothing.

When I interviewed the now late William G. Williamson, one of the co-authors of the book on Robertson Gladstone, *A Visit to Demerara 1828–1829*, which was published by the Liverpool Athenaeum – a private members' club founded in 1797 by enslaver George Case and abolitionist William Roscoe 'to provide a meeting place where ideas and information could be exchanged in pleasant surroundings'[18] – he shared some of his own impressions about how John Gladstone MP managed such a coup for the slave-owners: 'My impression of John Gladstone, the patriarch, was he was a very, very astute, clever, dry, miserable, penny-pinching Scot, who really just lived for business, and was very controlling of his family and his business . . . that comes across very easily.'[19]

As chair of the West India Association, and also a sitting MP, John Gladstone knew that slavery was going to be abolished, and he wanted compensation for the loss of the enslaved Africans that he saw as his rightful property. Yet, as one of the biggest slave-owners in the country at the time, he could not really advocate for himself, so he groomed his son William for political office. As Nicholas Draper notes, 'it is hard not to see John Gladstone's influence working not only through his own undistinguished spell as an MP, but through his son William, whose first speech, famously, defended his father's record as a slave owner in British Guiana'.[20] Interestingly, Draper adds that during the June 1831 election, the finance committee behind pro-West Indies Tory candidate Lord Sandon included enslavers John Moss, George Grant and Samuel Sandbach, illustrating how John Gladstone MP was not the only one in the family using politics to push his agenda. W. E. Gladstone owed his political rise in part to Sandbach also.

This wasn't the first time that slave-owners had sought compensation for the loss of people they had enslaved. We have already seen how, after Fédon's rebellion in 1795, the King agreed to give Grenada's plantation owners a substantial loan (some of which was never paid back) to re-establish their investments. Looking at the careful language of abolitionists such as Buxton, it is not too hard to see how the planters were able to convince Parliament of their need. While he may have toughened his stance in the ten years since his 1823 speech, it is worth remembering Buxton's anxiety not to offend. He described the West India merchants as 'rather unfortunate than culpable' that their manner of business (i.e. slavery) had changed from being generally acceptable to unacceptable, adding, 'I do consider it no slight matter to introduce any motion painful to their feelings.'

As John Gladstone MP and his son William Ewart Gladstone concentrated their energies on getting the best deal out of abolition, the wider family firms ensured everyone kept making money off the back of enslaved labour. In 1831, McInroy Sandbach & Co. in Demerara listed John Gladstone & Co. as a consignee on a manifest of the ship the *Parker*, cleared for sailing to Liverpool on 12 May, marking the Gladstones down for ten hogsheads of sugar. They were also busy discussing the future, diversifying their investments, and continuing to make plans for life after abolition. On 12 June 1824, for instance, a letter from McInroy Sandbach & Co. in Demerara to Sandbach Tinne & Co. in Liverpool, briefly mentioned 'the shares you have taken in the New West India Company', demonstrating that, by investing in the Dutch trading company, the Sandbach Tinne dynasty at this time saw the slave trading of their European neighbour as less precarious, which would have been a fair prediction given that the Netherlands did not abolish slavery in Suriname and the Dutch West Indian colonies until 1863.[21] Another letter, from 'N. French, Eliza French, Donna French' to McInroy Parker & Co., dated 13 May 1823, refers to a dispute over their brother's plantation, Phoenix Park, and a concern that the slaves were being sold too cheaply: '11 effective Negroes were picked out the gang & sold much under the value, in proportion as my brother was charged for 5, the demand on him for the small number was £1230, whereas he only gets credit for £1440 for 11 disposed of.' McInroy Parker & Co., acting as agents for the French family estate, sold eleven people on their behalf for almost the price of five they had previously charged them for.

They demand that 'no further sale of Negroes or estate shall take place until a general & impartial appraisement is made by two respectable planters, the one an English or Irishman & the other a Dutchman'. It is clear that the three writers are not only well informed as to the selling process but also to the political situation of the time, which is evidenced in their further statement that 'As for the bill talked of in Parliament to be brought out & passed against the slave trade, that ought to enhance the value in the different colonies.' In 1833, as the ink on the Emancipation Act was still drying, Thomas Garnett and William Jones in Demerary wrote to 'W. R. Sandbach Esq, Messrs Sandbach Tinne & Co., Liverpool' referring to an ongoing conversation about plantation labour. In the letter, dated 10 October 1833, they mention the need for more workers to be brought in, perhaps to replace the enslaved Africans shortly to receive their freedom. It reads, 'We notice your remarks about immigrants. It is certain that without a regular supply of them, our crops must fall off, and the government is so lukewarm about it and makes us pay so high for anything it undertakes on our behalf, that we have no confidence in it.'

Meanwhile, a succession of letters from the same year appear to show the main founders of the family business planning their exit from merchant life. A letter dated 21 December 1833 from Samuel Sandbach to Philip Frederick Tinne seeks approval for his retirement plans. In the response, dated 27 December, Tinne not only accepts the proposal, but expresses his wish to retire at the same time and transfer his shares to his son, John Abraham Tinne. Whilst Sandbach's retirement is confirmed, Tinne's was not, and he was forced to stay on before eventually transitioning his shareholding to his son.

CHAPTER 10

EMANCIPATION, FINALLY – BUT NOT REALLY

Silence is half of consent.
– Native American proverb

On 28 August 1833, an Act for the Abolition of Slavery throughout the British Colonies was passed, but what is less well known is the rest of its lengthy title, which reads . . . 'for Promoting the Industry of the Manumitted Slaves; and for Compensating the Persons Hitherto Entitled to the Services of Such Slaves'.[1] Slavery was to be abolished, but under two conditions. Firstly, that the enslaved Africans, once emancipated on 1 August 1834, should receive 'Provision' to promote their 'Industry' and 'good conduct'. This was the excuse given for the introduction of a system that would force the newly emancipated population to remain bonded for a period of four to six years as 'apprentices' in roles they had already been performing whilst enslaved. Secondly was the proviso that 'a reasonable compensation should be made to the persons hitherto entitled to the services of such slaves for the loss which they will incur by being deprived of their right to such services'. Henry Dalton, somewhat absurdly, describes this as 'an act of pure magnanimity'. He asserts that 'The concession was voluntary; it was neither extorted by threats, nor founded upon sordid calculations of profit.'[2] Nothing could have been further from the truth.

The scale of the compensation awarded – as proposed to the Treasury – was at first a loan of £15,000,000, which then was extended to £20,000,000. What had been meant for the enslaved victims was now to be divided among the perpetrators of the evil enterprise, the enslavers. What's more, the idea that the loan, which the Exchequer would pay back over the next 170 years with taxpayers' money, was also flipped from loans to the enslavers by way of compensation to non-repayable grants. Montgomery Martin reports that the proportion allotted to British Guiana was £4,297,117 – over a fifth of the total.[3] From the Sandbach Tinne dynasty, the claims came rolling in. According to the invaluable UCL Legacies of British Slavery database, in addition to individual and separate claims, Philip Frederick Tinne, Charles Stuart Parker, Henry Robertson Sandbach, George Rainy, William Robertson Sandbach, James Patrick McInroy, John Abraham Tinne and George Parker received substantial sums of money through a number of shared claims, including £20,752 14s 3d for 402 enslaved Africans on Plantation Leonora,[4] £15,482 14s 8d for 292 enslaved Africans on Plantations La Jalousie and Fellowship,[5] and £14,231 7d for 261 persons enslaved on Java, Bordeaux and Regt Door Zee.[6] When you aggregate the claims of the Sandbach Tinne partners for their own plantations, and contested claims over other plantation owners who were mortgaged or otherwise indebted to them, they were the second highest recipients of compensation. Additional claims by non-partners within the family, such as Peter Miller Watson and others, would see that proportion increase further.

Using the National Archives currency converter, the compensation for Leonora alone – a plantation that Sandbach Tinne paid £600,000 for and which yielded around £100,000 per year – their claim works out at approximately £1 million in today's money.[7] There were claims and counter claims as everyone rushed to squeeze what they could out of the Treasury. Famously, John Gladstone MP was the largest individual recipient of slavery compensation – over £112,000, the equivalent of £11,954,297 today[8] – for the 'loss' of over 2,500 enslaved Africans from his plantations in Demerara and Jamaica.

Gladstone had been transformed from the pariah of 1823, held responsible for the insurrection and the losses of the Demerara planters, to the toast of the West India Association of Liverpool, who presented him with a commemorative silver salver. The inscription reads:

> Presented to John Gladstone, Esquire, by the West India Association of Liverpool in Testimony of the High Sense They Entertain of the Value of his Services so Actively and Beneficially Employed in Settling the Conditions of the Emancipation of the Slaves in the West India Colonies AD.1833.[9]

This is clear evidence that Gladstone was in fact the architect of the scheme, and it is therefore unsurprising that he was its largest single beneficiary. Emancipation may have technically arrived, but many planters still saw their workers as slaves, and even referred to them as such. In a letter to McInroy Parker & Co., dated 16 May 1835, James Cooke wrote advising the company on engines for their plantations, suggesting two 12hp engines rather than one 25hp engine. 'In case of accident, always one of them might be calculated on, and that engine in case of need, might by two relays of slaves, go on without intermission.'

In British Guiana, news of the apprenticeship scheme had been greeted by the newly so-called 'emancipated' African population with protest. On 3 August 1834, two days after what is now known in Guyana as Emancipation Day, strike action commenced on plantations in Essequibo. *The Guyana Story* records the events, which began when 'Charles Bean – proprietor of Plantation Richmond – joined with the other planters to kill sixty-five pigs belonging to his workers, after claiming that the animals destroyed the roots of the young canes.' The real reason, Odeen Ishmael adds, was 'to cut off any alternative livelihood for their workers, so that the apprentices 'would remain bound to estate labour' – the same reason that some planters cut down fruit trees, to eliminate the sources of free food, thus further perpetuating dependency upon their former enslavers for basic survival.

Nonetheless, the protest grew and on 9 August, about 700 workers downed tools and assembled at Trinity churchyard in the somewhat inappropriately named area of 'La Belle Alliance', named after the command post where Napoleon famously 'met his Waterloo'. The troops were called and descended on the protest. Out of the crowd emerged a leader, a worker from Plantation Richmond called Damon. He hoisted a flag on a pole 'as a sign of their freedom and independence from the planters'. Charles Bean and other planters called on the soldiers to open fire, but they did not. The crowd dispersed two days later, on 11 August, with the arrival of the new governor, James Carmichael Smyth (who served from 26 June 1833 to 27 June 1838). The next day, Smyth ordered the arrest of Damon and the other leaders. They were tried for rebellion and found guilty. Some were sentenced to imprisonment and severe floggings, others to transportation to Australia, but Damon was sentenced to be hanged. Unlike the case of Jack Gladstone, however, there was no last-minute reprieve. Damon was hanged in front of the newly opened Parliament Buildings in Georgetown on midday on 13 October 1834. Today, those same buildings house Guyana's National Assembly. Compared to the likes of Cuffy, Damon comes in for much less attention, observes Alvin O. Thompson, 'but he is also gaining recognition as a freedom fighter'.

Damon and a number of his colleagues could not reconcile the notion that they were liberated from slavery with the fact that they were compelled by the Emancipation Act to work for their overlords on the same plantations or other locations, for a period of four to six years, as so-called 'apprentices', depending on whether they had worked in predial enslavement[10] (mostly land-based or as field hands) or non-predial enslavement (mostly as domestic or house servants) at the time of emancipation. Anyone under the age of six was automatically exempted and freed by default. The intense despair of the enslaved at their lack of freedom upon emancipation, despite the huge sums paid to their owners that should have gone to them, enraged them, but sensing that freedom was somehow inevitable, they opted to lay down their tools and 'engaged in passive forms of resistance'.[11] Thompson, however, points to the work of Hugh Tommy Payne (a former Guyanese archivist and the writer of the only detailed study of this revolt), who he says believed that the planters, in association with certain members of the colonial government, 'goaded them [the protestors] into physical confrontation that led to bloodshed'.

For years, Damon was remembered simply by a large cross located in the graveyard where he protested – and where, some say, he was buried.[12] In 1988, a monument by Guyanese sculptor Ivor Thom was unveiled in what is now known as 'Damon Square', featuring a defiant Damon, wielding a flag. The square, adds Thompson, 'has become the focal point for commemorative events, especially those involving struggle and martyrdom, in Essequibo county'.

Apprenticeship was essentially an extension of enslavement, providing an additional four years of mandatory cheap labour to the plantation owners, already enriched by their substantial compensation. Yet that was still not enough for the avaricious Gladstones. In a speech to the House of Commons on 30 March 1838, William Ewart Gladstone, long erroneously regarded as an 'abolitionist', urged the government for the 'apprenticeship system to be prolonged for an extra two years', no doubt at the behest of his greedy father:

> I beseech the House to consider the utter impossibility of any adequate legislative preparation for the abolition of the apprenticeship in August 1838. Let me suppose . . . that you could carry your resolution and pass your Bill in June. It might arrive in the West Indies by the 1st of August. We require poor laws, police laws, jury laws, electoral laws,

vagrant laws, laws for prison discipline. We require at least a currency in which it may be physically possible to pay wages to the mass of the apprentice population.[13]

Lord J. Russell responded, referring to British Guiana specifically by citing a speech by the governor of the colony of 3 February 1838, in which he reportedly echoed Gladstone's suggested extension: 'I consider the continuance of the present system until the 1st August 1840, as identified with the future welfare of this magnificent province. It appears to me, that if in British Guiana we are allowed to continue as we are, there is every prospect of our being enabled to slide almost imperceptibly into a state of perfect freedom.'

Russell went on to paint a rosy picture of the apprenticeship system in British Guiana and daily life for the 'apprentices', noting that the 'lash' was 'only used in cases of theft', and that 'women are not sent to the treadmill' – a pretty low bar for workers' rights. 'The advantages resulting from labour are becoming daily more understood and better appreciated by the apprentice,' he continued, patronisingly, as if the apprentices were doing a different job than the backbreaking labour they were forced to carry out while enslaved. He claimed that a 'kind and a good feeling between the employer and the labourer is everywhere rapidly gaining ground'. The paltry token sum the apprentice was paid was apparently enough to allow him to 'take care of his wife and family, and to provide himself and them, with those articles of comfort and luxury to which they have become habituated'. Russell concluded, 'When things are going on so well as in British Guiana, it appears to me, that it would be little short of an act of folly to offer any interruption to the present system.'

There was support for the extension of apprenticeship in British Guiana too. At a meeting of the Court of Policy on 20 June 1838, Dr Michael McTurk gave notice of a motion to bring in a bill to abolish the system of apprenticeship.[14] According to Emília Viotti da Costa, 'Peter Rose (1787–1859) business partner of Peter Miller Watson, brother-in-law to Philip Frederick Tinne and uncle of Anna (or Hannah) Rose (the mother of footballer Andrew Watson) voted against McTurk's motion. This followed a debate on the slave trade on Monday 29 January 1838 in the House of Lords where Lord Brougham castigated the unscrupulous and greedy planters – such as Gladstone, Sandbach, Tinne, Watson et al. – stating that not only had the people of Britain been burdened with this debt 'for nothing' but that if 'the Bill of 1833 would occasion a loss to the planter, not one million, or one pound, or one penny of this enormous sum would ever have been granted to the owners of slaves? When it is found that all this money has been paid for nothing, have we not an equal right to require that whatever can be done on the part of the planters to further a measure which has already been so gainful to them, shall be performed without delay?'[15]

No matter how much they received, they always wanted more, and they pushed it to the limits.

Peter Rose was also embroiled in the Sandbach Tinne business as they carried cargo for him on their ships. Despite his role at the Court of Policy, a letter of 15 March 1838 from McInroy Sandbach & Co., Demerara, to Sandbach Tinne & Co., Liverpool shows a cargo manifest for the ship the *Johnson*, where Peter Rose is recorded as having on board '10 Hogsheads (Hhd) of sugar, 10 Puncheons of rum, 36 Hhd of rum, 36 barrels of rum, 11 Puncheons of molasses, 36 bales of cotton, and a Hhd of wine', just five months before the end of the so-called 'apprenticeship' system.

Apprenticeship had allowed plantation owners to carry on production almost seamlessly. A document titled 'Export of Staple Articles of Produce of Berbice from 1824 to 1839' shows that gallons of rum exported from the colony dropped from 555,170 in 1832 to 246,510 in 1833 and 240,790 in 1834, before quickly bouncing back and even exceeding pre-abolition figures with 584,210 gallons exported in 1835. At this time, other types of products exported from British Guiana are not related to sugar and cotton. A 'Return of Sugar, Rum, Molasses, Coffee, Cotton and other Productions of the Colony of British Guiana, exported therefrom', produced by the Custom House in Georgetown, Demerara, in 1850, shows the changing market demand. After 1838, exports of sugar and rum fluctuate but generally follow a downturn, molasses and coffee too, with cotton exports stopping completely (or not recorded) in 1844. We see the emergence of charcoal, the export of which appears to begin in 1843, while 'cocoa nuts' (or coconuts) are on the rise also. Other more niche items listed include 'Horns', 'Hides' and 'Wallaba Shingles'. A shipping manifest cleared on 11 September 1849 mentions cargo from shipper James Stuart containing fifteen barrels of rum, with the consignee listed as 'Gladstone & Co.', alongside the plantation 'mark' or cipher 'GV', suggesting Plantation Goedverwagting on the east coast.[16]

During this period, John Gladstone continued to reap the benefits of cheap labour on the back of a new scheme that he'd pioneered – that of 'indentureship' – within the colony. Not content with the end of the apprenticeship scheme, Gladstone re-purposed old legislation around indentured labour, reapplied it to the Caribbean and sought permission from the government in a letter to Sir George Grey in 1837 to import 'Coolies' from India and China.[17]

We get a more direct insight into the position of other Sandbach Tinne family members regarding the end of so-called apprenticeships, from a letter written by Peter Miller Watson to Samuel Sandbach the day after the motion was passed:

> A motion [was] made yesterday by Dr McTurk for the abolition of the apprenticeship on the 1st August . . . we think it probable that the system cannot last. McTurk will have the support of a large number of the resident proprietors . . . some representatives of considerable estates are impowered by their constituents to accede to an immediate abolition . . . some gentlemen . . . have made up their minds to *'free their people . . .'* whether there is a legislative enactment to that effect or not . . . unconditional

emancipation cannot be averted & that too immediately. It has caused a great sensation in town . . . the news must spread among the labouring classes in the Country and revived their anxieties and expectations . . . [18]

The motion having prevailed meant that 'on August 1st 1838, the slaves were made free'.[19] This also demonstrates that Peter Miller Watson – despite the Emancipation Act of 1833 – still considered his 'apprentices' prior to 1 August 1838 as 'slaves'.

In a bid to show that 'apprenticeship continues to bear a marketable value', William Ewart Gladstone referred in his speech to the case 'of about 100 Negroes, whose time was purchased at the same period (December 1837) by the Government of British Guiana, at about £100. sterling, for each labourer'. That the government of British Guiana, the administrators of British rule, were purchasing African labour after the emancipation of the enslaved, at the epicentre of British power – Westminster – shows the incongruity and entanglements of the British state with enslavement. Gladstone even seems to call for further money to be paid out to former slave owners, citing the case of an unnamed planter 'holding four estates in British Guiana' who received £72,100 in compensation money, leaving £227,600 'against the estates'. Gladstone goes on, 'He would gladly agree to dispose of his interest in them after 1840 for £100,000 payable at that time; leaving a loss of £127,600 or about 42½ per cent on the entire value.' What he appears to be suggesting is a second batch of compensation for his own father for the loss of his 'apprentices', after having already had over £112,000 for the loss of his enslaved Africans. It appears that John Gladstone's sons followed his obsession with money while tragedy befell their sister. Willie Williamson from the Liverpool Athenaeum told me in our interview that, after their father's death, William and Robertson Gladstone fell out over his estate, while their sister, Helen Jane, joined a nunnery and later became addicted to 'laudanum' (opium).

The Act for the Abolition of the Slave Trade 1807 in Britain was, in theory, the last nail in the coffin for the official practice of kidnapping people from their homes, shipping them across oceans and forcing them to work on plantations. Yet legality had rarely been a priority for plantation owners. Though the transatlantic trade in enslaved Africans had been outlawed in 1807 by the British, others had not yet banned it. The trade continued. The ban on the importation of enslaved Africans, while still permitting the existence of chattel slavery in the British colonies, meant that the children of enslaved Africans in Demerara and throughout the British Empire between 1807 and 1833 were not born free. Even Dalton admits that in the colonies of British Guiana, 'slaves continued under certain restrictions and regulations to be imported into the colony, in limited numbers, from other sources for many years afterwards'.[20] The trade was also still legal in the Netherlands until 1814 and in Brazil until the 1830s, with Brazilian internal enslavement permitted until the 1880s. I found documentation that between 1840 and 1847, a total of 111,039 enslaved Africans were listed as 'Casualties on Passage' on voyages from West Africa into Brazil and the Spanish colonies. In this seven-year period alone, 332,007 Africans were transported onto plantations, and a mere 31,180 are listed as 'captured by cruisers' – meaning the British Navy, who were tasked with enforcing a naval blockade off the coast of West Africa to enforce the Abolition Act of 1807.

According to a *Missionary Intelligencer* of 1847,[21] unregulated slave trading existed 'south of the line' (i.e. the equator) on the west coast of Africa, and also 'upon the eastern coast, between the settlements of the Red Sea'. A House of Lords Select Committee referred to the matter in a summary of evidence which stated, 'With the actual and direct effect of the squadron in suppressing the slave trade, it has been proved that, when its operations began, the traffic extended over almost every part of Africa, from the equator as far as Cape Verde, a distance of almost 2500 miles.' It went on to say that removal of the squadron would lead to a proliferation of piracy and that would 'destroy the legitimate trade now daily increasing between Great Britain and Africa; whilst all the beginnings of civilization and all attempts to Christianise Africa would be wholly defeated and destroyed'. The so-called 'legitimate trade' he was referring to was one that had been enjoyed by, among others, the abolitionist William Roscoe, who had two ships employed in the Africa trade prior to his demise in 1831, while, notably, John Gladstone also named a ship after him, the *Roscoe*. This reinforces the notion that the new business model proposed by the missionaries, to 'civilise' and 'Christianise' the Africans, would provide more income through colonisation in Africa than trafficking enslaved Africans to the colonies, a paradigm to which Roscoe wholeheartedly subscribed and from which he profited directly as one of its pioneers, along with the Church.

The *Missionary Intelligencer* also makes mention of a 'Commander D. Robertson' who served on the southern west coast and appeared before a House of Lords committee. He reported that from February 1849 to February 1850, 'in addition to the efforts of our own cruisers', who were enforcing the British blockade against the slave trade, 'the Portuguese cruisers', which until recently had not enforced their own ban (which came into effect in Portugal itself in 1761, but not in the Atlantic until 1836), 'have latterly become very active, and their Commodore appeared to be perfectly in earnest in putting down the slave trade'. Prior to this period, the Portuguese were often free to trade south of the line, for example shipping enslaved Africans from Angola to Brazil, as the British ships were mainly patrolling north of the line. Also, due to the ongoing territorial tensions with its former colony of America, Britain mostly left North American ships alone to avoid triggering another war. Some slave traders took advantage of this loophole, decking their ships with an American flag and sailing through the British blockade.

When the British did seize so-called 'illegal vessels', the issue arose of what to do with the enslaved on board. Some were taken to the British Overseas Territory of St Helena in the South Atlantic, and the women and girls were sold into prostitution to be used as so-called comfort women for the Portuguese seamen passing through. Others were indentured and sent on to the Caribbean as labourers, or returned to other parts of Africa, often thousands of miles away from their homes, in some cases, only to be re-enslaved. The missionaries often questioned the cause of the British blockade, crediting the British naval force for progress made while noting that 'we would ask whether the preventative squadron is justly designated a costly absurdity. Let the British public candidly weigh the evidence of the facts and then decide whether it is indeed the case that after 20 years trial, the African squadron has been proved wholly ineffective for the purpose other than the very mischievous one of injuring our commerce and endangering our national friendship with well-disposed powers.' This was a reference to the seizure of vessels from other European slave traders and the damage to relations with countries like the Netherlands, Spain, Portugal and France.

Whether or not the blockade was actually effective at reducing the transatlantic slave trade, it offered a secondary bonus. Looking at the shipping registers for Liverpool, I noticed that in many cases the registration date of the ship was much later than the year it was built. Sometimes this was a case of a ship being scrapped and a new one built with the same name, but at other times it suggested a more cunning (and cost-effective) process. A stream of European wars gave merchant companies an excuse to seize the ships of their enemies, in the name of defending Britain and its colonies, and then re-registering them as British. During the Napoleonic Wars, for instance, French ships could be seized – and those of their allies too. The 'Short History of the Tinne Family' records that the Sandbach Tinne & Co. flag (horizontal stripes of blue, white and blue) 'was hurriedly made from a seaman's shirt and blue canvas trousers in response to the challenge of the French privateer'. In 1805, the narrative continues that King George III granted the firm 'Letters of Marque and Reprisal . . . which entitled them to fly the Royal Navy's pennant at the main'.[22] This rendered them officially as 'privateers'.

Following the British blockade, the number of prize vessels being re-registered (and renamed) in Liverpool grew exponentially. If they intercepted a Spanish galleon with enslaved Africans on board, they would often seize the ship, disembark the slaves, bring the galleon back to Liverpool and re-register it under an English name. Some ships were cut up in Sierra Leone, then reassembled and refloated. A whole commerce grew out of prize vessels. Given that the Portuguese and Spanish had superior ships to the British, the chance to acquire vessels without the time and costs of commissioning the building of a new ship was enticing.

From 1786 to 1805 there were '2,178 primary registrations of ships in Liverpool' – in addition to 1,013 marked *'de novo'*.[23] Registrations *de novo* were re-registrations of captured prize vessels, built elsewhere at another time and flagged in another country. So the date of construction, the port of registration and the name of the ship would differ when re-registered in Britain. A ship built and registered in 1815 in Lisbon, Portugal, and flying a Portuguese flag, might have a registration in Liverpool in 1820 and be flying a British flag. The name would also be changed, but it would be the same ship. From 1786 to 1805, 370 ships were built in Liverpool, but about the same number were seized by British privateers and registered as prize vessels,[24] an almost 50-50 split. The Navy could only be in so many places at once after 1807, so the shipping companies were now in a position where, having gained Letters of Marque as privateers, they could go out, arm their ships and seize any vessels carrying enslaved Africans – all in the name of the King. A Letter of Marque was all that distinguished a privateer from a pirate. Sandbach Tinne ships often came to Liverpool to be fitted out with cannon by Fawcett & Preston, a Lancashire firm of armourers and engineers who also supplied them with sugar machinery for their plantations. William Fawcett appears in a family album, along with Samuel Sandbach, P.F. Tinne and others. There is no doubt that Sandbach Tinne were also privateers, and as mentioned earlier, it is my firm belief that they also engaged in illegal slave trading as late as 1847.

In the letter I referred to, from Peter Miller Watson in Demerary to Sandbach Tinne in Liverpool, which I came across on the website of Swann Auction Galleries, dated 3 June 1847, Watson lists a 'cargo of Negro's' on the Sandbach Tinne ship the *Parker* as including '115 adult males, 86 adult females, 82 under 14 years, and 41 under 4 years'. Despite being warned of 'contrary winds and calms' that would prolong the voyage, it seems they decided to push ahead. The deaths of 'only' three – one man and two children – are not blamed on this rough, lengthy voyage but instead are attributed by a 'Captain R . . . to the wretched state in which they had lived ashore'. Where these people came from is not clear, but their destination was undoubtedly the plantations of Sandbach Tinne – or perhaps their store, where they would be sold secretly to the highest bidder. This indicates that they had not come from another colony but from Africa, as their 'wretched condition ashore' is attributed to themselves, rather than a master or the ship's captain. In any event, the trafficking of Africans had been outlawed forty years before, by the British, and Sandbach Tinne had been royally compensated for emancipating their enslaved Africans in 1838. Yet here they are, landing 'a cargo of Negro's' in British Guiana in 1847.

Watson's cousin Robertson Gladstone headed out to Demerara at the age of twenty-three to see his father's investments (and his inheritance) at close quarters. The Gladstone family have long been portrayed in the public imagination and many history books as 'absentee planters', benefiting from enslavement but never actually setting foot on a plantation. This whitewashing was perhaps intended to protect the image of William Ewart Gladstone, the future Prime Minister. The evidence about Robertson Gladstone scuppers this narrative – and it is likely that he was not the first Gladstone to go to British Guiana.

I came across his journal at the Liverpool Athenaeum. The club's website boasts that 'Early proprietors played a major part in the national movement to abolish slavery'.[25] What it fails to mention is that the part they played was to claim as much money as possible for the emancipation of the people they had enslaved. Similarly, in the case of people like Roscoe and Traill, they had benefited handsomely from the proceeds of their enslavement, while never getting their own hands tarnished with the dirty business itself.

At the Liverpool Athenaeum there are only ever 500 equal shares to be had, and upon each share certificate you can see the signature of each former holder back to 1797. My own share ironically was once held by Thomas Harrison, owner of the shipping line T & J Harrison & Co., another member of the Sandbach Tinne dynasty who traded Cognac from France to the enslavers of the Americas, bringing back slave-produced commodities to Liverpool and Europe.

Dr Thomas Stuart Traill, stepfather of Peter Miller Watson, was one of the earliest leading figures of the Athenaeum, serving as its president from 1823 to 1825.[26] A bust of Traill still sits proudly in the Athenaeum's newsroom to this day. To get a sense of how the Watson family were interlinked with the Athenaeum, Traill's daughter, Mary Eliza Traill, was a co-executrix of her half-brother Peter Miller Watson's estate and administered funds to both Andrew Watson and his sister Annetta, until Andrew attained his majority, and until Annetta's marriage and beyond.

The roster hanging on the wall at the Athenaeum's reception also includes Philip Frederick Tinne, Samuel Sandbach, Charles Stuart Parker, John Gladstone MP and John Abraham Tinne.

CHAPTER 11

'THESE GOOD-NATURED SAVAGES'

I have more respect for a man who lets me know
where he stands, even if he's wrong, than the one
who comes up like an angel and is nothing but a devil.
— Malcolm X

In Guyana and much of the former British Caribbean today, Emancipation Day is on 1 August. Crowds of Guyanese, particularly those of African descent, gather and remember the freedom their ancestors fought for. In Georgetown, the National Park is filled with colourful West African Kente cloth prints and whole families are dressed in matching patterns. There are posters sharing key moments in African and Guyanese history, the roll of many drums, the sweet smell of cook-up, and piles of conkee wrapped in banana leaf. Guyanese people are acutely aware of what it means not to be free, but also that 'emancipation' still does not mean liberation from enslavement and colonialism, even today. In 1838, the African population of British Guiana sought to build a new life as a free people. There was no compensation for them, no financial redress for the centuries of unpaid labour, abuse and torture that saw Liverpool and Glasgow go from provincial towns to sprawling cities, fuelled and funded by the brutality, barbarity and injustice dished out by their most prominent white merchant clans upon the Black African and indigenous Amerinidian victims of their incessant greed, perverse lust and boundless ambition.

If the Black people were to survive, it would not be through the savings banks owned by the colonial authorities. Instead, they used traditional African systems of saving, which can be found across the Caribbean under different names, such as *pardner*, *boxhand* or *susu*. The idea is that a group of people agree to each put a small amount of money in a pot, say every month, and once a month one person is given all the money collected – and so it goes around until everyone has had their windfall. It is a way of saving so that you receive a lump sum and can make a large purchase you would perhaps not otherwise be able to afford on your own. It was through such savings schemes that African villagers were able to purchase their own land from their former masters, as my relatives attested to when I met them in Georgetown.

The fortitude of those early freed communities, and the communal spirit fostered amongst them, brought about the emergence of what became known locally as the 'Village System'. The names of the villages were often drawn from the 'mother country', perhaps to honour, or even to mock, certain individuals. For example, the village is called Victoria after the former British queen. Others kept their colonial names, such as Plaisance in Region 4 (Demerara-Mahaica), which had once been a French plantation and cost the freed Africans who purchased it $39,000. This coastal village, located just a five-minute drive from Plantation Success, where Jack Gladstone was once enslaved, is best known today as the birthplace of Guyanese superstar Eddy Grant, the creator of hits such as 'Electric Avenue' and 'Do You Feel My Love?'.

For Sandbach Tinne, of course, the newly freed population represented yet another business opportunity. In a letter to William Robertson Sandbach (son of Samuel Sandbach and Elizabeth Robertson) in Liverpool, dated 25 September 1853, their agents and wider family members in Demerara, Garnett and Jones, mention leasing land on the Edinburgh estate to 'some Negroes' which they add 'will yield a handsome rental'.[1]

The Sandbach Tinne dynasty, continued to draw on their investments in cheap labour, plying their trade as individuals outside the House of Sandbach Tinne, but utilising the power of the House when it suited them. A letter from Peter Miller Watson of McInroy Sandbach & Co., in Demerara, to Messrs Sandbach Tinne & Co., in Liverpool, dated 26 May 1838, includes a 'Memorandum of coal transfers', which lists plantations: Leonora, William, Le Resouvenir, Vriesland, Providence, Retrieve, De Kinderen, Industry (all Sandbach Tinne plantations) and others, with 'ex Henry' or 'ex Parker' written next to each, possibly referring to the exclusion of those partners from the fortunes of that particular family enterprise for some reason. It may perhaps have been an evaluation of the value of commodities on hand prior to their leaving or joining the firm's shareholders and to which they had – at that point – no right. In another letter, Peter Miller Watson states, 'The writer here begs to advise . . . £200 on account La Bonne Intention – £150 on account Zeeburg'.[2] These were not Sandbach Tinne plantations at that time. According to a list from the *Demerara Gazette* of 1857, Watson's qualification to vote cites his co-ownership of these two plantations as evidence of his eligibility. Due to the date of this letter (during the early period of indentureship) we can gain a sense of the scale of Watson's personal exploitation of post-enslavement indentured labour, alongside his role in McInroy Sandbach & Co.

The Colonial Registrar's Office also lists George Rainy as 'Absent'. His qualification to vote is given as 'Proprietor' of 'Plantation Industry and one undivided moiety of Plantation Providence, having more than three acres under cultivation'.[3] Also, between 1861 and 1875, Rainy placed multiple orders for sugar machinery with Scottish firm Mirrlees Watson & Co., in Glasgow, for delivery to plantations Industry and Providence, in partnership with Sandbach Tinne & Co. Again, here is a member of the Sandbach Tinne dynasty with shares in plantations in his own right, but this time he's also a shareholder in the house too. Also mentioned are Henry Robertson Sandbach, William Robertson Sandbach and John Abraham 'Tinne', each listed as a 'Possessor' of Plantations Leonora, Groenveld and Anna Catharina (which are all Sandbach Tinne plantations). Being an absentee planter at this time may have been the most financially sound course of action, given Eric Williams' claim that a 'very large' part of the compensation money never reached British Guiana at all, and 'was paid to absentee owners and creditors in England'.[4] No doubt the Sandbach Tinne multinational conglomerate further benefited from the misfortunes of the small slave owner in British Guiana, of whom Williams contends, 'not infrequently was forced to sell out his claim to speculators, and ultimately received sometimes no more than £12 instead of £50 per head'.

Although Peter Miller Watson was listed as 'absent' when his voting qualification was registered by his attorney in 1855, he must have been in Demerara at some point between that date and when the document was created in January 1857, during which time his Black son Andrew Watson was born to Anna Watson (née Rose) in 1856. This is supported by a letter from Demerara dated 11 January 1857 and signed 'Peter M. Watson, McInroy Sandbach & Co.' The letter refers to sending rum from Plantation La Bonne Intention, and notes, 'we have endorsed the draft of Mr Watson of account of La Bonne Intention . . . payable in London £200'. It also refers to an amount 'in favour of Peter Rose Esquire for £600 in our own account and £200 on account of Pl'ns. Providence and Sage Pond'.[5]

We are further reminded of the family's influence and local connections in other correspondence. A letter from Peter M. Watson of McInroy Sandbach & Co., in Demerara, dated 20 January 1851, states: 'We may here mention that no proceeding of the Court of Policy or Combined Court have been printed since the date of those in Mr Tinne's possession'.[6] This suggests a close entwinement with the colony's central policy and enforcement body, of which both Peter Rose and the now late P.F. Tinne were both, at one point, in charge of. The 'Tinne' mentioned here was most likely John Abraham Tinne, who had by that time assumed his late father P.F. Tinne's shares in Sandbach Tinne & Co. Another letter of 25 October 1853 refers to a business request from Governor William Walker, demonstrating that the Governor was desirous of doing business with them.

Peter Rose is again mentioned in a letter from Peter M. Watson of McInroy Sandbach & Co., dated 6 July 1848, where he is referred to as the manager of the Colonial Bank. This alone would have made him incredibly important in British Guiana,[7] but according to Rose's epitaph on the wall of St George's Cathedral in Georgetown, he was in fact one of the most influential people in nineteenth-century Guiana, with a prominence that spanned over fifty years.

Slavery had ended, but the family were not willing to renounce their Demerara investments. They simply pivoted while everyone else either sold up or abandoned their holdings. For Sandbach Tinne, their subsidiaries and wider family concerns such as those of the Gladstones and the Watsons, the changing legislative landscape was just a prelude to a new business model.

Profits were clearly still to be had, even if it meant navigating both new labour dynamics, and a series of successive health crises. Yellow fever struck British Guiana in 1837, continuing into 1838, and again in 1842, according to a table of deaths in Guiana from 1838 to 1846.[8] Yellow fever, the document notes, is 'very fatal to Europeans and seamen'. Within that eight-year period, other conditions listed include smallpox in 1839, measles and 'hooping-cough' in 1842, and scarlatina ('very fatal') in 1844. Another obstacle for post-emancipation planters was labour unrest. This was of course nothing new: enslaved workers had campaigned for rights during the 1763 Berbice Rebellion, the 1823 Demerara Rebellion and Damon's Rebellion, to say nothing of smaller, unrecorded, lesser-known protests. The newly emancipated Africans continued in the same vein; a McInroy Sandbach & Co. letter of 17 August 1840 refers to a 'workers strike' in Demerara where 'on La Bonne Intention, the people struck for six bitts on the first of August and have not turned out since'. Later, we're told, the workers agreed to return to work for five bitts, not their initial goal but still an increase of one bitt on the wages usually given for cane cutting on the East Coast at the time. The date of the African workers' protest, 1 August, is also significant, marking two years to the day since they were finally officially emancipated.

Nine years later, there were hints that at least some of the African-owned plantations were proving prosperous. A letter from Peter M. Watson of McInroy Sandbach & Co. in Demerary, dated 5 July 1849, to Messrs Sandbach Tinne & Co., noted, 'The plantation work at Edinburgh, is in good order but the estates Amstel and Fellowship – now owned by Negroes – produce large quantities. There are also many of the sugar estates selling and the prices are consequently very low.'9 There is a hint of frustration that the 'Negroes' should be producing large amounts, perhaps more than some of Sandbach Tinne's estates and plantations. Indeed, it was not beyond plantation owners to sabotage and even destroy the farms and livelihoods of those they had formerly enslaved, and especially those who had since become competitors, producing at volume for export under their own auspices, and contributing to price reduction.

Eric Williams illustrates the vindictive and greedy machinations of the planters when he examines the tightly entwined history (and legacy) of western capitalism and slavery. He demonstrates how 'emancipation' was more an economic necessity than a humanitarian good deed. In the *Journal of Negro History* (1945), Williams cites German-born explorer and surveyor of British Guiana Robert Hermann Schomburgk, who declared that emancipation 'was one of the most powerful means of promoting the in-born and hereditary indolence of the Negro'. He went on to say:

> Every former labourer tried to purchase at the lowest rates, his own piece of land. He could get his living from out of its produce with the minimum of trouble, because his ordinary wants and the inexhaustible productiveness of the tropics forced him to no great efforts. The scarcity of labour arising from this

cause, increased the daily pay to such an extent that the free Negro who worked for one or two days could earn enough to live as he liked, comfortably, for the remainder of the week.[10]

Williams also quotes Henry Barkly, then Governor of British Guiana, writing in 1849: 'The acquisition of a plot of ground . . . has not been so much the sign of superior intelligence or manly independence, as of un-founded suspicions or a love of uncivilized ease; the freeholders being, I am inclined to think, as a body far less industrious than the older and steadier Negroes, who from confidence in their employers and a desire to work continuously have remained on the plantations.'

British colonial attitudes towards the freed African population were clearly still infused with a condescending notion of superiority and interlaced with a plethora of colonialist stereotypes. A colonialist such as Henry G. Dalton serves as an example of the racist attitudes prevalent at the time. In his *History of British Guiana* published in 1855, Dalton depicts the African and the native Arawak populations with a series of offensive stereotypes according to their nations of origin or tribes, referring to the earliest missionaries' interaction with the indigenous Arawaks as having 'soon gained the love and confidence of these good-natured savages',[11] after describing the Creoles as having lost their African features through forced breeding with their white masters: 'Elaborately tattooed skin, the cannibal appetite, the flattened forehead and nose, the prominent jaws and mouth, have more or less disappeared but, unfortunately, the indolence, the superstition, the immorality of the African character remains to an extent deplorable and alarming.'[12]

Interestingly, he notes, 'Up to this hour cargoes of liberated Africans are still imported to these shores', a nod to the African indentured labourers who came (at least nominally) as free labourers.[13] Though he recognises there were inadequate numbers to do all the work, Dalton still attributes the 'abandoned cane-piece and uncultivated lands' to 'the want of energy and industry among the lower classes'.[14]

Conversely, people like John Abraham Tinne, who was by now one of the largest plantation owners in Guiana, enjoyed a different experience. He wrote to his brother Fred (in 1908) of life on Plantation Leonora, which he claimed has 'without doubt one of the finest atmospheres in the world. In the evening with the trade winds blowing through the gallery of the manager's house and your feet up in a Berbice chair after a ride aback round the cultivation, and a boy to take your boots off and brings your slippers and a swizzle, you feel thoroughly at peace and comfortable.'[15]

As Williams concludes, 'The myth of the "laziness" of the Negro is one of the most mischievous legacies of the slavery period.' Formerly enslaved Africans were willing to work after 1838, 'but positively not as wage earners'. Being a landholder was easier in British Guiana than Barbados, adds Williams, 'where all the land was appropriated'. Yet the planters in both situations were keen to see their former enslaved Africans fail. The British Guiana planters themselves deliberately destroyed all the fruit trees to deprive the emancipated Africans of a source of sustenance, to compel them to seek employment on their sugar plantations, and 'seriously considered, as late as 1917, a repetition of this sabotage when indentured immigration came to an end'.[16]

Profit was still the bottom line and so, even after slavery was abolished and the apprenticeship scheme concluded, the plantation owners did everything they could to keep wages as low as possible. Some formerly enslaved Africans continued to work for the same master, whilst other so-called 'liberated Africans' arrived in the colony to fill the gaps. Dalton refers to them as 'cargoes of liberated Africans', which suggests they had been enslaved in Africa, liberated by the blockade, indentured and sent on to the colonies – not as 'free people' but as 'cargo'. The plantation owners needed an alternative labour force at a scale that none of the available options seemed to offer, so a period of economic uncertainty loomed over the colony. They needed a cheap and subservient workforce, operating under the system that had been entrenched during the period of enslavement but was not forbidden in post-emancipation law. The Guiana planters' competitive edge was maintained only by the imposition of tariffs on foreign sugar. Some, who were solvent, particularly from the vast sums paid out through the slavery compensation scheme, such as Gladstones and members of the Sandbach Tinne dynasty, could continue to fill their coffers, availing themselves of the available labour and purchasing even the produce of the so-called 'Negro plantations'. Others who were not so astute could barely stay afloat; some went under or abandoned the colony altogether. Anne-Marie Lee-Loy explains that in the mid-nineteenth century the sugar industry found itself 'in dire straits' after the removal of foreign sugar tariffs and the importation of cheaper beet sugar from the emerging markets in India: 'Its difficulties were caused by a complex combination of factors including soil depletion, the removal of protective tariffs on West Indian produced sugar in Great Britain, and the emancipation of the slaves. So extreme had the situation become that by 1850, one observer had claimed that three quarters of West Indian planters were on the verge of absolute financial ruin.'[17]

Eric Williams, too, charted the rise and fall of the sugar industry, and noted that 'In British Guiana, sugar exports fell 62% between 1839 and 1842, as compared with the period 1831–1834.' He gave the example of Windsor Castle Plantation in the 1840s, which was valued at '$199,520' but was unable to fetch '$40,000'. 'It was all very sad,' he concludes, with perhaps a lack of genuine sympathy and a tinge of sarcasm. 'The sugar planter in Cuba was a millionaire, in British Guiana he was a bankrupt.' Williams attributed the crash to the role played by 'free trade'.

Free trade was becoming a religion in England. The blow which knocked out British Guiana and the British West Indies came not in 1838, with the abolition of apprenticeships, but in 1846, with the equalisation of sugar duties. West Indian production between 1831 and 1846 had declined in the following proportions: Sugar: By ½. Rum by nearly ¾. Coffee by nearly ¾. Britain had now renounced 'those provisions of an exploded mercantile system, whereby failing trades have been supported, and uncongenial productions forced. It was the abolition of monopoly and not of slavery, it was free trade and not free labor, that ruined British Guiana and the British West Indies'.[18]

Despite the various factors that contributed to the decline of the sugar industry, Lee-Loy adds, 'planters put the blame on their inability to have total control over the ex-slave plantation workforce as the main cause of the failing industry'. Indentured labour, they hoped, would be a way of retaining 'some measure of control that they had held within the slave system'. A McInroy Sandbach & Co., letter of 5 July 1849 provides an illustration of how one set of cheap labour was replaced by another. The writer warns: 'The Negroes' houses at Tuschen de Vrienden (one range having fallen & another likely to be soon in the same state) must be immediately repaired to prevent the Coolies leaving the estate.'[19] This is proof that they housed the Indians in the slave huts. The 'Coolies', as they derogatorily referred to them, had their passage to Guiana paid, but in return they had to work for little – if any – wages, for a set number of years, in order to pay back their 'debt' or 'indenture' as it was referred to in law. These indentured labourers came not only to the Americas, British Guiana and neighbouring Dutch Guiana (later Suriname), but also Jamaica, Trinidad and Tobago, and beyond the Caribbean, to countries such as Mauritius and Fiji. Many of these changes in the labour force and economy are captured in 'A Short History of the Tinne Family' in which Philip Frederick Tinne's descendant, Dr John Ernest Tinne, provides more details on the products (and people) shipped by the house:

> Coolies were transported to the West Indies and tropical products such as sugar, cotton and copra (dried pieces of coconut flesh) were brought to Liverpool in vast quantities, as well as more exotic products such as the rubber-like balata gum, and even rubber itself, with which McInroy had experimented in the early plantations. One of the biggest shipments was greenheart timber, commonly used only in

fishing rods or the construction of the Liverpool landing stage, one of the largest floating structures in the world.[20]

Kinghorn's research discovered that in November 1839, the Bristol West India Association received a 'Copy of Resolutions passed at a meeting of the West India Association of Liverpool, respecting the necessity of promoting the emigration of free labourers in the British West India Colonies'. The West India Association of Liverpool, she explains, 'sought to apply to the Government for some immediate measures to encourage free emigration from all parts of the world, into the British West India Colonies'.[21] The signatories include Henry Sandbach (Samuel Sandbach's son and successor at Sandbach Tinne & Co.) and Robertson Gladstone, John Gladstone MP's son.

The plan for indentureship had been long in the making. Thomas Harding notes that on 4 January 1836, John Gladstone wrote to Gillanders, Arbuthnot & Co., of Calcutta, asking them to send indentured labourers to Demerara and Jamaica, deceptively promising: 'Labour is very light . . . They are furnished with comfortable dwellings and abundance of food . . . it may be fairly said, they pass their time agreeably and happily.'[22] This brazen deception from a man whose plantation had been used in 1823 as a case study in Parliament of the barbarity of slavery, was now conspiring, with fallacies of great opportunity and comfort, to compel another group of unsuspecting victims into his barbarous lair. His claims were of course directly contradicted in that letter of 1849 from Peter Miller Watson of McInroy Parker & Co., where the old Negro houses, or 'logies', as they were known in Guiana, that used to house enslaved Africans were repurposed for the new arrivals from India and were 'falling down' when they arrived.

The first 407 indentured labourers from India arrived in British Guiana on 18 May 1838, a date celebrated in Guyana today as Indian Arrivals Day. In 1908, when John Abraham Tinne wrote home from British Guiana, his impressions gave a sense of the way the Indian workers were viewed – even decades after they first arrived in the colony: 'I did a few days for him (Busby, the cashier) booking passengers for the Canadian steamer, which is not great fun, and receiving money from these confounded Coolie shopkeepers, who bring out a filthy $5 note from their baba, smeared with rancid coconut oil and wrapped round their coin, the silver blackened, and the copper verdigrised with sweat.'[23] As disgusted as he clearly was, he still took their soiled cash.

On 11 March 1859, James Stuart wrote to Philip Frederick Tinne from Demerara, of having had 'two vessels in – with Coolies – since the departure of last mail'.[24] Later that year, Stuart wrote again to Tinne stating: 'Our last ship of Coolies has just arrived, they are all going to Essequibo . . . 43 having died during the voyage of 83 days . . . the mortality I regret to say, is great.'[25] Other indentured labourers came from Shanghai, Amoy and Canton in China and a revealing letter from Peter Miller Watson in Demerara to William Robertson Sandbach Esq., dated 24 August 1853, paints a picture of life for these new arrivals, who he refers to as 'The Chinese immigrants'. It is clear from both the mortality rates on board and the condition of their health upon arrival, that what Gladstone had presented as a joyous experience was in fact a nightmare of grotesque tragedy, on a par with what we see today in the worst examples of human trafficking.

Watson stated, 'Since I last mentioned the Chinese immigrants, great sickness has presided amongst them and when I was a few days ago at Anna Catharina,[26] about half of them were in the hospital with sores of the worst description. I am afraid that sufficient attention has not been paid to them.'[27] This first-hand account is supported by David Aitkin's thesis on 'Plantation Medicine to Public Health' in Guiana, where he states: 'two years after the arrival of Chinese immigrants, planter dissatisfaction began to emerge. On some plantations, sickness prevented the Chinese from performing any work. At plantation Anna Catharina the cause of their sickness was attributed to their "filthy" state. Managing the new immigrants was also proving more problematical than expected.'[28]

Watson further contended that even the medical attendant of the

'Barbarities of the West Indies' cartoon by James Gillray, 23 April 1791.

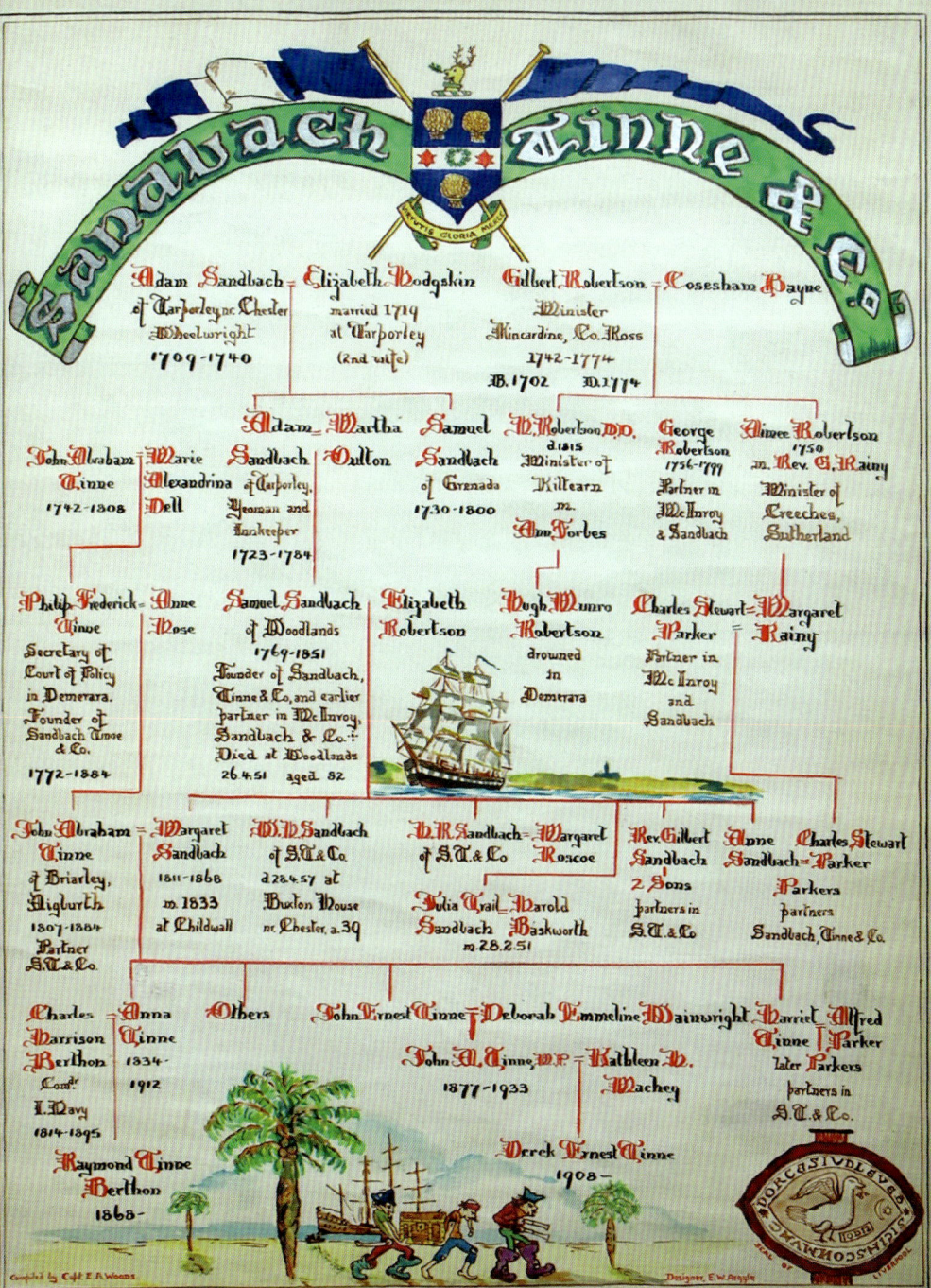

Family tree of key Sandbach Tinne family members.

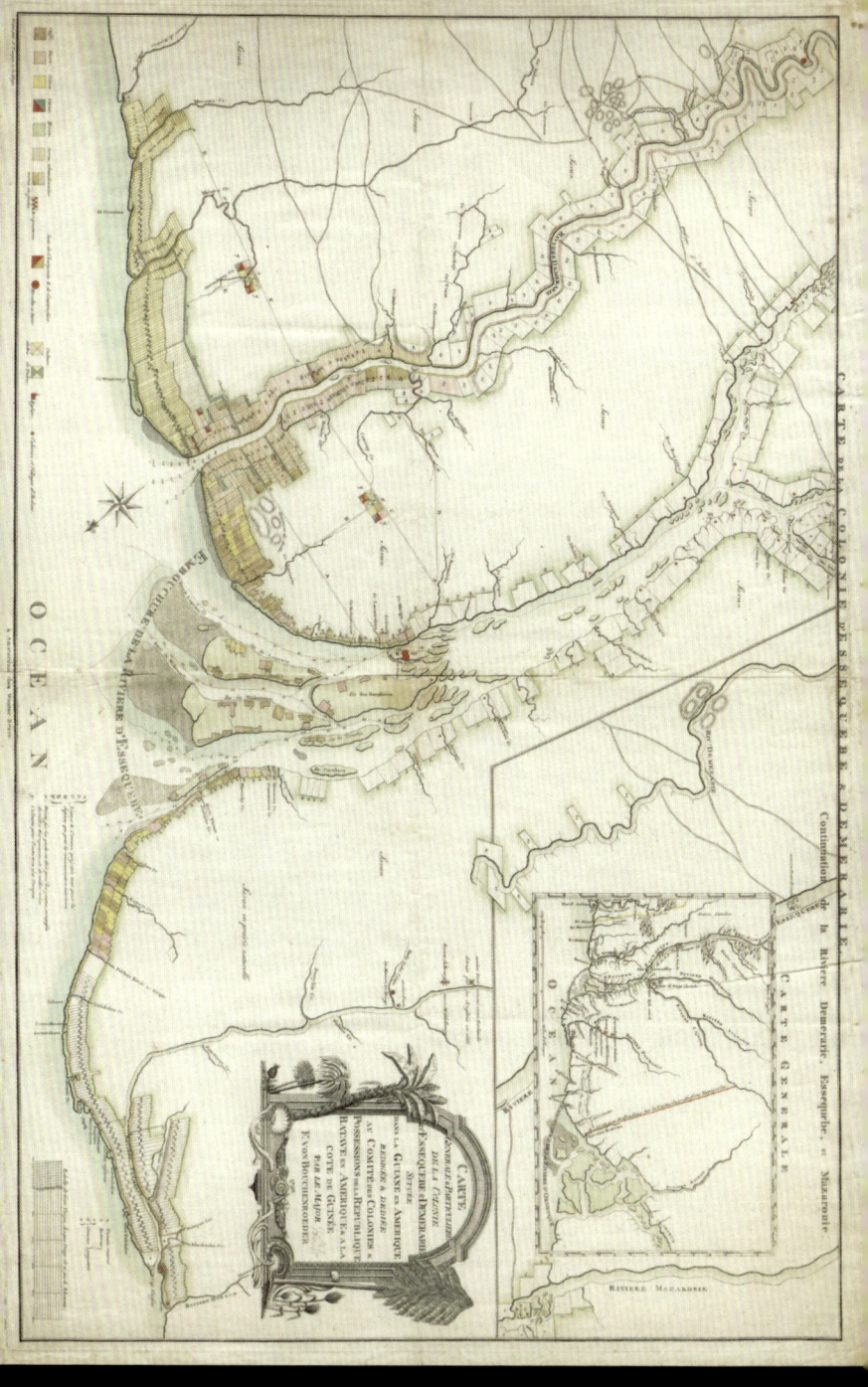

Late eighteenth-century Dutch map of 'Essequebe' and 'Demerarie' by Friedrich von Bouchenroeder

THE DOUGLASSES OF MULDERG.

Edward I., King of England, m. Margaret of France, daughter of Philip, King of France.

Edmund of Woodstock, Earl of Kent, m. Margaret, daughter of John, Lord Wake.

Thomas de Holland, Lord Holland, K.G., m. Joan Plantagenet, "The Fair Maid of Kent," sole heiress.

Thomas de Holland, 2nd Earl of Kent, m. Lady Alice Fitzalan, daughter of Richard, 9th Earl of Arundel.

John de Beaufort, Marquis of Dorset, Earl of Somerset, m. Lady Margaret de Holland.

Sir James Stewart, "The Black Knight of Lorn," m. Joan de Beaufort, Queen Dowager of Scotland, died 1445.

John Stewart, 1st Earl of Athol, m. Lady Eleanor Sinclair, daughter of William, Earl of Orkney, Chancellor of Scotland, son of Henry, Earl of Orkney, and Egadia, daughter of Sir Wm. Douglas of Netherdale, by his wife, Princess Egadia, daughter of King Robert II., and great granddaughter of King Robert Bruce.

John Stewart, 2nd Earl of Athol, m. Lady Mary Campbell, daughter of Archibald, Earl of Argyll, by his wife Elizabeth, daughter of John, Earl of Lennox.

Kenneth Mackenzie, feudal baron of Kintail, m. Lady Elizabeth Stewart.

Roderick Mor Mackenzie, I. of Redcastle, m. Catherine, daughter of Robert Munro, feudal baron of Fowlis, by his wife Margaret, daughter of James Ogilvie of Cardell.

Colin Mackenzie, I. of Kincraig, parish of Rosskeen, m. Catherine, daughter of the Rev. John Mackenzie, I. of Tolly, minister of Dingwall (son of Murdo Mackenzie, I. of Fairburn, by his wife Margaret, daughter of Urquhart of Cromarty), by his first wife Margaret, daughter of John Grant of Ballindalloch.

Gilbert Robertson, II. of Kindeace, merchant of Inverness, living 1650. m. Margaret Mackenzie. Sasine to her, 18th July, 1638, as future spouse of Gilbert Robertson, fiar of Kindeace. Issue— three sons and one daughter.

- William, predeceased his father.
- Colin Robertson, III. of Kindeace, married Rebecca, only dau. of Sir Robert Munro of Fowlis, 3rd Baronet, and had issue.
- Francis Robertson m. Helen, daughter of Hugh Ross of Easterfearn. in Balcony, parish of Kiltearn, living 12th April, 1697, buried at Kiltearn.
- Janet Robertson, mar. Alex. Ross of Easterfearn.

- Gilbert Robertson in Balcony, living 1704.
- Hugh Robertson m. ——— in Balcony, farmer.
- George Robertson in Balcony, farmer, married Christina Douglas as above.

- Hugh Robertson (junior), in Balcony, farmer, married Ann Douglas.
- Janet Robertson, married to Robert Douglas, farmer of Balcony.

The royal bloodline of the Robertsons. George Roberson and Christian Douglas, bottom right, were Andrew Watson's great-great-great-grandparents.

BAPTISMS solemnized at St. George's Church, in the Colony of Demerary, in the Year 1829.

No.	When Baptized	Child's Christian Name	Parents' Name (Christian / Surname)	Abode	Quality, Trade, or Profession	By whom the Ceremony Performed
	Nov 19th	Samuel (Aged 8 months) Son of	Joseph Forte & Free Bl[ac]k Woman Sarah Blunt	G[eorge]town		Jas. Luger
	"	Lady (Aged 4 yrs) Daughter of	Joseph Forte & Free Blk Woman Sarah Blunt	"		Jas. Luger
	"	Adult Slaves Jenny Betsey Halleluiah George Rosetta Lavilliers	Belongs to J.D. Pattison Wm Quintinburg	Demerara River		Jas. Luger
	"	Adult Slave Aridge	Belongs to Government	G[eorge]town		Jas. Luger
	"	Adult Slave Grace	Belongs to Patience Smith	"		Jas. Luger
	Nov 25th	William Luther (Born 20th Sept 1829) Son of	Sweetman & Anna Maria Chaska	G[eorge]town		Jas. Luger
	"	Adult Slaves Cupido January	Belongs to J.D. Pattison	Demerara River		Jas. Luger
	"	Infant Slave Thomas	Belongs to Mary Wishart	G[eorge]town		Jas. Luger
	"	Infant Slaves Frances Mary Margaret Jacob	Belongs to Government	"		Jas. Luger
	"	Adult Slaves Eleanor Philista Jemima Judy Charles John	Belongs to Saby Lucens	"		Jas. Luger
	"	Adult Slaves Peggy Lennox Rhodes	Belongs to J.H. Robinson	"		Jas. Luger

St George's Cathedral records, Georgetown, Guiana, showing mass baptisms of enslaved Africans in 1828, probably at the behest of their owners.

Chronological Chart of the Progress of the Church Missionary Society

A.D.

Authorized English Version of THE BIBLE, 1613
1661 S.P.C. in New Engl. founded at the instance of the Hon. R. Boyle. Eliot, preaches to the N.A. Indians, 1646.
Eliot (the Apostle of the Indians) d. 1690, aged 86.
1698 S.P.C.K. founded.
1701 S.P.G. founded.
Ziegenbalg & Plütscho, arrived in India, July, 1706.
Hans Egede, landed in Greenland, 1708.
Ziegenbalg, d. 1719. S.P.C.K. adopted Danish Missions in S. India, 1710.
Schmidt, commenced Moravian Mission among the Hottentots, 1736.
Brainerd, d. 1747. Schwartz, arrived in India, 1750.
1786 Wesl. M. S. founded. First Col. B.ꝑᵍⁱᶜ (Nova Scotia) 1787. Carey, arrived in India, 1793.
1792 Bapt. M. S. do.
1795 Lond. M. S. do.
1796 Scottish M. S. do.
1797 Netherlands M. S. do.
Schwartz, d. 1798, aged 72.

Mission founded	Income All Sources	Income Associat.ⁿˢ	N.º Clergy Sub.ᵗ	N.º Clergy Total	Labourers Total	Labourers including Native	Scholars Total	Scholars including Females	Communicants	
1799										C.M.S. founded April 12
1800	£911									Jänicke, d.
1801										
1802	356									
1803	566									Gericke, d.
1804 W. AFRICA	611		1	2	2					BIBLE SOCIETY FOUNDED
1805	1682		1	2	2					
1806	2449		1	5	5					
1807	1974		1	5	5					Morrison arrived in China
1808	1849		1	4	4					LONDON JEWS' SOC.ᵗ FOUNDED
1809	2331		2	3	3					N Zealand Miss.ⁿ decided on
1810	3366		3	4	6		35	13		American Board of Missions
1811	2476		3	4	6		42	17		
1812	2401		3	6	8		"	"		D Brown, d.
1813	3046		3	6	11	1	92	38		FORMATION OF ASSOCIAT.ⁿˢ
1814 {S. INDIA, N. ZEALAND}	11,024	7321	5	8	14	1	"	"		Basle M.S.
1815 {N. INDIA, MEDITER.ⁿ}	17,107	9942	8	13	21	2	201	"		
1816	19,663	9464	17	13	34	12	1003	"	6	Basle Seminary
1817	20,087	15,423	20	17	43	15	1115	"	21	
1818	25,783	18,862	28	25	95	55	3262	"	60	Sierra Leone occupied
1819	28,965	24,174	38	26	123	70	5152	"	120	Antigua occupied
1820 WESTERN INDIA	31,058	25,684	41	34	201	134	6125	"	318	Tinnevelly occupied
1821	33,066	28,158	38	35	2	217	155	6846	434	Bᵖ Coll. Calcutta
1822 N.W. AMERICA	34,144	28,135	40	36	2	252	184	9916	508	
1823	34,913	30,400	43	42	2	286	238	12,311	1347	689
1824	41,239	32,571	42	38	2	380	313	13,618	2609	675
1825	43,209	34,612	46	41	2	398	321	14,090	2957	477 C.M. Institution
1826 W. INDIES	46,569	38,861	51	52	2	425	344	13,637	2795	644 Jamaica, Egypt and Malta occupied
1827	46,473	36,972	54	52	3	407	334	13,447	3086	646 Br. Guiana occupied
1828	44,783	37,633	47	55	1	442	351	12,561	2364	750
1829	54,221	45,184	51	46	1	260	206	12,419	1686	1044 Syra Schools
1830	47,214	41,639	54	53		495	390	14,791	2169	1051 Abyssinian Mission
1831	47,795	39,661	56	58	4	550	457	15,791	2340	1071
1832	40,823	34,815	48	59	4	609	504	16,881	2404	1271
1833	49,381	41,087	46	66	4	620	504	18,318	2495	1598 Wilberforce, d.
1834	52,587	40,862	50	54	4	561	464	18,283	2607	1352
1835	69,682	47,759	64	61	6	593	487	18,361	2150	889 Amer. Episc. M.S.
1836	68,354	52,093	64	73	3	597	466	21,648	2730	1315
1837 S. AFRICA	71,727	54,210	81	75	5	487	374	19,706	2591	1514 Timneh Country occupied
1838	83,447	61,871	95	84	5	541	375	21,591	2066	1901 Awakening at Krishnaghur, Marsden d. aged 73
1839	71,306	58,522	95	92	6	607	434	26,230	4311	2721
1840	100,912	81,687	95	104	9	820	643	28,849	3049	3050
1841	91,471	69,242	97	112	11	1165	988	35,396	5900	4603 Bᵖ of N. Zealand. Telugu Mission
1842	90,821	71,986	107	117	10	1353	1179	41,335	6324	6050
1843	115,100	78,628	92	110	10	1263	1096	37,212	5975	6315
1844 {E. AFRICA, CHINA}	104,323	75,301	93	113	9	1181	1027	35,742	5608	8205 Himalaya Mission
1845 YORUBA	105,249	74,642	100	125	10	1265	1109	36,721	5564	9628 Sir T.F. Buxton, d.
1846	102,458	74,337	101	127	11	1394	1233	38,482	6211	11,714 Bᵖ of Madras Spencer
1847	116,827	77,923	100	124	10	1435	1280	23,693	5053	11,970 Bᵖ of Bombay Carr.
1848	101,293	74,067	102	139	14	1481	1313	26,484	5188	13,010 JUBILEE, NOV. 1.
1849	101,003	76,021	104	140	15	1505	1336	28,316	5378	13,352 Bᵖ of Victoria & Rupert's Land
1850 SCINDE	104,273	74,355	106	147	15	1726	1549	32,268	5748	13,551
1851										

*Incomplete returns from New Zealand.

British Slave Trade abolished March 24th 1807.
British Dominions abolished Aug. 1ˢᵗ 1834.
H. Martyn.
Corrie, (Bᵖ of Madras)
Middleton.
Heber.
Turner, James
Slavery in the British.

Chronological chart of the worldwide presence and financial gain of the Church Missionary Society, 1661–1851.

Christ Church in Cummingsburg, Georgetown, Guyana.

Construction of British Guiana Railway through Sandbach Tinne and Co. plantations, Enterprise and Providence, c.1890.

estate had been 'at death's door'. He also talked of a woman on the estate named Mirelle who should not be there and although I consent to be linked to Mr Cameron, my desire that we should get rid of him, he is still retained, and I think it is only due to you to inform you that no respectable young man of any feeling can be got to remain on the Estate. This is a delicate subject and one in which you will no doubt use due discretion, if you think it necessary to broach it to Mr McLagan.[29] The constant changes of overseer must show you that the system present is bad.'

An 1856 publication entitled *A Manual of Plantership in British Guiana* by Alexander MacRae, 'a resident planter in that colony for half a century', gives a snapshot of the population of British Guiana at that time: 'The colony generally has a population of about 120,000 souls of a very mixed character, viz., European and Creole whites, native and African Blacks, Hindoo Coolies, and natives of Madeira, with a few Chinese.'[30] The 1851 census for British Guiana breaks it down further. At the time, the most populous region was Demerara with 75,767 people; Essequibo had 24,925 and Berbice 27,003 – an overall total of 127,695. This figure did not include the indigenous population, which was estimated here at 7,000. Of those surveyed, 103,277 were recorded as 'Not ascertained or wholly illiterate'. A substantial number – 86,451 – are listed as 'Natives of British Guiana', with another 7,168 named 'African Immigrants', as opposed to the 'Old Africans' who numbered 7,083. The distinction between the two presumably refers to their arrival dates: perhaps the 'Old Africans' came before slavery was abolished, and the 'African immigrants' came after emancipation; one would assume, the 'liberated Africans' referred to earlier as having been 'indentured' after being 'liberated'. Other members of the population include 3,665 'Coolies from Madras' and 4,017 from Calcutta.

In his manual, McRae estimates that some 25,000 of the labourers were cultivating sugar cane for the manufacturing of sugar and rum. Written with the colonialist contempt for non-Europeans that was typical at the time, he uses every opportunity to reinforce a variety of imposed racial stereotypes, with repeated instances of pejorative terms such as 'these people' the 'coolies, half Creoles and African Blacks'. He states that 'the Coolies – in particular – do not on an average perform more than three days of industrious labour every week, the rest of their time is consumed in idleness and debauchery'.[31] He goes further still, claiming that 'One of the greatest evils which the planter has to contend with here, is the almost total absence of any active sense of moral obligation on the part of the great bulk of the labouring population, more particularly among the Coolies and Negroes. These people are addicted to the vices of thieving and lying to an extent that is fearful to contemplate.'[32]

As usual, hierarchies of 'evil' are established. We are told that when they first arrived, the Portuguese 'were not so much addicted to these vices, but the lower classes of them . . . are, I fear, beginning to be contaminated by the bad example shown by their compeers'. The Chinese, meanwhile, are dismissed as 'a very immoral set of people'.[33] As has long been customary with colonial administrators, McRae attributes characteristics and physical competences to particular racial or tribal groups. He asserts that 'The coolies are generally best employed at weeding and moulding, the Creole men at shovel work, the women at weeding and moulding, and the Africans at cutting canes and shovel work.' The Portuguese apparently are best suited to cutting cane and fuel-wood, and the Chinese to weeding, moulding and cane-cutting. 'If these castes would amalgamate kindly,' he grumbles, 'labour could be better concentrated and more cheaply performed.'[34]

While much of McRae's manual is devoted to the planting of agricultural crops and what appears to be his personal obsession, drainage, other details reveal how planters treated their workers. As under slavery, the focus is on economic efficiency. McRae advises prospective planters regarding the distribution of food, suggesting: 'The overseer in charge of this department ought either to weigh, measure, or reckon every article of stores given out by him for consumption.'[35] The treatment of illness is encouraged not as a duty or a human right but as 'the most powerful means of eliciting gratitude from a Negro or coolie', which McRae says 'paves the way to the exercise of a commanding influence over their minds'.[36] Religious instruction is also strongly advised, with the insistent demand that 'the minister of the Gospel, in order to accomplish the conversion of such sinners, must go amongst them in their private dwellings, and address them in their own language'.[37] Interestingly there is also a suggestion of growing divisions within the indentured population. McRae refers to 'a furious riot of the Creole and African black population' on 19 and 20 February 1856, which 'took place throughout the rural districts from one end of the colony to the other'.[38] He claims, 'They broke in by violence to almost every Portuguese shop and rifled them completely of their contents.'[39]

Seven years later, we can see the growth of the Portuguese traders in a letter from Sandbach Parker & Co. in Demerara to Sandbach Tinne & Co. in Liverpool:

> . . . matters in Water Street are in a very uncomfortable state. The failure of De Jongues . . . not only cripples many of the Portuguese traders but has brought to light the fact that the whole system of Water Street business is anything but admirably conducted. Many names who ought to be above such meanness condescending to ease the wind by means of Portuguese names on paper . . . mainly at the Colonial Bank.[40]

Today's Guyanese still refer to the 'Portuguese' as separate from 'Europeans' when explaining the country's 'Land of Six Peoples' moniker (usually listed as Indigenous, European, African, Indian, Portuguese and Chinese). This indicates the continued racialisation of the Portuguese in Guyana not as white Europeans, but as former indentured workers who escaped the cane field; it may also be due to their darker Mediterranean complexion, having emerged in the late fifteenth century from 700 years of Black and Arab

Moorish rule in the former Iberian Emirates of Muslim Spain and Portugal.

The Portuguese, however, like other Europeans, could not abide the arduous, back-breaking work on the plantations in the blistering heat and humidity of the Caribbean coast. Eric Williams asserts that 'The Portuguese died like flies on the plantations, they multiplied when they took to retail trade.'[41] However, the 1851 census cited earlier listed 7,928 'Madeirans' as distinct from the 2,088 'English, Scotch, Irish, Dutch, and Americans'. The Portuguese were not the only ones to strive for higher positions. In the Who's Who – *Guyanese Sugar Plantations in the late Nineteenth Century*, edited by Walter Rodney – 'an unnamed reporter' talks of the journey of a man named Harry Rose, an illiterate day labourer at Plantation Smythfield 'who rose from the ranks to become trusted foreman and later manager'. The proprietor, James Laing, went on to entrust him with the management of the plantation known as 'Friends'. The account goes on to say that 'Harry Rose became proprietor of Pln. Highbury when the Administrator General brought it to the hammer, and Harry Rose and his partners, the two brothers McWatt, became the proprietors.'[42] It is likely that this mixed-race person was of the progeny of either Peter Rose or his brother Andrew Rose, both influential in the colony. This would also potentially establish a familial connection through Anna Rose to the footballer Andrew Watson.

Social mobility, it seems, was at times possible for at least some of the mixed-race children or their mothers and wider relatives – particularly of the Sandbach Tinne dynasty. Perhaps the starkest example of this is the remarkable case of Dorothy 'Doll' Thomas (or Kirwan, a name derived from her owner in Montserrat). A mixed or so-called 'mulatto' woman, she was born enslaved around 1756 in Montserrat, was taken to Grenada and then – like the Sandbach Tinne founding partners – moved to Demerara, where she rose through the ranks of British Guianese society, and later also British society. Her daughter Eliza Thomas married Gilbert Robertson, thus bringing her into the Sandbach Tinne dynasty.

In a letter to his wife, Sandbach Tinne partner Charles Stuart Parker the elder sarcastically sneered, 'Who do you think is in Glasgow but Gilbert Robertson's mother-in-law [Doll Thomas], with about 19 other children & grandchildren come home for education?'[43] Dorothy 'Doll' Thomas is remarkable for many reasons; she inherited a fortune from her former master in Grenada, who freed her and brought her to Demerara. She bought her children out of enslavement, ran a team of hucksters selling wares all over the colonies of Demerara, Essequibo and Berbice and had business interests, including brothels, across the Caribbean and South America. In the 1863 letter quoted earlier regarding the Portuguese traders in Georgetown, the sender Sandbach Parker & Co., referring to certain financial accounts, added, 'this, however, does not include invoices of goods on the way or ordered, which including that of Dorothy, we estimate at about £3000'.[44] This amount is worth approximately £177,388 today.[45] How did a mixed-race woman of colour in British Guiana, less than three decades after the legal abolition of slavery, amass so much money that in one invoice she could be placing such significant orders?

Many instances occurred in which persons of colour of both sexes intermarried with some of the most high-profile inhabitants of British Guiana. The question of colour appears to have not always operated entirely as a 'social obstacle'.[46]

From the first encounters with indigenous peoples, through enslavement to indentureship, interracial mixing, or miscegenation as it is called, was entrenched in the British colonisation model across the Caribbean, and the Sandbach, Robertson, Watson, Parker, Rainy and Tinne families were no exception. On 24 April 1821, George Rainy wrote to Charles Stuart Parker, sharing the latest gossip from Demerara: 'I am sorry to say that my cousin Mrs Fraser has turned out in the way in which almost all of her colour & description are sure to end.'[47] While Rainy does not give further details as to his relative's racial background, it is clear that he sees her as belonging to a particular group typified by their colour, perhaps someone who at the time would have been described as a 'mulatto' or 'quadroon' (of one-quarter African ancestry), however, he clearly acknowledges her as his 'cousin'.

He goes on to say, 'She has eloped from her husband (who whatever his due failings, was not deficient in duty to her) and taken up with a miserable . . . hypocrite with who she formed an acquaintance at a missionary or methodist chapel, and I believe now lives with him. I am only sorry for her poor mother who had expended all her slender means on this shameless wretch and her sister.'

As Dalton had claimed that the question of colour may not have always operated as a 'social obstacle', there was a shifting set of rules and attitudes as regards to when mixing was permissible and open and when it was to be hidden. An imbalance in the white, English male to female ratios in British Guiana, and made 'miscegenation'[48] inevitable. Looking at the demographics for the colony in 1856, the year Andrew Watson was born, I found there were only 200 adult white women in the whole colony compared to over 40,000 adult Black and Indian women. You could travel for a month and never see a white woman. In the census of 1851, a few more had been there. 'English, Scotch, Irish, Dutch and American' adult white women in Demerara were 318, in Essequibo 43, and in Berbice there were 49, a grand total of 410 adult white females, in the colony with a total population of 127,695.[49]

William Windham provides us with a first-hand account which explains the protocol for the rape and general sexual exploitation of enslaved women by white Europeans in the colony. The description is both brazen and absurd, in that this could have ever been considered as 'legalised'. He states:

> When a European arrives in the West Indies and gets settled, or set down for any length of time, he finds it necessary to provide himself with a housekeeper, or mistress. The choice he has an opportunity of making is various, a Black, a

Tawney, a Mulatto, or a Mestee; one of which can be purchased for L 100 or L 150 (sterling), fully competent to fulfil all the duties of her station. Some of them are so much educated as to be able to read and write. They are tasty and extravagant in their dress; but when once an attachment takes place it is inviolable. The strictest scrutiny of their conduct in general cannot glean one particle of impropriety, by which their fidelity or constancy can be brought into question. They embrace all the duties of a wife, except presiding at the table, [a condition imposed also upon Dido Belle] so far as decorum is maintained, and a distinction made . . . Their usefulness in preserving the arts and diffusing the habits of cleanliness is felt and allowed by all, there being a lack of civilized European women.

What he perhaps should have been saying is that there was 'a lack of civilised European men', such was their so-called 'dignified' depravity.

In Alston's 'A Forgotten Diaspora' he says, 'And in 1830 a young doctor of Highland descent, Pierre Antoine Munro, wrote to his mother in Montreal saying, "We are living here like hermits, being so few whites in the place. You will probably not believe that I have not seen the face of a white lady for three months."'

A Scottish soldier quoted in *Rebecca's Ordeal*, a paper centring the experiences and resistance of an enslaved African woman, puts it more brutally. Recounting his experience of examining a slave ship after its arrival in British Guiana in the early nineteenth century, we are told he was 'appalled to find a group of five or six young girls, as naked as they were born' confined in the captain's quarters, where they were shared by the captain and his first mate'.[50]

The inevitable result of this grotesque and systemic sexual abuse by white men of enslaved African female children was mixed-race offspring. Interracial sexual relationships, whether forced, coerced or in some limited cases consensual, led to a diverse local population, stratified by their skin tones and afforded a range of privileges ranging from none at all for the blackest, to in some cases freedom for those closest to white. While there was a general perception that so-called 'Mulattos' on the plantation were treated more favourably by their masters and given roles within the house rather than in the field, life was far from easy. Abuse, violence, rape and cruelty were endemic and ingrained in the very fabric of the colony, from the accepted cultural norms, which included child rape by white masters, to flogging, cutting off ears, being broken at the wheel (tied naked to a cartwheel and having each limb broken with a club, one by one and left out in the scorching sun to die slowly), being boiled alive in a vat of molten sugar and stripping your skin off the flesh. This was all considered 'civilised' by white Europeans.

I found that on one of Thomas Cummings' estates, a so-called 'Mulatto' woman was whipped while she was heavily pregnant for insubordination, having refused to come to his bed to be raped. She was stripped naked, hung from a tree and whipped so violently with the cat o' nine tails that it broke almost every bone in the unborn baby's tiny body. When she gave birth to the baby it was horribly deformed but, incredibly, it survived. As it was a public spectacle, the horrific scenes were witnessed by others on the plantation, demonstrating what would happen to any Black woman who refused to be raped by her white master. The matter was brought by way of complaint to the Protector of Slaves appointed after Canning's amelioration measures of 1823 came into force. The judicial question was not about the white man wanting to rape the Black woman, nor about the despicable deformity of the newborn child battered to a pulp in its mother's womb, nor still about the barbarity and degradation of the callous and depraved brutality exerted by a grown man against a defenceless pregnant woman; in law, the question at hand was whether or not she had received more than the prescribed thirty-nine lashes, permitted under British colonial legislation. As the woman passed out during the torture, she was unable to attest to the number of lashes she had received, so the white master was acquitted of all wrongdoing, his reputation intact.

Henry Dalton, in his *History of British Guiana*, charts a changing picture for the so-called 'Mulatto' in the colony at this time: 'The slave, though raised to her master's embraces, was still his menial; her children became his property, were still accounted slaves, and were often compelled to the labour of the field, without being allowed to derive any advantage from their European descent. This, however, was not the general rule. The mother and her offspring were frequently made free by purchase, and the children brought up to some trade or business.'

He goes on to explain the terminology used to categorise mixedness; from the 'Mulatto' who was gradually whitened, to the 'Tercerones' and 'Quadroon', then the 'Quarterones', with 'all distinction finally vanishing in the 'Quinterons', who owed their origin to a white and 'Quarteron', called also 'Mustees'.[51] He tops this off with an unflattering sketch of the so-called 'Mulatto' man: 'He was marked by some of the most conspicuous traits of his descent on both sides, the prejudices and haughtiness of his European father, and the levity and the idleness of his African mother . . . his means were restrained; jealous of his parentage, he was denied its privileges. Such is the desire of the free coloured population for light and frivolous occupations and their contempt for agricultural pursuits.' Dalton tells us that 'they are not unfrequently outstripped in worldly prosperity by the plodding and unambitious Negro', and eventually were 'the worst off in a community where, at one time, they held a middle rank' – although, he adds, they do have 'some smattering of education'. In reality, there was no single mixed experience, and certainly more than Dalton's two thin portrayals of the 'enslaved Mulatto' or the 'light and frivolous' free coloured.

CHAPTER 12

'MERCANTILE MONSTERS'

The path to riches is paved with deceit,
but the reward is a barren soul.
– Old saying

When Black and mixed-race women are referred to in texts about enslavement, the subject is often the subjugation of their physical selves and, more particularly, their sexual exploitation at the hands of their ravenous and depraved white owners. The depths of this abhorrent historic episode in the lives of the enslaved are still emerging. As the archives gradually unfurl, the true horrors are becoming more evident. Despite these atrocities, what we rarely hear of is the notion that some of these Black and Brown women had any sort of agency.

In all historic periods, there are prevailing narratives and invariably there are also exceptions, such as Lord Mansfield's mixed-race great-niece Dido Elizabeth Belle, mentioned earlier. Whilst growing up amid relative opulence at the Lord Chief Justice's mansion, Kenwood House, she enjoyed the trappings of wealth, while still being subject to racial codes, which, due to her African heritage, disallowed her from sitting at the table when guests came to dinner. Though her mother, Maria Belle – an enslaved child who had been captured by the British aboard a Spanish galleon at the age of fourteen – had no agency when she was raped by Sir John Lindsay (1737–1788), 3rd Baronet of Evelix, captain of HMS *Trent*, and nephew of Lord Mansfield, Dido – the offspring of that rape – somehow did. Dido inherited from her great-uncle, Lord Mansfield; she was educated to a high standard and later married.

There is also the case of Annetta (or Annette) Watson, the sister of Andrew Watson. In the census of 1871, we find Annetta, aged twenty-one, living in Innerleithen in Scotland with William Robertson Watson, her uncle (recently returned from Demerara), now aged sixty-five, who is listed as an 'accountant'. Interestingly, under 'Occupation', Annetta's entry records 'D/O' or 'ditto', suggesting she was following in the footsteps of her uncle.

Two years later, Annetta declares her marriage to John Hunter Stephenson, Esq., of London, in the *Glasgow Herald* dated 2 October 1873, and is listed as 'daughter of the late Peter M. Watson, Esq., Georgetown, Demerara, and of Weylea, near Guildford, Surrey'.[1] The marriage was not a happy one, as we know from the legal documents of Annetta's application for a 'Protection Order' dated 5 February 1875. At the time, she stated her residence as the 'furnished apartments at No. 6 Weymouth Street, Portland Place (London) in the County of Middlesex'. For the first month of their marriage, the couple lived in Brighton, before moving to 138 Kensington Park Road, London. Six months later, on 16 May 1874, Stephenson abandoned his wife, as Annetta recounts in her statement:

> He left me without reasonable cause and did not return for any purpose except on the 29th day of August 1874, when he stayed only one hour and on the 1st day of September 1874, when he stayed about three quarters of an hour, his expressed object at both such visits being to persuade me to leave the said house 138 Kensington Park Road, and go on a visit to my friends which I did on the 4th day of September 1874.

Annetta returned to their Kensington Park Road home a month later and lived there alone for a few days. She bumped into her husband in the city, and he promised to return home the next day, but never showed up. A few days later, Annetta reported, he told her that he was 'planning to rent out the house' and that 'I must find a home with friends or where I could'. She eventually took up lodging in a private boarding establishment, where she was visited for one hour by Stephenson, who promised again to come and live with her as his wife. He returned on 15 December and stayed one night, telling her he 'cannot reside at the boarding establishment on account of the expense'.

What now becomes clear is that the mixed-race Annetta is more solvent than her white merchant husband. She has dividends on shares left to her under the will of Peter Miller Watson, her 'deceased father', and she was entitled to a half-yearly income paid annually in January and July.

Since 16 May 1874, she said, 'I have become entitled to receive the sum of £99.7'11/- cash and which sum I expect very shortly will be paid to me.' That her husband first left her on exactly the day she was entitled to receive a large sum of money may seem counterintuitive, but it seems Stephenson expected to have his cake and eat it. Annetta continued, 'I have lately received the portion of the income due to me in January last past' – adding that, 'the said John Hunter Stephenson did on the 2nd day of the present month of February, apply to and prevail upon me to give him the sum of £50 of my said own monies.' The background that Annetta gives suggests that this is not a one-off; on 1 June 1874, she claimed, Stephenson 'has never given me any money for housekeeping lodging or other expenses and I have maintained myself and continue to maintain myself from my own property' – this despite her merchant husband having 'a good annual income of at least three hundred pounds'. In one sad line, she captures a different kind of sorrow she has faced: 'That we have had issue of our marriage – one child which is now dead.' It appears that they had a form of informal marriage in Scotland, she then became pregnant and before the birth in early 1874, they registered the marriage in London. The purpose of her legal claim, she concludes, is 'That I am desirous, and I am advised and believe it is necessary, that an order should be made by this Honourable Court for the protection of my monies and property acquired since the said 16th day of May 1874, from the said John Hunter Stephenson and from all Creditors and persons claiming under him.' It does not state who had advised her, but the executor and executrix of her father's estate, Dr Robert Ormond and his wife Mary Eliza Traill, would have had a fiduciary responsibility in their trusteeship to protect her inheritance, even from her white merchant husband.

Annetta applied on 17 July 1875 for a divorce petition (decree nisi) in Her Majesty's Court for Divorce and Matrimonial Causes. Although in her earlier filing she still seemed to hope for a reconciliation, saying 'there is no reason why he should not reside with me', it now seemed that things had become more toxic after the first filing, and any hope of reconciliation was dashed. Llew Walker refers to additional allegations in the subsequent case, stating that; 'in the second filing, she described the abandonment in October 1873, a month after their marriage. She said Hunter Stephenson had contracted a venereal disease and in December, "wilfully" passed it on to her. She described this, saying he ". . . committed adultery with Selina Deacon. That on diverse occasions, he committed adultery with diverse women – to your petitioner, unknown."' This should have been grounds for an immediate divorce, but he denied it.

Annetta died on 31 March 1889, at 15 Florence Place, Glasgow, at the age of forty. She was still listed as being married to John Hunter Stephenson, as the embarrassment of having her case heard before a jury – which had been the decree of the judge hearing her petition – had caused her to drop the proceedings. This meant that the application for divorce was never made final (decree absolute). The cause of death is given as 'Cirrhosis of liver – 6 years' which could conceivably have been caused by a venereal disease such as hepatitis. The Probate Scotland records list the value of her estate at death as £213 7s. 7d. (about £17,507 in today's money).

On her death certificate, Annetta's parents are listed as 'Hannah Watson, M.S. Rose (deceased)' and 'Patrick Watson, Sugar Planter (deceased)' – 'Patrick' presumably being an administrative error. After all, we know well that she was the daughter of Peter Miller Watson and Anna (or Hannah) Watson, née Rose, the so-called 'Mulatto' daughter of Andrew Rose and an enslaved African woman, Minkey. This is the same Andrew Rose whom we find listed as a contact in a 'for sale' advertisement from around 1808, offering '20 to 50 or 60 prime seasoned Negroes, who have been for some years employed in a task-gang, among them are from eight to ten complete brick-makers and an excellent driver'. Andrew Rose's sister Anna (the wife of Philip Frederick Tinne), also living in Demerara, wrote to her mother in June 1807, saying, 'I told you in my last letter that Andrew had lost his little Mary. On the whole it is a fortunate circumstance as 'tis next to impossible to bring up a girl of that colour virtuously, a reference to the high demand amongst white men for the sexual exploitation of 'Mullato' girls.'[2] It seems therefore that Anna (or Hannah) was not Andrew Rose's first mixed-race child. While many business records of Peter Miller Watson remain, we know little of Anna (or Hannah) Rose, or their relationship, beyond their two children Andrew and Annetta. The online resource of British Guiana Colonists lists 'Rose, Hannah . . . married Watson, Peter Miller', but no date or location is given. And what of Minkey, Hannah's mother? Few scraps remain. In the *Demerary and Essequibo Royal Gazette* of 12 October 1811, a notice appears: 'The following persons have petitioned . . . the Court of Policy of the colonies of Demerary and Essequibo, for letters of manumission for the after-named slaves, as follows . . . Andrew Rose for the Negro woman named Minkey, and her mulatto child Anna.'

Interestingly, the notice is signed 'Courthouse, Stabroek, Demerary, 12th October 1811', which gives us some idea that the mixed-race Anna Rose was an infant in 1811. This would have made her perhaps forty-five or forty-six years old when she gave birth to Andrew Watson and either thirty-eight or thirty-nine years old when she had Annetta. Peter Miller Watson was born in 1805, so he was fifty-one at Andrew's birth and forty-four at Annetta's. We know Peter Miller Watson was in Demerara in 1823 from the letters he wrote home to his family about the uprising when he was barely eighteen years old. This raises the question of what he did for the satisfaction of his manly needs between the age of eighteen, which is the earliest account of his presence in Guiana, and the age of forty-three when he and Anna conceived Annetta? There is a gap of twenty-five years in his adult life with no mention of any other woman or children, despite the tradition of white men taking a mistress as soon as they arrived in the colony. Perhaps this explains the Watson children of Demerara, Mahaica and Berbice, who were – and, in some cases still are – landowners, including my own late grandfather George Edward Watson, and the oral histories of other Watsons about the 'three white Scottish brothers'.

The document manumitting the enslaved Minkey and her mixed-race daughter Anna (or Hannah) Rose, was signed by 'P.F. Tinne, Dy. Secty.' Having married another Anna Rose (1785–1827), Andrew Rose's white Scottish sister, Tinne then became Andrew Rose's brother-in-law. When Peter Miller Watson had a civil union with Anna (or Hannah) Rose, P.F. Tinne became Anna (or Hannah)'s uncle by marriage, making P.F. Tinne Andrew and Annetta Watson's great-uncle by marriage.

In a later edition of the *Demerary and Essequebo Royal Gazette* dated 18 February 1815, we find a further reference to Minkey (or Mincky): 'At the Commissary Court of the 6th of March 1815, will be passed the following Transports and Mortgages . . . 6. By E. J. Henery, n. ux. transport of the lot No. 229, Cummingsburg, with the buildings thereon, to the free Mincky Rose, with remainder to her children Ann and George Rose [Anna's mixed-race brother].'[3]

In the same edition of the newspaper, we can find a possible motive for the transfer of the property to Minkey under the heading, 'This is to inform the public, that the following persons intend quitting the colony.' On the list is Peter Rose, who is expected to leave British Guiana 'in 14 days or 6 weeks, from January 25th 1815', when he was about twenty-eight years old. With his departure imminent, Peter Rose left the property in the custody of his brother Andrew, who gifted it to Mincky for her and the children.[4] Peter Rose later returned to the colony and died there.

Other individuals named on the same departure list give us some insight into the lives and opportunities open to members of the free coloured population at this time, such as 'John Vial, free coloured man, with a servant' and 'Sarah Ann Hinds, free Mustee woman'. In September of that year, Minkey made another appearance in the *Royal Gazette*, a few months after her property acquisition, though this time she was the vendor: 'The Free Coloured Minkey Rose, Transport of the Concession or Lot No. 229 with all the buildings thereon, situated in Cummingsburg district – to M. Viret.'[5] Clearly, she had ownership of the land and buildings to enable her to sell the property and realise its value. Cummingsburg, where Samuel Sandbach and many of the rich merchants and dignitaries lived, was perhaps the wealthiest area of Georgetown.

Harry Robertson Watson, the oldest of James Watson's sons with Christian Robertson, had travelled to Demerara ahead of his brothers, as recorded by Dr Traill:

> In the month of April . . . (1817) Mrs Traill had to sustain a severe trial in parting with Harry Watson, her first born. He had acquitted himself highly to the satisfaction of his employers in the counting houses of Mr John Gladstone and Messrs Ewart & Rutson; and with very flattering testimonials, from these eminent merchants, of his steadiness and talent, he embarked for Demerary, under the auspices of Mr Gladstone; & the immediate care of a friend of experience in that colony. I loved him as one of my own children. Mrs Traill's maternal solicitude was received by hearing of his safe arrival in the colony, in the month of May, after a passage of 5 or 6 weeks.[6]

Harry would have been about seventeen years old at the time.

We have mixed accounts of Peter Miller Watson. His brother,

Andrew Watson (uncle of the footballer Andrew Watson), wrote to their mother, Christian, now Mrs Traill, from Georgetown on 15 October 1828, taunting his brother that 'Peter is just the same crabbed body he was at home, must have his own way in everything.' Although he does add, 'He is quite well and I think a good deal stronger in constitution than he was twelve months ago.'[7] The 'Memoir of Mrs Traill' (written by her second husband Dr Thomas S. Traill), records Traill's stepson's journey more favourably:

> On the 9th of November, (1822) Peter Watson, who had been for two years in the counting house of his uncle, Mr Sandbach,[8] where he gave the highest satisfaction, left England for Demerary. He had attempted to sail the previous day but was driven back; but on the second trial, they got well off. I, accompanying him beyond the floating light. Peter arrived in Demerary on the 19th of December, after a favourable passage, and immediately took an active share in the business, the vast concerns of the house of McInroy, Parker & Sandbach in that colony. He was especially under the guidance of his cousin George Rainy, a partner in that house – and has ever since maintained the highest character, as a man of business & integrity. Two of the Brothers were thus settled in British Guiana, both highly respected, Harry had about this time became a partner in a respectable mercantile house, and Peter became a great favourite with his cousin, the managing partner of that establishment, and one of the most able and respected men, who had ever lived in that colony.[9]

William[10] and Andrew[11] would later join them (after Andrew's stint with Messrs Gifillan in Bahia in Brazil in 1819–1820 and in Rio de Janeiro from 1820 to 1822). After a brief trip home and a falling out with a partner at the firm in Bahia, Andrew set off for Demerary in March of 1823 arriving in April, just four months prior to the Demerara uprising.

It appears that Peter Miller Watson had felt somewhat isolated in Demerara, perhaps due to the long periods he spent there, or to his serious approach to work and his vast portfolio of slave concerns. On 12 March 1855, just over a year before his mixed-race son Andrew Watson was born, he wrote from London to his brother William Robertson Watson, who by now had left the colony, and lamented, 'I only hear from Liverpool occasionally on business & have no idea of what is going on in the family circle . . . I have not been clear of cough & cold since November, & don't expect to be until there is a fixed change in the weather. When it regularly takes up, I intend going North.'[12]

Peter did provide for his mixed-race children – the ones that we know of – as is clear from Annetta's court statement. That is not to say, though, that they were incredibly wealthy, but they did have a comfortable income which assured their financial independence. The houses they are recorded as living in are in middle-class areas and although both siblings did work at various points in their lives, so did the richer members of the family. What is heartening is that it seems that Andrew and Annetta remained close. Annetta's death certificate records the address where she passed away in March 1889 as 15 Florence Place, Glasgow. Two years earlier, on 10 February 1887, her brother married his second wife, Eliza Kate Tyler (1861–1949) at the same address, suggesting that he either lived with his sister at this time or chose to have her host his wedding. We have no account of any other children of Peter's in Demerara, but it is unlikely that Andrew and Annetta – both born past his middle age – were the only ones. It is possible that there were others with enslaved women who were perhaps gifted land in Guiana by Peter but not brought out of the country, or who were dealt with in his will by means of prior gifts. Peter was never married in the UK. Furthermore, both Harry Robertson Watson (1801–1836) who died in Demerara and his brother Andrew Watson (1803–1837), who died on Plantation William in Guiana,[13] were recorded as 'unmarried' and both predeceased their mother Christian, who died in 1842.

Plantation William was owned in 1852 by Parker, Garrett & Co.,[14] another iteration of the Sandbach Tinne dynasty's vast business portfolio.

Andrew Watson was clearly connected to the white side of his family. His father Peter Miller Watson died while he was at school, but his aunt Mary Eliza Traill and her husband Dr Robert Ormond, acting as his father's executors, kept Andrew very much in the family fold. Annetta, while older, was the ward of Peter's brother William Robertson Watson, prior to her beleaguered marriage, as her inheritance was conditional upon her marriage. However, Andrew's career path – apart from the football – seems closely aligned to the family firm's own modus operandi.

His Glasgow address on Shields Road, located next to a railway yard, was likely not accidental. Shields Road in Pollokshields, Glasgow, is where three railway stations – Pollokshields, Shields Road and Shields – were constructed in the late 1800s, and were later replaced by the new Shields Road station, which opened in 1925 and closed in 1966. Even today it is a major rail hub, and it may have been a place where Watson gained experience in the now mature steam engine business that Sandbach Tinne championed globally. By the time Watson was old enough to be apprenticed, Sandbach Tinne were already shipping steam trains and rail track throughout the empire and globally. Captain Angel – an employee both of Sandbach Tinne and occasionally Messrs. R. Gladstone & Co. – recounted one such consignment: 'I was appointed to the command of the composite barque[15] "Mora", a fine craft in which I made four voyages to Demerara, and a long one to Japan, loaded with locomotives and iron railway bridgework.'[16]

The railway industry was burgeoning worldwide during this period, and Andrew Watson, as an engineer, was well placed to take advantage. His former tutor, who a few years later became Lord Kelvin, not only patented the then experimental gyrocompass,[17] but tested it out first on a Sandbach Tinne ship, the *Sheila*. According to a narrative by its master, Captain Angel, as they sailed out of the port of Glasgow, 'Scotland's grand old man was with us, accompanied by his assistants. We, being the first ship fitted with his celebrated compass . . . Of course, it goes without saying, the intercourse which we had with William [later Lord Kelvin] was an intellectual treat. He was most kind and patiently explained everything we wanted to know.'

The gyrocompass was a necessary step in the field of navigation. When ships with metal hulls were first introduced, the metal affected the accuracy of magnetic compasses, which rely on the earth's magnetism to read magnetic north. Kelvin (then William Thomson) had to come up with a design that could show true north (i.e. the North Pole) without being affected by the magnetism of the earth or any interference. Like Andrew Watson, I am an ex-seaman, and in 1986 while working for British Petroleum (BP) on one of their oil tankers, the MV *British Skill*, I took my steering certificate, spending the requisite hours at the wheel, steering this tanker across the South Atlantic between Angola and the Caribbean. Before the satellite navigating system came in, we navigated using the same gyrocompass.

Peter Miller Watson's mixed-race children were typical of this family. George Robertson had a so-called 'mulatto son', known as 'Black George'. Robertson's Scottish brother John, in Trinidad, had two 'mulatto' sons, Charles and Daniel. George Rainy had two 'mulatto' daughters, Mary Augusta (1828–1854) and Elizabeth Jemima (1830–1899). Charles Stuart Parker is said to have had 'natural-born mulatto' children, James (Jim) Parker and Charles Parker, and Samuel Sandbach of Grenada had a 'mulatto' daughter, Roza Catherina. Philip Frederick Tinne's brother Chrétien Tinne had a Black son by an enslaved woman called Mary. In a letter from Peter Miller Watson in Demerara to his brother William, dated 2 November 1845, he wrote with some irritation: 'I have since received your 2 notes by the Packit . . . I have not a sixpence of yours in my hands . . . I know that Mr Munro so clearly laid down the state in which you left your affairs, that you must look to providing for yourself.'[18]

What interests me most is what follows: 'Today the boy Henry came to Town. What am I to do with him? Not having been downstairs for some days I have not seen the Boy!' As William was a plantation overseer in Berbice, it is my belief that the 'boy Henry', clearly William's offspring, had 'come to town', denoting that he was not from Demerara, and Peter's contention that 'I have not a sixpence of yours in my hands' is a clear indication that the boy is William's responsibility and Peter has not been left any provision to deal with him. He has clearly come to his uncle Peter for some support. It is therefore likely that the Berbice Watsons are descended of William Robertson Watson, through 'the boy Henry' or William's brother Andrew Watson who was also in Berbice at the time.

Another hint of a mixed-race child in the family is suggested by Peter and William's brother Andrew Watson, writing again to their mother, Mrs Traill, from Berbice on 16 May 1837. In this letter he seems to be referring to a previous exchange when he writes, 'I thought that you were aware that Mr Robertson had a daughter',[19] presumably referring to his uncle Gilbert Robertson. He goes on: 'The old man (as we call him) has been most particular as to her instruction in every way which he could afford and has been more strict with her than many fathers would be, conscious of her colour. She attends to all my household affairs, although at the same time I have servants who do not require to be told what to do.'

Other examples of this racial and gendered nuance can also be found in the mixed-race women of the period. Doll Thomas had white men hanging off her daughter's arms (and purse strings) and was determined to protect their independent means – much like the other free coloured women of Demerara. 'Far from being just madams or mistresses, these were savvy, well-connected, and resourceful women who operated substantial businesses in a complex world of material wealth. It took skill to maintain the kinds of property portfolios that these women enjoyed, and even more skill to move in the circles that brought them opportunities they could use to their advantage.'[20]

Gilbert Robertson (brother of Christian Robertson – later Watson, then Traill) is recorded in *The Families of Douglas of Mulderg* as a bachelor who 'died unmarried in Edinburgh, on his return from Demerara, 10 September 1839'. In reality, he 'married' Eliza Thomas, the so-called 'quadroon' daughter of Dorothy 'Doll' Thomas, known by some as 'the Queen of Demerara', and the pair bore two children: Henry Robertson (1807–1881) and Ann Robertson. A letter from his brother Hugh Munro Robertson to Dr Traill adds more details: 'I have met in Gilbert a most affectionate kind-hearted brother, who does everything to make me comfortable and happy. He is distressed at present by the loss of a sweet little girl of his called Ann; she was indeed one of the finest engaging children I ever saw. She was quite fair haired, & at first sight struck me as being very like little Ann Sandbach. She died after 14 days illness of a teething fever.'[21]

Ironically, just two years earlier in April 1804, Gilbert's sister-in-law Anne Robertson wrote to her daughter regarding meeting the mixed children of Dr George Bethune – or what she calls the 'two little foreigners'. She goes on to say, 'Their mother was a brigand. They are yellow, ugly things. I think it would be best to leave them in their own country, but their aunt seems very tender of them and much interested.' The Bethunes were married into the family through the Sandbachs. What Anne would have made of her own mixed nieces and nephews in Demerara is impossible to know.

The amazing life of Doll Thomas is well captured in the book *Enterprising Women: Gender, Race, and Power in the Revolutionary Atlantic* by Kit Candlin and Cassandra Pybus. She also makes an appearance in the Sandbach Tinne archives, while David Alston quotes a letter from Charles Stuart Parker to his wife in which Parker sneers: 'Who do you think is in Glasgow but Gilbert Robertson's Mother-in-Law Doll Thomas, with about 19 of her children & grandchildren come home for education.' Their father, Gilbert Robertson, however, seems to have wished the best for his children. When he came to London in 1824, records Alston, 'he wrote to Dr Traill saying that he was "very much rejoiced to find my poor boy

Henry settled with so respectable a man as Mr Bowman of Harley Street, a surgeon and apothecary whose clients included the Duke of Dorset and the Marquis of Waterford".' Credit falls to Henry's grandmother, Doll Thomas, 'who had found him the position and paid the £400 fee for the seven-year apprenticeship'. Gilbert adds, 'Mrs Thomas is here well & hearty & sends her best respects. She makes herself quite at home among a numerous circle of acquaintances.'

Doll Thomas's wealth was derived in part from her own ownership and employment of enslaved people. The UCL Legacies of British Slavery database lists under 'British Guiana 1621 (No. 38 Cummingsburg District George Town)' a claim dated 21 December 1835 for fifty-five enslaved persons at a cost of £2,691 17s 8d.[22] The recipient is Dorothy Thomas. Her daughter Charlotte is also recorded as entering 'ten-year old Henry's "ownership" of three females in the Register of Slaves', showing a perpetuation of slave ownership as an extension of the life to which she had been conditioned and the society which had normalised this abhorrent practice. The UCL database entry includes a quotation from Cheveley's journal referring to Georgetown in 1821, a time when 'Quite the head of the coloured class was Mrs Dorothy Thomas, usually styled Miss Doll, a dark mestizo (or mustee as we English will call it) with the deportment of an empress and reputed to be wealthy. She lived alternately in a splendidly furnished handsome house in Georgetown, and on her cotton estate up the coast, called Kensington.'[23] He continues, with an air of condescension, 'like most of her contemporaries, she had in her establishment, a white gentleman who was not rich but submitted to the degradation of being domineered by this imperious old Dame. Her balls and entertainment's . . . were not for black or coloured, but for white young gentlemen, who were not ashamed to dance with coloured young ladies.'[24]

Gilbert Robertson had perhaps been one of those men, who enticed Doll's daughter, Eliza – or was persuaded to court her by the state of his own bank balance, for we find that Gilbert had become reliant on the Thomas family for his occupation. 'In 1820 he was listed as joint manager for Mrs Thomas of the Kensington plantation, along with Eliza's half-sister, Charlotte Thomas.'[25] Gilbert Robertson, who had been joint owner with Gilbert Rainy of the Kiltearn plantation in Berbice, acquired L'Amitié en Libertie with Charles Stuart Parker, and managed Woodlands in Demerara for Parker, however the family were not altogether impressed: 'I am sorry to say that accounts of Gilbert Robertson (from him we have heard nothing) are far from flattering, he is over his head in debt, I see nothing for it but compulsive measures to get what can be got out of his hands.'[26]

In the nineteenth century, one of the family firm's acquaintances was a man by the name of Banastre Tarleton. At the time he was known as 'the most feared officer in the British army during the War for American Independence'; today he is probably better known indirectly through the fictional characters he has inspired, such as Colonel William Tavington in Mel Gibson's 2000 film *The Patriot*.[27] Banastre Tarleton was the brother of Thomas Tarleton, whose company Thomas Tarleton & Co. was listed as the owner of Plantation La Resource in Demerara in 1798.[28] Thomas was also a business associate of Samuel Sandbach, as I discovered through an 1824 indenture document between the two.[29] Their father, John Tarleton, had property in the Aigburth Hall estate, a gated community created by Sandbach Tinne and sold to slavers and bankers and prominent merchants. He had married Jane Parker (1726–1797), daughter and co-heir of Banastre Parker of Cuerden, Lancashire – possibly a family member.[30] John Tarleton was also the neighbour of Samuel Sandbach, who resided at 35 St Anne Street in Everton – while Banastre was at no. 34, right next door.

The place where Lieutenant Colonel Banastre Tarleton had been born incorporated the King's Arms Inn and Tavern, a complex which included the Talbot Hotel. It was where many of the slave-ship captains used to stay, a stone's throw from the pier head where the ships disembarked their cargoes. A news clipping from the

Stamford Mercury dated 20 October 1786 highlights how slavery had long been a visible, familiar part of Liverpool life – even at the inn itself: 'A curious Negro boy, who came in the James, Capt. Caton, from Jamaica, is now at Mr. Dale's, the King's Arms tavern in Liverpool . . . He is about 14 years old, part of his forehead, part of his hair, breast, and the back of his legs, are white, with a few spots.'[31] Its reputation was such that, 117 years later, in his 1903 book *Birkenhead and its Surroundings*, Henry Kelsall Aspinall would mention the inn standing near the churchyard of St Nicholas' Church on Water Street: 'This old public-house was at one time, to all intents and purposes – a slave-mart. Before the abolition of slavery, some hundreds of merchants resided in or about Liverpool, who carried on a large trade in buying and selling slaves.'[32]

Back in September 1832, on the cusp of emancipation, Water Street was widened, and a new institution was opened on the site of the former Talbot Hotel, which had been located next to the King's Arms. This was the Bank of Liverpool.[33] Formed in December 1830 under the chairmanship of Sir William Brown, it began trading in May 1831 as Samuel Sandbach took up the post of Mayor of Liverpool. The Bank of Liverpool was Britain's first joint stock bank, with multiple shareholders to spread financial risk, but its major shareholders were the Sandbach Tinne dynasty who also monopolised its board of directors for decades. Table 1 lists some examples of the roles of family members in the early years.

Table 1: Sandbach Tinne Family Members on the Executive Board of the Bank of Liverpool

Name	Institution	Role	Date
Samuel Sandbach	Bank of Liverpool[34]	Deputy Chairman	1843–45

		Chairman	1845–47
		Director	1833–37, 1838–42, 1843–47
John Abraham Tinne	Bank of Liverpool	Deputy Chairman	1871–72, 1875–76
		Chairman	1876–77, 1880–81
		Director	1868–72, 1873–77, 1878–82
William Robertson Sandbach	Bank of Liverpool	Deputy Chairman	1855–56
		Director	1847–51, 1852–56, 1857–58
Charles Stewart Parker	Bank of Liverpool	Director	1837–39, 1840–44
Alfred Traill Parker	Bank of Liverpool Ltd	Chairman	1892–93
		Director	1884–88, 1889–93, 1894–98, 1899–1900
Edward Hodgson Harrison (T & J Harrison Ltd Shipping Line)	Bank of Liverpool Ltd	Chairman	1888–89
		Deputy Chairman	1886–88
		Director	1880–84, 1885–89, 1890–94, 1895–99, 1900–04, 1905–06

Source: Chandler, G., Op-cit. pp.539–45.[35]

Table 2: Sandbach Tinne Family Members as shareholders of the Bank of Liverpool[36]

Name of Shareholder	No. of Shares
Samuel Sandbach	971
John Abraham Tinne	560
Henry Robertson Sandbach	172
George Rainy	1032

According to a history of the bank, its 'fortunes were linked with those of Liverpool's merchants trading in sugar, rum, tobacco and cotton from the Americas' – not least Samuel Sandbach, who became its deputy chairman, chairman and director.[37] The bank continued to grow, buying up local and regional banks including Haywood's Bank, once the pride of slave traders Benjamin and Arthur Haywood, and in 1918, it acquired and merged with London-based Martins Bank. Founded on Lombard Street by Sir Thomas Gresham in the reign of Queen Elizabeth I, Martins was the nucleus of what became the City of London financial centre. The combined bank became Bank of Liverpool & Martins Bank Ltd, later shortened simply to Martins Bank. Such was its liquidity and renown that in May 1940, during the Second World War, 280 tons of the nation's gold reserves were 'transported from the Bank of England to Martins' Head Office in Water Street, Liverpool for safekeeping before being shipped to safety in Canada' – under what was known as 'Operation Fish'. In 1969 the bank merged with Barclays.[38] At the time of the Barclays merger it had over 3,000 employees, 600 branches and was Britain's sixth largest bank, its success built almost entirely upon the proceeds of enslavement and colonialism. Its head office in Water Street – next door to Liverpool Town Hall – continued as Barclays' regional headquarters until 2007; the building is characterised by the stone engravings of two enslaved African boys holding money bags, beneath the fins of the sea god Neptune, as well as the bank's combined crest bearing a cricket, symbolic of Gresham's Martins Bank (and still of London's Gresham College), and a Liver Bird, a cormorant symbolic of the Bank of Liverpool and also the City of Liverpool.

As well as investing in the future of banks, the Sandbach Tinne dynasty invested in industry. A partnership agreement between Samuel Sandbach, Henry Robertson Sandbach and other parties dated 1848 records that in 1841, 'the said parties thereto did thereby mutually promise and agree to carry on the trade or business of iron founders and engineers and co-partners for the term of seven years'.[39] Meanwhile, in British Guiana, the work of producing lucrative goods using cheap labour continued. Even Dr Traill was involved. In the *Memoir of Mrs Traill*, he writes:

> Early in 1830 I was consulted by Mr Moss & Mr Gladstone, respecting the application of Howard's patent process to the production of sugar in the West Indies. I pointed out what modifications were necessary in applying it to the first production of sugar, and highly recommended it to both my friends: my views were adopted, and sugar with us produced, so fine and crystalline, that when sent home, there was a long demur about admitting it as unrefined sugar; and it was not entered, until affidavits were made to show that it was only once boiled. Mrs Trail had pride and pleasure in exhibiting at tea or breakfast this new sugar; in producing which she felt that her husband had some share.[40]

Dr Traill also had a keen interest in the development of the railway. In his diary, he wrote that 'the great experiment of locomotive steam engines, as a mode of conveyance of persons, was rapidly going on near Liverpool . . . I had contributed a small sum, in the beginning, to aid the original survey I could not afford to hold shares in the concern; but it had my warmest wishes for its success; and

I took much pleasure in our occasionally viewing the stupendous works, which I often brought strangers to behold.'[41]

In May 1829, Dr Traill took his wife (the former Mrs Watson), his daughter and some friends including Margaret Sandbach (née Roscoe), Samuel Sandbach's daughter-in-law and granddaughter of William Roscoe, to see the progress of the railway at Rainhill, a few miles from Liverpool. There they watched the steam locomotive *Novelty* 'gliding up and down, with an agreeable motion, that seemed more like the operations of magic, than the result of machinery'. Its inventors John Ericsson and John Braithwaite whispered to Dr Traill that they would like to offer his party a ride, 'adding, that hitherto they had been unable to persuade any ladies to venture on riding in a steam carriage'. So it was that the Traills 'first set the example to their countrywomen of travelling by steam on a railway', sitting in the open carriage and travelling at 25–30mph 'amid the cheers of a great crowd'. In 'A Short History of the Tinne Family', Dr John Ernest Tinne goes even further, describing them as 'the first ladies to travel by railway train in the world'.[42] This account is also recorded by Margaret Sandbach. Mrs Sandbach and her ladies (including, it would appear from Dr Traill's account, Mrs Traill – Andrew Watson's grandmother) were therefore the first women in the world to ride a train.

Although *Novelty* lost out to George and Robert Stephenson's *Rocket* in the locomotive trials later that year, the family had their fingers in that pie too.[43] The Liverpool Athenaeum holds the original maps of the track, including the first route which was rejected by Parliament and the subsequent route, which was finally adopted in the Liverpool and Manchester Railway Act 1829. It shows the colour-coded parcels of land that were bought up by the investors to facilitate the founding of the world's first commercial railway. Robert Gladstone, Sandbach Tinne and many of the other proprietors at the Athenaeum, such as fellow slave traders like John Moss, and fellow bankers like William Rathbone (of Rathbone's Bank) bought up all the plots of land through which the line was to run, and then determined where the stations would be along the way, situating them strategically through their personal estates and on the routes to their Lancashire cotton mills.

They commissioned a competition to see who could build the fastest and best steam engine to run on the line.[44] Moreover, a series of papers compiled and bound by John Gladstone, entitled 'The Liverpool Tracts', included the original prospectus for the founding of the Liverpool and Manchester Railway, with Robert Gladstone as its deputy chair along with slave trader John Moss and directors including Harrisons, Ewarts, Rathbones and Garnetts, all family members or business associates of the Sandbach Tinne dynasty.[45] Philip Frederick Tinne also put money towards the survey for the line, and Robert Stevenson, who made the *Rocket*, was Gladstone's engineer.[46] This was to be one of many railways with which the family would be involved. Tinne in his memoir stated that they also became directors of the Demerara Railway Co., and Andrew Watson was a 'railway shareholder' in the East Kilbride station in New South Wales, Australia. A report from the West Hartlepool Harbour and Railway Company, dated 21 February 1862, names committee members including Henry Robertson Sandbach of London and Hafodunos, Denbighshire, who was the chair of the shareholders at their meeting.

There is a photo of William Robertson Sandbach at the International Exhibition, or Great London Exposition, which was held from 1 May to 1 November 1862 in South Kensington, London, on a site that now houses the Natural History Museum and the Science Museum.[47] Sponsored by the Royal Society of Arts, Manufactures and Trade, the exhibition featured more than 28,000 exhibitors from thirty-six countries and some exhibits that would have greatly interested the family, including vast machines used for crushing sugar cane. One contemporary report recounts the awe of encountering the machine up close:

> We come upon a massive structure of beams, wheel, cranks, pistons, and cylinders, occupying so vast a space, and rearing

its iron limbs so high that, even were it motionless, it would inspire awe, but moving with that ponderous deliberation and steadiness which suggests unlimited power, a creeping sensation is felt. Yet is this huge monster only the docile minister of the simplest of our domestic comforts, and all this show of colossal power is but to fill the sugar-basin on our tea-table.[48]

The technology transfer from enslavers and their families, along with new developments in mechanisation and industrialisation, were evident everywhere in this family. Dr Traill, for instance, is often referred to as having no direct connection to enslavement, but this is not true. Despite being endowed by his wife from the proceeds of enslavement she received from her uncle George Robertson (Grenada/Demerara), he was also instrumental in developing technologies for the plantations including, as mentioned earlier, how to better refine sugar.

A report of the exhibition in *The Times* also described a line of British railway locomotives and huge foreign locomotives: 'The Great North of France Railway Company have sent a perfect monster of a locomotive, which has its boilers, cylinders, water-tank, and coal-bunk built up one above another, to such a height that the wonder is that it can pass under an ordinary bridge. Its chimney instead of standing straight upright, as is the manner with ordinary locomotives, has to be curled over its back like an elephant's trunk.'[49]

It was not only in the UK that the family saw the lucrative potential of the railways. When Rupert Andrew Watson inherited shares from his father, Andrew Watson, in the East Kilbride railway in New South Wales, Australia, he followed so many of the family out to that region and also followed his father in the field of steam engineering. In British Guiana, Peter Rose is listed in 1847 as a shareholder of the new Demerara Railway Company, which sought to build a line 'from the city of Georgetown, the capital of said colony, to Mahaica with extensions and branches and for other purposes'. A prospectus issued beforehand listed the capital investment proposed as '£100,000, or about $480,000, in 10,000 shares of £10, or $48 dollars each'.[50] When I interviewed Willie Williamson, one of the co-authors of the book on Robertson Gladstone in Demerara, I asked about the family's involvement in the railways. He recalled seeing in the archives at the Gladstone Museum in Hawarden – a village and community in Flintshire and the Gladstones' country estate – that there is a quotation from George Stephenson on building a railway line at Plantation Vreed-en-Hoop in Guiana. Williamson described the idea: 'To take the slaves from their housing in the morning – rather than they walk for about a mile or two – up to where they are cutting cane and working . . . and then of course they'd also be used to bring the sugar cane back, loaded to the factories where they crush it and all the rest of it.'

Despite their newfound interest in the emerging railway industry, the family's reputation (and wealth) was still tightly entwined with shipping. Sandbach Tinne even provided weather reports to the Met Office. In an issue of the journal *Nature* dated 28 June 1892, Robert H. Scott, Secretary of the Meteorological Office, shared an extract of a letter from Captain S.P. Hearn of the ship *Genista* telling of his experience battling whirlwinds in the Indian Ocean in May of that year. Scott notes that the letter was 'supplied to the Meteorological Office by Messrs. Sandbach, Tinne & Co., of Liverpool'.[51] This practice is still enacted to this day by shipping lines who now take daily soundings and refer them to the Met Office in London.

The influence of the Sandbach Tinne dynasty extended to all aspects of life in the colonies. In British Guiana, most stamps between 1863 and 1920 'bore a design of a full-rigged ship which was the 435-ton "Sandbach" built in 1823'. 'This ship', writes Dr John Ernest Tinne,

> held the Atlantic Blue Riband for the fastest crossing in her day and had two notable innovations for a sailing ship; She was the first vessel to use only chain cables instead of rope hawsers, and also her masts and bowsprit were fitted with

iron caps . . . She was one of the great and most popular ships of the port and sailed regularly from Liverpool for 50 years. But her draft being too great to cross the bar at Demerara the Sandbach had to lie out some 10 miles and be offloaded by lighters.

The *Sandbach* was finally retired from service, and due to the sentimentality of the firm's owners towards her, she was not sold but rather broken up in Birkenhead in 1878, each member of the company and crew taking some item of memorabilia from her. By this time, the focus was less on sailing ships with the emergence of the steamship. Basil Lubbock's book *The Coolie Ships and Oil Sailers* contains many fascinating details about the changing nature of the shipping trade. Between 1865 and 1871, it records that six composite clippers were launched for Sandbach Tinne & Co., namely: the *Fairlie* (1865), named after Charles Stuart Parker's residence of Fairlie in Largs in North Ayrshire, Scotland. The *Kiltearn* (1865), named after a parish in Scotland, and also the name of a Sandbach Tinne plantation in Guiana. The *Ron* (1867), the *Saint Kilda* (1868), the *Aisla* (1870), and *Mora* (ex-Lothair, 1871) – all of which were built in Glasgow (except the *Mora*). Then came eight iron ships. The *Brenda*, writes Lubbock, 'was the last of Sandbach Tinne's clippers.'

In order to fund their new investments and ventures, after emancipation the Sandbach Tinne dynasty relied not only on the extensive compensation they had received as former slave-owners, but the continued flow of income from their interests in British Guiana, which had shifted from enslaved labour, through apprenticeships and then finally to indentured labour, affording them longevity where others had long since wound up operations. I discovered an agreement signed in 1869 by Sandbach Tinne & Co. (at this point comprising Philip Frederick Tinne (1836–1869),[52] Samuel Sandbach Parker and Alfred Traill Parker), Henry Tinne Garnett and George Henry Oliver, the latter two comprising 'the Demerara Partners who shall reside there'.[53]

The sums are considerable. Sandbach Tinne & Co. pledge £100,000 and the others £50,000 each. The source of their 25 per cent share is explained in another document, which records a loan of '$80,000 dollars from Thomas Garnett and Alexander Garnett, to be repaid with interest by Henry Tinne Garnett (1827–1879)[54] and George Henry Oliver' signed 1 July 1869.[55] The articles of agreement are an interesting read and give further insight into the operations of the Sandbach Tinne dynasty, now in its third generation of familial ownership with the founders' grandchildren at the helm. Article V instructs that 'The business and all correspondence relating to it shall be carried on in the name of the firm and not in the name of individual partners, and all letters shall be copied in the books of the firm.'[56]

In this, there are glimpses of what is today a familiar tool, abdicating personal responsibility by hiding behind brand and company names to limit liability. There is also an awareness of conflicts of interest or perhaps insider trading, with Article II declaring: 'No partner shall enter into any other business in British Guiana than that of the co-partnership the intention of the partners being that such business as they can influence shall be transacted by Sandbach Parker & Co., in British Guiana and by Sandbach Tinne and Company in England.' This is also essentially a no-competition clause, creating a monopoly within the business.

Other agreements from the period show the family buying and selling plantation lots. A memorandum of agreement between Sandbach Tinne & Co. and Quintin Hogg refers to the sale of Plantation Industry, purchased by Hogg for £16,500 'as cash in London on 31st December 1875' – with payments incurring what appears to be the company's standard interest rate of 5 per cent.[57] Earlier that year, on 22 September 1875, a letter from Sandbach Parker & Co., to Messrs Sandbach Tinne & Co., Liverpool notes: 'Sugar making is now going on vigorously and we hope to see the account improve rapidly.' An article by Charles S. Parker (iii) in the July 1898 edition of *Fortnightly Review* entitled 'Free Trade and Cheap Sugar' provides a further sense of the scale of investment still pouring into the colony: 'The imports of sugar machines into British Guiana alone during the past twenty-five years exceed £2,000,000 in value.' Parker quotes a West India Royal Commission, which predicts that 'In Jamaica, in Trinidad, in British Guiana, in St Lucia, in St. Vincent, and to some extent in Montserrat and Nevis, the sugar industry may in time be replaced by other industries, but only after the lapse of a considerable period, and at the cost of much displacement of labour and consequent suffering.'

That is not to say the family were struggling. Another company agreement between Samuel Sandbach Parker, Alfred Traill Parker, John Ernest Tinne and Gilbert Robertson Sandbach and 'the Demerara Company Limited' shows the overall value of the company: 'The nominal capital of the company is two hundred thousand pounds divided into five hundred preference shares of one hundred pounds each, and one thousand five hundred ordinary shares of one hundred pounds each.'[58]

The document is dated 1891 (although this has later been overwritten as 1892) and mentions the registering of the company under the Companies Acts of 1862 and 1890, 'having for its objects, amongst other things, the acquisition and working of the hereditaments and property specified in the schedule' – a schedule which include Plantations Diamond and Providence.[59]

Politics was also a popular career move for members of the Sandbach Tinne dynasty. Having William Ewart Gladstone in the family's pocket had proved useful when it came to pushing policy regarding sugar. He had also demonstrated how a family's reputation could be turned around in one generation, from slave-owner to moral abolitionist. Other members of the family to join the Houses of Parliament included John Abraham Tinne (1877–1933), who was MP for Liverpool Wavertree from 1924 to 1931, and Liberal MP Charles Stuart Parker (1829–1910), who represented Perth in Parliament from 1868 to 1874 and 1878 to 1892.[60] Parker is also recorded in The Douglas & Robertson genealogies book as sitting on several commissions, acting as 'sometime Public Examiner', and later becoming 'Private Secretary to his uncle by marriage, Mr Cardwell, at the Colonial Office from 1864 to 1866' and 'Chairman of Referees on Private Bills'. Of course, in the wider family, there were among others Sir John Gladstone MP and Peter McLagan Jr, the first Black Scottish MP, with a tradition in civic office that has continued in this family even up to recent history.

Given their constant desire to make the system work for them, it is little wonder that the family's interests also expanded into law-making and enforcement. Henry Robertson Sandbach is remembered in his obituary as 'a magistrate and deputy-lieutenant for Denbighshire', and a relative of 'Mr. Samuel H. Sandbach, J.P. of Cherry-hill'.[61] The Douglas & Robertson genealogies book adds that Samuel Sandbach also 'served the offices of Bailiff, Coroner, and Mayor for the Borough of Liverpool, and also as High Sheriff of Denbighshire in 1839'. In British Guiana too, of course, many members of the family had long been connected to law enforcement and creation, such as Matthieu Tinne and his cousin Philip Frederick Tinne in the Court of Policy in Demerara. In 1851, a letter from McInroy Sandbach & Co., & Peter M. Watson in Demerara to Messrs Sandbach Tinne & Co. refers to the fact that 'no proceeding of the Court of Policy or Combined Court have been printed since the date of those in Mr Tinne's possession',[62] suggesting that such was his grip on the Court of Policy that after his departure he was still kept up to date with proceedings that could affect the business enterprise.

In 'A Short History of the Tinne Family', Dr John Ernest Tinne records that the career of his ancestor Philip Frederick 'culminated as Commissioner for Peace for Lancashire in 1835, and High Commissioner for Denbighshire in 1838'. Meanwhile John Abraham Tinne 'similarly rose to prominence as a JP and Deputy Lord Lieutenant for Lancashire'. There is a sense here of wanting to hold the moral high ground, to be moral custodians – perhaps to assuage their guilty consciences for their systemic abuses and the sheer barbarity of their conduct in the colonies.

It is worth remembering that in 1829, Home Secretary Robert Peel established the first police force. Peel later made William Ewart Gladstone a Junior Lord of the Treasury and then Under-Secretary at the Colonial Office. The two inspired each other, Gladstone identifying as a 'Peelite' and Peel later promoting the values of what became known as 'Gladstonian Liberalism', the type of free-trade, laissez-faire approach to government that was ultimately to be employed to devastating effect by Margaret Thatcher. Gladstone did, however, approve of a hands-on approach in some matters. His biography on the UK government website notes that 'In 1840 Gladstone began his "rescue and rehabilitation" of London's prostitutes. Even while serving as Prime Minister in later years, he would walk the streets, trying to convince prostitutes to change their ways. He spent a large amount of his own money on this work.'

The misplaced notion of a moral superiority suggested by such behaviour gives us further indication of the whitewashing mission that the Sandbach Tinne dynasty and their extended family – through all of its branches, mercantile, political and ecclesiastical – were pursuing, in a systematic attempt to eradicate not only the history of their atrocities and those of their peers, but to write themselves into the history of the nation as the antithesis of what they actually were: mercantile monsters.

CHAPTER 13

'WE THE PEOPLE'

I've learned that people will forget what you said, people will forget what you did, but people will never forget how you made them feel.
— Maya Angelou

There is a fallout from all this social engineering, political conspiring, religious misguidance and ruthless capitalist exploitation. That fallout is only now beginning to unravel in the public realm. For generations it has been swept under the colonial rug, suppressed in the political discourse, contained by the force of empire, degraded in popular culture, omitted from the national curriculum, ignored in the ghettoised residue of the former colonies, assimilated out of the collective mindset and disguised by the philanthropic veneer of 'aid' or 'development' or 'democratisation', and brutally suppressed by force of arms or counter-insurgency whenever it raised its head and sought redress. But the call for reparations, restitution and reparative justice is gathering momentum as technology and mass communications gradually facilitates the possibility of decolonising the archives, the institutions of knowledge production. The correcting of the historical record, in the interests of all those affected, has become a reality, much to the horror of all but the most enlightened of the beneficiaries of that exploitation.

It is no accident that a country known for producing sugar and rum should struggle with health conditions such as hypertension and other cardiovascular diseases, cancer, diabetes and chronic respiratory disease, the top causes of premature death in Guyana. Professor Sir Hilary Beckles, the author of *Britain's Black Debt: Reparations for Caribbean Slavery and Native Genocide*, points this out. In a public discussion held by the CARICOM[1] Reparations Commission, Beckles described the Caribbean as 'the diabetic and hypertensive centre of the world' and highlighted that, as a result, more amputations are carried out in the Caribbean per capita than any other part of the world: 'For 300 years the people of this region were forced to consume a diet based on what we produced, sugar. In this part of the world, sugar was not consumed as a sweetener, it was consumed as a meal, as part of the dietary plan. If we take the marker of chronic diseases, the black people in the Caribbean are the sickest in the world on a per capita basis, this is a direct consequence and legacy of slavery and colonisation.'

In Guyana, people call diabetes 'sugar'. There is a recognition that the products of sugar cane have caused many of the country's health and social issues. It is a story of sweet pastries and slavery, rum shops and rivers, black bodies and brown bodies, drunkenness and domestic abuse. Sugar also symbolises the wealth extracted from Guyana.

Unlike 'Champagne', the name 'Demerara sugar' is not legally protected by Geographical Indication, as you can see by looking at the label on any packet of Demerara sugar in the supermarket today. Connoisseurs of rum may know of El Dorado, Guyana's award-winning spirit, which is still made in traditional wooden coffers at Plantation Diamond on the East Bank of the Demerara River by Demerara Distillers Limited (DDL), a Sandbach Tinne subsidiary. In the Liverpool Maritime Museum Archives, I found a number of references to rum companies in British Guiana and Guyana, such as 'Caribbean Distillers Ltd. (Formerly Demerara Co. (Stocks) Ltd.) 1958–1981', 'Demerara Co., Ltd. c.1916–1989', and 'Diamond Rum Co., Ltd., (Formerly Savile Row Gin Co., Ltd. Another Sandbach Tinne subsidiary) 1968–1989'. All are included in one deposit: of Sandbach, Tinne & Co. among the Bryson collection.

A timeline on the DDL website illustrates that rum-distilling companies were 'totally owned by the British companies Booker-McConnell and Sandbach-Parker, producers of bulk rum'. Booker and Sandbach Parker & Co. were not just rum producers working in the shadows, however, but part of the fabric of Guyanese society. An article from the *Guiana Graphic* dated Sunday 7 March 1948 records a visit from Mr. T.H. Nayor, Chairman of the Demerara Co., to Plantation Diamond where he meets a series of Boys' Brigades and Girls' Life Brigades. 'The proprietors of the Demerara Co.,' he tells the brigade leaders, 'recognise the useful part that your Brigade is capable of playing in the training of the rising generation to become useful members of the community.' He adds: 'It is my wish that they . . . may become the future foremen and leaders on this estate, and we therefore watch your work with very keen interest.' Once again, a seemingly benign institution is being used to shape and prepare children for the hierarchies of the plantation system – just as with religious instruction and colonial education in the latter days of enslavement.

After independence, adds the DDL website, 'both distilling companies became public companies as shares were sold to Guyanese institutions and the general public'. The former chairman of DDL, the late Yesu Persaud, was the son of cane workers and grew up on Plantation Diamond, which was then still the property of Sandbach Parker & Co. After studying in England he returned to Guyana in 1966 and soon joined Sandbach Parker & Co., by then 'the oldest British company in Guyana'. In 1975, the same year Sandbach Tinne's operations ceased trading in the UK, the Guyanese government nationalised the Demerara Sandbach Group. By this point, the Demerara Company, Sandbach Parker & Co. and Diamond Liquors had been acquired by Jessel Securities, a holding company.

Under the Vesting of Property (Acquisition or Purchase) Act, 1975, Jessel Securities Ltd (Sandbach Parker & Co. Limited) was nationalised with effect from 26 May 1975. The company had been ailing for some years, its factory capacity (Diamond Estate in particular) was grossly under-utilised and its agricultural practices inefficient. Jessel had attempted to dispose of its assets to another expatriate-owned company, but such a transfer of local corporate assets was prohibited by law, and the government therefore decided to acquire them.

Persaud became executive chairman of Diamond Liquors Ltd (DLL) and managing director of the Demerara Sugar Company. In 1983, Diamond Liquors Ltd merged with Guyana Distilleries Ltd to form the current Demerara Distillers Ltd. DDL is celebrated in Guyana as a local company producing one of the country's finest and most famous exports, but its roots lie in a company that grew rich from slavery and indentured labour. In terms of sugar production, the website of the Guyana Sugar Company (GUYSUCO) now lists just four estates: Albion Estate in Berbice, Blairmont Estate on the West Bank of the Berbice River, Uitvlugt Estate, named after Dutch planter Ignatius Charles Bourda Uitvlugt, and Rose Hall Estate in Canje, East Berbice, which reopened in 2023 after closing in 2020. The industry, which still uses many of the techniques employed during slavery and indentureship, just cannot compete with other sugarcane and sugar-beet producing nations and relies on government funding and subsidies.

Other estates have been turned into housing developments and villages, many retaining the name of the plantation that once stood there, such as Diamond, La Bonne Intention, Leonora, Caledonia, Industry, Vreed-en-Hoop and many others. The tall, white wooden house on Main Street in central Georgetown where Samuel Sandbach once lived was purchased in 1911 by Booker. Later it was sold to the British government and became the official residence of the British High Commissioner. In 1987, the building was bought by the government of Guyana, and today it is the official residence of the Prime Minister. The preamble to the 1980 Constitution of Guyana was defiant in its rejection of colonialism and assertion of national pride, declaring:

> We the people of the co-operative republic of Guyana, the proud heirs of the indomitable spirit and unconquerable will of our forefathers who by their sacrifices, their blood and their labour made rich and fertile and bequeathed to us as our

inalienable patrimony for all time this green land of Guyana, saluting the epic struggles waged by our forefathers for freedom, justice and human dignity and their relentless hostility to imperialist and colonial domination and all other forms and manifestations of oppression; . . . inspired by the glorious victory of 26th May, 1966, when after centuries of heroic resistance and revolutionary endeavour we liberated ourselves from colonial bondage, won political independence and became free to mould our own destiny.

The latest version of Guyana's constitution, dated 2012, makes no reference to 'imperialist and colonial domination' or the 'blood' of our forefathers. Even in Guyana, the revolutionary spirit of the past is being muted by some. New colonisers now come in the form of mineral extraction companies, international charities, and oil giants seeking to exploit Guyana's considerable offshore oil and gas reserves. However, other narratives are bringing the stories of Guyana's revolutionaries – and the ordinary people making small, quiet revolutionary acts – to the foreground.

This book started out as a search for my roots, but it has become so much more than that. It is a way of reasserting my dignity and my cultural identity, of understanding and acknowledging my ancestors upon whose shoulders I stand and whose cries of anguish echo in my very soul. It has become a roadmap of my roots for future generations who will inevitably one day need to find their way home. That seemingly insignificant statement by my father to his eight-year-old son – 'Spartacus! One day I gwan take you back to de sugar cane' – blended in my troubled soul with the racist litany of 'Go back to where you came from', by those who knew less about their own history than they did about mine, and had compelled me to embark upon this epic journey of discovery. For it was only in Guyana, and more specifically in Berbice, that I was to find the keys that unlocked all these mysteries, that had lain dormant for hundreds of years.

EPILOGUE

> *Cream rises to the top,*
> *sediment sinks to the bottom*
> *and water seeks its own level.*
> *– Jalal Nuriddin (The Last Poets)*

When I first discovered my cousin, the now late Whithyelene Amelia Watson (b. 26 May 1926), in Rosignol, West Bank Berbice, in 2008, I met a man called Mercurius, who was her son-in-law and her daughter Adamay's husband. Whithyelene was the daughter of Reginald Daniel William Watson and Henrietta Smith. Mercurius was not the father of Vanessa Joan Johnson, Adamay's daughter, but was in fact Vanessa's stepfather. Mercurius was very quiet when I visited, not saying much at all, but paying keen attention to all that was being said. Adamay was the one who'd known most about the grandfather that my cousin Amelia and I shared. She'd grown up with her grandmother, Henrietta Smith (Netta), who was the partner of my uncle Reginald Daniel William Watson, my father's half-brother. Netta had told Adamay lots of things about the family that even Withyeline didn't know.

I didn't pay much attention to Mercurius. He was a late addition to the family and wouldn't have known my father. Also, he never volunteered any information; why would he?

Some years later, after the death of my cousin Whithyelene, my niece Adamay also passed away. I had kept in touch, so Vanessa informed me. With Adamay's passing went a lot of family history. When I'd met her and Whithyelene in 2008, I'd asked about the land they'd owned. I figured it was the only way to connect me to Sandbach Tinne, as the birth records were so vague, first from slavery, where the records of the enslaved were deliberately obscured, writing first names with often no surnames; with baptismal accounts recording 'name of owner' rather than parents of the person baptised, and with the systemic sexual exploitation so engrained in the abusive and depraved colonialist mentality of the white Europeans, tracing lineage by any means other than transfer of property would be all but impossible, as most birth records continued post-slavery to record 'father not stated'.

In 2008 Whithyelene had offered me the adjoining piece of land to her plot, but we never formalised it, so it passed to Adamay, who never formalised it either. Then Adamay died and the hitherto benign Mercurius swung into action. I later found out that after Adamay's death he'd challenged Vanessa, her daughter, for ownership of the house and the land, including the adjoining plot. I had no idea of this at the time, Vanessa didn't trouble me with it. However, while the dispute continued, Mercurius got sick and required care. Despite his attempts to dispossess Vanessa of her rightful property, Vanessa cared for Mercurius. She felt that he'd been a father figure to her and that he deserved that. Mercurius subsequently died in February 2023 in Berbice, and so that land dispute died with him. Vanessa contacted me at the time, as it had fallen to her to organise Mercurius's funeral, without, it seemed, much help from his family. Still unaware of the land dispute, I obliged, and sent money to pay for the burial, despite not knowing the man and having only a tentative connection to him by marriage to my niece. The funeral went ahead, and Vanessa sent me some pictures to mark the occasion. I was happy that she could lay her stepfather to rest.

What I also didn't know was that a competing claim to the adjoining plot that Whithyelene had promised me had now emerged. Sybil Melvinna (b. 28 October 1928 in D'Edward Village, Berbice) was Whithyelene's sister, and so was my first cousin. I'd met her also in 2008, when she told me she'd inherited a lot of land from her father – my uncle Reginald – and our grandfather George Edward Watson, but that she'd sold it all, and at that time she was living in rented accommodation in New Amsterdam with her children and grandchildren, so this counterclaim made no sense to me. Vanessa said she'd spent too much money fighting it, and was about to throw in the towel, when I decided to come back to Guyana in 2024.

While writing this book, I knew that there were still pieces of the puzzle that needed to be discovered to establish my connection to Andrew Watson and thus the Sandbach Tinne dynasty. And it had become apparent that the land held the key.

I returned to Guyana on 22 August 2024 and set about a series of visits to the Walter Rodney Archives where the deputy archivist Karen Budhram kindly helped me a lot, and through her relationship with the General Register's Office Guyana, she referred me to the Registrar General himself, Mr Raymon Cummings. Mr Cummings thankfully agreed to see me. I soon realised he was a very serious man, clearly about his business, with an air of authority that befitted his title. I spread out all my documentation in front of him: my father's birth certificate, my own birth certificate and subsequent deed polls for name changes, an affidavit from the court in which my mother attested to the paternity of my father before a magistrate, and my father's death certificate. Things soon took a nosedive. Mr Cummings informed me that 'We do not accept documents from the UK courts as evidence.' I retorted, 'I thought as a former British colony, a document from a UK court would be recognised in a common law jurisdiction?' He appeared somewhat angry and a bit challenged by my response and snapped back, 'We are a sovereign independent republic since 1966. We do not recognise the jurisdiction of the UK courts.' 'Not even under the auspices of the Privy Council as a Commonwealth nation?' I asked. He shifted in his chair and looked visibly uncomfortable with this line of questioning. He may have been correct, but I sensed that he also understood that I was not his average client, so he softened his approach and began to describe the protocols in detail to me. As I explained my dilemma – no doubt one he'd heard many times – and how far I'd come at great expense to piece together the puzzle of my colonial past, he said, 'Come with me.' I did as I was told. He called over Ms Camelle, who proceeded to work with me over the next couple of days, to attempt to unravel the mystery of the missing links in my lineage.

My father was not on my birth certificate because he was not married to my mother, although we grew up in the same home with his wife, Florence Mary Watson (née Caldwell). On his marriage certificate to Flo, as we called her, his father is cited as 'George Edward Watson – School master'. The problem that arose in 2008 when I first visited the GRO and obtained my father's birth certificate was that he was recorded as 'Reginald Wilcox' (with July being his mother's surname), and on his certificate father is also 'not stated'. The same scenario occurs with my cousins Whithyelene Amelia and Sybil Melvinna: on both of their birth certificates, their father (my uncle), Reginald Daniel William Watson, was recorded as 'father not stated', but they inherited his land, and Whithyelene at the time of my first visit in 2008 had inherited the house where he'd lived with Henrietta Smith, Whithyelene and Sybil's mother, named on both of their birth certificates. This was the woman who'd raised Adamay; this was the house that Whithyelene's granddaughter, my great-niece Vanessa Joan Johnson, had been born in, and now inhabited.

After some time, Ms Camelle called me and told me she'd discovered something in the original register of my father's birth. I rushed back to the GRO and was astonished at what she'd found. There is an extra category on the original birth register that does not get transcribed onto the birth certificate: the 'name of the informant', i.e. who registered the birth. Lo and behold, there it was – the evidence that I had long sought connecting my father and my grandfather. It stated, 'Name of and, qualification of informant; George Edward Watson – Friend of the mother, present at the birth.' My mind raced, as did my heart seeing my grandfather's signature for the first time. This was my only visible connection to him, to my roots, to the Watson clan, to the man who gifted our family all that land in Berbice. It was the conduit to Andrew Watson, his father Peter Miller Watson and his brothers, and, by extension, to the whole Sandbach Tinne dynasty. What woman in 1918 would have a random man as a 'friend – present at the birth' and then allow him on the same day to wander off and register a child, if it was not his child? It was a messy conclusion, but a conclusion none the less. What remained was to connect his land to that of Sandbach Tinne, to ascertain how a Black school master in a rural sugar colony came to be in possession of dozens of acres of land. It could only be by inheritance; no school master could afford such costs, even today.

Ahead of my trip to Guyana, I had asked my friend Eric Phillips, who is the deputy chair of the CARICOM Reparations Commission, if he could put me in touch with someone who might be able to assist me with tracing the land. The hope was that it might lead to a former Sandbach Tinne plantation in Berbice. Eric connected me with several people, including lawyer Robert Forrester. He was a remarkable man, and he resolved to help me out as a friend of Eric's, so I explained my dilemma. 'You need to get the Transport,' he explained. 'What's the Transport' I asked. 'It is the legal conveyance of the land from one owner to another. This is how land is conveyed in Guyana. Get the Lot Number, and get the Transport, from this you'll see the transition of ownership.'

I messaged Vanessa to ask for her lot number, as hers was the only piece of land pertaining to my grandfather that I could be sure of. Vanessa said she'd take a look and get back to me. The next day she called me. 'Uncle Malik, I was going through a briefcase that Mercurius used to keep all his important documents in, and I found a document which mentions the land.' I was shocked. He knew when I came in 2008 that I was asking about the land, but he never mentioned anything about any document. He had been completely silent on the issue. I asked her to come to Georgetown and bring the document, which she did. I photographed it and took it to Robert Forrester and asked him to decipher it. He'd never seen one like it before, but intimated that it was from the *Gazette* (an official newspaper where announcements were made formally during the colonial period). The document was a Local Government Board Notice dated 1959. He advised me to take it to the Land Registry, as this document contained owners' names and lot numbers for the villages of D'Edward and Rosignol, where my grandfather's land was, and the adjoining sugar plantation of Blairmont – formerly owned by Sandbach Tinne.

The following day I went and presented the document at the desk. The woman looked confused. 'In all my years here, I have never seen a document like this,' she said. 'I will have to speak to my manager.' I waited nervously and after about fifteen minutes the manager came over and offered to help. 'It seems like there was a land survey commissioned for Berbice between 1956 and 1959 by the former colonial government. They will have then drawn up a list of ownership decisions, to the satisfaction of the appointed surveyor and published it in the *Gazette*. I have never seen one of these before.' I asked, 'Does it help me to find my father's land? His name is on that list on at least five plots in D'Edward and Rosignol.' Yes, you have the lot numbers, so the local land registry in Berbice will have the transports,' said the manager. 'So, I have to go all the way back to Berbice?' I asked. 'Hold on a minute, let me see what I can do.' She called over the young lady I'd first presented the curious document to, and gave it to her. She scurried off. I waited about twenty minutes more and then she called me over. She had a stack of papers in her hand. 'I contacted the registry in Berbice, gave them the lot numbers, and they emailed me all the transports for your father's land. The award was split, a single plot which was sold by Sibyl Boilers with a power of attorney from her father Reginald Watson' – my uncle Reginald – 'and four other plots that are together which until now are unsold, by the same name. This suggest to me that a part went to your uncle, which his daughter sold, and a part went to your father which is as yet unclaimed. You'll need to get the plans from Land & Surveys to ascertain where exactly each lot is situated. Anyhow here's all the transports.'

I never imagined I'd ever get this far, and to think that Mercurius knew this all along and hid the information from me, Vanessa and possibly even Adamay, his wife, was a sobering thought. Vanessa too was becoming agitated and began to reflect on fragments of memories that had now taken on new relevance. One such memory was that of others in the locale coming to the house to ask Mercurius about local land ownership when they had disputes. He seemed to have the definitive evidence to resolve those disputes. Vanessa began to understand why he had hidden the information from her; it was a ploy to disinherit her after her mother died. She was angry. When she told me this, I was also angry. He'd deliberately withheld this information from me too, and I unknowingly and in good faith had actually paid for the man's funeral.

The pieces were gradually coming together, but there was still a part of the puzzle that was missing. If D'Edward and Rosignol bordered a Sandbach Tinne plantation, how could I prove that Sandbach Tinne had once owned the land? The document only went back as far as 1959. I had a few maps from my last visit to the Land Registry in 2008 which showed how the villages bordered the plantation, but they were relatively recent maps, so were not particularly helpful in solving this new puzzle. I needed to get into the Blairmont plantation and find out what records they might have.

I had already uncovered evidence of Sandbach Tinne owning Blairmont at one point from the Bryson collection, an archive at Liverpool Maritime Museum. Bryson was a man who collected the files of solicitors in Liverpool who'd closed down. Solicitors held important documents for clients such as title deeds and mortgages. When Bryson deposited them with the museum, they were not categorised by their contents, simply filed under 'Bryson'. This obscured the substantial Sandbach Tinne collection which was held there, with few if any of the archivists even knowing of its existence. Upon examining the Sandbach Tinne files within the collection, I found extensive documents pertaining to their ownership of the Blairmont plantation in Berbice, once also owned by rival firm Booker Bros., and now owned by the Guyanese Sugar Corporation (GUYSUCO). The nationalisation of the sugar concerns in Guyana was the final nail in the coffin of Sandbach Tinne multinational conglomerate; soon after, in 1975, their holding company held their last board meeting, and the company was liquidated.

I met up again with the lawyer Robert Forrester in Georgetown and told him what I'd found. He said, 'I know the chairman of GUYSUCO, he's a dear friend of mine. I can take you to meet him at his house if you like?' This was amazing: I had already asked Vanessa to go to Blairmont and see if a visit could be arranged, but she reported back that they said I would need to write a letter and await a response. I only had a few days left and this was the last piece in the puzzle. I needed to close this chapter once and for all and establish the connection to Andrew Watson and Sandbach Tinne. I needed to get onto that plantation.

While in Georgetown, I'd arranged to meet with some of the wider Watson family. Geoffrey and Andrew Watson were originally from Berbice, but the family had long been resident in Georgetown. Geoffrey had reached out to me in 2020 after the BBC article that was the trigger for this book had broken, and we had stayed in touch on social media. Inspired by my story, Geoffrey had decided to trace the Berbice Watsons in his family. He had an elderly grandmother in Florida, whom his wife and kids had never met, and he began to think they might lose a lot of the family history when she passed away. So he'd arranged to take his family to Florida to meet her and connect the Berbice Watsons with their Floridian cousins. On that trip he'd amassed a wealth of knowledge from his grandma, as well as some documentation and the beginnings of a Berbice Watson family tree. I invited him to my apartment in Campbellville when Vanessa arrived from Berbice, and I also invited Judy Watson, one of the Mahaicony Watsons. I'd met Cheryl Watson when I came in 2008, and she had connected me with a cousin in Canada, who'd connected me to her sister Judy in Georgetown. What became apparent was that several of the Berbice Watsons had intermarried with the Benn family, thus further complicating my search for the person Adamay had described as 'Nanny Benn Watson'.

Meanwhile, the lawyer Robert had arranged a meeting with the CEO of GUYSUCO, Paul Cheong. He picked me up in Campbellville and took me to Paul's house, which was on the other side of the Demerara River. On the way we passed through Plantation Vreed-en-Hoop, the Dutch-named plantation I had seen many times in the Sandbach Tinne correspondence and financial accounts. Paul was a born and bred Guyanese of Chinese extraction. He welcomed us and was very friendly and helpful. When I explained what I was researching, it became clear that he was a descendant of one of the Chinese indentured labourers trafficked by Sandbach Tinne from Shanghai or Canton in the post-emancipation period. He also told me that the GUYSUCO headquarters was on La Bonne Intention, Peter Miller Watson's plantation, suggesting that it was – and still is – of particular significance to the Guyanese sugar industry. Paul himself was traveling to Berbice the next day and said he would speak to his plant manager and arrange a formal visit. Robert Forrester had come through yet again.

A few days later my driver arrived with a minivan. Judy took a taxi over to my apartment that morning with her friend, and set off together; first to Mahaicony, and then on to Berbice. We picked up Cheryl Watson in Mahaicony, who insisted on feeding us with the most delicious local cuisine, before showing me the maps with the extent of her Watson land, which was massive and went on for miles. Judy Watson stopped off at her mother's house in Mahaicony; I also interviewed her mother, and she showed us the extent of her Watson land, which was as big as Cheryl's – if not bigger. We also stopped by Amelia Watson's business in Mahaicony, which included a gas station, a hotel and an amusement park. After many years in the US, Amelia and her husband had invested back home and were now developing their retirement nest egg in the heart of Mahaicony. What had become abundantly clear about almost all the Watsons that I'd met in Guyana was that they all had vast lands. Geoffrey, Amelia, Adamay and Cheryl all had different versions of the same story about the three white Scottish Watson brothers, and they knew that all the Guyana Watsons were related somehow – although before my article and visit, they had never met each other. The story was almost complete. I just needed to get onto that Blairmont plantation and see what evidence they had.

After dinner we headed eastwards along the coast road in the direction of New Amsterdam and Suriname. The next stop was Rosignol to pick up Vanessa and her daughter Nyresha. We met them and they jumped aboard, then we headed off to the Blairmont sugar plantation and refinery. When I arrived, the first thing that struck me was the vastness of the cane fields with the massive 12–15ft crop waving in the breeze. All I could see for miles was cane on my left, bordering the road, and canals on the right. My first thoughts were, 'How the hell did men hand-dig these canals and chop down those whole crops with their bare hands, walk on those cropped cane shards in their bare feet, and endure this scorching heat and humidity while doing it?' I imagined my own father cutting that cane as he'd told me he did as a young teenager, and my heart sank at the overwhelming reality of the cruelty of Samuel Sandbach, George Rainy, Peter McLagan, Philip Frederick Tinne, Peter Miller Watson, John Abraham Tinne, George Robertson, Peter Rose, James McInroy, William Robertson Watson, Hugh Munro Robertson, Henry Robertson Sandbach, John Gladstone, Robertson Gladstone, and many others in the family, who practised or promoted this barbarity. They wrought so much death, pain, torture, rape, murder, dismemberment, fratricide and genocide on African people; my people, my ancestors, and through their depravity and disregard for Black humanity raped their way into my family tree with such hubris.

Paul Cheong had sent me the details of the plantation manager Shiv Persaud whom I'd contacted on 5 September 2024 to arrange my trip to Blairmont. After driving past miles of sugar cane, we arrived at the entrance to the plantation. There were a series of detached colonial wooden houses on stilts, some quite grand and clearly nineteenth- or early twentieth-century constructions. As we drove in, the first building that caught my eye was an orange timber colonial mansion house with a pitched tiled roof and a porch with white wooden pillars, elevated on stilts, meticulously maintained and surrounded by potted plants. It had a vast open-plan garden space and beside the road were some nineteenth-century engines on display. At this point I was filled with anticipation at what else I might uncover. As we drove down the main esplanade, the true scale of this gargantuan former slavery operation began to sink in. We passed detached residence after detached residence on both sides, at least two dozen in total, and Vanessa explained to me that they were all the supervisors' houses; all the key people lived on the plantation. It was like a town.

We passed a sign that read 'Guyana Sugar Corporation Inc. Entrance to the Field Workshop and Primary Health Care Centre'. Before long we crossed the railway line and Vanessa explained to me that Blairmont had its own railway, from the sugar refinery across the plantation to the wharf at the mouth of the Berbice River, where the sugar was loaded directly onto the ships for export. I recalled Philip Tinne stating in his biography that he was a director of the Demerara railway company, and clearly Sandbach Tinne had used their knowledge of the railways to further their mercantile ambitions on their own plantations as well as across the colonies and in the UK. This was a private railway and is still operating long after the Demerara railway was decommissioned post-independence by Prime Minister Burnham. A sign on the left read 'Blairmont Estate Meteorological Station'. Again, the colonials were preoccupied with sciences that affected crop production, the weather being the single most important variable. We arrived at the administrative building and were greeted by the estate manager and two security guards armed with pump-action shotguns. I thought that was a bit of overkill– why the need for armed guards? I later asked and they said, 'We still deal with cash here, so security is necessary.' I assume that's how they did payroll for the hundreds of employees in the gangs in the cane fields, as well as the workers in the vast sugar refinery that adjoined the plantation.

As I embarked upon the tour, I saw hundreds of massive rollers and gear cogs rusting in the forecourt. The manager explained to me that they had all been dismantled at Plantation Diamond, another former Sandbach Tinne plantation, and shipped to Blairmont as part of a plan to incorporate additional capacity, but it soon turned out that the gear was incompatible. So now the forecourt is littered with massive chunks of British Victorian engineering debris that has no apparent use.

The manager explained the production process to me and some aspects haven't changed since the times of enslavement. All the cane that is cut is loaded onto punts and sailed along the canals to the dock at the refinery. It is then lifted into a hopper and weighed to determine the payments to the field harvesters, the bear loaders and the machine harvesters. Next, it passes through a cutting system, the first knife, the level knife, then the heavy-duty knife, which exposes the cells of the cane so that you can extract the sucrose. Afterwards it passes through three mills, where there is a crusher, then the juice goes to the process house for sugar processing and the bagasse (the shredded and crushed chaff from the cane) goes to the boilers where it is used as fuel for steam generation. They also have a huge vat of sugar juice containing tons of liquid which passes into a pan where it's boiled; then it passes into a 'pugmill' where the molasses is separated into what's called the high-grade basket to 'spin-out' (which I assume is a form of centrifuge). The molasses is then shipped off to distillers to make rum. Sandbach Tinne would have shipped it to their subsidiary, Demerara Distillers, for their famous rum brands like El Dorado and Black Diamond. GUYSUCO still supply Demerara Distillers with molasses for their alcohol production, although this Sandbach Tinne subsidiary was part of the nationalisation decades ago.

After a tour of the refinery, I went to the manager's office and he brought out some maps. I immediately located Rosignol and D'Edward villages adjoining Blairmont plantation, and I asked him if he had any maps that predated the 1956–1959 Berbice land survey. 'Sure,' he said. My face lit up as he riffled through a range of rolled-up plans. He pulled out a map that was about 1.5m wide and 2.5m long which, when he rolled it out, covered the entire boardroom table from edge to edge. I immediately located the villages, but they were not delineated by boundaries as on the previous maps I'd seen. 'Where are the village boundaries for D'Edward and Rosignol?' I inquired. 'The railway was the boundary,' he replied. At that time everything north of the railway was the village and everything south of the railway line was Blairmont. This was the silver bullet I was looking for. About 40 per cent of D'Edward and about 85 per cent of Rosignol was in Blairmont – which meant that during my father and grandfather's time most if not all of their land had previously been owned by Sandbach Tinne. By a process of deduction, the only way my grandfather could possibly have come into that much land would have been if it was gifted or bequeathed from a Watson of the Sandbach Tinne dynasty.

Having now visited the crime scene, I felt violated and traumatised at the mere thought of it. To add insult to injury, I had endured the pseudo-narratives of their gentlemanly conduct, their philanthropic works and the veneer of propriety provided by their vassals whom they endowed with vast fortunes to fund their every endeavour, such as William Roscoe, Liverpool's favourite son, and Dr Thomas Stuart Traill, the founders respectively of what are today the University of Liverpool and John Moores University, and the sculptor John Gibson who immortalised them in marble reliefs, in one case with Henry Robertson Sandbach in a marble relief with Jesus.

I had started this journey to find out who I am and where I come from, and if I am in any way connected to the footballer Andrew Watson. What I discovered was an epic tale that will redraw the boundaries of our historical understanding of a dynasty that shaped not only the British Empire, but our present society, in ways we could never have imagined and in ways we have yet to uncover.

'History despite its wrenching pain, cannot be unlived,
but if faced with courage, need not be lived again.'

Maya Angelou, 'On the Pulse of Morning'

LIST OF ILLUSTRATIONS

Andrew Watson (*Scottish Athletic Celebrities Album, 1886*)
Scotland 6-1 victory against England (*courtesy of the Scottish Football Museum*)
Queen's Park FC (*courtesy of the Scottish Football Museum*)
Andrew Watson's graveside (*courtesy of the author*)
Malik arriving at Cheddi Jagan (*courtesy of the author*)
Rossignol Ferry Stelling (*courtesy of the author*)
Map of Berbice and Suriname, 1767
Statue of Cuffy (*courtesy of the author*)
George Rainy (*Sandbach Tinne, Bookers Collection of John Platt*)
Machinery at Blairmont (*courtesy of the author*)
Mr James Parker deemed a prisoner of war (*Parker Papers. Liverpool Record Office*)
Letter from George Robertson (*Parker Papers. Liverpool Record Office*)
Arms of the Company of Scotland
Peter Miller Watson's voyage (*Parker Papers. Liverpool Record Office*)
Epitaph of Hugh Munro Robertson (*Parker Papers. Liverpool Record Office*)
Map of Grenada (*The History Collection / Alamy Stock Photo*)
'Barbarities of the West Indies' (© *National Portrait Gallery, London*)

Black Diamond Rum

Sandbach-Tinne family tree (*Compiled by E. A. Woods. Designed by E. W. Argyle. Image courtesy of Liverpool Central Library and Archives.*)

Map of 'Essequebe' and 'Demerarie' (*Bibliothèque Nationale de France*)

Bloodline of the Robertsons (*Genealogy of the families of Douglas of Mulderg and Robertson of Kindeace (1895)*)

Baptisms of enslaved Africans (*St George's Cathedral, Georgetown, Guyana*)

Progress of the Church Missionary Society (*The Church Missionary Intelligencer, A Monthly Journal of Missionary Information, Vol. II, 1851*)

Christ Church (*courtesy of the author*)

Construction of British Guiana Railway through Sandbach Tinne and Co. plantations, Enterprise and Providence, c 1890 (photographer unknown, held by National Museums Liverpool, Archives Centre, reference D/B/176B/34)

ACKNOWLEDGEMENTS

I would like to acknowledge Ed Thomas and Ben Milne who first broke this story on BBC online and brought it to the attention of the world. I would also like to thank Prof. David Olusoga, who has been an inspiration both by his work and his support in helping this story reach a broader global audience. I would like to thank my agent, Charles Walker, and his assistant Olivia Martin at United Agents, for their representation and guidance throughout this process. My sincere gratitude to my publishing director Arabella Pike at the William Collins imprint of HarperCollins UK, for her stalwart support, expert advice, and considerable patience, which has allowed me to get this work finished in the best possible way. I'd also like to thank the HarperCollins team: My editor, Alex Gingell; publicist, Nicola Webb; marketing, Hope Butler; editorial, Sam Harding; Georgie Proctor (superb promo and cover design) and publicity director, Katherine Patrick.

I also acknowledge Guyanese specialists David Dabydeen, Juanita Cox and Carinya Sharples, for helping me to structure my ideas, and validate the Guyanese elements of my research. Your collective and individual input was invaluable. I would also like to acknowledge those in Guyana who assisted me in my fieldwork: Eric Phillips,

(CARICOM); Karen Budhram and Nadia Carter, at the Walter Rodney National Archives; Robert Forrester, who assisted with land law; Estherine Adams, and Paloma Mohamed Martin, (Vice Chancellor) of the University of Guyana; Ms Camile and Ms Stanton, (GPO) in the Guyana Records Office; and Vanessa Joan Johnson (my great-niece), Geoffrey Watson, Judy Watson, Cheryl Watson, and Amelia Watson (my distant cousins), who provided valuable familial information.

I extend my sincerest gratitude to Dr John Henry (Hank) Gonzalez, at the Faculty of History, University of Cambridge, who has mentored me throughout this process, in conjunction with supervising my PhD on a similar topic. He saw the potential in my research before it was in the public domain and has supported me ever since. I also send my sincere gratitude to Julie Coimbra, formerly Librarian & Events coordinator at (CLAS) Centre of Latin American Studies, at University of Cambridge, whose decision to invite me to present my archival research at the Centre in 2017 led me to researching this story at Cambridge.

To my family, who have sacrificed their quality time with me to allow me to write this work, I extend my eternal love and gratitude to you all.

I would also like to give my sincere thanks to Prof. Phil Taylor (former Pro-Vice Chancellor at University of Bristol, and current Vice Chancellor of the University of Bath), for partnering with me and sponsoring the Sandbach Tinne Conference. The conference allowed me to bring together universities, galleries, museums, libraries, and expert practitioners studying Sandbach Tinne-related collections, artifacts, and historical figures, to widen the knowledge base and create new and exciting projects that give prominence to the voices of the enslaved, and the descendants of the victims of enslavement, within the Academy, and the arts and cultural sectors, through positive action and decolonisation.

I would like to give a special thank you to Ged O'Brian, founder of the Scottish Football Museum, whose discovery of the black

Victorian footballer, Andrew Watson, started me on this roots quest. Without Ged's discovery, none of this would have been possible. Also, a special thank you to Rich McGinnis, (Live Nation) who has been a stalwart support system for me and my work for over a decade, and has never wavered in his belief in me and the significance of my work, seeking nothing in return other than my success. Also, to Indy Vidyalankara, who worked tirelessly to ensure that my work got the widest possible exposure and always exceeded all expectations. I also acknowledge Jim Bellew (Liverpool Atheneum), and Fran Hollinrake, Cathedral Curator, Orkney Islands Council.

Thanks to my fellow researchers who have adopted a collegiate approach to the discoveries around Andrew Watson and Sandbach Tinne, with whom I have shared many of my research findings, and who have also shared their findings with me. These include: Lucy Moynahan (University of Liverpool); David Alston, (Slaves and Highlanders); Dr. Stephen Mullen, and Dr Christine Whyte (University of Glasgow); Moira Rankin (Scottish Business Archives); Dora Petherbridge, Patrick Hart, and Chris Cassells (National Library of Scotland); Phyl Hall, Shenagh Leiper, Phil Tinne, Katie Tinne, and Alison Clark (descendants of the Sandbach Tinne dynasty) and Miranda Kaufman (author of 'Heiresses' and 'Black Tudors').

Thanks to Lisa Marie Rand, who was the first to report on my discovery in the *Liverpool Echo*, before it made the national and international press; Huw Jones, Dr Mark Purcell, Katrina Dean, and Maciej Pawlikowski at Cambridge University Library, who facilitated the digitisation of the Sandbach Tinne Collection on Cambridge Digital Library; Kat Steer at St Catharine's College Cambridge; Sarah Williams and Anne Alexander at Cambridge Digital Humanities.

GLOSSARY OF TERMS

Derogatory or pejorative racial terms
Mulatto (Feminine – Mulatess) – a person with one white and one black parent.
Tercerones (Spanish *Terceron*) – a person with one white parent and another Mulatto.
Quadroon – a person who is one-quarter black by descent.
Quinteron (Spanish) or Quintroon – offspring of a Quadroon and a white person.
Quarterone (Spanish *Mestizo*) also Mustee (or Mestee) – a person of one-eighth Black ancestry.
Tawney – light-skinned Mulatto.
Mahomedan – a European misrepresentation of a Muslim.
Coolie – a person of Asian descent, usually an indentured labourer.
Creole – (Spanish *criollo*) someone of European descent born in the Americas usually of mixed ethnicity.
Negro or Negroe – Spanish or Portuguese, from *negro* black, Latin *nigr-*, *niger*.
Miscegenation – sexual relationships or reproduction between people of different ethnic groups, especially when one of them is white.

Maroon – a Black person of the Americas who escaped slavery and formed or joined a free and often secluded settlement of the West Indies or Guiana in the 17th and 18th centuries or a descendant of such a person. Derived from the term Marooned (abandoned in a secluded place).

Buck or Buck skin – reference to a Native American, derived of a Roe Buck or Red Deer, hence Redskins. Used to denote trinkets traded with Native people, hence the term for US currency 'Bucks'.

Mandingos – a member of any of a number of peoples forming an extensive linguistic group in western Africa including Mande and Malinke. Mandingo is primarily known as a pejorative term, historically used to describe enslaved Black men used to 'breed' enslaved black women and thought to be hyper-sexual.

Logies – term used to describe the dilapidated slave huts.

Commercial terms

Transport – means of land conveyance in Guiana.

Indenture – form of contracted debt.

Indentured labour – a system where individuals are contracted to work for a specific period, to repay a debt.

The House – a trading entity, usually a close company or a family enterprise.

Close company – UK resident company with five or fewer participators.

Verenigde Oost-Indische Compagnie (Dutch East India Company).

Plaisterers – Old name for plasterers. The Worshipful Company of Plaisterers has a guild to this day.

GUYSUCO – Guyanese Sugar Corporation.

Units of measurement

Barrel* – used to transport rum. A barrel contains 1/8 of a tun.

Tun – a large barrel used for wine. A tun contains 210 imperial gallons (c. 955 litres).

Hhs. – a hogshead, a type of barrel used to transport sugar. A hogshead contains 1/4 of a tun.

Puncheon, tertian – a type of barrel used to transport rum. A puncheon contains 1/3 of a tun.

lb. – a pound in weight, contains 16 ounces.

cwt. – a hundredweight. In UK measurements, a hundredweight is 112 pounds.

Bale – a standard trading unit for cotton on the market, weighing 500 (lb) pounds (USA).

Gallon – a unit of liquid or dry capacity, equal to 8 pints.

Units of currency

Joe – a Portuguese gold Johannes coin.† After 1830, a paper Joe was issued in Guiana = *fl*22.

fl – a guilder or florin. A unit of currency in Holland prior to the advent of the Euro in 2002.

L or £ – a pound sterling. Before decimalisation (in 1971), a pound = 240d (pence) or 20s (shillings).

s. – a shilling = 12d (pence), pre-decimalisation (in 1971).

d. – a penny, pre-decimalisation (in 1971).

Bitts – referred to coins with a low value of several named units (e.g. threepenny bit).

---

* NB: Units used here are based upon the imperial measurements used in British colonies. American and other colonial jurisdictions had differing volumes for each of these measurements.

† Issued by the 'Court of Policy of the Colonies of Demerary and Essequebo' [*sic*], https://bankofguyana.org.gy/bog/images/communications/history_notescoins/History_of_Guyana_Notes.pdf (accessed 6 February 2025).

Nautical terms

Sloop – a one-masted sailing ship.

Brig or Brigantine – a two-masted sailing ship.

Clipper – a three-masted sailing ship.

The Line – the equator; distinguishing the tropics of the northern and southern hemispheres.

Letter of Marque – a government licence allowing private individuals to attack and seize the foreign ships of a state at war with their own.

Prize vessel – a foreign ship seized by the government or a privateer using a Letter of Marque.

Registration *de novo* – new registration, usually for a ship seized by privateers and renamed, and / or re-registered in the country that seized it.

Gyrocompass – a non-magnetic compass that uses the principles of gyroscopic motion and the Earth's rotation to determine true north.

Familial terms

Praenomina – forenames passed down.

Plantagenets – a royal dynasty that ruled England from 1154 to 1485, establishing the longest period of English rule by a single dynasty. Their name is derived from Geoffrey of Anjou's use of the broom plant as a badge, 'planta genista' in Latin.

Religious terms

Surah – a chapter of the Quran.

Moravian – a group of Protestants who trace their origins to the Czechia.

SPCK – Society for Promoting Christian Knowledge.

SPG – Society for the Propagation of the Gospel in Foreign Parts, was a Church of England missionary organisation founded in 1701.

Manse – in Scotland, the house provided by a church for its minister to live in.

Mammon – in the Gospels Jesus warns against 'serving both God and Mammon'; personified, especially in the Middle Ages, as a demon or god of greed.

Legal or Latin terms

de novo – anew; from the beginning.

fons et origo – the source and origin of something.

Commandant General des Forces de la Republique Francaise, et Officiers en Service actual (French) – Commander General of the Forces of the French Republic, and Officers in Current Service.

Remainderman – a person who is entitled to receive a future interest in property.

Place names no longer used

Demerary – now called Demerara.

Batavian Republic – now called The Netherlands.

Saint-Domingue – now called Haiti.

Guiana – now called the Co-operative Republic of Guyana.

Gold Coast – now called Ghana in West Africa.

Mahaica and 'Maicouny' – now called Mahaicony in Guyana.

Linguistic terms, foreign phrases and vernacular

Patois – a language that has developed from a mixture of other languages such a Jamaican Patois which whilst based upon English, incorporates also Arawak, Spanish and remnants of African languages.

Taki Taki (Talk Talk) – a language derived of Sranan Tongo, (Surinamese tongue) a.k.a. Ningre-Tongo, (*nigger + tongue* – derogatory) or Suriname Creole English spoken by the Djuka people of Suriname.

Jookootoo – Grenadian patois meaning 'right up to you'.

Liberté, Égalité, Fraternité (French) – Liberty, Equality, Fraternity.

Liberté, Egalité, ou la Mort' (French) – Liberty, Equality or Death.

Conkee – a sweetcorn-based dish, similar to Ghanaian kenkey or Banku, traditionally made with cornmeal, pumpkin, coconut, sugar and warm spices.

Pardner, Boxhand or Susu – a community-based lending model where individuals contribute money regularly to a shared fund, and then members take turns receiving the entire accumulated sum.

Scarlatina – (a.k.a. scarlet fever), is a contagious bacterial infection primarily affecting children. During colonial times it was often fatal.

Swizzle – during the colonial period, a 'swizzle' referred to a type of mixed drink, particularly a frothy one, often made with rum or gin, and stirred with a special tool called a swizzle stick. The term 'swizzle' also described the act of mixing the drink with the swizzle stick, creating a frothy texture.

Gwan (Guyanese patois) – means 'going to'.

De (Guyanese patois) – means 'the'.

Tribes, groups and titles

Chantee – (a.k.a. Asante or Ashanti) people, specifically from the Gold Coast region of West Africa.

Fantee (a.k.a. Fante or Fanti) – a confederacy of Akan people and aboriginal Guan people, of central and western Ghana.

Coromantee (a.k.a. Kormantine) – primarily Akan people from present day Ghana who were shipped to the Americas from the Ghanaian slave fort Fort Kormantine.

Hausa – a large ethnic group in West Africa, made up of several tribal groups. Hausa is also a language in West Africa.

Fulani – also known as the Fula or Fulbe, a large and dispersed ethnic group predominantly found in West and Central

Africa, particularly in the Sahel region. Fulani is also a language in West and Central Africa.

Kongo (a.k.a. Congo) – a Bantu ethnic group, primarily defined by their language, Kikongo. They are also referred to as Bakongo. The Kongo people are a diverse group with subgroups like the Yombe, Vili and Beembe.

Popo – refers to several different tribal groups, primarily the Mina (or Mina-Aja) people who are a major ethnic group in Togo and Benin, concentrated along the coast from Lomé to Ouidah in West Africa.

Khoesān (a.k.a. the Hottentots – derogatory) – an ancient people of South Africa.

Djuka (a.k.a. Ndyuka) – one of six Maroon peoples in the Republic of Suriname. Also called 'Bush Negroes' (derogatory).

Arawak – a group of indigenous peoples, primarily found in South America and the Caribbean.

Amerindian – a European term for a member of one of the indigenous peoples of the Americas.

Kru – a group of tribes from Liberia, Ivory Coast and Sierra Leone in West Africa.

Factor (Scottish) – a landlord's agent responsible for managing and overseeing the administration of their property, tenants, rents, and overseeing repairs.

Raadpensionaris (Dutch) – the Grand Pensioner. The grand pensionary of Holland was the political leader of the entire Dutch Republic when there was no Stadtholder at the centre of power.

Heren Regeerders (Dutch) – ruling lords.

The Fiscal General – acted as an adjudicator and was assigned the role of insuring that the judiciary and the colonial administration complied with the law.

Regis – the monarch. An 'Act of Regis' generally refers to an Act of Parliament or other legislative body in which a king or queen is named or recognised, or an act related to the royal prerogative.

Greffier (French) – clerk.

CARICOM (Caribbean Community) – a regional group of nations that encourage common policy and economic goals and consists of 20 countries, of which 15 are actual member states.

NOTES

PREFACE

1 'A Guyanese version of the British term (cunt) passed on from the colonial period', https://www.urbandictionary.com/define.php?term=Skunt
2 The National Health Service Act had come into force in England and Wales in 1948.
3 Enoch Powell's speech, often known as the rivers of blood speech, was delivered to a Conservative Association meeting in Birmingham on 20 April 1968, https://anth1001.files.wordpress.com/2014/04/enoch-powell_speech.pdf [accessed Dec. 2023].

CHAPTER 1: ANDREW WATSON

1 *A Popular History of The Grammar School of Queen Elizabeth at Heath, Near Halifax, by Thomas Cox, M.A., Master of the School* (Halifax, 1879). The school is referred to in the census as the Fau Grammar School, Halifax. In both cases Andrew Watson is listed as being from Demerara.
2 Source: Ged O'Brian Scottish Football Museum.
3 West India & Pacific Steamship Company Ltd, Liverpool Ship's name 'Darien (2)' Built 1888. 1900 transferred to Frederick Leyland & Co., 1907, wrecked at Barranquilla: https://www.theshipslist.com/ships/lines/wip.shtml [accessed 18 Dec. 2023].

4 https://www.newspapers.com/newspage/76467378/ [accessed 18 Dec. 2023].
5 A.H. Keane and Sir Clements R. Markham, *Central & South America, Vol. 2: Central America & West Indies*, Stanford's Compendium of Geography & Travel (London: E. Stanford, 1911), p. 268, https://archive.org/details/centralandsoutha02kean/page/266/mode/2up?q=Goajira [accessed 18 Dec. 2023].
6 BBC Scotland documentary, *Scotland's Lost Captain* (2003).

CHAPTER 2: BACK TO DE SUGAR CANE

1 Whisky is generally 70–80° proof containing 40% alcohol. Overproof rum contains over 50% and up to 80% alcohol, making it between 100° and 160° proof, also known as 'Navy strength'. 'The term "proof" as it pertains to alcohol, has origins that date back to the 18th century, when soldiers in the British Royal Navy would add rum to their gunpowder to test its strength. If the weapon still fired with gunpowder doused in liquor, the soldiers had "proof" that the rum was strong enough for them. The official proof system was established by the government in 1848 when they dictated that any liquor bottle with 50% ABV (alcohol by volume) would be labelled as 100 proof for tax purposes', https://resetiv.com/blogs/news/what-does-proof-mean-in-alcohol [accessed Dec. 2023].
2 'To close the accounts of a naval ship when she reached the end of a commission—when the crew received any pay owing to them—or, in the case of a merchant ship, to close the accounts at the end of a voyage.' Oxford Reference, https://www.oxfordreference.com/display/10.1093/oi/authority.20110803100312117 [accessed Dec. 2023].
3 'Possibly the most famous townships are in South Africa and were a creation of the apartheid system and its predecessor regimes of white rule. Apartheid was formally instituted as state policy in 1948 but dating from the white settlers' permanent landing at what is now Cape Town in 1652, racial segregation was formal practice. The townships were racially discriminatory in that "black" African, "colored" (mixed-race), and "Indian" people were ordered by the Land Act of 1913 and the Group Areas Act of 1950 to live separately. Even within black townships, ethnic groups were often segregated into separate areas for Zulus, Xhosas, Sothos, and others. These laws existed until the early 1990s, and since then there has

been only gradual desegregation of formerly white, colored, and Indian areas.' Encyclopaedia, https://www.encyclopedia.com/social-sciences/applied-and-social-sciences-magazines/townships [accessed Dec. 2023].

4 Nanny Benn is known as the person who raised Reginald Daniel William Watson. For a time, I suspected that Marion Benn was Nanny Benn, which would make Frederick Adolphus Watson a relative. It doesn't tell us if Marion Benn was Reginald's mother or grandmother. If it was his grandmother who raised him, that would accord with Adamay's statement that Nanny Benn's husband was William, which would make William Watson Frederick Adolphus Watson's father or uncle and Beryl Watson's grandfather or great-uncle. To further complicate things, it has since emerged that there were other marriages in Berbice between Watsons and Benns. So 'Nanny Benn Watson' is still a mystery, although the Benn connection definitively links with the history of the Berbice Watsons whom I met in Georgetown in 2024, namely Geoffrey Watson and his brother Andrew Watson.

5 Born Whithyelene Amelia Watson on 26 May 1926 in Rosignol, West Bank, Berbice, British Guiana, died Fort Wellington Hospital Berbice on 28 December 2010. Her first husband was Charles Gordon Bevan, born c.1924 in New Amsterdam, died 31 October 1999 in Georgetown. Her second husband was Ronald Breinburg, from Paramaribo in Suriname, born 1925, died 15 May 2000.

6 American Indians of the Greater Antilles and South America. The Taino, an Arawak subgroup, were the first native peoples encountered by Christopher Columbus on Hispaniola. It was long held that the island Arawak were virtually wiped out by Old World diseases to which they had no immunity (see Columbian Exchange), but more recent scholarship has emphasised the role played by Spanish violence, brutality and oppression (including enslavement) in their demise. Moreover, in *A Short Account of the Destruction of the Indies* (1542), Bartolomé de Las Casas paints a horrifying portrait of depredation, slaughter and sexual abuse by the Spanish. A small number of mainland Arawak survive in South America. Most (more than 15,000) live in Guyana, where they represent about one-third of the Native American population, https://www.britannica.com/topic/Arawak [accessed Dec. 2023].

7 'A semantic change whereby a word acquires unfavourable connotations', https://www.collinsdictionary.com/dictionary/english/pejoration

CHAPTER 3: I HEARD HIM CRY IN A MOST AFFECTING MANNER

1. B.L. Blair, 'Wolfert Simon Van Hoogenheim in the Berbice Slave Revolt of 1763–1764', in *Bijdragen Tot de Taal-, Land- En Volkenkunde* 140:1 (1984), p. 61.
2. J. Rodway, *The History of British Guiana*, Vol. I, *1668–1781* (Georgetown, Guyana: J. Thomson, 1891), p. 170.
3. Ibid., p. 173.
4. Ibid., p. 174.
5. Blair, 'Wolfert Simon Van Hoogenheim', p. 62.
6. A. Thompson, *Colonialism and Underdevelopment in Guyana 1580–1803* (Bridgetown, Barbados: Carib Research & Publications, 1987), p. 154.
7. Morton C. Khan, *Djuka: The Bush Negroes of Dutch Guiana* (New York: The Viking Press, 1931), p. 12.
8. M. Kars, *Blood on the River: A Chronicle of Mutiny and Freedom on the Wild Coast* (London: Profile Books, 2022), p. 55.
9. C. Goslinga, 'Dutch in the Caribbean and Guianas 1680–1791', pp. 463 in Thompson, *Colonialism and Underdevelopment in Guyana*, p. 129.
10. Kars, *Blood on the River*, p. 55.
11. Rodway, *The History of British Guiana*, Vol. I, p. 173.
12. Kars, *Blood on the River*, p. 22.
13. Khan, *Djuka*, pp. 10–11.
14. Ibid., p. 11.
15. https://newworldjournal.org/british-guyana/a-birth-of-freedom/ [accessed 1 Sep 2022].
16. Thompson, *Colonialism and Underdevelopment in Guyana*, p. 156.
17. Kars, *Blood on the River*, p. 76.
18. Rodway, *The History of British Guiana*, Vol. I, p. xxx.
19. Governor Van Hoogenheim was in post in Berbice from 1760 to 1764.
20. Thompson, *Colonialism and Underdevelopment in Guyana*, p. 130.
21. Roelof C. Hol, Johan van Langen, Veronique Vos (2020) Inventaris Van De Digitale Duplicaten Van De Lokale Bestuursarchieven Van De Nederlandse Koloniën Essequibo, Demerara en Berbice en notariële akten [tezamen 'Dutch Series' genoemd], aanwezig in de National Archives of Guyana te Georgetown, (1685) 1720–1814 (1827).
22. *Raadsheer* is a Dutch word for a municipal official, such as a councillor.

23 Extract uit een ander fchryver. Surinamen 27 April 1763. In Staatkundige Historie Van Holland, Veertiende Deel. Met Kunft Plaaten opgehelderd., Boekverkooper in de Nes, by de groote Vlees- Hal. Bernardus, Mourik. *Staatkundige Historie van Holland*, v. 14–15 (1863), p. 636.

24 Dutch jurist Hugo Grotius and his 1625 work 'The Rights of War and Peace' (De Jure Belli ac Pacis).

25 *Sommersett v. Steuart* (1772), 98 ER 499 (1772) 20 State Tr 1, (1772) Lofft 1 King's Bench, 22 June 1772.

26 Jim Powell, *The Triumph of Liberty: A 2,000-Year History, Told Through the Lives of Freedom's Greatest Champions* (New York: Free Press, 2000). p. 110.

27 Owner in 1794 of Plantation Standvastigheid Eigenaar in Berbice. Standvastigheid Eigenaar [Owner] J.A. Charbon; Adminis. [Attorney] G. Mahler; Directeur [Manager] G. Mahler. Naam-Lyst . . . op de colonie de Berbice (1794) [Transcribed by Paul Koulen, 2011] p. 10, https://www.ucl.ac.uk/lbs/estate/view/789 [accessed 24 Jan. 2024].

28 Louise Collis, *Soldier in Paradise: The Life of Captain John Stedman 1744–1797* (New York: Harcourt, Brace & World, 1965), p. 38.

29 French term for a ditch.

30 'Some Particulars relating to the Insurrection at Berbices, being an Extract of the Letter from Curaçao, dated May 12th 1763 and signed by John Abraham Charbon.' *Norwich Gazette* or *The Norfolk & Suffolk Advertiser* III: 61, Saturday 6 August 1763, p. 336.

31 Collis, *Soldier in Paradise*, p. 39.

32 Kars, *Blood on the River*, p. 161.

33 https://newworldjournal.org/british-guyana/a-birth-of-freedom/ [accessed 1 Sep. 2022].

34 https://guyaneselanguagesunit.com/lecture-the-last-last-berbice-dutch-speaker/ [accessed 24 Aug. 2022].

35 Khan, *Djuka*, p. 162.

36 Ibid., p. 176.

37 https://www.stabroeknews.com/2013/02/27/news/guyana/the-1763-monument/ [accessed 24 Aug. 2022].

38 Excerpt: Guyana SPEAKS event- Sun, 25 Oct 2020, featuring Dr Nigel Westmaas on the 1763 Berbice Rebellion, https://www.youtube.com/watch?v=oml2CoM3PWE [accessed 1 Sep. 2022].

39 https://en.wikipedia.org/wiki/Amina [accessed 24 Jul. 2024].

40 Thompson, *Colonialism and Underdevelopment in Guyana 1580–1803*, p. 162.

41 Kars, *Blood on the River*, p. 78.

42 Ibid., p. 76.
43 Ibid., p. 79.
44 Ibid., p. 100.
45 Thompson, *Colonialism and Underdevelopment in Guyana*, p. 137.
46 Kars, *Blood on the River*, p. 83.
47 Ibid., p. 84.
48 Rodway, *The History of British Guiana*, Vol. I, p. 200.
49 Ibid., p. 198.
50 Kars, *Blood on the River*, p. 94.
51 Translated from the original Dutch text using Google Translate: 'Op 19th December een groot offensief tegen de opstandige Afrikanen. Een kleine vloot voer de Berbice op en vanuit Demerara trokken een contingent compagniestroepen over land op. In maart 1764, ruim een jaar na aanvang van de opstand, werden de vijandigheden gestaakt.' Hol, van Langen, Vos, p. 9. 1.05.21.
52 Rodway, *The History of British Guiana*, Vol. I, p. 207.
53 Thompson, *Colonialism and Underdevelopment in Guyana 1580–1803*, p. 173.
54 Appendix p.
55 T. Burnard, 'A Voice for Slaves: The Office of the Fiscal in Berbice and the Beginning of Protection in the British Empire, 1819–1834', *Pacific Historical Review* 87:1 (2018), pp. 30–53, https://www.jstor.org/stable/26419878
56 https://www.stabroeknews.com/2009/02/24/opinion/letters/maroons-and-amerindians/ [accessed 1 Sep. 2022].
57 https://newworldjournal.org/british-guyana/a-birth-of-freedom/ [accessed 1 Sep. 2022].
58 Kars, *Blood on the River*, p. 263.
59 Catherine Porter, Constant Méheut, Matt Apuzzo and Selam Gebrekidan, *New York Times*, 20 May 2022, updated 16 Nov. 2022 [accessed 1 Sep. 2022], https://www.nytimes.com/2022/05/20/world/americas/haiti-history-colonized-france.html
60 David Olusoga, 'The Treasury's Tweet Shows Slavery is Still Misunderstood', *Guardian*, 12 Feb. 2018 [accessed 13 Feb. 2024], https://www.theguardian.com/commentisfree/2018/feb/12/treasury-tweet-slavery-compensate-slave-owners
61 Ibid. [accessed 1 Sep. 2022].

CHAPTER 4: THE AIR OF ENGLAND WAS TOO PURE FOR SLAVERY

1. (Childs, 1984)
2. Kirkwall, 26 May 1810. Test. Dative Umq James Watson Esquire, signed by 'Mrs Christian Robertson otherwise Watson Relict of the said deceased James Watson and only Executrix Dative qua Relict deceased to him'.
3. 'An Act to carry into further Execution Provisions of an Act for completing the full Payment of Compensation to Owners of Slaves upon the Abolition of Slavery.' This 1837 Act finalised the compensation provisions built into the preceeding 1833 Act formally titled 'An Act for the Abolition of Slavery throughout the British Colonies; for promoting the Industry of the manumitted Slaves; and for compensating the Persons hitherto entitled to the Services of such Slaves'.
4. James McInroy (ii) of Lude, 1st Laird, born 12 Aug. 1759, Balnabruich, Moulin, Perthshire, Scotland, died 12 Jul. 1825, Lude House, Atholl, Perthshire, Scotland.
5. Mason, Keith. 'A Loyalist's Journey: James Parker's Response to the Revolutionary Crisis.' *The Virginia Magazine of History and Biography*, vol. 102, no. 2, 1994, p. 148. JSTOR, www.jstor.org/stable/4249428. Accessed 10 Apr. 2021.
6. Mason, Keith. 'A Loyalist's Journey: James Parker's Response to the Revolutionary Crisis.' *The Virginia Magazine of History and Biography*, vol. 102, no. 2, 1994, p. 161. JSTOR, www.jstor.org/stable/4249428. Accessed 10 Apr. 2021.
7. Mason, Keith. 'A Loyalist's Journey: James Parker's Response to the Revolutionary Crisis.' *The Virginia Magazine of History and Biography*, vol. 102, no. 2, 1994, p. 166. JSTOR, www.jstor.org/stable/4249428. Accessed 10 Apr. 2021.
8. M.S. Weiner (2002) Notes and documents – New Biographical Evidence on Somerset's Case, 23:1, 121–136, DOI: 10.1080/714005226. p. 123.

CHAPTER 5: HUNTED VICTIMS

1. National Archives CO 101/28/85, https://discovery.nationalarchives.gov.uk/details/r/C9188200; CO 101/32/47, https://discovery.nationalarchives.gov.uk/details/r/C9226155 [accessed 8 Feb. 2023].
2. From transcription of the will of Samuel Sandbach, kindly provided via email by David Reade (Phyllis Hall).

3   The Loyalist Collection PDF.
4   Liverpool Records Office, Parker Papers, 920 PAR I : 49 / 1-52, Correspondence from Robertson, Parker & Co., to James Parker, 1793–1797.
5   Thomas Laurence Dundas, 1st Baron Dundas, FRS (16 February 1741–14 June 1820), was a Scottish politician and peer who sat in the British House of Commons from 1763 to 1794 when he was raised to the peerage of Great Britain as Baron Dundas. He was responsible for commissioning the *Charlotte Dundas*, the world's 'first practical steamboat'. Wikipedia [accessed 27 May 2024].
6   Associated records, GB241/D1/48. Dutch frigate *Utrecht*, salvage papers, 1807.
7   UCL, Legacies of British Slavery: Claim Details, Associated Individuals and Estates Grenada 604 (Dougalston Estate), £4,818 0s 6d.
8   Edith Haden-Guest, 'Dundas, Thomas (1741–1820), of Castlecary, Stirling and Aske, Nr. Richmond, Yorks.', in L. Namier and J. Brooke (eds), *The History of Parliament: The House of Commons 1754–1790* (1964).
9   Edward L. Cox, 'Fédon's Rebellion 1795–96: Causes and Consequences', *The Journal of Negro History* 67:1 (1982), pp. 7–19, https://doi.org/10.2307/2717757 [accessed 8 Feb. 2023].
10 Kit Candlin, *The Last Caribbean Frontier, 1795–1815*, p. 12.
11 Ibid.
12 C. Soriano, 'The Impact of the French Revolution on the Caribbean' (Aug. 2022),
    DOI: 10.1093/OBO/9780199730414-0369 [accessed 25 May 2024].
13 Raymund P. Devas, *The Island of Grenada: 1650–1950*, 1960, p. 110.
14 Home to Dundas, 9 Feb. 1793, 1 Aug. 1794, CO 101/33, cited in Cox, 'Fédon's Rebellion 1795–96', p. 12 [accessed 14 Feb. 2023].
15 Cox, 'Fédon's Rebellion 1795–96', p. 7.
16 National Archives CO 101/34, cited in https://blog.nationalarchives.gov.uk/excessive-severity-treason-and-the-grenadian-rebellion-of-1795/
17 D.G. Garraway, *A Short Account of the Insurrection, St. George's*, 1877. Cited in *The Island of Grenada*, p. 117.
18 Devas, *The Island of Grenada*, p. 111.
19 Ibid., p. 112.
20 Cox, 'Fédon's Rebellion 1795–96', p. 14 [accessed 13 Feb. 2023].
21 Gregory E. O'Malley, *Final Passages: The Intercolonial Slave Trade of British America, 1619–1807* (Williamsburg, 2014), pp. 30, 370; Kit Candlin and Cassandra Pybus, *Enterprising Women: Gender, Race and Power in the Revolutionary Atlantic* (Georgia, 2015), p. 109, both cited in D. Alston, *Slaves and Highlanders*, p. 264.

22 National Archives, CO 101/28/34.
23 G. Morgan and Rushton, *The British and French in the Atlantic 1650–1800: Comparisons and Contrasts* (Routledge, 2019), Ch. 3, https://doi-org.ezp.lib.cam.ac.uk/10.4324/9780429202643
24 Devas, *The Island of Grenada*, p. 117.
25 Encyclopaedia Britannica 1800-10 edition cited in *History of Grenada*, pp. 117–18.
26 Thomas Turner Wise, *A Review of the Events, Which Have Happened in Grenada* (1795), pp. 4–6, https://books.google.co.uk/books?id=8q9XAAAAcAAJ&lpg=PA11&ots=P7WyeMJnVO&dq=%22port%20of%20liberty%22%20%22february%20stile%20of%20the%20slaves%22&pg=PA5#v=onepage&q=%22port%20of%20liberty%22%20%22february%20stile%20of%20the%20slaves%22&f=false [accessed 9 Mar. 2023].
27 Kit Candlin, *The Last Caribbean Frontier*, 1795–1815, 2012.
28 Altson, *Slaves and Highlanders*, p. 264.
29 Devas, *The Island of Grenada*, p. 121.
30 Letter quoted in Wise, *A Review of the Events, Which Have Happened in Grenada*.
31 A.M. Tulloch, 'On the Sickness and Mortality Among the Troops in the West Indies', *Journal of the Statistical Society of London* 1:3 (Jul. 1838), pp. 129–42, https://www.jstor.org/stable/2337906
32 'Report on the Petition of the Proprietors of Estates in the Island of Grenada' Appendix No. 17, cited in *The Island of Grenada*, p. 114.
33 Letter quoted in Wise, *A Review of the Events, Which Have Happened in Grenada*, pp. 16–17 [accessed 9 Mar. 2023].
34 'Report on the Petition of the Proprietors of Estates in the Island of Grenada' Appendix No. 19, cited in *The Island of Grenada*, pp. 123–4.
35 National Archives, CO 101/34/91795.
36 Ibid.
37 Cox, 'Fédon's Rebellion 1795–96', p. 8 [accessed 13 Feb. 2023].
38 National Archives, CO 101/34/12.
39 https://blog.nationalarchives.gov.uk/excessive-severity-treason-and-the-grenadian-rebellion-of-1795/ [accessed 9 Mar. 2023].
40 Cox, 'Fédon's Rebellion 1795–96', p. 15 [accessed 13 Feb. 2023].
41 Ibid.
42 https://www.britishmuseum.org/collection/term/BIOG206143 [accessed 11 May 2023].
43 D. Hollett, *A Passage from India to El Dorado: Guyana and the Great Migration* (Cranbury, NJ: Associated University Presses (1999), p. 38,

https://books.google.co.uk/books?id=SJtJoNvUx3gC&lpg=PA40&ots=00QR

44 Hollett, *A Passage from India to El Dorado*, p. 39.
45 National Archives, CO 101/34/47.
46 Cox, 'Fédon's Rebellion 1795–96', p. 15 [accessed 13 Feb. 2023].
47 National Archives, CO 101/34/51.
48 Nicholas Draper, 'The British State and Slavery: George Baillie, Merchant of London and St Vincent, and the Exchequer Loans of the 1790s', UCL 15. www.ehs.org.uk/dotAsset/ [accessed 13 Feb. 2023].
49 Ibid.
50 https://www.historyofparliamentonline.org/volume/1790-1820/member/baillie-evan-1741-1835 [accessed 13 Feb. 2023].
51 https://www.ucl.ac.uk/lbs/estate/view/3648 [accessed 13 Feb. 2023].
52 Draper, 'The British State and Slavery' [accessed 13 Feb. 2023].
53 https://face2faceafrica.com/article/the-bravery-of-julien-Fédon-the-grenadian-warrior-who-led-a-giant-revolt-against-the-british-in-1795 [accessed 17 Feb. 2023].
54 Cox, 'Fédon's Rebellion 1795–96', p. 7 [accessed 13 Feb. 2023].
55 https://www.spanglefish.com/slavesandhighlanders/index.asp?pageid=552969 [accessed 16 May 2023].
56 MacInroy of Lude – Red Book of Scotland [accessed 11 Jun. 2023].

CHAPTER 6: THREE OR FOUR HATCHETS

1 Not to be confused with his son 'James P. McInroy (1799–1 Oct. 1878) of Lude Blaire Athol was grandfather of Colonel William McInroy C.B. (1838–1919) of The Burn Edzell, who served in India, Burma and Africa, and who was also Deputy Lieutenant for Kincardineshire and a Justice of the Peace for Forfar and Kincardine shires in Scotland. The Colonels wife was Emilia Katharine Hamilton of Edinburgh'. Obituary, *Perthshire Advertiser*, 12 Feb. 1919, p. 4.
2 Both James McInroy Sr and James Patrick McInroy Jr were partners in McInroy Parker & Co. The profit and loss account of 1824 shows James McInroy Sr as second largest shareholder with 20% (Samuel Sandbach being the largest at 25%) and James P. McInroy Jr a minor shareholder with 5%. 'McInroy Parker and Co., Glasgow, balance sheet and profit and loss account', 1824-12-31 (STC 5/26), Cambridge Digital Library.

3 https://www.rct.uk/collection/1072088/the-discovery-of-the-large-rich-and-beautiful-empire-of-guiana-with-a-relation-of [accessed 22 Feb. 2023]. Manoa is another name for El Dorado.
4 https://www.gutenberg.org/files/2272/2272-h/2272-h.htm [accessed 22 Feb. 2023].
5 Hollett, *A Passage from India to El Dorado*, p. 15.
6 Ed. C.W. Eliot LLD, 'Voyages and Travels, Ancient and Modern', Vol. 33, The Harvard Classics (New York: P. F. Collier & Son, 1910), https://archive.org/stream/Harvard-Classics/033_Harvard_Classics_djvu.txt [accessed 1 June 2024].
7 Now part of the territory of Suriname also known previously as Dutch Guiana.
8 Hollett, *A Passage from India to El Dorado*, p. 16.
9 W. Rodney, *A History of the Guyanese Working People, 1881–1905* (Johns Hopkins University Press, 1981), pp. 2–3.
10 https://gallica.bnf.fr/ark:/12148/btv1b53102808s#; https://bostonraremaps.com/inventory/bouchenroeder-essequibo-demerara-1798/ [accessed 22 Feb. 2023].
11 W.R. van Diepen, 'Act of Measuring', copied by W. V. Cooten, Sworn Land Surveyor, on 6 December 1776 [Translated 2 Sep. 1792].
12 Captain Thomson Walter, 'A Chart of the Coast of Guyana, comprehending the Colonies of Berbice, Demerary & Essequibo', 1 October 1798, https://www.atlasofmutualheritage.nl/en/page/10217/map-of-the-plantations-around-the-berbice-demerara-and-essequibo [accessed 23 Oct. 2023].
13 Gilbert Robertson in Demerary to Charles Stuart Parker in London, 24 May 1799. Parker Papers, Liverpool Records Office, 920 PAR II 6/1. pp1–4.
14 Traill papers NLS GB233 MS19331 ff 1–54, Letters by Rev Harry Robertson 1800–14.
15 Rev Harry Robertson to James Watson, from Kiltearn, 24 May 1803. Traill papers NLS GB233 MS19331 ff 1–54, Letters by Rev Harry Robertson 1800–14. National Library of Scotland, Letter 13, NLS MS 19331 f25r.
16 Diary entry; 4 December 1797. Parker Papers, Liverpool Records Office, 920 PAR I 84–129.
17 Parker Papers at Liverpool Records Office, 920 PAR III 107/1.
18 https://www.bankofengland.co.uk/monetary-policy/inflation/inflation-calculator

19 In the Sandbach Tinne accounts you can see payments to the 'estate of George Robertson' for several years after his demise. His will of 1799 depicts how his share of that subsequent income would be sub-divided between his heirs, of whom Christian Robertson, his niece, was one.
20 Christian Robertson was nineteen and a half when she married James Watson in Kiltearn, Scotland, on 6 June 1800.
21 It is possible that Mr Miller was the namesake of James's subsequent son, whom he named Peter Miller Watson.
22 T.S. Traill, 'Memoir of Mrs. Traill', Pt. 1. p. 3.
23 Although the letter makes reference to his setting up a 'House' in Rotterdam, Holland.
24 The signature has been cut out, but in pencil it is given as 'Gilbert Robertson' and a note on the enclosing address page is signed 'GR'.
25 Hugh Munro Robertson was fifteen years old at the time, his parents being the Revd. Harry Robertson DD and Ann Robertson, née Forbes.
26 A puncheon is a type of wooden barrel holding 450–500 litres or 1/3 tun. A butt (or pipe butt) is another which holds ½ tun.
27 Traill Papers, NLS GB233 MS19331 ff 1–54, Letters by Revd Harry Robertson 1800–14, Letter 16, NLS MS 19331 f371r., Revd Harry Robertson to James Watson, from Kiltearn, 3 Dec. 1804.
28 Alston, David. https://urldefense.com/v3/__https://www.spanglefish.com/slavesandhighlanders/index.asp?pageid=605729 n.d. McBean (Tomatin). Accessed February 4, 2025.
29 Hollett, *Passage from India to El Dorado*, Appendix 1, pp. 276–84.
30 *Essequebo and Demerary Gazette* re Woodlands.png.
31 JP to CSP, by Thomas Thompson Esq. Barbados 9 Aug. 1776. Edinburgh University Library Special Collections, originals in Liverpool Record Office, Liverpool Central Library Archives PAR 920. Sourced by Alison Clark.
32 Bristol Record Society's Publications, Vol. xlv, Microfiche – 3298, 3299, 3300, prepared by Walter Minchington, Professor of Economic History, University of Exeter (1964), ii, p. xxii.
33 Bristol Record Society's Publications, Vol. xlvii, p. xxvi.
34 National Archives currency converter as at 2017, https://www-nationalarchives-gov-uk.ezp.lib.cam.ac.uk/currency-converter/#currency-result [accessed 31 Jul. 2024].
35 McInroy Parker and Co., Glasgow, profit and loss account, 1810–12–31 (STC 5/1) Sandbach Tinne Collection, Cambridge Digital Library.

36 'Sandbach, Parker and Company', *Sunday Times* magazine (Guyana), 6 Dec. 2015.
37 Prof. Cassandra Pybus, 'The Colourful Life of Gilbert Robertson', transcript of The Examiner – John West Memorial Lecture (2011), in Launceston Historical Society, P&P.
38 National Library of Scotland, Gilbert Robertson to Doctor Traill, St Ann Street, Liverpool, Plant Brothers, Demerary, 23 Oct. 1832. NLS GB233/MS 19332. f21.
39 *Hansard*, 'Condition of the Slaves in the West Indies', Volume 22: debated on Monday 8 Feb. 1830.
40 LRO PAR 1/53, C.S. Parker to E. Parker, 28 Jun. 1810. Cited in David Alston, ' "Once again destined to mourn": Christian Robertson (1780–1842) and a Highland network in the Caribbean'. Kindly provided by David Alston.
41 Letter 12 NLS MS 19331 f23r
42 Extract from letter from Charles S. Parker to Peter McLagan Esqr., Glasgow, 18 Dec. 1819.
43 Bouchenröder, Friederich von Turpin, Jacobus, 18e E. *Carte Géneralé & Particulière de La Colonie d'Essequebe & Demerarie, Située Dans La Guiane, En Amérique, Redigée & Dédiée Au Comité Des Colonies & Possessions de La République Batave En Amérique, & À La Côte de Guinée Par Le Major F. Von Bouchenroeder, 1798; Gravé Par J. Turpin À La Haye. A.* (Amsterdam: Chez Wouter Brave, 1798), https://hdl.handle.net/11245/3.38621 [accessed 20 Nov. 2024].
44 Legacies of British Slavery, 'Woodlands and L'Amitie, British Guiana, Demerara', https://www.ucl.ac.uk/lbs/estate/view/956 [accessed 15 Jul. 2024].
45 https://discovery.nationalarchives.gov.uk/details/r/C4302 [accessed 22 Feb. 2023].
46 Henry, G. Dalton MD, *History of British Guiana*, Vol. 1 (London: Longman, Brown, Green and Longmans, 1855), p. 246. Other reproductions give the signature as 'M.S. Tuine', 'M. Sinne' to name just two.
47 The son, Alexander, we are told, 'had two sons and four daughters on the Albion Berbice Sugar Estate'. Fred. Oudschans Dentz, *History of the English Church at the Hague 1586–1929*.
48 Dr John Ernest Tinne, 'A Short history of the Tinne Family for three centuries', which includes translated extracts from Philippe Frederick Tinne, '1772–1844', 'Reminiscences d'une Vie Unimportant'.

49 P.F. Tinne, '1772–1844' in J.E. Tinne, 'A Short History of the Tinne Family'.
50 P.F. Tinne, '1772–1844', 'A Short History of the Tinne Family'.
51 Dentz, *History of the English Church at the Hague 1586–1929*.
52 Names of companies outlined in archive document: Sandbach Tinne DB/176A, A1/A4, Agreements, Bryson Collection, Liverpool Maritime Museum. Also, British Museum https://www.britishmuseum.org/collection/term/BIOG206143 [accessed 17 May 2023].
53 University of London, SOAS Library, Journal of J.C. Cheveley, ii, 124. Cited in David Alston, 'A Forgotten Diaspora: The Children of Enslaved and Free Coloured Women and Highland Scots in Guyana Before Emancipation', *Northern Scotland* 6 (2015), pp. 49–69, DOI: 10.3366/nor.2015.0087
54 David Clover, 'Exploring Caribbean Shipping Company Records: The Case of Sandbach Tinne and Co.', in Society for Caribbean Studies (UK) Annual Conference (2011) hosted by the International Slavery Museum, Liverpool, 29 Jun.–1 Jul. 2011, International Slavery Museum, Liverpool, https://sas-space.sas.ac.uk/5169/1/SCS2011_Sandbach_Tinne_and_Co.pdf [accessed 8 Mar. 2023].
55 Journal of J.C. Cheveley, Georgetown, British Guiana, 1821–1825, Vol. 2, p. 124, held in London Missionary Society archives, SOAS CWM/LMS/12/05/03. cited in Clover, 'Exploring Caribbean Shipping Company Records' [accessed Mar. 2023]. Date of journal entry from https://www.spanglefish.com/SlavesandHighlanders/index.asp?pageid=245741 [accessed 8 Mar. 2023].
56 Ibid.
57 An old name for plasterers.
58 National Library of Scotland, 'Traill Papers – Letters by Mrs Anne Robertson 1800–13', NLS GB233 MS19331 ff 55–152. NLS MS 19331 f115r.
59 National Library of Scotland. In a letter to her daughter Christian Watson in Orkney from 14 March 1810, Anne Robertson, in Kiltearn, writes of 'my dear Hugh . . . He now lives with Gilbert at his place called Kiltearn in Berbice.' It seems therefore that there are two Woodlands Plantations: one in Demerara/Mahaica, the other in Berbice. Woodlands is also the name of the final home of Samuel Sandbach in Aigburth, Liverpool. NLS MS 19331 f147r. Woodlands Hospital in Cummingsburg, Demerara is about ½ km from Samuel Sandbach's Demerara residence, which is now the President of Guyana's residence. Woodlands in Berbice is close to the Watson family land in D'Edward and Rosignol villages, bordering Plantation Blairmont, also formerly owned by Sandbach Tinne.

60 Dalton, *History of British Guiana*, Vol. 1, p. 307.
61 [From Sandbach Tinne archive, correspondence letters, pp. 182 of 247].
62 West India Committee brochure No. 73, Monday 23 Jun. 1903. [From Sandbach Tinne archive]
63 Dalton, *History of British Guiana*, Vol. 1, p. 287.
64 [From Sandbach Tinne archive correspondence and financial accounts] the symbol ƒ was used for several currencies, including the former Dutch guilder. The exchange rate to the British pound was initially fixed at 1 pound = ƒ12 Guilders. So ƒ600,000 was equal to c.£50,000 in 1820 (the nearest year available in the calculator); £50,000 would be worth £2,871,520 in 2017 (the last year available in the calculator), https://www-nationalarchives-gov-uk.ezp.lib.cam.ac.uk/currency-converter/#currency-result [accessed 1 Aug. 2024].
65 [Sandbach Tinne correspondence archive pp.172 of 247].
66 Reference: Anonymous. '(189) British Slave Indenture, 1814' on Cowan Auctions Online, https://www.cowanauctions.com/lot/british-slave-indenture-1814-134682 [accessed 10 Jun. 2021].
67 Alston, 'Once again destined to mourn'.
68 National Library of Scotland, Edinburgh, Hugh Munro Robertson to Thomas Traill, 9 Sep. 1806. NLS, GB233/MS19332, fo. 69.
69 National Library of Scotland, Edinburgh. 'Hugh Munro Robertson to Thomas Traill, 9th September 1806.' [NLS] GB233/MS19332, fo. 69.
70 Alston, 'A Forgotten Diaspora', p. 50.
71 National Library of Scotland, Traill Papers. Transcribed by David Alston in *Slaves and Highlanders*.
72 National Library of Scotland, Edinburgh. Cited in Alston, 'Once again destined to mourn', NLS MS 19332 f67 & 69, p. 9.
73 See document 'Hugh Munro Robertson perished 1819'.

CHAPTER 7: THE DEMERARA REBELLION – A LICENCE TO PREACH TO THE NEGROES

1 W.D. Rubinstein, 'Who were the rich? A biographical directory of British wealth-holders', Vol. 1: 1809–1839 (2009), p. 308, reference 1829/34.
2 M.R.D. Foot (ed.), *The Gladstone Diaries*, Vol. 1, *1825–1832* (Oxford: Clarendon Press, 1968) p. 137. [Entry, Mon 17 Sep. 1827 – Footnote 1].
3 Charles Stuart Parker the elder, family member and partner in Sandbach Tinne.

4   Foot (ed.), *The Gladstone Diaries*, p. 402 [Entry, Fri 6 Jan. 1832 – Footnote 9]. This denotes more than one female unmarried Traill girl. There were in fact three Traill sisters: Ann Traill (1812–73) aged twenty at the time, Lucia Traill (1814–50) aged eighteen, and Mary Eliza Traill (1817–98) aged fifteen; they were the half-sisters of Peter Miller Watson. Mary Eliza Traill and her husband Robert Ormond were later Peter Miller Watson's executors, administering his estate on behalf of Peter's Black children Annetta and Andrew Watson, the footballer.

5   Probably refers to his first cousin, Robert Gladstone the younger (Feb. 1811–1872), aged twenty-one in Jan. 1832, the son of Robert Gladstone (1773–1835), Sir John Gladstone's brother.

6   Checkland, S.G. *op-cit*. Cambridge University Press (1971), p. 94.

7   UCL, Legacies of British Slavery, https://www.ucl.ac.uk/lbs/person/view/1648741604 [Accessed 6 Oct. 2024].

8   Foot (ed.), *The Gladstone Diaries*, p. 74. [Entry, Mon 18 Sep. 1826 – Footnote 2].

9   *Hansard*, HC Deb, 17 May 1833, 'Abolition of slavery', Vol. 17, cc1345-7. 1345 §.

10 *Richmond and Twickenham Times*, 'Deaths', Vol. XLVII, No. 5239, 19 March 1921, p. 1.

11 *Genealogy of the families of Douglas of Mulderg and Robertson of Kindeace* (Dingwall: A.M. Ross & Co., 1895), p. 64, https://digital.nls.uk/histories-of-scottish-families/archive/95618599 [Accessed 3 Aug. 2024].

12 Ann McKenzie Gladstone (née Robertson, 1772–1835), second wife of Sir John Gladstone and mother of Prime Minister W.E. Gladstone.

13 NLS MS 19331 f96r [2019-11-02 11.43.10.jpg] Mrs Anne Robertson, Kiltearn, to her daughter Christian (Mrs Watson), Crantit, Orkney, 14 Feb. 1805.

14 Harry Watson (1801–36) was the brother of Peter Miller Watson. He died in Demerara aged thirty-five.

15 'A Visit to Demerara 1828–1829 comprising Letters Written from Demerara by Robertson Gladstone to his Father' (transcription by William G. Williamson) and 'The Journal of a Visit to the Colony of Demerara by Robertson Gladstone' (transcription by Nancy M. Rudd), published by Athenaeum Liverpool, pp. 27–8.

16 Checkland, S.G. *op-cit*. Cambridge University Press (1971) Cambridge. p. 117.

17 Checkland, S.G. *ibid*, Appendix II (i) 'The growth and composition of the fortune', p. 414.

18 Calculated using the National Archive currency calculator with historical records such as those of the royal household and Exchequer.

19　The Bank of England's inflation calculator checks how prices in the UK have changed over time, from 1209 to now. The calculator uses Consumer Price Index (CPI) inflation data from the Office for National Statistics from 1988 onwards.

20　The Emancipation Act was passed in 1833 but came into force on 1 August 1834 in most British dominions.

21　T. Rain, 'The Life and Labours of John Wray, Pioneer Missionary in British Guiana: Compiled chiefly from his own mss. and diaries', reprint of the 1892 edition (Hansebooks, 2018).

22　H. Townsend, letter of 22 Aug. 1850 in *The Church Missionary Intelligencer, A Monthly Journal of Missionary Information,'* II:4 (Apr. 1851), pp.77.

23　Ibid., p. 76.

24　Checkland, p. 185.

25　Checkland, p. 186.

26　'Amelioration of the Condition of the Slave Population in the West Indies', *Hansard*, HC Deb, 16 Mar. 1824, Vol. 10. cc1091-198.

27　S. A. Simeonov, 'Amelioration or abolition? British consulship, Haitian recognition, and the question of colonial emancipation', *Atlantic Studies* 20:4 (2023), pp. 698–718, https://doi.org/10.1080/14788810.2022.2149235

28　Thomas Harding, *White Debt* (Hachette, 2022), p. 35.

29　https://www.vc.id.au/fh/jsmith.html, Wednesday 10 Nov. 1819.

30　Emília Viotti da Costa, *Crowns of Glory, Tears of Blood: The Demerara Slave Rebellion of 1823* (Oxford University Press, 1997), http://ebookcentral.proquest.com/lib/leicester/detail.action?docID=271271. Created from Leicester on 2023-09-14 13:53:14.

31　P.F. Tinne to 'Henry', The Hague, 13 Aug. 1832.

32　P.F. Tinne, 21 Aug. 1822, Letters to Sandbach, Tinne & Co., Merchants & Shipowners. Maritime Museums Archive, Liverpool. B/STI. Acc. No.: MMM.1995.16.

33　Fridor Van der Haas, 14 Aug. 1832. Letters to Sandbach, Tinne & Co., Merchants & Shipowners. Maritime Museums Archive, Liverpool. Ref. Code: B/STI. Acc. No.: MMM.1995.16.

34　Harding, *White Debt*, p. 66.

35　Ibid., p. 193.

36　Sources: 2139 to 2145 slave register David Alston 2019-11-30 15.09.44

37　Letter from McInroy Sandbach & Co., Demerara to Sandbach Tinne & Co.

38　Dalton, *History of British Guiana*, Vol. 1, p. 357.

39　Letter from McInroy Sandbach & Co., Demerara, to Sandbach Tinne & Co., Liverpool (STC 1/40b), Cambridge Digital Library.

40 From McInroy Sandbach and Co., Demerara, to Sandbach Tinne and Co., Liverpool (copy), 1823-06-24 (STC 1/40a) Sandbach Tinne Collection, Cambridge Digital Library.
41 Peter Miller Watson in Demerary to Sandbach Tinne and Co., Liverpool. 11 February 1825. Parker Papers – photocopies (STC/2) pp. 6–7, Sandbach Tinne Collection, Cambridge Digital Library, from: Parker Papers 920 PAR III 57/1, Liverpool Records Office.
42 Da Costa, *Crowns of Glory, Tears of Blood*, p. 172.
43 Harding, *White Debt*, p. 20.
44 Ibid., p. 30.
45 Da Costa, *Crowns of Glory, Tears of Blood*, p. 145.
46 https://www.soas.ac.uk/library/archives/specialist-guides/subject/file76132.pdf
47 This code of law outlining how slaves should be treated was introduced by the Dutch in 1772. From Trevor Burnard, 'A Voice for Slaves', *Pacific Historical Review* 87:1 (Winter 2018), pp. 30–53 at p. 33, https://www.jstor.org/stable/10.2307/26419878.
48 Harding, *White Debt*, p. 57.
49 Ishmael (ed.), British Parliamentary Debate 'Trial of Rev. John Smith.' p. 41.
50 Harding, *White Debt*, p. 171.
51 Ishmael (ed.), British Parliamentary Debate, p. 193.
52 Harding, *White Debt*, pp. 68–9.
53 Letter from Quamina, Satin, Bristol, Asaar and Moses Chisholm, Plantation Success, Demerara, 14 Dec. 1817, https://digital.soas.ac.uk/EK00000142/00001/2x [accessed 1 Sep. 2023].
54 The term 'babes' is taken from instructions given to Smith before his departure for Demerara, cited earlier by Da Costa (p. 131), which in reference to the enslaved Africans notes: 'You need not be informed that they are deplorably ignorant; you will probably find them mere babes in understanding and knowledge; and that you must teach them as you would teach children.'
55 Da Costa, *Crowns of Glory, Tears of Blood*, pp. xvii–xviii.
56 Ibid., p. 98.
57 From Appendix, pp. 534. [file name: Sugar Prices 1781-1829.png]
58 From Appendix, pp. 527 [file name: Guiana produce & exports 1810-1824.png]
59 From McInroy Sandbach and Co., Demerara, to Sandbach Tinne and Co., Liverpool (copy), 1823-06-24 (STC 1/40a), Cambridge Digital Library, Sandbach Tinne Collection.

60 Da Costa, *Crowns of Glory, Tears of Blood*.
61 Appraisement of Georgetown & Population 1789–1834. p. 538 [Appendix, not clear from document which book].
62 Da Costa, *Crowns of Glory, Tears of Blood*, p. 195.
63 Ibid., p. 67.
64 Ibid., p. 192.
65 Ibid., pp. 197–8.
66 Ibid., p. 211.
67 Odeen Ishmael (ed.), British Parliamentary Debate on the Trial of Rev. John Smith, pp.7–8.
68 Harding, *White Debt*, pp. 130–2.
69 Ibid., pp. 146–8.
70 Ibid., p. 138.
71 J. Baillie, 'Resolution: Minutes of the British Guiana Association' (23 Oct. 1823), The Thatched House, Bristol. p. 161.
72 'Governor of Demerara 1813–April 1824, and a plantation owner in Berbice'. See Legacies of British Slavery, https://www.ucl.ac.uk/lbs/person/view/8236 [accessed 9 Oct. 2024].
73 An archipelago stretching from the Bahamas to Trinidad and Tobago to the north of Demerara.
74 Ishmael (ed.), *British Parliamentary Debate*, pp. 56–7.
75 Baillie, 'Resolution: Minutes of the British Guiana Association', p. 160.
76 British Library, MS 38297 ff.159–60.
77 Document name McInroy Sandbach & Co 1823.
78 McInroy Sandbach and Co., Demerara, to Sandbach Tinne and Co., Liverpool, 1824-04-14 (STC 1/42), Cambridge Digital Library.
79 Alston, 'Once Again Destined to Mourn', National Library of Scotland, Peter Watson to his mother (Mrs Traill), Demerara 4 Sept. 1823, NLS MS 19334, f63r MS 19334 f63.
80 Da Costa, *Crowns of Glory, Tears of Blood*, pp. 246–7.
81 National Library of Scotland, NLS MS 19334 f51r.
82 National Library of Scotland, Peter Watson to his mother (Mrs Traill), Demerara 24 Dec. 1823, NLS MS 19334 f65r.
83 McInroy Sandbach and Co., 1824-04-14 (STC 1/42), Cambridge Digital Library.
84 D. Alston, 'The Guyana Maroons, 1796–1834: Persistent and Resilient until the End of Slavery', *Slavery & Abolition* (2023), p. 2, DOI: 10.1080/0144039X.2023.2165065.
85 Ibid., p. 16.

86 Da Costa, *Crowns of Glory, Tears of Blood*, p. 173.
87 Quamina is widely described as being born in Africa, although the slave register of 26 Aug. 1817 lists him as a forty-six-year-old Black carpenter who is 'weakly' and born in Demerary; this could be an administrative error. Source: '2041 slave register David Alston, 2019-11-30 15.09.44'.
88 Da Costa, *Crowns of Glory, Tears of Blood*, p. 229.
89 Ishmael (ed.), *The Trial of Rev. John Smith*, p. 12.
90 https://www.theguardian.com/world/2022/feb/13/david-lammy-requests-pardon-for-1823-slave-rebellion-convicts [accessed 27 Sep. 2023].
91 Ishmael (ed.), *The Trial of Rev. John Smith*, pp. 10–11.
92 Harding, *White Debt*, p. 166.
93 Ibid., p. 179.
94 Ibid., p. 173.
95 Source: '2141 slave register David Alston2019-11-30 15.09.44'
96 Harding, *White Debt*, photo insert after p. 156.
97 Quoted by Juanita in Zoom chat with Malik
98 Ishmael (ed.), *The Trial of Rev. John Smith*, p. 21
99 Harding, *White Debt*, p. 98.
100 Da Costa, *Crowns of Glory, Tears of Blood*, pp. 63–4
101 Transcript of B/STI/2. Letters to Sandbach, Tinne & Co., Merchants & Shipowners. Maritime Museums Archive, Liverpool. B/STI. Acc. No.: MMM.1995.16.
102 Ishmael (ed.), *The Trial of Rev. John Smith*, p. 88.
103 Harding, *White Debt*, p. 52.
104 Ibid., p. 183.
105 *The Correspondence Between John Gladstone, Esq., M.P. and James Cropper, Esq., on the Present State of Slavery in the British West Indies and in the United States of America; and on the Importation of Sugar from the British Settlements in India. With an Appendix Containing Several Papers on the Subject of Slavery* (Liverpool West India Association, 1824), cited in Richard B. Sheridan, 'The condition of the slaves on the sugar plantations of Sir John Gladstone in the colony of Demerara, 1812-49', *NWIG: New West Indian Guide / Nieuwe West-Indische Gids* 76:3/4 (2002), pp. 243–69, at p. 251, http://www.jstor.org/stable/41850197
106 Harding, *White Debt*, p. 237.
107 Da Costa, *Crowns of Glory, Tears of Blood*, p. xiv.
108 Harding, *White Debt*, p. 239.

109 Ishmael (ed.), *British Parliamentary Debate*, p. 221.
110 Da Costa, *Crowns of Glory, Tears of Blood*, p. 12.
111 Ishmael (ed.), *British Parliamentary Debate*, p. 55.
112 Release from enslavement, usually at the discretion of the owner rather than by force of the law.

CHAPTER 8: LARGE AND LIBERAL ATONEMENT

1 McInroy Sandbach and Co., Demerara, to Sandbach Tinne and Co., 1824-04-14 (STC 1/42) Cambridge Digital Library.
2 Ibid.
3 Ibid. Lambeth Palace [accessed 2 Oct. 2023].
4 https://www.lambethpalacelibrary.info/exhibitions/enslavement-voices-from-the-archives/ Lambeth Palace [accessed 2 Oct. 2023].
5 Dalton, *History of British Guiana*, Vol. 1, p. 288.
6 Ibid., p. 360.
7 G. Pinckard, MD, 'Notes on the West Indies, Including Observations Relative to the Creoles and Slaves of the Western Colonies, and the Indians of South America; Interspersed with Remarks Upon Seasoning or Yellow Fever of Hot Climates, 2nd Edn, With Additional Letters from Martinique, Jamaica, and St. Domingo', Letter XLI, p. 359.
8 H. Townsend, letter of 22 Aug. 1850 in *The Church Missionary Intelligencer*, Vol. II, No. 4 (Apr. 1851), p. 77.
9 In the Will of Charles Stuart Parker, we see a bequest to the Moravian Mission.
10 Townsend. 1851. 'Original Communications.' *Church Missionary Intelligencer – A Monthly Journal of Missionary Information* 2 (4): 73–96.
11 S90. Marriages (PR) England. Collection: Marriages and Banns, Liverpool, England 1813–1821. Location: Provo, Utah, USA, 13 Nov. 1816, Liverpool, Lancashire. Ref 283 HOL/3/2. p. 88; No. 263. 'Abraham Garnett, Batchelor of this parish and Anne Mewburn, of this parish, minor, were married in this church by license this thirteenth day of November. Wit. P.F. Tinne; Anna Tinne.'
12 *Report of the Incorporated Society for the Conversion and Religious Instruction and Education of the Negro Slaves in the British West India Islands for the year MDCCCXXVI* (London, 1827), pp. 1–107 (Pamphlet of the West India Association). Microfiche.

13 'Refuse men' refers to those Africans freed from the slave ships captured by the British blockade in West African waters after the abolition of the slave trade in 1807 and returned to Africa.

14 F. Buxton, Parliamentary debate: 'Abolition Of Slavery' Volume 9: debated on Thursday 15 May 1823. *Hansard*, https://hansard.parliament.uk/Commons/1823-05-15/debates/1de6491b-9868-45d3-a21c-183198f32d97/AbolitionOfSlavery [accessed 19 Oct. 2024].

15 *Report of the Incorporated Society for the Conversion and Religious Instruction and Education of the Negro Slaves in the British West India Islands for the year MDCCCXXVI*, p. 9.

16 Dalton, *History of British Guiana*, Vol. 1, p. 366.

17 Townsend. 1851. 'Original Communications.' *Church Missionary Intelligencer – A Monthly Journal of Missionary Information* 2 (4): 73–96.

18 Townsend. 1851. 'Original Communications.' *Church Missionary Intelligencer – A Monthly Journal of Missionary Information* 2 (4): 73–96.

19 'Missions of the Church in British Guiana', from *The Colonial Church Chronicle and Missionary Journal* xxiv (Nov. 1849), pp. 161–72, http://anglicanhistory.org/sa/gy/missions1849.html [accessed 3 Oct. 2023].

20 https://www.churchofengland.org/media-and-news/press-releases/equality-advocate-appointed-church-englands-first-racial-justice [accessed 2 Oct. 2023].

21 https://www.churchofengland.org/about/leadership-and-governance/church-commissioners-england/who-we-are/church-commissioners-links [accessed 3 Oct. 2023].

22 'Church Commissioners' Research into Historic Links to Transatlantic Chattel Slavery' (2022), https://www.churchofengland.org/sites/default/files/2022 [accessed 3 Oct. 2023].

23 *Genealogy of the Families of Douglas of Mulderg and Robertson of Kindeace*, https://digital.nls.uk/histories-of-scottish-families/archive/95618599 [Accessed 3 Aug. 2024].

24 Ibid.

25 *The Chester Courant and Advertiser for North Wales*, 13 Nov. 1907. p. 8.

26 https://www.stannesaigburth.com/st-annes/history/ [Accessed 3 Oct. 2023].

27 Dentz, *History of the English Church at the Hague*, p. 104.

28 P.M. Watson Esq. Demerary to C.S. Parker Esq. Glasgow, 11 February 1826, Parker Papers – photocopies (STC/2) pp.6–7, Sandbach Tinne

Collection, Cambridge Digital Library, from: Parker Papers 920 PAR III 157/3, Liverpool Records Office.
29 Slave populations Demerara Berbice 1829 1828_ Erh4Fl7XMAADQhQ
30 Sandbach Tinne plantation in Guiana.
31 From Charles S. Parker, Glasgow, to Sandbach Tinne and Co., Liverpool, 1826-02-06 (STC 1/54c) p. 2, Sandbach Tinne Collection, Cambridge Digital Library.
32 From H. van Cooten, Demerara, to McInroy Parker and Co., Glasgow (copy), 1825-12-03 (STC 1/54a) p.1, Sandbach Tinne Collection, Cambridge Digital Library.
33 P.M. Watson Esq. Demerary to C.S. Parker Esq. Glasgow, 11 February 1826, Parker Papers – photocopies (STC/2) pp.1–2, Sandbach Tinne Collection, Cambridge Digital Library, from: Parker Papers 920 PAR III 157/3, Liverpool Records Office.
34 Henry R. Sandbach to Lord Derby, Woodlands, 12 September [No year, c. 1830–1831] Source: Derby Papers, Liverpool Record Office, Ref. 920/DER (13)/144/1.
35 £172,913 in 1925 to 2017 money converter, £7,099,617.58, https://www.nationalarchives.gov.uk/currency-converter/#currency-result [accessed 10 Nov. 2024].
36 https://www.iron-church.com/the-changing-community/ [accessed 3 Oct. 2023].
37 https://lan-opc.org.uk/Liverpool/Everton/stgeorge/burials_1815-1873.html#TAIL and https://lan-opc.org.uk/Liverpool/Everton/stgeorge/burials_1874-1932.html [accessed 3 Oct. 2023].

CHAPTER 9: EXTENDING TO SLAVES PRACTICALLY ALL CIVIL RIGHTS BUT FREEDOM

1 Scottish Gaelic: Neach-casaid a' Chrùin (Procurator Fiscal) is a public prosecutor in Scotland, who has the power to impose fiscal fines.
2 Trevor Burnard, 'A Voice for Slaves: The Office of the Fiscal in Berbice and the Beginning of Protection in the British Empire, 1819–1834', *Pacific Historical Review* 87:1, Special Iss. Protection: Global Genealogies, Local Practices (Winter 2018), pp. 30–53, https://www.jstor.org/stable/10.2307/26419878

3 Adela Tinne was freed (along with any future children) by her former owner P.F. Tinne. This suggests that as well as being Philip Frederick Tinne's property, she was also likely his child. Freeing their Black women – with whom they had children, and their Black children also – was typical of Sandbach Tinne when they had no further use of them, having left the colony – as Andrew Rose had also done with Minky and Anna Rose.
4 It is highly likely that Sophia was a Black child of James McInroy or his brother Peter McInroy (b. 2 Feb. 1751 in Moulin, Perthshire, Scotland and who died in the Caribbean in 1821).
5 'Protectors of Slaves Report', ordered by the House of Commons, 10 March 1831, pp. 143–144.
6 'Our Records: Peter McLagan (1823–1900), British Liberal Party politician and Scotland's first Black MP', Scotland's People, https://www.scotlandspeople.gov.uk/article/our-records-peter-mclagan-1823-1900-scotlands-first-black-MP [accessed 19 Nov. 2024].
7 From Peter McLagan, Demerara, to McInroy Parker and Co., Glasgow (copy), 1822-01-03 (STC 1/36b) (Then referred by McInroy Parker and Co., to Sandbach Tinne & Co., Liverpool, on 4 Mar. 1822). Cambridge Digital Library.
8 Da, Costa, *Crowns of Glory, Tears of Blood*, p. 372.
9 Ibid, p. 158.
10 'Hard toil of sugar cultivation'; Appendix to the Sixty-Fourth Volume of the Journals of the House of Lords Session 1831–2.
11 https://api.parliament.uk/historic-hansard/commons/1831/oct/07/sugar-refining-bill [accessed 25 Oct. 2023].
12 8 Bristol Archives, Society of Merchant Venturers Collection: SMV/8/3/3/2/39. From Alice Kinghorn, 'Bristol's connections to Sandbach Tinne & Co. Initial Findings' (undated).
13 Alston, 'Once again destined to mourn', p. 103.
14 Buxton, 'Abolition Of Slavery', Volume 9: Debated on Thursday 15 May 1823, House of Parliament. *Hansard*. Col: 275.
15 British Guiana Association Minutes (British Library (BL), Correspondence and papers of the 2nd Earl of Liverpool, Vol. CVIII: 1820–1827 (MS 38297) ff.159-162) F 159.
16 Ibid.
17 Not to be confused with the London West India Committee.
18 https://theathenaeum.org.uk/history-of-the-athenaeum/ [accessed 5 Nov. 2023].

19 Malik interview with Willie Williamson in 2021.
20 Nicholas Draper, 'The rise of a new planter class? Some counter currents from British Guiana and Trinidad, 1807–33', *Atlantic Studies*, 9:1 (2012), pp. 65–83, at p. 76, DOI: 10.1080/14788810.2012.636996
21 It now becomes clear how Peter Miller Watson was landing a 'cargo of Negroes' in 1847 if they were invested in the Dutch 'New West India Company' trading in Suriname, where enslavement was lawful until 1863, despite it being unlawful to traffic enslaved people into Dutch colonies since 1814 under Dutch law. However, it would have been a simple task to smuggle them across the border into Berbice.

CHAPTER 10: EMANCIPATION, FINALLY – BUT NOT REALLY

1 https://beta.nationalarchives.gov.uk/explore-the-collection/explore-by-time-period/georgians/1833-abolition-of-slavery-act-and-compensation-claims/#:~:text=In%20August%201833%2C%20Parliament%20passed,protect%20their%20work%20and%20wellbeing [accessed 30 Oct. 2023].
2 Dalton, *History of British Guiana*, Vol. 1, p. 396.
3 Ibid, p. 409.
4 30 Nov. 1835, UCL Legacies of Slavery, https://www.ucl.ac.uk/lbs/claim/view/8880
5 30 Nov. 1835, UCL Legacies of Slavery, https://www.ucl.ac.uk/lbs/claim/view/8875
6 30 Nov. 1835, UCL Legacies of Slavery, https://www.ucl.ac.uk/lbs/claim/view/8071
7 £15,482 14s 8d in 1830 is worth approximately £1,049,749.45 in 2017, https://www.nationalarchives.gov.uk/currency-converter/
8 Using the Bank of England inflation calculator for the year that most of the money was received, which was 1835. https://www.bankofengland.co.uk/monetary-policy/inflation/inflation-calculator [Accessed 3 Nov. 2024].
9 'Shaped circular and on four cast shell and foliage feet, with similarly cast border, engraved with foliage scrolls and lattice work, the centre engraved with a coat-of-arms and an inscription, marked underneath 26 3 A in. (68 cm.) diam. 207 oz. 10 dwt. (6,453 gr). The arms are those of Gladstone impaling Robertson, for Sir John Gladstone (1764–1851) and

his second wife Anne MacKenzie, the daughter of Andrew Robertson, whom he married in 1800.'

10 The word derives from the Latin noun for 'landed property', *praedium*. *Praedium* in turn is based on *praed-*, meaning 'bondsman' – that is, one who is legally liable for the debt of another.

11 Alvin O. Thompson, 'Symbols Legacies of Slavery in Guyana'. New West Indian Guide / Nieuwe West-Indische Gids 80: 3/4 (2006), pp. 191–220, https://www.jstor.org/stable/41850454

12 https://ntg.gov.gy/monument/damons-cross/ [accessed 7 Nov. 2023].

13 https://api.parliament.uk/historic-hansard/commons/1838/mar/30/negro-apprenticeship-adjourned-debate#S3V0042P0_18380330_HOC_10 [accessed 5 Nov. 2023].

14 Dalton, *History of British Guiana*, p. 429.

15 Lord Brougham, Lords Chamber, 'Slave Trade', Vol. 40: Debated on Mon 29 Jan. 1838. HOL Col. 597.

16 From McInroy Sandbach and Co., Demerara, to Sandbach Tinne and Co., Liverpool (copy), 1849-09-15 (STC 1/106a) p.1, Sandbach Tinne Collection, Cambridge Digital Library.

17 Letter from John Gladstone to Sir George Grey, Assistant Secretary at the Colonial Office, 25 March 1837. Catalogue ref: CO 111/161.

18 Peter M. Watson, Signed Letter, from McInroy Sandbach & Co., Demerary, British Guiana, 20 Jun. 1838 to Sandbach Tinne & Co., Liverpool, England. 4pp. Auction lot PBA Galleries [accessed 2 Nov. 2024].

19 Da Costa, *Crowns of Glory, Tears of Blood*, p. 372.

20 Dalton, *History of British Guiana*, Vol. 1, p. 287.

21 Select Committee, House of Lords Sessions 1849–1850 in *The Church Missionary Intelligencer*, II:4 (Apr. 1851), p. 73.

22 Tinne, 'A Short History of the Tinne Family', p. 22.

23 Craig and Jarvis, 1967, p. 187.

24 From 1793 to 1805, approximately 377 'Total Prizes' were taken and registered at Liverpool. Craig and Jarvis, 1967.

25 https://theathenaeum.org.uk/history-of-the-athenaeum/ [accessed 5 November 2023].

26 https://theathenaeum.org.uk/some-proprietors-of-note-traill-booth/ [accessed 6 Nov. 2023].

CHAPTER 11: THESE GOOD-NATURED SAVAGES

1. From Thomas Garnett and William Jones, Demerara, to R. Sandbach, Liverpool (copy), 1855-09-25 (STC 1/113a) p.1, Sandbach Tinne Collection, Cambridge Digital Library.
2. From McInroy Sandbach and Co., Demerara (Peter M. Watson) to Sandbach Tinne and Co., Liverpool (copy), 1853-08-25 (STC 1/111a)), p.2, Sandbach Tinne Collection, Cambridge Digital Library.
3. Colonial Registrar's Office in and for the counties of Demerara and Essequibo - Electoral College, in Gazette 29 Nov 1857 p. 681 – (Photocopy). Voter lists with plantation details and qualification to vote (STC/20) p.6, Sandbach Tinne Collection, Cambridge Digital Library.
4. Eric Williams, 'The Historical Background of British Guiana's Problems', *The Journal of Negro History* 30:4 (1945), pp. 357–81, https://doi.org/10.2307/2715026
5. From McInroy Sandbach and Co., Demerara, to Sandbach Tinne and Co., Liverpool (copy), 1851-01-11 (STC 1/107a) p.1, Sandbach Tinne Collection, Cambridge Digital Library.
6. From McInroy Sandbach and Co., Demerara, to Sandbach Tinne and Co., Liverpool, 1851-01-20 (STC 1/107b), p.1, Sandbach Tinne Collection, Cambridge Digital Library.
7. From McInroy Sandbach and Co., Demerara (Peter M. Watson) to Sandbach Tinne and Co., Liverpool , 1849-07-18 (STC 1/105b), p.2, Sandbach Tinne Collection, Cambridge Digital Library.
8. 'Synoptical Statement of the Mortality in Georgetown, from the Year 1838 to the Year 1846' from Appendix p. 552. [file name: Deaths in Guiana 1838-1846.png]
9. From McInroy Sandbach and Co., Demerara (Peter M. Watson) to Sandbach Tinne and Co., Liverpool (copy), 1849-07-05 (STC 1/105c) p.2, Sandbach Tinne Collection, Cambridge Digital Library.
10. Williams, 'The Historical Background of British Guiana's Problems'.
11. Dalton, *History of British Guiana*, Vol. 2.
12. Dalton, Vol. 1, pp. 163–4.
13. Ibid., p. 164.
14. Ibid.
15. Tinne, 'A Short History of the Tinne Family', p. 21.
16. Ibid.

17. Anne-Marie Lee-Loy, 'Saying No to Chineseness: The Possibilities and Limits of a Diasporic Identity in Janice Lowe Shinebourne's Fiction', *Journal of Chinese Overseas* 5 (2009), pp. 291–309, brill.nl/jco
18. Williams, 'The Historical Background of British Guiana's Problems', *The Journal of Negro History* 30:4 (1945), 357–81, (p. 380).
19. From McInroy Sandbach and Co., Demerara (Peter M. Watson) to Sandbach Tinne and Co., Liverpool (copy), 1849–07–05 (STC 1/105c) p.2, Sandbach Tinne Collection, Cambridge Digital Library.
20. Tinne, 'A Short History of the Tinne Family', p. 23.
21. Kinghorn, 'Bristol's Connections to Sandbach Tinne & Co. Initial Findings'.
22. Harding, *White Debt*, p. 256.
23. Tinne, 'A Short History of the Tinne Family', p. 22.
24. From James Stuart, Demerara, to P. F. Tinne, 1859–03–11 (STC 1/116) p.2, Sandbach Tinne Collection, Cambridge Digital Library.
25. From James Stuart, Demerara, to P. F. Tinne, 1859–11–25 (STC 1/117) Sandbach Tinne Collection, Cambridge Digital Library.
26. The name of a Sandbach Tinne plantation in Guiana. Not to be confused with the Sandbach Tinne ship the *Anna Catharina*.
27. From Peter M. Watson, Demerara, to R. Sandbach, 1853–08–24 (STC 1/110) p.2, Sandbach Tinne Collection, Cambridge Digital Library.
28. D. Aitkin, 'From Plantation Medicine to Public Health: The State and Medicine in British Guiana 1838–1914', Ph.D Thesis, UCL (London) Aug. 2001, p. 131.
29. It is not clear from this letter which McLagan is being referred to or why it was sensitive, but it will undoubtedly be a descendant or relative of the founding partner, still associated somehow with the firm after the death of Peter McLagan (the early partner in firms that became Sandbach Tinne) and his son John McLagan, a surgeon in Demerara who died in 1850.
30. A. MacRae, 'A Manual of Plantership in British Guiana, as it Has Heretofore Been Practised, and as it is at Present in Operation; With Some Suggestions for Improvement on the Present Practice' (London: Smith, Elder & Co., 1856). pp. 7–8.
31. Ibid., p. 9.
32. Ibid., p. 65.
33. Ibid.
34. Ibid., p. 58.
35. Ibid., p. 50.

36 Ibid., p. 52.
37 Ibid., p. 66.
38 Ibid., pp. 67–8.
39 Ibid., p. 68.
40 From Sandbach Parker and Co., Demerara, to Sandbach Tinne and Co., Liverpool, 1863-12-08 (STC 1/118) Sandbach Tinne Collection, Cambridge Digital Library.
41 Williams, 'The Historical Background of British Guiana's Problems'.
42 'Harry Rose snippet Walter Rodney'.
43 Parker, C.S. to Margaret Rainy, Parker Family Papers, 920 PAR, 1/53, 11 Aug. 1810. Liverpool Record Office.
44 From Sandbach Parker and Co., Demerara, to Sandbach Tinne and Co., Liverpool, 1863-12-08 (STC 1/118)) p.1, Sandbach Tinne Collection, Cambridge Digital Library.
45 Using the National Archives currency converter, £3,000 in 1860 is worth approximately £177,387.60 in 2017.
46 Dalton, *History of British Guiana*, Vol. 1, pp. 313–14.
47 Letter From George Rainy, Demerara, to Charles S. Parker (copy), Sandbach Tinne Collection, Cambridge Digital Library, 1821-04-24 (STC 1/31a).
48 Oxford Reference: '"Literally mixing of races", a racist term denoting sexual relations between different races, especially White and Black. Miscegenation was promoted in some systems—for example Portuguese colonialism and the Baha'i religion—as a means of overcoming artificial ethnic barriers. The concept is treated pejoratively in racist ideology as a source of social and economic degeneration', https://www.oxfordreference.com/display/10.1093/oi/authority.20110803100201137 [accessed 16 Nov. 2024].
49 1851 Census, Guiana, Appendix, 'Abstract of the Census of the Population, &c. Continued: Race', p. 562.
50 Randy M. Browne, Lisa A. Lindsay and John Wood Sweet, 'Rebecca's Ordeal, from Africa to the Caribbean: Sexual Exploitation, Freedom Struggles, and Black Atlantic Biography', *Slavery & Abolition* 43 (2021), pp. 40–67. doi:10.1080/0144039X.2021.1938399.
51 Dalton, *History of British Guiana*, Vol. 1, p. 174.

CHAPTER 12: MERCANTILE MONSTERS

1. 'Persons Affiliated w/ B. Guiana in British Newspapers', https://sites.rootsweb.com/~nyggbs/Transcriptions/LisaB/MarriagesTrans2015.pdf, Transcribed by Lisa Booth.
2. Alston, 'A Forgotten Diaspora'.
3. Transcription from *Royal Gazette* March 1815, Guyana Genealogy Society, p. 5, https://gbggs.org/resources/RoyalGazette/PropertySales.pdf [accessed 16 Nov. 2024].
4. *Essequebo & Demerary Royal Gazette*, 10 Dec. 1808. The Executors of James Robinson, Esq. M.D. deceased, are listed as 'Andrew and Peter Rose'.
5. *Essequebo & Demerary Royal Gazette*, 16 Sep. 1815.
6. Traill, 'Memoir of Mrs. Traill', Pt. 2, p. 156.
7. National Library of Scotland, NLS MS 19334. f57r.
8. Peter Miller Watson would have started in Samuel Sandbach's counting house aged sixteen. As we see from this account from Dr Traill, Peter arrived in Demerara in Nov. 1822 after two years' apprenticeship with his 'uncle' Samuel Sandbach, presumably in Liverpool where his mother had relocated with Dr Traill. Upon arrival in Demerara, Peter was mentored by 'his cousin' (fellow partner with Sandbach) George Rainy.
9. Traill, 'Memoir of Mrs. Traill', Pt. 2, pp. 174–2.
10. 'William Watson has made arrangements last year with an Anglo-American Company to go out as their mining agent . . . But that Company was dissolved, and he was thrown out of the prospect of employment. On this he expressed a wish to join his brothers in Demerary and he obtained an engagement as a sugar planter in that colony. He left England in the month of April this year, (1826) and his mother's anxieties were reduced by letters informing us of his arrival there, after a favourable passage, on the 20th of May. He kept his health and became a very expert manager of an extensive sugar plantation.' Traill, 'Memoir of Mrs. Traill', Pt. 2, p. 187.
11. '14th of March, (1823) Andrew Watson again left Britain, which he was never more destined to revisit, and arrived on the 14th of April, in Demerary, where he was received into the flourishing establishment of his brother Harry.' Traill, 'Memoir of Mrs. Traill, Pt. 2, pp. 175–5.
12. MS 19334 f81r

13 'Nett proceeds Plantation William, dividend awarded to Parker, Garrett, and Co. 85 29c.' *The Gazette*, London, 2129, p. 465, https://www.thegazette.co.uk/London/issue/21291/page/465/data.pdf [accessed 20 Nov. 2024].

14 Parker, Garrett and Co of London, solicitors, 1783–1871 https://catalogue.gloucestershire.gov.uk/records/D2167 (accessed 27 April 2025) Still trading in London at St. Michael's Rectory, Cornhill, E.C.3, (THE LONDON GAZETTE, 30 MAY, 1933. p.3653).

15 'A composite barque is a sailing ship with a wooden planking over an iron frame.'

16 Capt. W.H. Angel, 'The Clipper Ship "Sheila" – Angel Master' (London: Heath Cranton Ltd, 1919), p. 41.

17 Gyrocompass, Royal Museums Greenwich (rmg.co.uk) [accessed 21 Dec. 2023].

18 NLS Letters of the Watson boy's transcripts, by David Alston.

19 NLS MS 19334 f59r, Letter from Andrew Watson to his mother (Mrs Traill), from Kiltearn [Berbice], 16 May 1837. From letters transcribed by David Alston.

20 Candlin and Pybus, *Enterprising Women*.

21 NLS MS 19332 f67 Hugh M. Robertson to Thomas Traill, physician, 21 Islington, Liverpool from Demerary, pl Kensington (17 Aug, 1806) from Slaves and Highlanders | Gilbert Robertson (spanglefish.com).

22 Details of Claim | Legacies of British Slavery (ucl.ac.uk).

23 Cheveley, *Journal*, Vol. 2, p.126.

24 Alston, 'Once again destined to mourn'.

25 Alston, 'Once again destined to mourn'.

26 Letter from Charles Stuart Parker to his wife in 1810.

27 https://www.history.com/this-day-in-history/bloody-ban-tarleton-born-in-britain [accessed 6 Jan. 2024].

28 https://www.ucl.ac.uk/lbs/person/view/2146632009 [accessed 5 Jan. 2024].

29 Articles of Co-partnership between James McInroy and Charles Stuart Parker of Glasgow and Samuel Sandbach and Phillip Frederick Tinne of Liverpool and George Buchanan, George Rainy and Peter McLagan of Demerary; signed 13 June 1815, (Liverpool)18 December 1815 (Demerary) and 1 October 1816 (Glasgow). Bryson Collection: Sandbach Tinne, DB/176 A-A1/A4. Merseyside Maritime Museum.

30 https://en.wikipedia.org/wiki/John_Tarleton_(slave_trader).

31 The British Newspaper Archive via @Liverpool1207, https://twitter.com/liverpool1207/status/1448330188387852294 [accessed 5 Jan. 2024].
32 Henry Kelsall Aspinall, *Birkenhead and its Surroundings*, pp. 290–1
33 https://www.old-merseytimes.co.uk/lplstreetsandcorners.html [accessed 5 Jan. 2024]. Barclays Fact Sheet Martins Bank [accessed 28 Jun. 2022, no longer available online].
34 Formed initially as a 'joint stock bank' in 1831 (equivalent today of a listed company selling shares to the public) the corporate name was Bank of Liverpool from 1831–1882. After that it was reincorporated as a Limited Liability company and became Bank of Liverpool Ltd, between 1882-1918. When it acquired Martins Bank and became Bank of Liverpool and Martins Ltd, from 1818–1928 and then it became simply Martins Bank Ltd, from 1928–1968 when it was subsumed in a merger into Barclays Bank.
35 Chandler, G. ibid. pp. 539–545.
36 From the shareholders book at the Bank of Liverpool. Barclays Bank archive.
37 Barclays Fact Sheet [accessed 5 Jan. 2024]; Barclays Fact Sheet Martins Bank [accessed 28 Jun. 2022, no longer available online].
38 Barclays Fact Sheet [accessed 5 Jan. 2024 – downloaded version].
39 Articles of Agreement between Samuel Sandbach, Henry Robertson Sandbach and Walter Fergus McGregor for Co-partnership in the trade of Iron Founders and Engineers. Signed 11 September 1841, (Liverpool). Bryson Collection: Sandbach Tinne, DB/176 A. Merseyside Maritime Museum.
40 Memoir of Mrs Trail, Part II (Liverpool years: 1811 to 1833), transcribed and provided by David Alston.
41 Quoted in Tinne, 'A Short History of the Tinne Family', p. 26.
42 Tinne, 'A Short History of the Tinne Family'.
43 https://rainhilltrials.co.uk/rainhill-trials-and-the-liverpool-and-manchester-railway/ [accessed 9 Jan. 2024].
44 Joseph Sanders, 'Prospectus for the Liverpool Manchester Railway – bound into – The Liverpool Tracts. (1824). Appendix to 'A Letter on the Subject of the Projected Rail Road, Between Liverpool & Manchester, Pointing Out the Necessity for its Adoption and the Manifest Advantages it Offers to the Public – with an Exposure of the Exorbitant & Unjust Charges of the Water Carriers.' 2nd edn (Liverpool. W. Wales & Co., 1824) pp. 33–6.

45 Norwich Gazette, or Norfolk and Suffolk Advertiser, 1763–08–06 (STC 12/1), pp. 333–336 (whole issue), Sandbach Tinne Collection, Cambridge Digital Library.
46 Tinne, 'A Short History of the Tinne Family.'
47 London International Exhibition (1862) | Organisations | RA Collection | Royal Academy of Arts [accessed 22 Jan. 2024].
48 *St James's Magazine*, May 1862, p. 248. Cited in John Agnew, 'The 1862 London International Exhibition: Machinery on Show and its Message', *International Journal for the History of Engineering & Technology*, 85:1 (2015), pp. 1–30, DOI: 10.1179/1758120614Z.00000000053
49 *The Times*, 28 May 1862, p. 5, col. 5. Cited in Agnew, 'The 1862 London International Exhibition'.
50 Dalton, *History of British Guiana*, Vol. 1, p. 497.
51 [File name: 046294c0]
52 Son of John Abraham Tinne and Margaret Sandbach and grandson of founder Phillip Frederick Tinne (1772–1844).
53 Articles of Co-partnership Sandbach Parker Co of Demerara July 1869 and supplementary articles Nov. 1871. Bryson Collection, Liverpool Maritime Museum. D/B/176a.
54 I found Henry Tinne Garnett's epitaph in Christ Church, Cummingsburg in Georgetown on my visit to Guyana in 2024. He was sponsored for baptism as an infant by P.F. Tinne. He died on board the *Don*, 17 July 1879.
55 Articles of Co-partnership Sandbach Parker Co of Demerara July 1869 and supplementary articles Nov. 1871. Bryson Collection, Liverpool Maritime Museum. DB/176 A.
56 Ibid.
57 I28 73200, 'Sandbach Tinne' DB/176 A, Section 1, accession no. 73-200, City of Liverpool Museums Records.
58 Agreement between Samuel Sandbach Parker, Alfred Traill Parker, John Ernest Tinne and Gilbert Robertson Sandbach of Liverpool and The Demerara Company. Signed 25 March 1892. Bryson Collection: Sandbach Tinne, DB/176 A. Merseyside Maritime Museum.
59 Bryson Collection, Sandbach Tinne DB/176 A, Section 1, Accession No. 73–200, Liverpool Maritime Museum.
60 Nicholas Draper et al., *Legacies of British Slave Ownership* (Cambridge University Press, 2016), p. 87, https://api.parliament.uk/historic-hansard/people/mr-charles-parker/index.html [accessed 22 Jan. 2024].

61 *Liverpool Courier*, Wednesday 12 June 1895, 'Death of Mr. Henry R. Sandbach'.
62 From McInroy Sandbach and Co., Demerara, to Sandbach Tinne and Co., Liverpool, 1851–01–20 (STC 1/107b) Sandbach Tinne Collection, Cambridge Digital Library.

CHAPTER 13: WE THE PEOPLE

1 CARICOM is an acronym for 'Caribbean Community'. It is a regional grouping of twenty countries in the Caribbean.

INDEX

Abercromby, Lieutenant General Sir Ralph 137
Act for a Company Trading to Africa and the Indies (1695) 88
Act for the Abolition of Slavery throughout the British Colonies (1833) 91, 244
Act for the Abolition of the Slave Trade (1807) 115, 167, 252–3
Act of Regis (1806) 139–40, 339–40
Acts of Union (1706 and 1707) 87–8, 98
Aflakka 76
Africa 13, 22, 28, 32–4, 36–7, 52–3, 63–72, 75–97, 105–18, 120–21, 124, 127–32, 134–9, 141, 142, 144–5, 148, 151–2, 154, 156, 157, 166–70, 172, 175, 180–99, 202–7, 210, 211, 212–18, 220, 221, 223, 227, 228, 229, 231, 232, 236–8, 241, 243, 244, 245, 246, 253–7, 259–60, 263–6, 269, 271–3, 277–80, 284, 298, 322–3, 334, 337–9 slavery and 3, 14, 15, 22, 23, 34, 43, 53, 60, 62, 64–72, 75, 79, 80–82, 85, 87, 89, 91, 94–5, 104–9, 112–21, 127–32, 134–7, 139, 145, 151–8, 166–71, 172, 175, 180–99, 203–32, 236–81, 297–8 *See also individual nation name*
Aisla, The (ship) 303
Aitchison & Parker 108
Aitchison, William 98–9, 100, 101–102, 103, 104, 110
Akkara 66
Albion Estate, Berbice 311
Alexander Houston & Co. 140
Alfred, Gerald 38
Alleyne, John 112, 118
Alston, David 47, 129, 155, 165, 169, 202, 239, 277, 292–3, 331
'Amazing Grace' hymn 15–16

American Revolution / American War of Independence (1775–83) 82, 88, 102, 104, 105, 106, 120, 131, 153
Andersons (Bristol-based) 153
Anderson, John 153
Angelou, Maya 308, 326
Anglo-Dutch Treaty (1814) 179–80
Anti-Slavery Society 188
Archbishops' Anti-Racism Taskforce report ('From Lament to Action') 223–4
Armour, Agnes 26–7, 28
Armour, Jessie Nimmo 25
Armour, John 26–7, 29
Atta (rebel leader 1763) 79, 80, 81

Babington, Mary 225
Babington, Thomas 225
Bachelor's Adventure 197
Baillie, Evan xiii, 139–41, 219
Baillie, George xiii, 139–41
Baillie, James Evan 197, 198, 199, 207, 218, 219, 238–9
Bain, Christian 224
Bain, Revd. John 209, 224
Baldwin, James vii
Bank of Liverpool 165, 295–8
Barbados High Commissioner to the UK 223
Barclay, David 120
Barclays Bank 297–8
Barkey, Anthony (Anthonij Barkeij) 68
Barkly, Henry 265
Barnes, John 19
Barnes, Samuel 229

Batavian Republic 156, 163, 337
Bathurst, Lord 188
Grenville Baye, or La Baye, (town) 132–3
BBC 17, 18, 29, 30, 47, 58, 320
BBC Scotland 13, 14, 22
Bean, Charles 246, 247
Beckles, Professor Sir Hilary 309
Belle (film – re: Dido Elizabeth Belle) 115
Belle, Dido Elizabeth 115, 277, 280
Belle, Maria (mother of Dido Elizabeth Belle) 280–81
Benezet, Anthony 121
Benn, Marion 53, 55–6
Berbice 5, 38, 41, 43, 45, 47, 49, 50, 54, 56, 57, 61, 62, 93, 140–45, 154, 155, 159, 162, 168, 170, 179, 180, 190, 200, 227, 231, 234, 250, 263, 266, 271, 275, 276, 291, 294, 311–15, 317, 319–21, 323, 325
Berbice Association (aka Berbice Society or Company) 64
Berbice Dutch (extinct language) 76
Berbice Rebellion (1763) 62, 63–85, 87, 133, 137, 216–17, 263
Berbice Society (see Berbice Association) 64, 69, 81
Bethel Chapel, Plantation Le Resouvenir 179, 192, 200
Bethune, Dr George 292
Bevan, Adamay Amelia Patricia, xi, xv, 54, 55, 313–14, 316, 319, 321, 322
Bird, Charles 231

'Black Flash A Century of Black Footballers in Britain' (documentary) 16–17, 22
Blair, Barbara 64
Blair, James 239
Blairmont Estate 5, 45, 46, 55, 61, 311, 320
Blockman, Gerald Jocelyn 45
Boilers, Sibyl (née Watson) xvi, 318–19
Bonaparte, Napoleon 156, 247
Bonnie Prince Charlie 86
Booker Bros. 320
Boston Tea Party 102, 121
Botetourt, Norborne Berkeley, 4th Baron Botetourt, Lord 100
Boyd, Robert 108
Breinburg, Whithyelene (née Watson) see Whithyelene Watson
Brenda (ship) 303
Britain's Forgotten Slave Owners (documentary) 193
British Colonial Dependencies, Slave Registers (1813–1834) 127–8
British Empire 3, 16, 22, 84, 85–6, 88, 89, 100, 253, 326
British Guiana xiv, 5–6, 22, 23–4, 33–6, 40, 45, 46, 47–50, 52, 63–5, 75, 76, 77–8, 87, 93, 142–6, 156, 158, 159, 166, 172, 175, 181, 191, 193, 197, 199, 214, 223, 237, 240–41, 245–53, 257, 259, 262–70, 275–7, 279, 284–8, 293, 298, 301, 302–6, 309, 310, 334, 335, 337
British Guiana Association 197, 199, 240–41

British Overseas Territory of St Helena 254–5
British Slave Indenture 169
'Brothers' coffee plantation 154
Broughton, Henry 198
Brown, Sir William 295
Bryson collection 309, 319–20
Buchanan, George 165
'Buck (derogatory) 60
Budhram, Karen xiv, 315, 330
Burnard, Trevor 232
'Bush Negroes' (derogatory) 78, 161, 202, 339
Buxton, Thomas Fowell 183–4, 188, 219, 238, 239, 241, 242

Cade, Elizabeth 111
Cameron, A. J. McR.: *The Berbice Uprising* 78
Candlin, Kit 129, 133, 292
Canning, George 168, 184–5, 188, 205, 240, 278
CARICOM xiii, 340
  Reparations Commission 309, 317
Case, George 241
Chapman, Richard 196
Charbon, John (or Jan) Abraham 71–4, 345
Charles II, King of England, Scotland and Ireland 144
Checkland, Sydney 174, 207, 356, 357
Cheong, Paul 321, 323
Cheveley, J.C. 165, 191, 196, 197, 200, 293, 354, 370
Church Missionary Intelligencer 181, 216, 253, 254
Church Missionary Society 181, 214

Church of England 192, 200, 212, 214, 217, 336
    Racial Justice Unit 223–4
Clark, Alison 152–3, 331
Clarkson, Thomas 188
Clinton, General 103
Clonbrook 51
close company 334
Coercive Acts (1774) 102
Coffey, John 192
Coffin, Nathaniel 109
colonial patriots 102, 103
comfort women 255
Companies Acts (1862 and 1890) 305
Company of Scotland 88
Consolidation Slave Ordinance 236–7
Constitution of Guyana (1980) 311
Continental Association 102
Continental Congress 102
Cooke, James 246
Coolies (derogatory) 23, 251, 268–72
Council or Court of Policy 160, 188, 189, 262, 284, 306, 335n
Cox, Edward 139
Creoles 85, 129, 168, 191, 194, 197, 265, 272
Crombie, Alexander 169
Cropper, James 207
Cross Farm County Primary School, Netherley 1–2, 7
Cuffy (aka **Kofi or Coffij – Dutch**) 67–72, 75–81, 133, 247
Culloden, battle of (1746) 86
Cummings, Raymon 315
Cummings, Thomas 278
Cunningham, Laurie 20
Cummingsburg 217, 285, 286, 293

D'Aguiar, Fred 115
d'Urban, Sir Benjamin 212
da Costa, Emília Viotti 193, 194, 202, 206, 208, 249–50, 357
Dalton, Henry G. 187, 213, 220, 237, 244–5, 253, 266, 276 159, 166–7, 265, 279
Damon 247–8, 263
Davy, William 112
Déclaration des droits de l'homme et du citoyen (Declaration of the Rights of Man and the Citizen) 130
Declaratory Act (1766) 118
Demerara xi, xii, xiv, xv, xx, xxi, 5–6, 14, 24, 30, 36–7, 41, 43, 45, 49–51, 58–9, 64, 75, 80, 82, 84, 90–98, 125–6, 137–8, 140–41, 142–50, 152–5, 158–72, 175–6, 178–180, 186–8, 190, 192–4, 196–8, 203–208, 211–14, 219–21, 225–8, 230, 232–3, 240–42, 246, 250–51, 253, 257, 260–64, 269–70, 271, 273–8, 281, 284–94, 300–303, 309–11, 321, 337
Demerara Association 207
Demerara Company Limited 305, 310
Demerara Distillers Limited (DDL) 142–3, 309, 311, 324–5
Demerara Gazette 154, 261
Demerara Railway Company 301, 323
Demerara Rebellion (1823) 77, 155, 179, 188, 196, 206, 208, 211, 213, 219, 240, 263
Demerara Sandbach Group 310
Demerara Sugar Company 311

Demerary (old name for Demerara) 46, 90–91, 96, 140, 143, 146–7, 151–2, 165–8, 186, 193, 199, 204–5, 227, 243, 256–7, 264, 284–7, 335n, 337

Demerary and Essequebo Royal Gazette 285

Dentz, Fred. Oudschans 160, 226

de Salve, Colonel Jan Marius 80

Devine, T.M 103–4

Diamond Liquors Ltd (DLL) 310, 311

Djuka, (aka Ndyuka also Bush Negro – derogatory) 72, 76, 337, 339, 344–345,

Dochfour estate 196

Doddridge, Revd. Dr Philip 224

Donald, David 14–15

Doser Gaol 103

Douglas, Christian 177

Douglas, Sir William 177

Draper, Nicholas 139–40, 241

Dumas, Alexandre 135

Dundas of Kerse, Sir Lawrence xiv, 126

Dundas, Lord Henry xiv, 47, 92, 137

Dundas, Thomas, 1st Baron 126

Dunmore, Lord 102, 117

Dutch Republic 80, 81, 87, 339

Dutch West Indian Company (WIC) 64, 143

East India Company 102, 121

Edward I, King of England 177

Egidia (daughter of King Robert II of Scotland) 177

El Dorado 142–3, 309, 324–5

Elizabeth I, Queen of England 143, 297

Ellegood, Colonel James 99

Emancipation Act (1833) 95, 155, 157–8, 180, 202, 228, 243, 246, 247, 252, 259, 295

Encyclopaedia Britannica 132–3

Enterprising Women: Gender, Race, and Power in the Revolutionary Atlantic 292

Equiano, Olaudah 115

Essequebo & Demerary Royal Gazette 151, 152, 168

Evan Baillie & Sons 218–19

'Export of Staple Articles of Produce of Berbice from 1824 to 1839' 250–51

Fahie, Anthony 108

Fashanu, John 19

Fédon, Julien 129–41, 199, 242

Fileen, Jonas 175

Forbes, William 224

Forrester, Robert xvi, 316, 317, 318, 320, 321, 330

Fortnightly Review 304–5

Fothergill, John 114, 120, 121

Franklin, Benjamin 104, 117–21

free trade 267–8, 304–5

French Revolution (1789) 130

Garnett, Alexander 304

Garnett, George xiii

Garnett, Henry Tinne xiii, xiv, 217–18, 303, 304, 371

Garnett, Thomas 243, 304

Garraway & Baillie 139

Genista, The (ship) 302
George III, King of Great Britain and Ireland 6, 160, 255
George, J.C. (Johan) 67, 69
Gibbs, Michele xv, 141
Gibson, John 325
Gladstone Museum, Hawarden 302
Gladstone, Ann McKenzie (née Robertson) 174, 177
Gladstone, Helen Jane xiv, 252
Gladstone, Jack ('Black Jack') xiv, 178–9, 185, 189, 190–91, 199, 202, 203, 204, 205, 247, 260
Gladstone, Sir John xii, xiii, xiv, xvi, xvii, 172–80, 187, 193, 199, 204–5, 207–8, 224, 226, 238–40, 241, 246, 251, 252, 254, 258, 269, 286, 300, 306, 322
Gladstone, Robert 299, 300
Gladstone, Robertson xvi, 178, 241, 242, 257, 269, 302, 322
Gladstone, William Ewart xi, xiii, xv, xvii, 172–85, 197–9, 210, 242, 248, 252, 257, 305, 307
Glynne, John 112
Gold Coast, West Africa 53, 76, 78, 82–3, 145–6, 152, 171, 337, 338
Goodrich, Philip: *Somersett v Steuart* 110, 118, 120, 121
Gordon (the elder), William 169
Gordon (the younger), William 169
Gordon, Daniel 125
Goslinga, Cornelis Ch. 66, 344
Gouyave 133
Grant, Eddy 260
Grant, George 241
Grenada xiii, xvi, xvii, 22, 86, 93, 95–6, 97, 103, 106, 122–33, 135–6, 138, 139–41, 176, 199, 242, 274, 275, 290, 301
Gresham, Sir Thomas 297–8
Grotius, Hugo 71, 345
Grotius De, - 'De Jure Belli ac Pacis - On the Law of War and Peace', (1625), 71
Guiana, British (or Br.) xiv, 5–6, 23, 30, 33–5, 40, 45–9, 52, 63–5, 75–7, 87, 93, 142–3, 145–6, 156, 158–9, 166, 172, 175, 181, 193, 197, 199, 214, 223, 237, 241, 245–6, 249–53, 257, 259, 262–71, 275–277, 279, 284–5, 287–8, 293, 298, 301–6, 309–10, 334–5, 337, 343–4, 346, 351, 353–5, 357–9, 361–2, 364–8, 371,
Guiana Graphic 310
Guyana Distilleries Ltd 311
Guyana, Republic of xi, xvi, 6, 10, 18, 23, 31, 32–3, 35, 37, 38, 39–41, 43, 45–8, 50, 51–4, 56–9, 60–61, 67, 77, 78, 79, 92, 151, 178, 188, 198, 202–3, 217, 230, 246–7, 259, 269, 273, 309, 311–12, 315, 317, 320, 322, 323, 329–30, 335n, 337
Guyana Story, The 246
Guyana Sugar Company (GUYSUCO) 311, 321, 325, 334

Hafodunos xiii, xiv, 300
Haitian Revolution (1791-1804) 62, 64, 82, 84, 131, 132, 188
Haley, Alex 22
Hall, Phyl xvi, 127
Hamilton, Mr 44–5, 54

Hamilton, John 185
Harding, Thomas 189–90, 192, 204, 206, 269
Hargrave, Francis 112
Harte, William Marshall 220
Hartley, David 119
Haywood, Arthur 297
Haywood, Benjamin 297
Haywood's Bank 297
Hearn, Captain S.P. 302
Heskey, Emile 17
Hewitt, Guy 223–4
Highland Society of London 89
Hogg, Quintin 304
Hollett, David 151
Home, Ninian 124, 129–30, 134–5, 137–8
Horton, Robert John Wilmot 205, 206–7
Howe, Sir William 103
Hugues, Jean-Baptiste Victor 130, 135
Huguet, Victor 161
Hundred (aka James Small) 39–40, 42–3
Huskisson, William 183

illegal vessels 254–5
Incorporated Society for the Conversion and Religious Instruction and Education of the Negro Slaves in the British West India Islands 220
indentured labour 23, 34, 43, 94, 115, 117, 203, 251, 255, 261, 265, 266, 268, 270, 271, 272, 273, 303, 311, 321, 333, 334

Institute of Commonwealth Studies at the University of London 223
International Exhibition, or Great London Exposition 300
Ishmael, Odeen 196, 197, 203, 247
Islam 70, 82–3, 181–2

Jacobite uprising (1745–6) 86
James I, King of England 177
Jessel Securities 310
Joe (aka Josiah Sally) 110
John Moores University 325
John, Llewellyn 41
Johnson (ship) 250
Johnson, Vanessa Joan xvi, 313, 316, 330
July, Olivia 5–6, 38, 40–42, 54, 56, 59
July, Terrence 'Terry' 41–2

Kars, Marjoleine 66, 69, 77, 79, 80
Kenwood House 280
Kenyon, Lord 218
Khan, Ruth K. 65–6, 76
Kiltearn 303
Kiltearn Estate 166, 170, 177, 294
Kinghorn, Dr Alice 152–3, 268–9
Knight, Elsie 3
Knowles, Captain 109, 111
Kru tribe 144–5, 339
Kwayana, Eusi 68, 75, 82

L'Amitié 154, 156–7, 158, 294
L'Ouverture, Toussaint 64, 84
La Bonne Intention 46, 196, 197, 261, 262–4, 311, 321
La Valette, Jean Pierre 130
Lambert, Captain 102–3

Lammy, David 203
'Latest Returns' 227
Laval, Sophie de 162–3
Le Resouvenir 179, 185–6, 196, 227, 261
Leahy, Lieuten John Thomas 197
Lee-Loy, Anne-Marie 267, 268
Leslie, Alexander 103
Leslie, Tonya 38–9
Lewis, Kermit 2
Library at Timbuktu 82, 182
Lindsay, 3rd Baronet of Evelix, Sir John 281
literacy 82–3, 191
Liverpool xii, xv, xvi, xvii, 1–3, 8, 15, 18–20, 24, 27, 28, 29, 32, 34, 35–6, 37, 39, 50, 90, 91, 92, 93, 97, 99, 149, 151, 153–4, 159, 164–6, 169, 170, 171, 173, 174, 175, 176, 180, 181, 183, 184, 185, 187, 193, 207, 211, 218, 224, 225, 227, 228, 229, 233–4, 235, 236, 240–43, 246, 250, 255–8, 259–61, 268–9, 273, 288, 295–300, 302–3, 304, 305, 308, 325, 331
   Liverpool and Manchester Railway Act (1829) 299
   Liverpool Athenaeum 241, 252, 257, 258, 299
   Liverpool Corporation 6
   Liverpool Maritime Museum 309, 319–20
   Liverpool West India Association 240–41
logies (term used to describe the dilapidated slave hut) 168, 334
London Chronicle 118

London Missionary Society 178, 193, 208
Long, Edward 114
Lothian, Duncan 90
Louis, King of the Netherlands 156
Lubbock, Basil 303

MacRae, Alexander 271
Mahaica 43, 57, 59, 146, 152, 158, 196, 204, 260, 285, 301–2, 337
Malcolm X 259
Mandingos (derogatory) 194, 334
Mansfield, Lord 104, 111–21, 280, 281
Marlow, John 111
Maroon (see also Djuka) 79, 82, 161, 202, 334
Martins Bank 297, 298
Massachusetts House Committee of Correspondence 121
Mathew, General 103
Matthew, Edward 132
Maxwell, Margaret xiii
McInroy, Catherine xii, xiv, 141
McInroy, Grace Ann xii, 141, 234
McInroy, James xiv, 97, 137, 138, 140, 141, 142, 149, 150, 151, 153, 158, 164, 167, 228, 234, 322
McInroy Sr, James xiii, xiv, 97, 137, 138, 140, 141, 142, 149, 150, 151, 158, 164, 167, 228, 234, 322
McInroy, James Patrick xiv, 245
McInroy Parker & Co. xiii, 90, 153, 164, 165, 167, 168, 169, 206, 227, 242, 243, 246
McInroy Sandbach & Co. xii, 92–3, 95, 96, 137, 167, 186, 187,

188–9, 193, 199, 201, 211, 237, 242, 250, 261–4, 268, 306
McKenzie, James 167
McKenzie, Kenneth Francis 135–9
McKenzie, Robert 108
McLagan, Janet 234–5
McLagan Jr., Peter xv, 156–7, 167, 234–5, 306, 322
McLagan Sr, Peter xv, 156
McTurk, Michael 190–91, 249, 250, 251
Meadow Bank 38, 40–42, 57, 58
Meertens, Anthony 159, 163
Melvinna, Sybil xvi, 315, 316
Mercurius xv, 313–14, 317–19
The Mirror of Literature, Amusement, and Instruction 191, 208
miscegenation 275, 276, 333
Moira, Samantha 51
Moore, Elizabeth xiii, 141, 234
Moore, Philip 77
Mora, The (ship – ex-*Lothair*, 1871) 303
More, Hannah 115
Moss, John 241, 299, 300
mulatto (mulatess) (person with one white and one black parent) 128–9, 130, 134, 136, 141, 162, 162, 274, 276, 277, 278, 279, 284, 290–91, 333
multi-culturalism 5
Munro, George 170
Munro, Pierre Antoine 277
Murray, Lady Elizabeth 115
Murray, John 188, 190, 196–8, 202, 203, 204
Murray, Richard 110

Napoleonic Wars 255
National Front 20
National Health Service 5
National Library of Scotland 126, 154
Nature 302
Nederlandsche Mercurius 68, 70
New Amsterdam 5, 46, 81, 315, 322
Nicholson, Robert 124–5
Nogues, Charles 130
Novelty 299
Nuriddin, Jalal (*The Last Poets*) 313

O'Brien, Ged 21–2
Oliver, George Henry 303, 304
Olusoga, David 123, 193
Ormond, Dr Robert xv, 283, 289

Paganini, Niccolò 173
Paisley, Bob 20
Paley, Ruth 111
Parker, Alfred Traill 94, 296, 303, 305
Parker, Ann (*née* Robertson) xi, 148, 224, 292
Parker Jr., Charles Stuart xii, 93, 275
Parker the elder, Charles Stuart xii, xiv, xv, 90, 95, 96, 97, 107–8, 121–5, 129, 137–8, 140, 142, 146, 147, 148–9, 152–6, 166, 173, 209, 218, 224–5, 228, 238, 258, 275, 290, 292, 294, 303
Parker, Charles 305
Parker, Evelyn Stuart xiii
Parker, James 97, 111
Parker, Jane 294
Parker, Margaret xii, 107, 126, 147, 150, 173, 224–5

Parker Papers, The 90, 91, 92, 93, 102, 140
Parker, Patrick xv, 98, 105–7
Parry, Elvin 2–3
Parry, Sonia 2–4
The Patriot (film) 294
Patterson, Elizabeth 235
Payne, Hugh Tommy 248
Peel, Robert 168, 218, 307
Penn, Thomas 120
Persaud, Shiv 323
Persaud, Yesu 310–11
Philadelphia Society for the Relief of Free Negroes Unlawfully Held in Bondage 119–20
Philip III, King of France 177
Phillips, Eric xiii, 317
Pitt, William 137, 139
Plantagenet, Joan 177
Plantation Diamond 309, 310, 324
Plantation Industry 261, 304
Plantation Nabaclis 195
Plantation Richmond 246, 247
Plantations Coffee Grove and Caledonia 235
Portugal 23, 55, 76, 83, 87, 114, 152, 254–6, 273–4, 335
potato famine (1845–52) 229–30
Powell, Enoch 4–5
Printed & Manuscript African Americana 92
Protector of Slaves 195, 231–6, 278, 279
Puri, Shalini 141
Pybus, Cassandra 154, 292

quadroon (person who is one-quarter black by descent) 276, 279, 292, 333
Quakers 110, 120, 121, 214
Quamina 77, 186, 190, 192, 193, 201, 202–5
Quarterone (Spanish Mestizo) 279, 333
Queen Ann Bounty 224
Queen's Park FC 22, 25, 26
Qur'an 83

racism 1–11, 12, 17, 19–21, 114, 159, 221, 223, 265, 312
Rainy, George xiii, 147–8, 151, 158, 165, 188, 206, 209–10, 224, 232, 233, 234, 245, 261, 275–6, 287, 290, 297, 322
Rainy of Creich, Revd. George 151, 224
Rainy, Elizabeth Jemima 290
Rainy, Gilbert 147–8, 294
Rainy, Mary Augusta (1828–1854) 290
Raleigh, Sir Walter 142
Rambler (ship) 138
Ramring, Jonas 69
Rathbone, William 299–300
Rawlins, Mabel 54, 61
Rebecca's Ordeal 277
Regis, Cyrille 20
Riddell, John 116
Robert II, King of Scotland 177
Robertson, Andrew 176
Robertson, Ann xi, 148, 224, 292

Robertson, Ann McKenzie (later Gladstone) xi, 173–74, 176–7, 183
Robertson, Anne xi, xvi, 165–6, 176, 177, 292
Robertson, 'Black George' 290
Robertson, Christian xi, xii, xiii, xvi, 48–50, 67, 91, 95, 97, 107, 126, 148–9, 165–6, 169, 173, 175, 176–7, 286, 287, 288–9, 292
Robertson, Colin xii, 174
Robertson, Divie xii, xiii, 174
Robertson, Elizabeth xiii, xvi, 97, 107, 150, 176, 177, 260
Robertson, George xi, xii, xiii, xvi, 49, 93, 94, 96, 97, 105, 107, 122, 124, 125, 137, 138, 140–41, 142, 146–50, 153, 154, 166, 176, 177, 290, 301, 322
Robertson, Gilbert xi, xiv, 146–50, 154–6, 166, 169, 170, 171, 196, 209, 224, 225, 275, 292–4, 305
Robertson, Gordon & Parker xii, 95, 124, 125
Robertson DD, Revd. Harry 49, 90, 91, 140, 147–8, 150–51, 155–6, 209, 224
Robertson, Hugh Munro xiv, 149–50, 169, 171, 292, 322
Robertson, Ian 76
Robertson Parker & Co. xii, xiii, 95–8, 105, 125, 149, 153
Robinson, Gilbert 154
Rocket (train) 299, 300
Rodney, Walter 145, 274, 330
Rodway, James 65, 66, 79–80
Roebuck, HMS (ship) 103
Ron, The (ship) 303

Ronald, Andrew 102–3
Roscoe (ship) 254
Roscoe, William xv, xvii, 180, 241, 254, 257–8, 299, 325
Rose Hall Estate 311
Rose, Andrew 29, 163, 164, 169, 236, 274, 284, 285, 315
Rose, Anna (or Hannah) 48, 163, 274, 284–5
Rose, Anne 163
Rose, Patrick 169
Rose, Peter 163, 169, 249–50, 262–3, 274, 285–6, 301–2, 322
Royal Bank of Scotland 88
Royal Institution 181
Royal Museum Greenwich 96
Royal Navy 6, 37–8, 255
Royal Society of Arts, Manufactures and Trade 300
'The Rules on the Treatment of Servants and Slaves' 231
Russell, Lord J. 249

Saffon, A.L. de 146
Saint Kilda, The (ship) 303
Sandbach, Adam 95–6
Sandbach, Ann xii, 292
Sandbach, Arthur Edmund xii, xiii
Sandbach, Charles Parker xii, 94
Sandbach, Elizabeth xii, xiii, 173–4
Sandbach, Gilbert xiii, 225, 229
Sandbach, Gilbert Robertson xiii, 225, 305
Sandbach, Henry Robertson xiv, xv, xvii, 228, 238, 245, 262, 292, 297, 298, 300, 306, 322, 325
Sandbach, Margaret xv, xvii, 173–4, 299

Sandbach, Mary Rosina xv, 174
Sandbach Parker & Co. 142, 149, 273, 275, 304–5, 310–11
Sandbach, Rose 127, 128–9
Sandbach, Samuel xii, xiii, xiv, xvi, xvii, 95–6, 124–5, 128, 137, 138, 140, 142, 149, 150, 153, 156–7, 169, 171, 177, 209–10, 217, 218, 219, 229, 238, 241, 243, 256, 258, 260, 269, 286, 290, 294, 295, 297, 298, 299, 303, 306, 311, 322
Sandbach Tinne & Co. xii, xiii, xiv, xv, xvii, 90, 92–3, 151, 152, 164–5, 168, 187, 202, 227, 234, 235, 242, 303, 306, 309–10
Sandbach, William xvi, xvii, 125, 128, 138, 245, 260–61, 270, 296, 300
Sandon, Lord 241
Schama, Simon 112, 116, 117
Schomburgk, Robert Hermann 264–5
Scott-Heron, Gil 77
Scott, Robert H. 302
Scottish Brigade 87, 89
Scottish Darién Company 88
Scottish Football Association 21–2
Scottish Football Museum 21, 330–31
Seaforth, Francis Humberston Mackenzie, 1st Baron 172, 176
Second Carib War (1795) 132, 136
Seven Years War (1756–63) 85–6, 88–9, 95
Sharp, Granville 111–12, 115
Simon, James 57, 59, 60
Simon, Richard Kato 57

Skeet 36–7
Slave Bible 192–3, 209–10
slave trade xi, xii, xiv, xv, xvi, 3, 5, 6, 14, 15, 16, 22, 23, 27, 30, 31, 32–4, 43, 47, 53, 56, 60, 62, 63, 64–72, 75, 76, 77, 79, 80, 81–4, 85, 87, 89, 91, 94–6, 98, 99, 104–21, 123–5, 126, 127–30, 131–2, 133, 134, 135, 136, 137, 138–9, 140, 142, 143, 144–5, 147, 148, 151, 152–8, 161, 166–71, 172, 174, 175, 178–99, 201, 202, 203–10, 211–32, 236–81, 284, 285, 288, 290, 293–5, 297–8, 299, 300–303, 305, 309–11, 314, 323, 324, 330, 334
  Act for the Abolition of Slavery throughout the British Colonies (1833) 91, 244
  Act for the Abolition of the Slave Trade (1807) 115, 167, 252–3
  Africa and *see* Africa
  Slave Trade Act (1807) 167
  Slavery Compensation Act (1837) 95
Small, Stephen xvi, 32–3
Smallie (Mr Small) 32–3
Smith, Henrietta 54, 55, 56, 206, 313, 316
Smith, Reverend John 179, 198, 203, 205, 209, 210, 212, 213, 214, 215, 222, 224, 227, 240
Smyth, James Carmichael (Governor) 247
Society for Promoting Christian Knowledge (SPCK) 181, 209, 215, 336

Society for the Propagation of the Gospel (SPG) 181, 215, 221, 336
Somerset, James (also Sommersett) 108–14, 117, 118–20
Sommersett v. Steuart (1772) 71, 104, 120–22
Sophia 234, 236, 363
Souness, Graeme 14, 16
Sour-pot (aka Gerald Alfred) 36, 37, 38, 43, 45, 51, 52, 59, 61
South Sea Company 86, 224
Speedwell, HMS (ship) 96
Speirs, Alexander 98
St George, Grenada xvi
St George's Cathedral, Georgetown 217, 220, 283
St John and St Philip (English Church at the Hague) 160, 225–6, 3534, 357, 362
St Nicholas Church 224
Stedman, Captain John 74–5
Stephenson, George 299, 302
Stephenson, John Hunter 281–3
Stephenson, Robert 299
Steuart, Charles 101, 104–11, 113, 114, 117, 120–21
Stevenson, Annetta (née Watson) 92
Stevenson, John Hunter 92
Stevenson, Robert 300
Success (plantation) 172
Sugar Act (1764) 100, 119
Sugar Refining Bill 238
Suriname 46, 74, 75–6, 80, 82, 144, 158, 242, 268, 322, 337, 339
Susannah, slave girl 170
Swann Auction Galleries 92, 257

Talkie Talkie (Taki Taki) 76
Tarleton, Banastre xii, 294–5
Tarleton, John 294
Tarleton, Thomas 294
Tavington, Colonel William 294
Tawney (light-skinned Mulatto - derogatory) 277, 333
Taylor, Steph 7
Tea Act (1773) 102, 121
Tercerones (a person with one white parent – derogatory) 279, 333
Thatched House, Bristol 197–8
Thatcher, Margaret 307
The House of Burgesses, 100
The House (commercial term) 334
The House of Lords 237–8, 250, 253, 254, 364
The House (McInroy, Parker & Sandbach) 287
The House (of Commons, Parliament) 155, 183, 209, 248, 305, 348
The House (Sandbach Tinne) 154, 261–2, 268
Thomas, Captain Joseph xiv
Thomas, Charlotte 293, 294
Thomas, Dorothy 'Doll' xiii, 274–5, 292, 293–4
Thomas, Eliza 275, 293–4
Thompson, Alvin 65, 69
Thomson, Jessie 235
Tiger Bay 6, 40
Tinne, Alexine 226
Tinne, Anna 217
Tinne, Chrétien (Christian) 290

Tinne, John Abraham xiv, xv, 173–4, 209, 225–6, 229, 238, 243–4, 245, 258, 262–3, 265–6, 269–70, 296, 297, 305, 306, 322

Tinne, Dr John Ernest xiv, 160, 268, 299, 302–3, 305, 306

Tinne, Jeanne Marguerite xiv, 160

Tinne, Matthieu 160, 162, 306

Tinne, Philip Frederick xi, xii, xiv, xv, 159, 160–64, 169, 176, 186, 188, 209, 217, 219, 225, 233, 234, 243, 245, 250, 258, 262–3, 268, 270, 284, 285, 290, 300

Tinne (Jr), Philip Frederick xv, 303, 306

Tinne, Théodore xii, 160

Townsend, Henry 181–2

Townshend Duties 101

Traill, Anne 107

Traill Papers 154

Traill, John 108

Traill, Marjorie 107

Traill, Mary Eliza xv, xvi, 47, 258, 283, 289

Traill, Thomas Stuart xi, xv, xvi, 49, 91, 107, 133, 148–9, 169–70, 180, 258, 287, 325

Treaty of Amiens (1802) 159, 163

Treaty of Breda (1667) 144

Treaty of Hubertusburg (1763) 86

Treaty of Paris (1763) 86

Treaty of Paris (1783) 123

Trinidad 23, 93, 136, 138, 139, 225, 231, 268, 290, 305

Tull, Walter 17

Turkeyen Estate 160, 206

Tuschen de Vrienden 268

Tyler, Eliza Kate 288

UCL Legacies 157–8, 245, 293

Uitvlugt Estate 311

Uitvlugt, Ignatius Charles Bourda 311

Uncle Lucky 35–6

University of Liverpool 325

Utrecht 126

Van der Haas, Adrianus 185–6

Van Hoogenheim, Wolfert Simon 69–70, 74–5

Van Peere, Abraham 69

Verenigde Oost-Indische Compagnie (Dutch East India Company) 86, 334

Vesting of Property Act, 1975 310

Viendri, Marie 162

Village System 260

Virginia General Court 101

Vreed-en-Hoop 175, 178, 311, 321

Walker, Llew 47

Walklin, Thomas 111

Walter Rodney Archives xiv, 314

Walters, Mark 14–16

Wardlaw, David 235

Watson, Agnes Maud xi, 25, 26, 29

Watson, Andrew (uncle of footballer) xi, 91-2, 287–9, 290, 291, 300, 301, 317

Watson, Andrew (footballer) xi, xv, xvi, 13–19, 34, 38, 46, 47, 48–9, 53, 56, 58, 59, 63, 90–92, 148,

163, 176, 178, 200, 228, 236, 250, 258, 262, 276, 281, 284–7, 301, 317, 320, 326, 331
family origins 17–24, 29–31
football career 13–17, 19, 21–7
grave 15–16
Watson, Annetta (or Annette – see also Annetta Stevenson) xi, xvii, 24, 47, 51, 92, 258, 281–5, 288, 289
Watson, Beryl xii, xiii, 51–6, 78
Watson, Cheryl 321–2, 330
Watson, Elaine 53
Watson Florence Mary (Flo – née Caldwell), xiii, 10–11, 54, 316
Watson, Frederick Adolphus xiii, 52–4, 56
Watson, George Edward 5, 38, 46, 54, 55, 285, 314, 316
Watson, Harry Robertson 49, 90–91, 93, 286–7, 288–9
Watson, James xii, xiv, 47, 48, 49, 91, 92, 126, 148–9, 286
Watson Jr, James 91
Watson, Joshua 218
Watson, Miller & Baird 25
Watson, Peter Miller xii, xiv, xv, xvi, xvii, 22, 29–30, 46, 47, 48–9, 50–51, 53, 56, 61–2, 90–96, 107, 126, 132–3, 154, 176, 178, 196, 199, 201, 205, 209, 212, 226, 228, 245, 249–50, 251–2, 256–7, 258, 261, 262, 269, 270, 282, 284–90, 317, 321, 322
Watson, Reginald Daniel William xvi, xvii, 54, 55, 57, 313–14, 316

Watson, Reginald Wilcox 1–10, 18, 19, 22, 28–9, 33–8, 40, 42–6, 53–60, 195, 313–14, 315–17
Watson, Rose 22
Watson, Rupert Andrew xvi, 25, 26–9, 301
Watson, Sybil Gwen (aka Elaine) 53–4
Watson, Whithyelene Amelia (aka Elaine) xvi–xvii, 54, 57, 64, 313–6, 322, 330, 343
Watson, William Robertson xvii, 49, 51, 55, 91–2, 245, 281, 282, 289, 291, 322
Weldaad 38, 43, 44, 45, 46, 51, 52, 53, 54
West Bromwich Albion 19–20
West India Association 159, 205, 238, 240–41, 246, 269
West India Company 69
West India Planters and Merchants of Glasgow 218
West India Planters and Merchants of Liverpool 218, 238
West India Planters and Merchants of London 218
West Indian Regiment 197
Westmaas, Nigel 77–8
Wharton, Arthur 17
Wilberforce, William xvii, 183, 188, 208–9, 218–19
Williams, Eric 274; *Capitalism and Slavery* 113, 116, 262; *Journal of Negro History* 264–7
Williams, John 191
Williamson, William G.: *A Visit to Demerara 1828–1829* 241
Williamson, Willie 252, 302
Windham, William 276–7

Windrush generation 4, 5
Windrush Scandal Research Project 223–4
Windsor Castle Plantation 267
Windward Islands 135
Wise, Steven M. 112, 118–19
Wise, Thomas Turner 133–4

Woodlands 97, 152, 154, 156–8, 194, 225, 235, 294
Wray, Charles 196
Wray, Revd. John 179, 180–81, 193

Zong massacre 114–15